Complete American Presidents Sourcebook

Complete American Presidents Sourcebook

Volume 3
Ulysses S. Grant through William Howard Taft
1869–1913

Roger Matuz
Lawrence W. Baker, Editor

AN IMPRINT OF THE GALE GROUP

DETROIT · NEW YORK · SAN FRANCISCO
LONDON · BOSTON · WOODBRIDGE, CT

150159

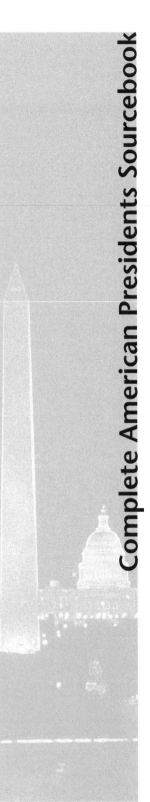

Complete American Presidents Sourcebook

Roger Matuz

Staff

Lawrence W. Baker, *U•X•L Senior Editor*
Gerda-Ann Raffaelle, *U•X•L Contributing Editor*
Carol DeKane Nagel, *U•X•L Managing Editor*
Thomas L. Romig, *U•X•L Publisher*

Rita Wimberley, *Senior Buyer*
Dorothy Maki, *Manufacturing Manager*
Evi Seoud, *Assistant Manager, Composition Purchasing and Electronic Prepress*
Mary Beth Trimper, *Manager, Composition Purchasing and Electronic Prepress*

Cynthia Baldwin, *Senior Art Director*
Michelle DiMercurio, *Senior Art Director*
Kenn Zorn, *Product Design Manager*

Shalice Shah-Caldwell, *Permissions Associate (text and pictures)*
Maria L. Franklin, *Permissions Manager*
Kelly A. Quin, *Editor, Imaging and Multimedia Content*
Pamela A. Reed, *Imaging Coordinator*
Leitha Etheridge-Sims, *Image Cataloger*
Mary Grimes, *Image Cataloger*
Robert Duncan, *Imaging Specialist*
Dan Newell, *Imaging Specialist*
Randy A. Bassett, *Image Supervisor*
Barbara J. Yarrow, *Imaging and Multimedia Content Manager*

Marco Di Vita, Graphix Group, *Typesetting*

Library of Congress Cataloging-in-Publication Data

Matuz, Roger.
  Complete American presidents sourcebook / Roger Matuz ; Lawrence W. Baker, editor.
    p. cm.
  Includes bibliographical references and indexes.
    ISBN 0-7876-4837-X (set) — ISBN 0-7876-4838-8 (v. 1) — ISBN 0-7876-4839-6 (v. 2) — ISBN 0-7876-4840-X (v. 3) — ISBN 0-7876-4841-8 (v. 4) — ISBN 0-7876-4842-6 (v. 5)
      1. Presidents—United States—Biography—Juvenile literature. 2. Presidents' spouses—United States—Biography—Juvenile literature. 3. United States—Politics and government—Sources—Juvenile literature. I. Baker, Lawrence W. II. Title.

E176.1 .M387 2001
973'.09'9—dc21
[B]

00-056794

Contents

Volume 2

Volume 3

Volume 4

Volume 5

Reader's Guide

An "embarrassed pause" fell on the gathering of delegates at the Constitutional Convention of 1787 when James Wilson of Pennsylvania suggested the idea of a chief executive. Wanting "no semblance of a monarch," as Edmund Randolph of Virginia put it, delegates moved on to other matters.

So went the first real "discussion" about the office of president, according to Virginia delegate James Madison. Madison, later nicknamed "the Father of the Constitution," took lengthy notes on the proceedings. They were published in 1840 in a book, *Journal of the Federal Convention*.

The Convention was called to address the weakness of the American government formed under the Articles of Confederation that was approved in 1781. By the end of the Convention of 1787, delegates had cautiously agreed on a new system. They had debated ideas of government ranging in history from ancient Greece and Rome to the "Age of Enlightenment" (eighteenth century) in Europe; they considered the workings of the Iroquois confederacy of Native American tribes as well as the state governments in America; and they held to their ideals of liberty and their dislike of monarchy, a system in which one person rules a country for life. The delegates eventually returned to Wilson's suggestion and debated it. The new system of government they cautiously agreed to in the end did indeed include an elected chief executive—the president.

"President" was a title used for the position of governor in three states—Delaware, Pennsylvania, and New Hampshire. They were among the first nine states to ratify the Constitution, helping provide the majority (nine of thirteen states) needed for the Constitution to become legally binding.

The process of ratification was not easy. In Virginia, for example, which finally approved the Constitution in 1788 by a slim majority (89-79), there were significant concerns about the powers of the president. Former Continental congressman and former Virginia governor Patrick Henry called it "a squint toward monarchy."

The delegates of Virginia, however, had an example of the kind of leader envisioned when the office of president was created. George Washington had presided over the Constitutional Convention. He introduced no ideas and seldom participated in debates, but he kept delegates focused on the cause of improving the system of government. Washington was known for his honesty and for not being overly ambitious. Americans had turned to him to lead their military struggle in the Revolutionary War (1775–81). After the Constitution was ratified (approved), delegates turned to him to lead the new nation as its first president.

Washington's example as president reveals the realities of political leadership. He was voted unanimously into office, and left office in the same high regard, but he had faced resistance in between. Some viewed his version of the federal government as being too powerful: he had called on state militias to put down a rebellion in Pennsylvania against taxes; and for economic reasons, he sided in foreign relations with Great Britain—still a hated enemy to some Americans—over France, the nation that had assisted Americans in winning independence.

Washington was among those presidents who made firm decisions, then awaited the consequences. Some had viewed the presidency as being more impartial. Such are the perils of the presidency. John Adams, the second president, followed the more forceful actions of members of his party and became so unpopular that he had no real hope for reelection. Thomas Jefferson, whose ideals shaped the Declaration of Independence, lost much popularity by the time he left office as the third president. Jefferson had ordered foreign trade restrictions to assert America's strength and to demand respect from Great Britain and France, but the action ended up hurting the American economy.

Like the Constitution, the office of the president was never intended to be perfect. The Constitution is flexible, meant to be used and adapted to form "a more perfect union." The presidency has ranged at times from being a near monarchy to having little real strength. President Andrew Jackson was dubbed "King Andrew" by his opponents, who felt he overstepped his power in several instances. Franklin D. Roosevelt was given tremendous powers and support, first in 1933 to combat the effects of the Great Depression (1929–41), and later to direct the nation's economy during World War II (1939–45). But when Roosevelt tried to change the Supreme Court, he was met with swift criticism. Roosevelt was the only president elected to office four times, the last time being 1944. (In 1945, he died only three months into his fourth term.) By 1951, a constitutional amendment was passed to limit presidents to two terms in office.

Other presidents were far less powerful or effective. Prior to the Civil War, two presidents from the North (Franklin Pierce and James Buchanan) supported the rights for states to decide whether to permit slavery. Abraham Lincoln was elected to challenge that notion, and the Civil War (1861–65) followed. Lincoln took a more aggressive approach than his two predecessors, and he emerged in history as among the greatest presidents.

After Lincoln's assassination in 1865, the presidency was dominated by Congress. In 1885, future president Woodrow Wilson criticized that situation in a book he wrote, *Congressional Government*, while he was a graduate student at Johns Hopkins University. By the time Wilson was elected president in 1912, a series of strong presidents—Grover Cleveland, William McKinley, and Theodore Roosevelt—had reasserted the president's power to lead.

The presidency, then, has passed through various stages of effectiveness. The dynamics of change, growth, and frustration make it fascinating to study. Different ideas of leadership, power, and the role of government have been pursued by presidents. Chief executives have come from various backgrounds: some were born in poverty, like Andrew Johnson and Abraham Lincoln, and others had the advantages of wealth, like the Roosevelts and Bushes; some were war heroes, like Ulysses S. Grant and Dwight D. Eisenhower, others were more studious, like Thomas Jefferson and Woodrow Wilson. Some came to the presidency by accident, like John Tyler and Gerald R. Ford, others campaigned long and hard for the position, like Martin Van Buren and Richard Nixon.

There are various ways to present information on the presidency. In 2000, a Public Broadcasting System (PBS) television series called *The American President* divided presidents into ten categories (such as presidents related to each other, those who were prominent military men, and chief executives who became compromise choices of their parties). The same year, a group of presidential scholars also used ten categories (such as crisis leadership, administrative skills, and relations with Congress) to rank presidents in order of effectiveness

Complete American Presidents Sourcebook uses a chronological approach, beginning with George Washington in 1789, and ending with George W. Bush in 2001. Each president's section contains three types of entries.

Biography of the president

Each of the forty-two men who have served in the nation's top political office is featured in *Complete American Presidents Sourcebook*.

- Each entry begins with a general overview of the president's term(s) in office, then follows his life from birth, through his service as president, to his post-presidency (if applicable).

- Outstanding events and issues during each presidential administration are described, as are the president's responses in his role as the nation's highest elected official.

- Sidebar boxes provide instant facts on the president's personal life; a timeline of key events in his life; a "Words to

Know" box that defines key terms related to the president; results of the president's winning election(s); a list of Cabinet members for each administration; and a selection of homes, museums, and other presidential landmarks.

- A final summary describes the president's legacy—how his actions and the events during his administration influenced the historical period and the future.

Biography of the first lady

Forty-four first ladies are featured in *Complete American Presidents Sourcebook*. Though some of the women died before their husbands became president, all had an important influence on the men who would serve as president. The profiles provide biographical information and insight into the ways in which the women lived their lives and defined their public roles. Like the presidents, first ladies have responded in different ways to their highly public position.

Primary source entry

Another important feature of interest to students is a selection of forty-eight primary source documents—speeches, writings, executive orders, and proclamations of the presidents. At least one primary source is featured with each president.

In the presidents' own words, the documents outline the visions and plans of newly elected presidents, the reasons for certain actions, and the responses to major world events. Students can learn more about key documents (such as the Declaration of Independence and the Monroe Doctrine); famous speeches (such as George Washington's Farewell Address and Abraham Lincoln's Gettysburg Address); presidential orders (the Emancipation Proclamation issued by Abraham Lincoln in 1863 and Harry S. Truman's executive order on military desegregation in 1946); responses to ongoing issues, from tariffs (William McKinley) to relations between the government and Native Americans (Chester A. Arthur); different views on the role of the federal government (from extensive programs advocated by Franklin D. Roosevelt and Lyndon B. Johnson, to reducing the influence of government by Warren G. Harding and Ronald Reagan); and many inaugural addresses, including the memorable speeches of Abraham Lincoln and John F. Kennedy.

Each document (or excerpt) presented in *Complete American Presidents Sourcebook* includes the following additional material:

- **Introduction** places the document and its author in a historical context.

- **Things to remember** offers readers important background information and directs them to central ideas in the text.

- **What happened next** provides an account of subsequent events, both during the presidential administration and in future years.

- **Did you know** provides significant and interesting facts about the excerpted document, the president, or the subjects discussed in the excerpt.

- **For further reading** lists sources for more information on the president, the document, or the subject of the excerpt.

Complete American Presidents Sourcebook also features sidebars containing interesting facts and short biographies of people who were in some way connected with the president or his era. Within each entry, boldfaced cross-references direct readers to other presidents, first ladies, primary sources, and sidebar boxes in the five-volume set. Finally, each volume includes approximately 70 photographs and illustrations (for a total of 350), a "Timeline of the American Presidents" that lists significant dates and events related to presidential administrations, a general "Words to Know" section, research and activity ideas, sources for further reading, and a cumulative index.

This wealth of material presents the student with a variety of well-researched information. It is intended to reflect the dynamic situation of serving as the leader of a nation founded on high ideals, ever struggling to realize those ideals.

Acknowledgments from the author

Many individuals, many institutions, and many sources were consulted in preparing *Complete American Presidents Sourcebook*. A good portion of them are represented in bibliographies and illustration and textual credits sprinkled throughout the five volumes. The many excellent sources and the ability to access them ensured a dynamic process that made the project lively and thought-provoking, qualities reflected in the presentation.

Compilation efforts were organized through Manitou Wordworks, Inc., headed by Roger Matuz with contributions from Carol Brennan, Anne-Jeanette Johnson, Allison Jones, Mel Koler, and Gary Peters. On the Gale/U•X•L side, special recognition goes to U•X•L publisher Tom Romig for his conceptualization of the project. Thanks, too, to Gerda-Ann Raffaelle for filling in some editorial holes; Pam Reed, Kelly A. Quin, and the rest of the folks on the Imaging team for their efficient work; and Cindy Baldwin for another dynamite cover.

The author benefited greatly through his association and friendship with editor Larry Baker and his personal library, tremendous patience, and great enthusiasm for and knowledge of the subject matter.

Finally, with love to Mary Claire for her support, interest (I'll miss having you ask me the question, "So what new thing did you learn about a president today?"), and understanding from the beginning of the project around the time we were married through my frequent checking of the latest news before and after the election of 2000.

Acknowledgments from the editor

The editor wishes to thank Roger Matuz for a year and a half of presidential puns, for putting up with endless Calvin Coolidge tidbits, and—above all—for producing a tremendously solid body of work. You've got my vote when Josiah Bartlet's time in office is up. Thank you, Mr. Author.

Thanks also to typesetter Marco Di Vita of The Graphix Group who always turns in top-quality work and is just a lot of fun to work with; Terry Murray, who, in spite of her excellent-as-usual copyediting and indexing, still couldn't resist suggesting a sidebar for Zachary Taylor's horse, Old Whitey (um, no . . . maybe if we do *Complete American Presidents' Pets Sourcebook);* and proofer Amy Marcaccio Keyzer, whose sharp eye kept the manuscript clean and whose election e-mails kept me laughing.

In addition, the editor would be remiss if he didn't acknowledge his first family. Decades of thanks go to Mom & Dad, for starting it all by first taking me to the McKinley Memorial in Canton, Ohio, all those years ago. Love and appreciation go to editorial first lady Beth Baker, for putting up with all of the presidential homes and museums and grave markers and books, but who admits that touring FDR's Campobello during a nor'easter storm is pretty cool. And to Charlie & Dane—please don't fight over who gets to be president first!

Finally, a nod to Al Gore and George W. Bush for adding some real-life drama to the never-ending completion of this book . . . and who *did* fight over who got to be president first!

Comments and suggestions

We welcome your comments on the *Complete American Presidents Sourcebook* and suggestions for other topics in history to consider. Please write: Editors, *Complete American Presidents Sourcebook,* U•X•L, 27500 Drake Rd., Farmington Hills, Michigan 48331-3535; call toll-free: 800-877-4253; fax to 248-414-5043; or send e-mail via http://www.galegroup.com.

Timeline of the American Presidents

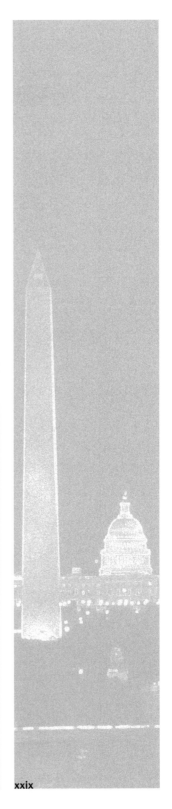

1776 The Declaration of Independence is written, approved, and officially issued.

1781 The Articles of Confederation are approved, basing American government on cooperation between the states. Congress is empowered to negotiate treaties, but has few other responsibilities.

1787 A national convention called to strengthen the Articles of Confederation develops the U.S. Constitution instead, defining a new system of American government. The powers of Congress are broadened. Congress forms the legislative branch of the new government, and the Supreme Court forms the judicial

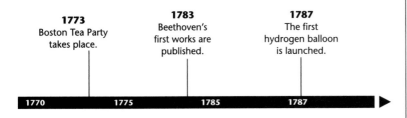

1773
Boston Tea Party
takes place.

1783
Beethoven's
first works are
published.

1787
The first
hydrogen balloon
is launched.

1770   1775   1785   1787

branch. An executive branch is introduced and will be led by an elected official, the president. The president and vice president are to be inaugurated on March 4 of the year following their election (a date that remains in practice until 1933, when the Twentieth Amendment is ratified, changing inauguration day to January 20).

1787 Three of the original thirteen colonies—Delaware, Pennsylvania, and New Jersey—ratify the Constitution, thereby becoming the first three states of the Union.

1788 Eight of the original thirteen colonies—Georgia, Connecticut, Massachusetts, Maryland, South Carolina, New Hampshire, Virginia, and New York—ratify the Constitution, thereby becoming the fourth through eleventh states of the Union. The Constitution becomes law when New Hampshire is the ninth state to ratify it (two-thirds majority of the thirteen states had to approve the Constitution for it to become legally binding).

1789 One of the original thirteen colonies—North Carolina—ratifies the Constitution, thereby becoming the twelfth state of the Union.

1789 The first presidential election is held. Voting is done by electors appointed by each state, and the number of electors are based on the state's population. Each elector votes for two candidates. Whomever finishes with the most votes becomes president, and whomever finishes second becomes vice president.

1789 Revolutionary War hero George Washington is elected president, receiving votes from each elector.

1789 The French Revolution begins.

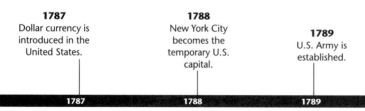

1787
Dollar currency is introduced in the United States.

1788
New York City becomes the temporary U.S. capital.

1789
U.S. Army is established.

1787   1788   1789

1789 George Washington is inaugurated in New York City. A site for the national capital is selected along the Potomac River in Washington, D.C., and the federal government will be situated in Philadelphia, Pennsylvania, until the new capital is completed.

1789 One of the original thirteen colonies—Rhode Island—ratifies the Constitution, thereby becoming the thirteenth state of the Union.

1789 Political factions solidify. Federalists, who support a strong federal government, are led by Secretary of the Treasury Alexander Hamilton, and Anti-Federalists, who support limited federal power and strong states' rights, are led by Secretary of State Thomas Jefferson.

1791 Vermont becomes the fourteenth state of the Union.

1792 President George Washington is reelected unanimously.

1792 Kentucky becomes the fifteenth state of the Union.

1794 American forces defeat a confederacy of Native American tribes at the Battle of Fallen Timbers in Ohio, opening up the midwest for settlement.

1796 When Vice President John Adams finishes first and former Secretary of State Thomas Jefferson finishes second in the presidential election, two men with conflicting political views and affiliations serve as president and vice president. Political parties—the Federalists and the Democratic-Republicans—become established.

1796 Tennessee becomes the sixteenth state of the Union.

1798 The United States engages in an undeclared naval war with France.

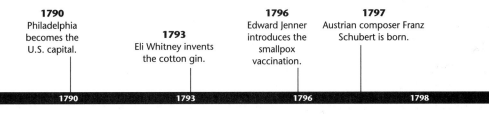

1790
Philadelphia becomes the U.S. capital.

1793
Eli Whitney invents the cotton gin.

1796
Edward Jenner introduces the smallpox vaccination.

1797
Austrian composer Franz Schubert is born.

1790 1793 1796 1798

1798 Federalists in Congress pass and President John Adams signs into law the Alien and Sedition Acts. The laws, which expand the powers of the federal government, prove unpopular and bolster the prospects of anti-Federalists.

1800 The seat of government moves from Philadelphia, Pennsylvania, to Washington, D.C.; President John Adams and first lady Abigail Adams move into the White House (officially called The Executive Mansion until 1900).

1800 In the presidential election, Vice President Thomas Jefferson and former New York senator Aaron Burr (both of the Democratic-Republican Party) finish tied with the most electoral votes. The election is decided in the House of Representatives, where Jefferson prevails after thirty-six rounds of voting.

1803 The historic *Marbury v. Madison* decision strengthens the role of the U.S. Supreme Court to decide constitutional issues.

1803 The Louisiana Purchase more than doubles the size of the United States.

1803 Ohio becomes the seventeenth state of the Union.

1804 The Twelfth Amendment to the Constitution mandates that electors must distinguish between whom they vote for president and vice president (to avoid repeating the problem of the 1800 election, where most voters selected both Jefferson and Burr with their two votes).

1804 President Thomas Jefferson wins reelection. He selects a new running mate, New York governor George Clinton, to replace Vice President Aaron Burr.

1799
Rosetta Stone found in Egypt.

1800
Washington, D.C., becomes the new U.S. capital.

1800
The Library of Congress is established.

1804
Lewis & Clark expedition begins.

1798   1800   1802   1804

1804 After losing an election for governor of New York, outgoing vice president Aaron Burr kills former U.S. secretary of the treasury Alexander Hamilton in a duel. Hamilton had influenced voters against Burr in the presidential campaign of 1800 and during Burr's campaign to be governor of New York in 1804.

1806 The Lewis and Clark expedition, commissioned by President Thomas Jefferson, is completed when explorers Meriwether Lewis and William Clark return to St. Louis, Missouri, after having traveled northwest to the Pacific Ocean.

1807 President Thomas Jefferson institutes an embargo on shipping to England and France, attempting to pressure the nations to respect American rights at sea. The embargo is unsuccessful and unpopular.

1807 Former vice president Aaron Burr is tried and acquitted on charges of treason.

1808 Secretary of State James Madison, the "Father of the Constitution," is elected president. Vice President George Clinton campaigns and places third as a member of the Independent Republican Party after having accepted Madison's offer to continue in his role as vice president.

1811 At the Battle of Tippecanoe, American forces (led by future president William Henry Harrison) overwhelm a Native American confederacy led by Shawnee chief Tecumseh.

1811 Vice President George Clinton casts the tie-breaking vote in the U.S. Senate (a responsibility of the vice president under the U.S. Constitution) against rechartering the National Bank, and against President James Madison's wishes.

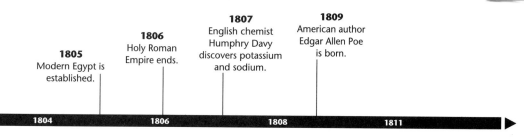

1805
Modern Egypt is established.

1806
Holy Roman Empire ends.

1807
English chemist Humphry Davy discovers potassium and sodium.

1809
American author Edgar Allen Poe is born.

1804 — 1806 — 1808 — 1811

1812	War of 1812 (1812–15) begins.
1812	President James Madison is reelected.
1812	Louisiana becomes the eighteenth state of the Union.
1813	After having suffered military defeats in Canada, U.S. naval forces win control of the Great Lakes.
1814	British military forces burn the White House and the Capitol during the War of 1812.
1815	The Battle of New Orleans, where American forces (led by future president Andrew Jackson) rout a superior British force, occurs after an armistice was agreed on, but news had not yet reached Louisiana. The War of 1812 officially ends a month later.
1816	Secretary of State James Monroe is elected president. The "Era of Good Feelings" begins: the war is over, America is expanding, and Monroe is a popular president.
1816	Indiana becomes the nineteenth state of the Union.
1817	President James Monroe moves into an incompletely reconstructed White House.
1816	Mississippi becomes the twentieth state of the Union.
1818	Illinois becomes the twenty-first state of the Union.
1819	Alabama becomes the twenty-second state of the Union.
1819	Bank Panic slows economic growth.
1820	President James Monroe is reelected by winning every state. One elector casts a vote for John Quincy Adams as a symbolic gesture to ensure that George Washington remains the only president to win all electoral votes in an election.

1812
The Brothers Grimm publish their book of fairy tales.

1814
Francis Scott Key writes the "Star Spangled Banner."

1818
Mary Shelley writes *Frankenstein.*

1818
Congress adopts a U.S. flag.

1812   1815   1818   1820

1820   The Missouri Compromise sets a boundary (the southern border of present-day Missouri): slavery is not permitted north of that boundary for any prospective territory hoping to enter the Union.

1820   Maine, formerly part of Massachusetts, becomes the twenty-third state of the Union.

1821   Missouri becomes the twenty-fourth state of the Union.

1823   In his annual message to Congress, President James Monroe introduces what will become known as the Monroe Doctrine. Although not very significant at the time, the Doctrine, which warns European nations against expansionist activities in the Americas, sets a foreign policy precedent several later presidents will invoke.

1824   Electoral votes are based on the popular vote for the first time. Tennessee senator Andrew Jackson bests Secretary of State John Quincy Adams with over 45,000 more popular votes and a 99-84 Electoral College lead, but does not win a majority of electoral votes, split among four candidates. The election is decided in Adams's favor by the House of Representatives. The support of powerful Speaker of the House Henry Clay, who finished fourth in the election, helps sway the House in favor of Adams. When Adams names Clay his secretary of state, Jackson supporters claim a "corrupt bargain" had been forged between Adams and Clay.

1824   John Quincy Adams is the fourth straight and last president from the Democratic-Republican Party, which held the White House from 1800 to 1829. The party splits into factions around Adams and his elec-

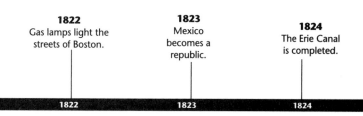

1822
Gas lamps light the streets of Boston.

1823
Mexico becomes a republic.

1824
The Erie Canal is completed.

1820   1822   1823   1824

tion opponent, Andrew Jackson (called Jacksonian Democrats), respectively.

1826 Former presidents John Adams and Thomas Jefferson die on the same day, July 4—fifty years to the day after the Declaration of Independence was officially issued.

1828 Former Tennessee senator Andrew Jackson defeats President John Quincy Adams. Modern-day political parties are established: Jackson leads the Democratic Party, and Adams leads the National Republican Party. The National Republicans are also represented in the 1832 presidential election, but most party members are joined by anti-Jackson Democrats to form the Whig Party in 1834.

1832 President Andrew Jackson is reelected. Candidates from the Nullifier Party (based on the proposition that states have the right to nullify federal laws) and the Anti-Masonic Party receive electoral votes. Future president Millard Fillmore was elected to the U.S. House of Representatives in 1831 as a member of the Anti-Masonic Party (a pro-labor group against social clubs and secret societies).

1832 The Black Hawk War leads to the taking of Native American land west to the Mississippi River. Future president Abraham Lincoln is among those fighting.

1832 President Andrew Jackson vetoes the charter for the Second National Bank (the federal banking system), creating great controversy between Democrats (favoring states' rights) and proponents for a strong federal government, who gradually unite to form the Whig Party in 1834.

1833 Running water is installed in the White House.

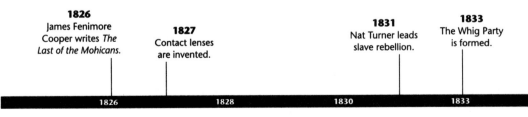

1826
James Fenimore Cooper writes *The Last of the Mohicans.*

1827
Contact lenses are invented.

1831
Nat Turner leads slave rebellion.

1833
The Whig Party is formed.

1826   1828   1830   1833

1834   Congress censures (publicly rebukes) President Andrew Jackson for having taken funds from the federal bank and depositing them in various state banks.

1836   Vice President Martin Van Buren is elected president after defeating three Whig candidates. Whigs hoped that their three regional candidates would win enough electoral votes to deny Van Buren a majority and throw the election to the House of Representatives, where Whigs held the majority.

1836   The last surviving founding father, James Madison, dies the same year the first president born after the American Revolution (Martin Van Buren) is elected.

1836   Arkansas becomes the twenty-fifth state of the Union.

1837   The Panic of 1837 initiates a period of economic hard times that lasts throughout President Martin Van Buren's administration.

1837   Michigan becomes the twenty-sixth state of the Union.

1840   Military hero and Ohio politician William Henry Harrision (known as "Old Tippecanoe") defeats President Martin Van Buren.

1841   President William Henry Harrison dies thirty-one days after being inaugurated president. A constitutional issue arises because the document is unclear as to whether Vice President John Tyler should complete Harrison's term or serve as an interim president until Congress selects a new president. Tyler has himself sworn in as president. Controversy follows, but Tyler sets a precedent on presidential succession.

1841   The President's Cabinet, except for Secretary of State Daniel Webster, resigns, and some congressmen con-

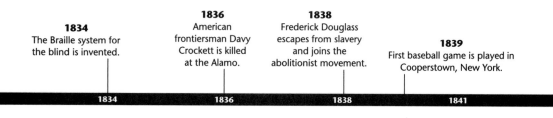

1834
The Braille system for the blind is invented.

1836
American frontiersman Davy Crockett is killed at the Alamo.

1838
Frederick Douglass escapes from slavery and joins the abolitionist movement.

1839
First baseball game is played in Cooperstown, New York.

1834   1836   1838   1841

sider impeachment proceedings against President John Tyler (but the impeachment fails to materialize). Though a member of the Whig Party, Tyler opposes the Whig program for expanding federal powers. He is kicked out of the Whig Party.

1842   The Webster-Ashburton Treaty settles a border dispute between Maine and Quebec, Canada, and averts war between the United States and Great Britain.

1844   Congress approves a resolution annexing Texas.

1844   Tennessee politician James K. Polk, strongly associated with former president Andrew Jackson, is elected president. The years beginning with Jackson's presidency in 1829 and ending with Polk's in March 1849 are often referred to historically as The Age of Jackson.

1845   Congress passes and President James K. Polk signs legislation to have presidential elections held simultaneously throughout the country on the Tuesday following the first Monday in November.

1845   Florida becomes the twenty-seventh and Texas the twenty-eighth states of the Union.

1845   The U.S. Naval Academy opens.

1846   The Mexican War begins.

1846   Iowa and Wisconsin expand the Union to thirty states.

1848   Gas lamps are installed in the White House to replace candles and oil lamps.

1848   The Mexican War ends. The United States takes possession of the southwest area from Texas to California.

1848   General Zachary Taylor, a Mexican War hero, is elected president in a close race. He had joined the Whig

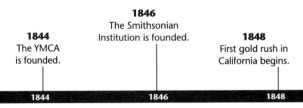

1846
The Smithsonian
Institution is founded.

1844
The YMCA
is founded.

1848
First gold rush in
California begins.

1842   1844   1846   1848

Complete American Presidents Sourcebook

Party but promised to remain above partisan causes and announced that he was against the expansion of slavery into new territories. Ex-president Martin Van Buren finishes a distant third as a candidate for the Free-Soil Party that also opposes the expansion of slavery into new territories. Van Buren likely drew enough votes from the Democratic candidate, former Michigan senator Lewis Cass, to tip the election to Taylor.

1849   The California Gold Rush brings thousands of people into the new American territory.

1850   President Zachary Taylor dies in office, and Vice President Millard Fillmore becomes president.

1850   President Millard Fillmore supports and signs into law the series of bills called the Compromise of 1850 that the late president Zachary Taylor had opposed. The Fugitive Slave Act, which forces northern states to return runaway slaves, becomes law.

1850   California becomes the thirty-first state of the Union.

1850   The Pony Express begins operation, providing mail service to the far west.

1852   Former New Hampshire senator Franklin Pierce is elected president.

1852   *Uncle Tom's Cabin,* by Harriet Beecher Stowe, is published and further fuels growing support in the North for complete abolition of slavery.

1853   The Gadsden Purchase adds southern areas of present-day New Mexico and Arizona as American territory.

1854   The Republican Party is formed by those against the expansion of slavery and by abolitionists wanting to outlaw the institution, drawing from the Whig Party

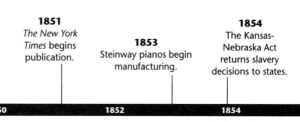

1851
The New York Times begins publication.

1853
Steinway pianos begin manufacturing.

1854
The Kansas-Nebraska Act returns slavery decisions to states.

1849   1850   1852   1854

(which becomes defunct) and Democrats opposed to slavery.

1854 Diplomatic and trade relations begin between the United States and Japan.

1856 Civil war breaks out in Kansas Territory between pro- and anti-slavery proponents.

1856 Former secretary of state James Buchanan, a states' rights advocate, is elected president. Former California senator John Frémont finishes second as the Republican Party's first presidential candidate. Former president Millard Fillmore finishes third with about twenty percent of the popular vote and eight electoral votes, as the nominee of the American Party (also nicknamed the Know-Nothing Party).

1857 The *Dred Scott* decision by the U.S. Supreme Court limits the power of Congress to decide on slavery issues in American territories petitioning to become states.

1858 The Lincoln-Douglas debates in Illinois, between U.S. Senate candidates Abraham Lincoln and incumbent Stephen Douglas, receive national press coverage.

1858 Minnesota becomes the thirty-second state of the Union.

1859 Abolitionist John Brown leads a raid on a federal arsenal in Harper's Ferry, Virginia (now West Virginia), hoping to spark and arm a slave rebellion.

1859 Oregon becomes the thirty-third state of the Union.

1860 Former Illinois congressman Abraham Lincoln is elected president despite winning less than forty percent of the popular vote. Democratic votes are split among three candidates. One of the party's candidates, Illi-

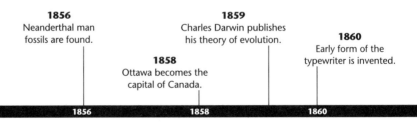

1856
Neanderthal man fossils are found.

1859
Charles Darwin publishes his theory of evolution.

1860
Early form of the typewriter is invented.

1858
Ottawa becomes the capital of Canada.

1854   1856   1858   1860

nois senator Stephen Douglas, finishes second in the popular vote but places fourth in electoral votes.

1860 South Carolina secedes from the Union.

1861 Confederate States of America formed; Civil War begins.

1861 Kansas becomes the thirty-fourth state of the Union.

1863 President Abraham Lincoln, sitting in what is now called the Lincoln Bedroom in the White House, signs the Emancipation Proclamation, freeing slaves in the states in rebellion.

1863 West Virginia becomes the thirty-fifth state of the Union.

1863 President Abraham Lincoln proposes a policy for admitting seceded states back into the Union on moderate terms.

1864 Pro-Union Republicans and Democrats unite as the National Union Party under President Abraham Lincoln (Republican) and Tennessee senator Andrew Johnson, who had remained in Congress after his southern colleagues walked out. The Lincoln-Johnson ticket wins 212 of 233 electoral votes.

1864 Nevada becomes the thirty-sixth state of the Union.

1865 The Civil War ends.

1865 President Abraham Lincoln is assassinated, and Vice President Andrew Johnson succeeds him as president.

1865 The Thirteenth Amendment to the Constitution, outlawing slavery, is ratified.

1867 Over objections and vetoes by President Andrew Johnson, Congress passes harsher Reconstruction

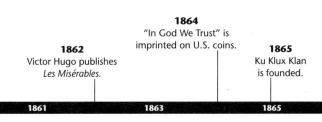

1862
Victor Hugo publishes
Les Misérables.

1864
"In God We Trust" is
imprinted on U.S. coins.

1865
Ku Klux Klan
is founded.

1861   1863   1865   1867

policies (terms under which former Confederate states can operate) than the Johnson (and Lincoln) plans.

1867 Nebraska becomes the thirty-seventh state of the Union.

1867 The United States purchases Alaska (a deal called "Seward's Folly" after Secretary of State William H. Seward, who negotiated the acquisition) from Russia.

1868 President Andrew Johnson becomes the first president to be impeached by the House of Representatives. He is acquitted by one vote in a trial in the U.S. Senate.

1868 Civil War hero Ulysses S. Grant is elected president.

1869 The Transcontinental railroad is completed.

1869 President Ulysses S. Grant fails in attempts to annex the Dominican Republic.

1872 President Ulysses S. Grant is reelected. His opponent, newspaper publisher Horace Greeley, dies shortly after the election, and his electoral votes are dispersed among several other Democrats.

1873 The Crédit Mobilier scandal reflects widespread corruption among some officials in the Ulysses S. Grant administration and some congressmen.

1876 Colorado becomes the thirty-eighth state of the Union.

1876 In the hotly contested presidential election, the Democratic candidate, New York governor Samuel J. Tilden, outpolls the Republican nominee, Ohio governor Rutherford B. Hayes, by over two hundred thousand votes, but falls one electoral vote short of a majority when twenty electoral votes (from the states of Florida, South Carolina, Louisiana, and Oregon) are contested with claims of fraud. The House of Representatives fails to resolve the issue.

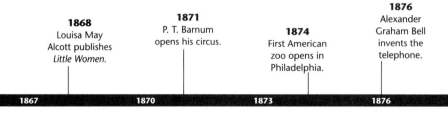

1868
Louisa May Alcott publishes *Little Women.*

1871
P. T. Barnum opens his circus.

1874
First American zoo opens in Philadelphia.

1876
Alexander Graham Bell invents the telephone.

1867 1870 1873 1876

1877 A special Electoral Commission is established to resolve the 1876 presidential election controversy. Days before the scheduled inauguration of the new president in March, the Commission awards the 20 disputed votes to Republican Rutherford B. Hayes, who edges Democrat Samuel J. Tilden, 185-184, in the Electoral College. Some historians refer to the decision as the Compromise of 1877, believing that Republicans and southern Democrats struck a deal: Hayes would be president, and Reconstruction (federal supervision of former Confederate states) would end.

1877 Federal troops are withdrawn from South Carolina and Louisiana, where troops had been stationed since the end of the Civil War to enforce national laws. Reconstruction ends, and southern states regain the same rights as all other states.

1878 Attempting to reform the civil service (where jobs were often provided by the party in power to party members), President Rutherford B. Hayes suspends fellow Republican Chester A. Arthur (a future U.S. president) as the powerful head of the New York Custom's House (which collects import taxes).

1879 The first telephone is installed in the White House. The phone number: 1.

1879 Thomas Edison invents the incandescent light bulb.

1880 Ohio congressman James A. Garfield is elected president.

1881 President James A. Garfield is assassinated by an extremist who lost his job under civil service reform. Chester A. Arthur becomes the fourth vice president to assume the presidency upon the death of the chief executive. Like the previous three (John Tyler, Millard

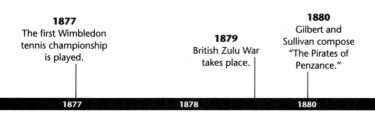

1877
The first Wimbledon tennis championship is played.

1879
British Zulu War takes place.

1880
Gilbert and Sullivan compose "The Pirates of Penzance."

| 1877 | 1878 | 1880 | 1881 |

Fillmore, and Andrew Johnson), Arthur is not selected by his party to run for the presidency after completing the elected president's term.

1883   The Pendleton Act, mandating major civil service reform, is signed into law by President Chester A. Arthur.

1884   New York governor Grover Cleveland is elected as the first Democrat to win the presidency since 1856. Tariffs (taxes on imported goods) and tariff reform become major issues during his presidency and the following three elections.

1885   The Statue of Liberty is dedicated.

1886   President Grover Cleveland marries Frances Folsom, becoming the only president to marry at the White House.

1888   Former Indiana senator Benjamin Harrison is elected president despite receiving 90,000 fewer popular votes than President Grover Cleveland. Harrison wins most of the more populated states for a 233-168 Electoral College advantage.

1889   North Dakota, South Dakota, Montana, and Washington enter the Union, expanding the United States to forty-two states.

1890   Idaho and Wyoming become the forty-third and forty-fourth states of the Union.

1891   Electric wiring is installed in the White House.

1892   Former president Grover Cleveland becomes the first person to win non-consecutive presidential terms by defeating incumbent president Benjamin Harrison (in the popular vote *and* the Electoral College). Iowa politician James B. Weaver of the People's Party (also

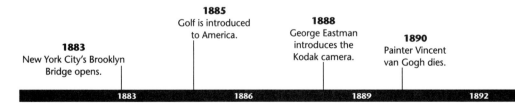

1885
Golf is introduced to America.

1883
New York City's Brooklyn Bridge opens.

1888
George Eastman introduces the Kodak camera.

1890
Painter Vincent van Gogh dies.

1883   1886   1889   1892

known as the Populists) finishes a distant third in the popular vote but garners twenty-two electoral votes.

1893   Lame duck (an official completing an elected term after having failed to be reelected) President Benjamin Harrison presents a treaty to annex Hawaii to the U.S. Congress.

1893   President Grover Cleveland rescinds former president Benjamin Harrison's treaty for the annexation of Hawaii and calls for an investigation of the American-led rebellion that overthrew the Hawaiian native monarchy.

1894   An economic downturn and numerous strikes paralyze the American economy.

1895   With gold reserves (used to back the value of currency) running low, President Grover Cleveland arranges a gold purchase through financier J. P. Morgan.

1896   Ohio governor William McKinley, the Republican Party nominee, is elected president over the Democratic candidate, former Nebraska congressman William Jennings Bryan.

1896   Utah becomes the forty-fifth state of the Union.

1898   The Spanish-American War takes place. The United States wins quickly and takes possession of overseas territories (the former Spanish colonies of Cuba, Puerto Rico, and the Philippines).

1898   President William McKinley reintroduces the Hawaii annexation issue and Congress approves it.

1899   President William McKinley expands U.S. trade with China and other nations through his Open Door Policy.

1900   President William McKinley is reelected by defeating William Jennings Bryan a second time.

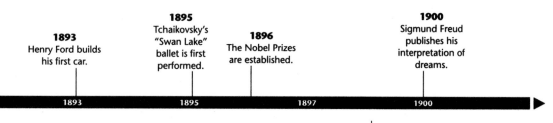

1893
Henry Ford builds his first car.

1895
Tchaikovsky's "Swan Lake" ballet is first performed.

1896
The Nobel Prizes are established.

1900
Sigmund Freud publishes his interpretation of dreams.

1893   1895   1897   1900

1900 Chinese nationalists take arms against growing foreign influences in their country, an uprising called the Boxer Rebellion. American military forces join those of other foreign nations to put down the uprising. American military forces are also stationed in the Philippines to combat revolts.

1901 President William McKinley is assassinated; Vice President Theodore Roosevelt assumes the presidency and, at age 42, becomes the youngest man to become president.

1902 To combat the growing influence of trusts (business combinations intended to stifle competition), President Theodore Roosevelt orders vigorous enforcement of antitrust laws, and an era of business and social reform gains momentum.

1903 The United States quickly recognizes and supports a rebellion in the nation of Colombia through which Panama becomes an independent nation. Through the Panama Canal treaty, which provides a strip of land to be developed by the United States, President Theodore Roosevelt spearheads plans to build a canal across Panama, linking the Atlantic and Pacific oceans.

1904 Theodore Roosevelt becomes the first president who assumed office upon the death of the elected president to win election for a full term.

1905 President Theodore Roosevelt serves as mediator during the Russo-Japanese War. His success at helping end the conflict earns him a Nobel Peace Prize.

1907 Oklahoma becomes the forty-sixth state.

1908 William Howard Taft, who served in the William McKinley and Theodore Roosevelt administrations, is

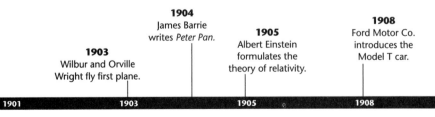

1904
James Barrie
writes *Peter Pan.*

1905
Albert Einstein
formulates the
theory of relativity.

1908
Ford Motor Co.
introduces the
Model T car.

1903
Wilbur and Orville
Wright fly first plane.

1901   1903   1905   1908

elected president. William Jennings Bryan loses in his third presidential bid.

1909   In a sign of the times, President William Howard Taft purchases official automobiles and has the White House stable converted into a garage.

1909   The North Pole is reached.

1912   New Jersey governor Woodrow Wilson is elected president. Former president Theodore Roosevelt, running as the Progressive Party candidate (nicknamed "the Bull Moose Party"), finishes second. Roosevelt outpolls his successor, President William Howard Taft, by about seven hundred thousand popular votes and wins eighty more electoral votes.

1912   New Mexico and Arizona enter the Union, expanding the United States to forty-eight states.

1912   The Sixteenth Amendment, authorizing the collection of income taxes, is ratified.

1912   The Federal Reserve, which regulates the nation's money supply and financial institutions, is established.

1913   The Seventeenth Amendment changes the system for electing U.S. senators. The popular vote replaces the system where most senators were elected by state legislatures.

1914   World War I begins.

1914   U.S. military forces begin having skirmishes with Mexican rebels in a series of incidents that last until 1916.

1914   The Panama Canal is opened.

1916   President Woodrow Wilson is reelected by a slim Electoral College margin, 277-254. He defeats the Repub-

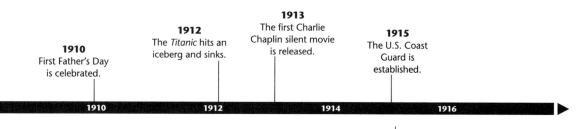

1910
First Father's Day is celebrated.

1912
The *Titanic* hits an iceberg and sinks.

1913
The first Charlie Chaplin silent movie is released.

1915
The U.S. Coast Guard is established.

1910   1912   1914   1916

lican candidate, former U.S. Supreme Court justice Charles Evans Hughes.

1916   President Woodrow Wilson acts as mediator for the nations in conflict in World War I.

1917   Citing acts of German aggression, President Woodrow Wilson asks Congress to declare war. The United States enters World War I. The Selective Service (a system through which young men are called on for military duty) is established.

1918   World War I ends.

1919   Congress rejects the Treaty of Versailles negotiated by President Woodrow Wilson and other leaders representing the nations involved in World War I. Congress also rejects American participation in the League of Nations that Wilson had envisioned.

1919   Attempting to rally support of the Treaty of Versailles and the League of Nations during a long speaking tour, President Woodrow Wilson collapses with a debilitating stroke. The public is not made aware of the severity of the affliction that leaves Wilson bedridden.

1919   The Eighteenth Amendment, outlawing the manufacture and sale of alcohol, is ratified.

1920   Women are able to participate in national elections for the first time.

1920   Ohio senator Warren G. Harding is elected president.

1922   Illegal deals are made by some officials of the Warren G. Harding administration. Two years later, they are implicated in the Teapot Dome scandal.

1923   President Warren G. Harding dies in San Francisco, California; Vice President Calvin Coolidge assumes the presidency.

1918
The U.S. Army's
Stars and Stripes
newspaper begins
publication.

1920
Joan of Arc is
canonized a saint.

1923
Jacob Schick
patents the
electric razor.

1917   1919   1921   1923

1924   Calvin Coolidge is elected president in a landslide, defeating West Virginia politician John W. Davis, the Democratic candidate. Progressive Party candidate Robert M. LaFollette, a future Wisconsin senator, garners over thirteen percent of the popular vote and wins thirteen electoral votes.

1925   The Scopes Trial is held in Dayton, Tennessee, after a public school teacher instructs his class on the theory of evolution in defiance of a state law.

1927   Charles Lindbergh becomes the first pilot to fly solo across the Atlantic Ocean.

1928   Former secretary of commerce Herbert Hoover, who also supervised international relief efforts during World War I, wins his first election attempt in a landslide (by over six million popular votes and a 444-87 Electoral College triumph).

1929   The stock market crashes.

1930   President Herbert Hoover assures the nation that "the economy is on the mend," but continued crises become the Great Depression that lasts the entire decade.

1932   The Bonus March, in which World War I veterans gather in Washington, D.C., to demand benefits promised to them, ends in disaster and death when military officials forcibly remove them and destroy their campsites.

1932   New York governor Franklin D. Roosevelt defeats President Herbert Hoover by over seven million popular votes and a 472-59 margin in the Electoral College.

1933   President Franklin D. Roosevelt calls a special session of Congress to enact major pieces of legislation to combat the Great Depression. Over a span called The

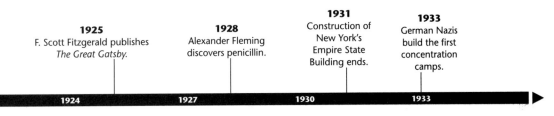

1925
F. Scott Fitzgerald publishes
The Great Gatsby.

1928
Alexander Fleming
discovers penicillin.

1931
Construction of
New York's
Empire State
Building ends.

1933
German Nazis
build the first
concentration
camps.

1924   1927   1930   1933

Hundred Days, much of Roosevelt's New Deal program of social and economic relief, recovery, and reform is approved.

1933 As part of the Twentieth Amendment to the Constitution, the inauguration date of the president is changed to January 20 of the year following the election.

1933 The Twenty-first Amendment repeals prohibition.

1936 President Franklin D. Roosevelt is reelected by a popular vote margin of eleven million and wins the Electoral College vote, 523-8.

1937 Frustrated when the U.S. Supreme Court declares several New Deal programs unconstitutional, President Franklin D. Roosevelt initiates legislation to add more justices to the court and to set term limits. His attempt to "stack the court" receives little support.

1939 World War II begins.

1939 Physicist Albert Einstein informs President Franklin D. Roosevelt about the possibility for creating nuclear weapons and warns him that Nazi scientists are already pursuing experiments to unleash atomic power.

1940 President Franklin D. Roosevelt wins an unprecedented third term by slightly less than five million popular votes and a 449-82 win in the Electoral College.

1941 Pearl Harbor, Hawaii, is attacked; the United States enters World War II.

1942 The success of the first nuclear chain reaction is communicated to President Franklin D. Roosevelt through the code words, "The eagle has landed." A secret program for manufacturing and testing atomic bombs begins.

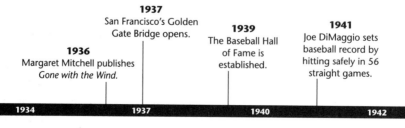

1937
San Francisco's Golden Gate Bridge opens.

1939
The Baseball Hall of Fame is established.

1941
Joe DiMaggio sets baseball record by hitting safely in 56 straight games.

1936
Margaret Mitchell publishes *Gone with the Wind.*

1934   1937   1940   1942

1944   President Franklin D. Roosevelt is elected to a fourth term by over five million popular votes and a 432-99 Electoral College triumph.

1945   President Franklin D. Roosevelt attends the Yalta Conference and meets with British prime minister Winston Churchill and Soviet leader Joseph Stalin to discuss war issues and the postwar world.

1945   President Franklin D. Roosevelt dies; Vice President Harry S. Truman becomes president. It is only then that Truman learns about development and successful testing of the atomic bomb.

1945   World War II ends in Europe.

1945   The United States drops atomic bombs on Japan. Japan surrenders, and World War II ends.

1946   The U.S. government seizes coal mines and railroads to avoid labor strikes and business practices that might contribute to inflation.

1947   An economic aid package called the Marshall Plan, named after its architect, Secretary of State George C. Marshall, helps revive war-torn Europe.

1947   The Cold War, a period of strained relations and the threat of nuclear war between the United States and the Soviet Union, and their respective allies, settles in and continues for more than forty years.

1948   Renovation of the White House begins. Four years later, the project has completely reconstructed the interior and added two underground levels.

1948   Despite the *Chicago Daily Tribune* headline "DEWEY DEFEATS TRUMAN" on the morning after election day, President Harry S. Truman wins the presidency,

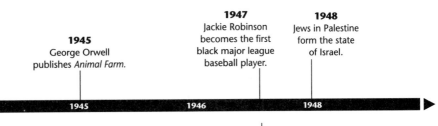

1945
George Orwell
publishes *Animal Farm.*

1947
Jackie Robinson
becomes the first
black major league
baseball player.

1948
Jews in Palestine
form the state
of Israel.

1944   1945   1946   1948

taking over two million more popular votes and winning 303-189 in the Electoral College. The State's Rights Party candidate, South Carolina governor J. Strom Thurmond, places third, slightly outpolling the Progressive Party candidate, former vice president Henry Wallace, and winning thirty-nine electoral votes. Thurmond led a contingent of Southern politicians away from the Democratic Party in protest of Truman's support for civil rights legislation.

1949   The North Atlantic Treaty Organization (NATO) is formed by the United States and its European allies to monitor and check acts of aggression in Europe.

1950   The United States becomes involved in a police action to protect South Korea from invasion by communist North Korea. The police action intensifies into the Korean War.

1951   The Twenty-second Amendment to the Constitution is ratified, limiting presidents to two elected terms and no more than two years of a term to which someone else was elected.

1952   Dwight D. "Ike" Eisenhower, famous as the Supreme Commander of Allied Forces during World War II, is elected president.

1953   An armistice is signed in Korea.

1954   The Army-McCarthy hearings are held. Wisconsin senator Joseph McCarthy presents accusations that the U.S. military and Department of State are deeply infiltrated by communists. McCarthy is eventually disgraced when most of his accusations prove groundless.

1954   In *Brown v. Board of Education,* the U.S. Supreme Court rules that racially segregated public schools are un-

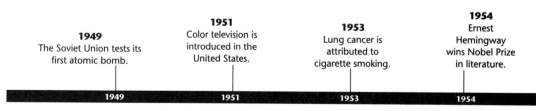

1949
The Soviet Union tests its first atomic bomb.

1951
Color television is introduced in the United States.

1953
Lung cancer is attributed to cigarette smoking.

1954
Ernest Hemingway wins Nobel Prize in literature.

1949   1951   1953   1954

constitutional. In 1957, President Dwight D. Eisenhower sends troops to Little Rock, Arkansas, to enforce desegregation of schools.

1956   An uprising in Hungary against Soviet domination is quickly crushed.

1956   President Dwight D. Eisenhower wins reelection, his second straight triumph over his Democratic challenger, former Illinois governor Adlai Stevenson.

1957   The Soviet Union launches the first space satellite, *Sputnik I.*

1958   The United States launches its first space satellite, *Explorer I,* and the National Aeronautics and Space Agency (NASA) is created.

1959   Alaska and Hawaii enter the Union as the forty-ninth and fiftieth states.

1960   The Cold War deepens over the *U2* incident, where a U.S. spy plane is shot down inside the Soviet Union.

1960   Massachusetts senator John F. Kennedy outpolls Vice President Richard Nixon by slightly more than 100,000 votes while winning 303-219 in the Electoral College. Kennedy, at age 43, is the youngest elected president. A dispute over nine thousand votes in Illinois, that might have resulted in Nixon winning that state instead of Kennedy, is stopped by Nixon. A change of electoral votes in Illinois would not have affected the overall electoral majority won by Kennedy.

1961   The District of Columbia is allowed three electoral votes.

1961   An invasion of Cuba by American-supported rebels at the Bay of Pigs fails when an internal rebellion does

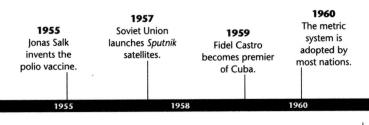

1955
Jonas Salk invents the polio vaccine.

1957
Soviet Union launches *Sputnik* satellites.

1959
Fidel Castro becomes premier of Cuba.

1960
The metric system is adopted by most nations.

1955   1958   1960   1961

not materialize and President John F. Kennedy refuses to provide military backing.

1962 The Cuban Missile Crisis puts the United States and the Soviet Union on the brink of nuclear war after the Soviets are discovered building missile launch sites in Cuba. After a tense, ten-day standoff, the missiles are removed.

1963 A military coup overthrows the political leader of South Vietnam, where American military advisors are assisting South Vietnamese to repel a communist takeover.

1963 A large civil rights march on Washington, D.C., culminates with the famous "I Have a Dream" speech by Rev. Martin Luther King Jr.

1963 President John F. Kennedy is assassinated; Vice President Lyndon B. Johnson assumes the presidency.

1964 President Lyndon B. Johnson steers major civil rights legislation through Congress in memory of the late president John F. Kennedy. The Twenty-fourth Amendment to the Constitution is ratified and ensures the right of citizens of the United States to vote shall not be denied "by reason of failure to pay any poll tax or other tax."

1964 President Lyndon B. Johnson is elected in a landslide, winning almost sixteen million more popular votes than Arizona senator Barry Goldwater.

1965 The Vietnam conflict escalates. President Lyndon B. Johnson is given emergency powers by Congress. Massive bombing missions begin, and U.S. military troops begin engaging in combat, although the U.S. Congress never officially declares war.

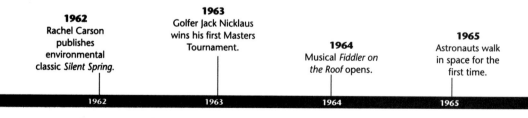

1962
Rachel Carson publishes environmental classic *Silent Spring*.

1963
Golfer Jack Nicklaus wins his first Masters Tournament.

1964
Musical *Fiddler on the Roof* opens.

1965
Astronauts walk in space for the first time.

1962   1963   1964   1965

1966   An unmanned American spacecraft lands on the moon.

1967   Protests, including a march on Washington, D.C., escalate against American involvement in the Vietnam War.

1967   Thurgood Marshall becomes the first African American Supreme Court justice.

1967   The Twenty-fifth Amendment to the Constitution is ratified and provides clear lines of succession to the presidency: "Section 1. In case of the removal of the President from office or of his death or resignation, the Vice President shall become President. Section 2. Whenever there is a vacancy in the office of the Vice President, the President shall nominate a Vice President who shall take office upon confirmation by a majority vote of both Houses of Congress."

1968   Civil rights leader Rev. Martin Luther King Jr. is assassinated in April, and leading Democratic presidential candidate Robert F. Kennedy is assassinated in June.

1968   Former vice president Richard Nixon is elected president, winning with 500,000 more popular votes than incumbent vice president Hubert H. Humphrey and a 301-191 Electoral College edge. Former Alabama governor George C. Wallace of the American Independent Party (for state's rights and against racial desegregation) nets over nine million popular votes and wins forty-six electoral votes.

1969   American troop withdrawals from South Vietnam begin.

1969   U.S. astronaut Neil Armstrong becomes the first man to walk on the moon.

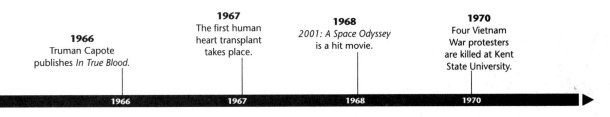

1966
Truman Capote publishes *In True Blood.*

1967
The first human heart transplant takes place.

1968
2001: A Space Odyssey is a hit movie.

1970
Four Vietnam War protesters are killed at Kent State University.

1966   1967   1968   1970

1972   President Richard Nixon reestablishes U.S. relations with the People's Republic of China that were ended after a communist takeover in China in 1949. He visits China and the Soviet Union, where he initiates a policy of détente (a relaxing of tensions between rival nations).

1972   An investigation of a burglary of Democratic National Headquarters at the Watergate Hotel and Office Complex in Washington, D.C., begins and leads to connections with officials in the Richard Nixon administration.

1972   President Richard Nixon is reelected in a landslide.

1973   The Paris Peace Agreement, between the United States and North Vietnam, ends American military involvement in the Vietnam War.

1973   Vice President Spiro T. Agnew resigns over income tax evasion; he is replaced by Michigan congressman Gerald R. Ford.

1974   Nationally televised U.S. Senate hearings on the Watergate scandal confirm connections between the 1972 burglary and officials of the Richard Nixon administration as well as abuses of power.

1974   The House Judiciary Committee begins impeachment hearings and plans to recommend to the House the impeachment of President Richard Nixon.

1974   President Richard Nixon resigns from office over the Watergate scandal. Vice President Gerald R. Ford assumes office.

1974   President Gerald R. Ford issues a pardon, protecting former president Richard Nixon from prosecution in an attempt to end "our national nightmare."

1972
Longtime FBI director J. Edgar Hoover dies.

1973
Skylab space missions take place.

1974
Hank Aaron passes Babe Ruth as baseball's all-time home run hitter.

1972   1973   1974   1975

1976   In a close election, former Georgia governor Jimmy Carter defeats President Gerald R. Ford.

1977   Beset by rising fuel costs and a continued sluggish economy, President Jimmy Carter calls an energy shortage "the moral equivalent of war" and attempts to rally conservation efforts.

1979   The Camp David Accords, the result of negotiations spearheaded by President Jimmy Carter, is signed by the leaders of Egyptian president Anwar Sadat and Israeli prime minister Menachem Begin in Washington, D.C.

1979   Fifty-two Americans are taken hostage in Iran following a religious revolution in that nation in which the American-supported leader was overthrown. The hostage crisis lasts 444 days, with the hostages released on the day President Jimmy Carter leaves office.

1980   Former California governor Ronald Reagan wins a landslide (489-49 in the Electoral College) over President Jimmy Carter. Independent candidate John Anderson, a longtime Republican congressman from Illinois, polls over five million votes. Reagan becomes the oldest president.

1981   Sandra Day O'Connor becomes the first female U.S. Supreme Court justice.

1982   Economic growth begins after a decade of sluggish performance.

1984   President Ronald Reagan is reelected in another landslide, drawing the most popular votes ever (54,455,075) and romping in the Electoral College, 525-13.

1987   A sudden stock market crash and growing federal deficits threaten economic growth.

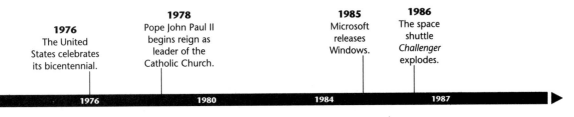

1976
The United States celebrates its bicentennial.

1978
Pope John Paul II begins reign as leader of the Catholic Church.

1985
Microsoft releases Windows.

1986
The space shuttle *Challenger* explodes.

1976   1980   1984   1987

1988 George Bush becomes the first sitting vice president since Martin Van Buren in 1836 to be elected president.

1989 Several East European nations become independent from domination by the U.S.S.R. Reforms in the U.S.S.R. eventually lead to the breakup of the Soviet Union; the former Soviet states become independent nations in 1991, and the Cold War ends.

1991 After the Iraqi government fails to comply with a United Nations resolution to abandon Kuwait, which its military invaded in August of 1990, the Gulf War begins. Within a month, Kuwait is liberated by an international military force. President George Bush's popularity soars over his leadership in rallying U.N. members to stop Iraqi aggression.

1992 An economic downturn and a huge budget deficit erode President George Bush's popularity. Arkansas governor Bill Clinton defeats Bush for the presidency. The Reform Party candidate, Texas businessman H. Ross Perot, draws 19,221,433 votes, the most ever for a third-party candidate, but wins no electoral votes. Clinton and running mate Al Gore are the youngest president–vice president tandem in history.

1994 An upturn in the economy begins the longest sustained growth period in American history.

1996 President Bill Clinton is reelected.

1998 President Bill Clinton is implicated in perjury (false testimony under oath in a court case) and an extramarital affair. The House Judiciary Committee votes, strictly on party lines, to recommend impeachment of the president, and the House impeaches the president for perjury and abuse of power.

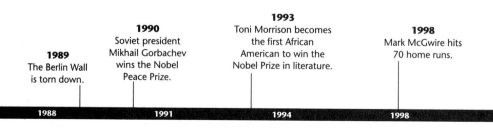

1989
The Berlin Wall is torn down.

1990
Soviet president Mikhail Gorbachev wins the Nobel Peace Prize.

1993
Toni Morrison becomes the first African American to win the Nobel Prize in literature.

1998
Mark McGwire hits 70 home runs.

1988   1991   1994   1998

1999 President Bill Clinton remains in office after being acquitted in a Senate trial.

2000 In the closest and most hotly contested election since 1876, Texas governor George W. Bush narrowly defeats Vice President Al Gore in the Electoral College, 271-266. Gore wins the popular vote by some three hundred thousand votes. The final victor cannot be declared until after a recount in Florida (with its twenty-five electoral votes at stake) takes place. Five weeks of legal battles ensue and Gore officially contests the results before Bush is able to claim victory in the state and, therefore, in the national election.

2000 Hillary Rodham Clinton becomes the first first lady to be elected to public office when she is elected U.S. senator from New York.

2000 In one of his last functions as president, Bill Clinton attends an international economic summit in Asia and visits Vietnam, twenty-five years after the end of the conflict that deeply divided Americans.

2001 George W. Bush is inaugurated the nation's forty-third president and becomes the second son of a president to become president himself.

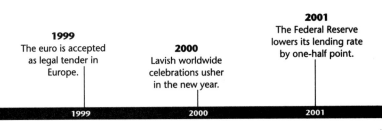

1999
The euro is accepted as legal tender in Europe.

2000
Lavish worldwide celebrations usher in the new year.

2001
The Federal Reserve lowers its lending rate by one-half point.

1999   2000   2001

Words to Know

A

Abolitionists: People who worked to end slavery.

Agrarian: One who believes in and supports issues beneficial to agriculture.

Alien and Sedition Acts: Four bills—the Naturalization Act, Alien Act, Alien Enemies Act, and Sedition Act—passed by Congress in 1798 and signed into law by President John Adams. The Naturalization Act extended from five to fourteen years the waiting period before citizenship—and with it, the right to vote—could be obtained by new immigrants. The two Alien acts gave the president the right to deport or jail foreign citizens he deemed a threat to the nation's stability, especially during wartime. The Sedition Act criminalized criticism of the government. To write or publish views that disparaged the administration was punishable by harsh fines and jail terms.

Allied forces (allies): Alliances of countries in military opposition to another group of nations. Twenty-eight nations made up the Allied and Associated powers in World War I. In World War II, the Allied powers included Great Britain, the United States, and the Soviet Union.

Anarchist: One against any form of government.

Annexing: Adding a new state or possession to the existing United States of America.

Annual Message to Congress: A speech the president delivers before Congress each year. Originally called the Annual Message to Congress and delivered each November, the speech became known as the State of the Union Address and is delivered each January.

Anti-Federalists: A group who wanted a limited federal government and more power for individual states.

Antitrust: Government action against businesses that dominate a certain industry or market and that are alleged to have stifled competing businesses.

Appropriations: Funds authorized for a particular project.

Armistice: An agreement to cease fire while warring parties negotiate a peace settlement.

Articles of Confederation: From March 1, 1781, to June 21, 1788, the Articles served as the equivalent of the Constitution (1787). The Constitution replaced the Articles, which had failed to produce a strong central government, and the present-day United States was formed.

Axis: The countries that fought together against the Allies in World War II. Germany, Italy, and Japan formed the first coalition; eventually, they were joined by Hungary, Romania, Slovakia, Finland, and Bulgaria.

B

Bar: A term that encompasses all certified lawyers—those who have passed all official requirements (the bar exam) to be certified as lawyers.

Bar exam: A test that lawyers must pass in order to become legally certified to practice law.

Battle of the Bulge: Battles surrounding the last German offensive (1944–45) during World War II. Allied forces moving toward Germany from France following the D-Day invasion were stalled by bad weather along the German border. Germans launched a counteroffensive to divide American and British forces. Germans created a "bulge" in the Allied lines, but they were halted and then withdrew.

Bay of Pigs invasion: Failed U.S.-backed invasion of Cuba at the Bay of Pigs by fifteen hundred Cuban exiles opposed to Fidel Castro, on April 17, 1961.

"Big stick" foreign policy: Theodore Roosevelt's theory that in diplomatic efforts, it was wise to "speak softly and carry a big stick," meaning that one should attempt peaceful solutions while at the same time being prepared to back up the talk with action when necessary.

Bill of Rights: The first ten amendments to the American Constitution of rights and privileges guaranteed to the people of the United States.

Black Codes: Laws and provisions that limited civil rights and placed economic restrictions on African Americans.

"Bleeding Kansas": The conflict in Kansas in 1854 between slavery advocates and abolitionists—in the form of both residents and transients, and two different governments—that led to bloodshed. It was the first indication that the issue of slavery would not be settled diplomatically.

Bloc: A unified group able to wield power through its size and numbers.

Boston Tea Party: An event in 1773 in which colonists spilled shipments of tea into Boston harbor to protest taxes imposed on various products.

Bull market: A stock market term that describes a period of aggressive buying and selling of stock that proves profitable for most investors; in contrast, "bear market" is used to describe a more sluggish trading period.

Bureaucracy: A government or big business set up to be run by bureaus, or departments, that strictly follow rules and regulations and a chain of authority.

C

Camp David Accords: An agreement of peace following negotiations led by President Jimmy Carter and signed by Israeli prime minister Menachem Begin and Egyptian president Anwar Sadat on March 26, 1979.

Capitol Hill: A nickname for Congress, since the Capitol building where Congress holds sessions is located on a small hill.

Carpetbaggers: A term of contempt used by Southerners about agents, humanitarians, politicians, and businessmen who came to the South to assist or to exploit Reconstruction policies. The term suggests that Northerners could stuff everything they owned into a bag made from carpet.

Caucus: An organized vote by registered and designated members of a political party to determine the amount of support within a state for the party's presidential candidates.

Censure: To publicly condemn an individual; in Congress, the act of censure expresses Congress's condemnation of an individual's actions and is entered into the *Congressional Record.*

Central Intelligence Agency (CIA): A U.S. government agency charged with accumulating information on foreign countries.

Checks and balances: The system in which the three branches of the U.S. government can review and dismiss acts passed by one of the other branches.

Civil service: Positions under the authority of the federal government.

Civil War: Conflict that took place from 1861 to 1865 between the Northern states (Union) and the Southern seceded states (Confederacy); also known in the South as the War between the States and in the North as the War of the Rebellion.

Coalitions: Groups of people supporting a political issue or cause.

Cold War: A term that describes a period from 1945 to the late 1980s characterized by tense conflicts and failed diplomacy between the Soviet Union and the United States and their respective allies.

Communism: A system in which the government controls the distribution of goods and services and limits individual freedom.

Compromise of 1850: Legislation passed by Congress and signed into law by President Millard Fillmore consisting of five bills: (1) California was admitted as a free state; (2) Texas was compensated for the loss of territory in a boundary dispute with New Mexico; (3) New Mexico was granted territorial status; (4) the slave trade—but not slavery itself—was abolished in Washington, D.C; (5) and most controversially, the Fugitive Slave Law was enacted, allowing slaveowners to pursue fleeing slaves and recapture them in free states.

Confederate States of America (Confederacy): The eleven Southern states that seceded (separated) from the United States during the 1860s and fought the Union during the American Civil War.

Congressional Record: A document that records all speeches and votes made in Congress.

Conservative: A political philosophy of limited government influence and support for conventional social values.

Constitutional Convention: The 1787 convention attended by delegates to strengthen the Articles of Confederation. Instead, delegates adopted the American Constitution that formed the United States.

Constructionist: One who bases decisions on literal readings of the Constitution.

Consul: A diplomat stationed in a foreign country who advises people from his or her own country on legal matters.

Continental Army: The American army during the Revolutionary War against Great Britain.

Continental Congress: The group of representatives who met to establish the United States.

Coup: A sudden overthrow of a government, often by the country's military.

Covert operations: Secret, undercover acts used to help influence the outcome of events.

Cuban missile crisis: A showdown in October 1962 that brought the Soviet Union and the United States close to war over the existence of Soviet nuclear missiles in Cuba.

D

D-Day: A military term that describes the day when an event can be scheduled. D-Day in World War II was June 6, 1944, when Allied forces landed in Normandy, France.

Dark horse: A little-known candidate with modest chances for success who might emerge surprisingly strong.

Delegate: A member of a party or organization who has a vote that represents a larger group and helps determine the leader of that party or organization.

Democratic Party: One of the oldest political parties in the United States, developed out of the Democratic-Republican Party of the late eighteenth century. Andrew Jackson was one of its first leaders. In the years before the Civil War (1861–65), Democrats became increasingly associated with the South and slavery. Following the war, the party gradually transformed and became associated with urban voters and liberal policies. In the twentieth and twenty-first centuries, Democrats have generally favored freer trade, more international commitments, greater government regulations, and social programs.

Democratic-Republican Party: One of the first political parties in the United States, led by Thomas Jefferson and James Madison in the 1790s to oppose the Federalist Party and close ties with Great Britain. It was also called the Republican Party and the Jeffersonian Republican Party at the time, but the term Democratic-Republican helps distinguish that early political group from the Democratic and Republican parties that were formed later. The Democratic-Republican Party dissolved in the 1820s. Many former members began supporting the formation of the Democratic Party led by Andrew Jackson, who was elected president in 1828 and 1832. The modern-day Republican Party was formed in 1854.

Depression: *See* **Great Depression.**

Deregulation: Removal of guidelines and laws governing a business or financial institution.

Détente: A relaxing of tensions between rival nations, marked by increased diplomatic, commercial, and cultural contact.

Draft cards: From the mid-1960s through the mid-1970s, all males had to register for the draft upon turning eighteen. After registering, an individual received a draft card that contained a draft number. A lottery system was used to determine which available males would be "drafted"—required to serve in the military.

E

Election board: A group authorized to operate elections and count votes.

Electoral College: A body officially responsible for electing the president of the United States. In presidential elections, the candidate who receives the most popular votes in a particular state wins all of that state's electoral votes. Votes are distributed among states in ratios based on population. A candidate must win a majority of electoral votes (over fifty percent) in order to win the presidency.

Electoral votes: The votes a presidential candidate receives for having won a majority of the popular vote in a state. In presidential elections, the candidate who receives the most popular votes in a particular state wins all of that states' electoral votes. Votes are distributed among states in ratios based on population. A candidate must win a majority of electoral votes (over fifty percent) in order to win the presidency.

Emancipation: The act of freeing people from slavery.

Enfranchisement: Voting rights.

Expansionism: The policy of a nation that plans to enlarge its size or gain possession of other lands.

Exploratory committee: A group established by a potential political candidate to examine whether enough party, public, and financial support exists for the potential candidate to officially announce that he or she is running for an elected position.

F

Federal budget: The list of all planned expenditures the federal government expects to make over a year.

Federal budget deficit: When government spending exceeds income (from taxes and other revenue).

Federal Reserve System: The central banking system of the United States, which serves as the banker to the financial sector and the government, issues the national currency, and supervises banking practices.

Federalist: A proponent for a strong national (federal) government.

Federalist Party: An American political party of the late eighteenth century that began losing influence around 1820. Federalists supported a strong national government. Growing sentiments for states' rights and rural regions led to the demise of the party. Many Federalists became Democratic-Republicans until that party was split into factions in the mid-1820s. Those favoring states' rights became Jackson Democrats and formed the Democratic Party in 1832.

First Continental Congress: A group of representatives from the thirteen colonies who met in Philadelphia in 1774 to list grievances (complaints) against England.

Fiscal: Relating to financial matters.

Fourteen Points: Famous speech given by Woodrow Wilson that includes reasons for American involvement in war, terms for peace, and his vision of a League of Nations.

Freedmen's Bureau: An agency that provided federal help for freed slaves.

Fugitive Slave Law: The provision in the Compromise of 1850 that allowed Southern slaveowners to pursue and capture runaway slaves into Northern states.

G

General assembly: A state congressional system made up only of representatives from districts within that particular state.

Gerrymandering: A practice whereby the political party in power changes boundaries in a voting area to include more people likely to support the party in power. This can occur when Congressional districts are rezoned (marked off into different sections) following the national census that occurs every ten years.

Gold standard: The economic practice whereby all of the money printed and minted in a nation is based on the amount of gold the nation has stored. (Paper money is printed; coins are minted, or stamped.)

GOP: Short for "Grand Old Party," a nickname of the Republican Party.

Grand jury: A group empowered to decide whether a government investigation can provide enough evidence to make criminal charges against a citizen.

Grass roots: A term that describes political activity that begins with small groups of people acting without the influence of large and powerful groups.

Great Depression: The worst financial crisis in American history. Usually dated from 1929, when many investors lost money during a stock market crash, to 1941, when the last Depression-related relief effort to help impoverished and unemployed people was passed by the government. When America entered World War II (1939–45) in 1941, many more employment opportunities became available in war-related industries.

Great Society: A set of social programs proposed by President Lyndon B. Johnson designed to end segregation and reduce poverty in the United States.

Gross national product (GNP): An economic measurement of a nation's total value of goods and services produced over a certain period (usually a year); the GNP became an official economic statistic in 1947.

H

House of Burgesses: A representative body made up of Virginia colonists but under the authority of British rule.

Human rights: Principles based on the belief that human beings are born free and equal; governments must respect those rights or they can be accused of human rights violations.

I

Immunity: Protection from prosecution; usually extended to someone who can help the prosecution win its case.

Impeachment: A legislative proceeding charging a public official with misconduct. Impeachment consists of the formal accusation of such an official and the trial that follows. It does not refer to removal from office of the accused.

Imperialism: The process of expanding the authority of one government over other nations and groups of people.

Incumbent: The person currently holding an elected office during an election period.

Independent counsel: A federal position established during the 1970s to investigate federal officials accused of crimes. The Independent Counsel Act, intended to perform in a nonpartisan manner in rare occasions, was not renewed in 1999.

Indictment: An official charge of having committed a crime.

Industrialization: The use of machinery for manufacturing goods.

Inflation: An economic term that describes a situation in which money loses some of its value, usually because the cost of goods is more expensive.

Infrastructure: The system of public works—the physical resources constructed for public use, such as bridges and roads—of a state or country.

Injunction: A legal maneuver that suspends a certain practice until a legal decision can be reached.

Insurrections: Armed rebellions against a recognized authority.

Integration: The bringing together of people of all races and ethnic backgrounds without restrictions; desegregation.

Interest rates: The percentage of a loan that a person agrees to pay for borrowing money.

Internationalism: Interest and participation in events involving other countries.

Iran-Contra scandal: A scandal during the Ronald Reagan administration during which government officials made illegal sales of weapons to Iran. Money made from those sales were diverted to secret funds provided to the Contras in the civil war in El Salvador. This was illegal, since Congress must authorize foreign aid.

Iran hostage crisis: A 444-day period from November 4, 1979, to Inauguration Day 1981 when Iran held 52 American embassy officials hostage following the toppling of the American-backed Shah of Iran.

Iron Curtain: A term describing Eastern European nations dominated by the Soviet Union.

Isolationism: A national policy of avoiding pacts, treaties, and other official agreements with other nations in order to remain neutral.

K

Kansas-Nebraska Act: A U.S. law authorizing the creation of the states of Kansas and Nebraska and specifying that the inhabitants of the territories should decide whether or not to allow slaveholding.

Keynote address: The most important speech during opening ceremonies of an organized meeting.

Korean War: A war from 1950 to 1953 fought between communist North Korea and non-communist South Korea; China backed North Korea and the United Nations backed South Korea.

L

Laissez faire: A French term (roughly translated as "allow to do") commonly used to describe noninterference by government in the affairs of business and the economy.

Lame duck: An official who has lost an election and is filling out the remainder of his or her term.

League of Nations: An organization of nations, as proposed by President Woodrow Wilson, that would exert moral leadership and help nations avoid future wars.

Legal tender: Bills or coin that have designated value.

Lobbyist: A person hired to represent the interests of a particular group to elected officials.

Louisiana Purchase: A vast region in North America purchased by the United States from France in 1803 for $15 million.

Loyalists: Americans who remained loyal to Great Britain during the Revolutionary War (1775–83).

M

Manifest Destiny: The belief that American expansionism is inevitable and divinely ordained.

Marshall Plan: A post–World War II program led by Secretary of State George C. Marshall that helped rebuild European economies (also benefiting U.S. trade) and strengthened democratic governments.

Martial law: A state of emergency during which a military group becomes the sole authority in an area and civil laws are set aside.

Medicare: A government program that provides financial assistance to poor people to help cover medical costs.

Mercenaries: Soldiers hired to serve a foreign country.

Merchant marine: Professional sailors and boat workers involved with commercial marine trade and maintenance (as opposed to branches of the military such as the navy and the coast guard).

Midterm elections: Congressional elections that occur halfway through a presidential term. These elections can affect the president's dealings with Congress. A president is elected every four years; representatives (members of the House of Representatives), every two years; and senators, every six years.

Military dictatorships: States in which military leaders have absolute power.

Military draft: A mandatory program that requires that all males register for possible military service. Those who pass a medical test receive a draft number. A lottery system is used to determine which available males must serve in the military. Those whose numbers are drawn are "drafted" into military service.

Military governments: Governments supervised or run by a military force.

Military tribunal: A court presided over by military officials to try cases in an area under a state of war.

Militia: A small military group, not affiliated with the federal government, organized for emergency service.

Missing in action: A term that describes military personnel unaccounted for. They might have been captured by the enemy, in which case they become prisoners of war; they might be hiding out and attempting to return to safety; or they might have been killed.

Missouri Compromise: Legislation passed in 1820 that designated which areas could enter the Union as free states and which could enter as slave states. It was repealed in 1854.

Monarchy: A form of government in which a single person (usually a king or queen) has absolute power.

Monroe Doctrine: A policy statement issued during the presidency of James Monroe (1817–25) that explained the position of the United States on the activities of European powers in the western hemisphere; of major significance was the stand of the United States against European intervention in the affairs of the Americas.

Muckrakers: A circle of investigative reporters during Theodore Roosevelt's term in office who exposed the seamier (unwholesome) side of American life. These reporters thoroughly researched their stories and based their reports on provable facts.

N

National Security Council: A group of military advisors assisting the president.

Nationalism: Loyalty to a nation that exalts that quality above all other nations.

Nazi: The abbreviated name for the National Socialist German Workers' Party, the political party led by Adolf Hitler, who became dictator of Germany. Hitler's Nazi Party controlled Germany from 1933 to 1945. The Nazis promoted racist and anti-Semitic (anti-Jewish) ideas and enforced complete obedience to Hitler and the party.

Neutrality: A position in which a nation is not engaged with others and does not take sides in disputes.

New Deal: A series of programs initiated by the administration of President Franklin D. Roosevelt to create jobs and stimulate the economy during the Great Depression (1929–41).

North Atlantic Treaty Organization (NATO): An alliance for collective security created by the North Atlantic Treaty in 1949 and originally involving Belgium, Canada, Denmark, France, Great Britain, Iceland, Italy, Luxembourg, the Netherlands, Norway, Portugal, and the United States.

Nuclear test ban treaty: An agreement to stop testing nuclear weapons.

Nullification: Negatation; the Theory of Nullification was proposed by John C. Calhoun, a South Carolina congressman who later served as vice president to Andrew Jackson. In Calhoun's theory, a state has the right to nullify federal laws that it deems harmful to the state's interests.

O

Open Door Policy: A program introduced by President William McKinley to extend trade and relations with China, opening up a vast new market.

Oppression: Abuse of power by one party against another.

P

Pacifist: A person opposed to conflict.

Panic of 1837: An economic slump that hit the United States in 1837.

Pardon: A power that allows the president to free an individual or a group from prosecution for a crime.

Parliamentary government: A system of government in which executive power resides with Cabinet-level officials responsible to the nation's legislature. The highest-ranking member of the political party with a majority in such a system of government is usually made the nation's chief executive.

Partisan: Placing the concerns of one's group or political party above all other considerations.

Patronage system: Also called spoils system; a system in which elected officials appoint their supporters to civil service (government) jobs.

Peace Corps: A government-sponsored program that trains volunteers for social and humanitarian service in underdeveloped areas of the world.

Peacekeeping force: A military force sponsored by the United Nations that polices areas that have been attacked by another group clearly defined as aggressors.

Pearl Harbor: An American naval station in Hawaii attacked without warning by Japanese forces in December 1941.

Pendleton Civil Service Reform Act: A congressional act signed into law by President Chester A. Arthur that established the Civil Service Commission, an organization that oversees federal appointments and ensures that appointees do not actively participate in party politics while holding a federal job.

Perjury: The voluntary violation of an oath or a vow; answering falsely while under oath (having previously sworn to tell the truth).

Platform: A declaration of policies that a candidate or political party intends to follow if the party's candidate is elected.

Political boss: A politically powerful person who can direct a group of voters to support a particular candidate.

Political dynasty: A succession of government leaders from the same political party.

Political machine: An organized political group whose members are generally under the control of the leader of the group.

Populism: An agricultural movement of rural areas between the Mississippi River and the Rocky Mountains of the late nineteenth century that united the interests of farmers and laborers. In 1891, the movement formed a national political party, the People's Party, whose members were called Populists. Populist ideals remained popular even when the party faded early in the twentieth century.

Presidential primaries: Elections held in states to help determine the nominees of political parties for the general election. Each party disperses a certain number of delegates to each state. A candidate must win support of a majority of those delegates to win the party's presidential nomination. In states that hold primary elections, delegates are generally awarded to candidates based on the percentage of votes they accumulate; in some states, the leading vote-getter wins all of those state's delegates.

Presidential veto: When a president declines to sign into law a bill passed by Congress.

Primaries: *See* **Presidential primaries.**

Progressive "Bull Moose" Party: Party in which Theodore Roosevelt ran as a third-party candidate in 1912. He came in second to incumbent president William Howard Taft, but lost to New Jersey governor Woodrow Wilson.

Progressivism: A movement that began late in the nineteenth century whose followers pursued social, economic, and government reform. Generally located in urban areas, Progressivists ranged from individuals seeking to improve local living conditions to radicals who pursued sweeping changes in the American political and economic system.

Prohibition: The constitutional ban on the manufacture and sale of alcohol and alcoholic beverages from 1920 to 1933.

Prosecuting attorney: The attorney who represents the government in a law case.

Protectorate: A relationship in which an independent nation comes under the protection and power of another nation.

Proviso: A clause in a document making a qualification, condition, or restriction.

R

Racial desegregation: A policy meant to ensure that people of all racial origins are treated equal.

Rapprochement: Reestablishment of relations with a country after it has undergone a dramatic change in government.

Ratification: A vote of acceptance. A majority of the representatives from each of the thirteen colonies had to vote for the U.S. Constitution (1787) in order for the document to become legally binding.

Recession: A situation of increasing unemployment and decreasing value of money.

Recharter: To renew a law or an act.

Reciprocal trade agreements: When participating nations promise to trade in a way that will benefit each nation equally.

Reconstruction: A federal policy from 1865 to 1877 through which the national government took an active part in assisting and policing the former Confederate states.

Reconstruction Act of 1867: An act that placed military governments (governments supervised by a military force) in command of states of the South until the Fourteenth Amendment was ratified in 1868.

Regulation: Monitoring business with an established set of guidelines.

Reparations: Payments for damage caused by acts of hostility.

Republican government: A form of government in which supreme power resides with citizens who elect their leaders and have the power to change their leaders.

Republican Party: Founded in 1854 by a coalition (an alliance) of former members of the Whig, Free-Soil, and Know-Nothing parties and of northern Democrats dissatisfied with their party's proslavery stands. The party quickly rose to become one of the most important parties in the United States, and the major opposition to the Democratic Party. Republicans are generally associated with conservative fiscal and social policies. The Republican Party is not related to the older Democratic-Republican Party, although that party was often called the Republicans before the 1830s.

Riders: Measures added on to legislation. Riders are usually items that might not pass through Congress or will be vetoed by the president if presented alone. Congressmen attempt to attach such items to popular bills, hoping they will "ride" along with the more popular legislation.

S

Sanctions: Punishment against a nation involved in activities considered illegal under international law; such punishment usually denies trade, supplies, or access to other forms of international assistance to the nation.

Satellite nations: Countries politically and economically dominated by a larger, more powerful nation.

Secession: Formal withdrawal from an existing organization. In 1860–61, eleven Southern states seceded from the Union to form the Confederate States of America.

Second Continental Congress: A group of representatives from the thirteen colonies who began meeting in Philadelphia in 1775 and effectively served as the American government until the Constitution was adopted in 1787.

Sectionalism: The emphasis that people place on policies that would directly benefit their area of the country.

Segregation: The policy of keeping groups of people from different races, religions, or ethnic backgrounds separated.

Social Security: A government program that provides pensions (a regular sum of money) to American workers after they reach age sixty-five.

Social welfare: A term that encompasses government programs that provide assistance, training, and jobs to people.

Solicitor: An attorney who represents a government agency.

Solicitor general: An attorney appointed by the president to argue legal matters on behalf of the government.

South East Asia Treaty Organization: An alliance of nations founded in 1954 to prevent the spread of communism in Asian and Pacific island nations. Original members included Australia, France, Great Britain, New Zealand, Pakistan, the Philippines, Thailand, and the United States. The alliance disbanded in 1977.

Speaker of the House: The person in charge of supervising activity in the House of Representatives. The Speaker is elected by colleagues of the party with a majority in Congress.

Spin doctoring: A late twentieth-century term that describes the practice of having political aides offer the best possible interpretation of a political statement or the effects of an event on their political boss.

State militia: An organized military unit maintained by states in case of emergency; often called the National Guard.

Stock market crash: A sudden decline in the value of stocks that severely affects investors.

Strategic Arms Limitation Treaty (SALT): Missile reduction program between the United States and the Soviet Union.

Strategic Defense Initiative (SDI): A proposed—but never approved—technological system (nicknamed "Star Wars," after the popular movie) that combined several advanced technology systems that could, in theory, detect and intercept missiles fired by enemies of the United States.

Subpoena: A formal legal document that commands a certain action or requires a person to appear in court.

T

Taft-Hartley Act: Act that outlawed union-only workplaces, prohibited certain union activities, forbade unions to contribute to political campaigns, established loyalty oaths for union leaders, and allowed court orders to halt strikes that could affect national health or safety.

Tariff: A protective tax placed on imported goods to raise their price and make them less attractive than goods produced by the nation importing them.

Teapot Dome scandal: Incident that became public following the death of President Warren G. Harding that revealed that Navy secretary Edwin Denby transfered control of oil reserves in Teapot Dome, Wyoming, and Elk Hill, California, to the Department of the Interior, whose secretary, Albert Fall, secretly leased the reserve to two private oil operators, who paid Fall $400,000.

Tenure of Office Act: A law passed by Congress to limit the powers of the presidency.

Terrorist: A person who uses acts of violence in an attempt to coerce by terror.

Theater: A large area where military operations are occurring.

Thirteenth Amendment: An amendment to the U.S. Constitution that outlawed slavery.

Tonkin Gulf Resolution: Passed by Congress after U.S. Navy ships supposedly came under attack in the Gulf of Tonkin, this resolution gave President Lyndon B. Johnson the authority to wage war against North Vietnam.

Tribunal: A court of law.

Truman Doctrine: A Cold War–era program designed by President Harry S. Truman that sent aid to anticommunist forces in Turkey and Greece. The Union of Soviet Socialist Republics (U.S.S.R.) had naval stations in Turkey, and nearby Greece was fighting a civil war with communist-dominated rebels.

U

Underground railroad: A term that describes a series of routes through which escaped slaves could pass through free Northern states and into Canada. The escaped slaves were assisted by abolitionists and free African Americans in the North.

Union: Northern states that remained loyal to the United States during the Civil War.

V

Veto: The power of one branch of government—for example, the executive—to reject a bill passed by a legislative body and thus prevent it from becoming law.

Vietcong: Vietnamese communists engaged in warfare against the government and people of South Vietnam.

W

War of 1812: A war fought from 1812 to 1815 between the United States and Great Britain. The United States wanted to protect its maritime rights as a neutral nation during a conflict between Great Britain and France.

Warren Commission: A commission chaired by Earl Warren, chief justice of the Supreme Court, that investigated President John F. Kennedy's assassination. The commission concluded that the assassination was the act of one gunman, not part of a larger conspiracy. That conclusion remains debated.

Watergate scandal: A scandal that began on June 17, 1972, when five men were caught burglarizing the offices of the Democratic National Committee in the Watergate complex in Washington, D.C. This led to a cover-up, political convictions, and, eventually, the resignation of President Richard Nixon.

Welfare: Government assistance to impoverished people.

Whig Party: A political party that existed roughly from 1836 to 1852, composed of different factions of the former Democratic-Republican Party. These factions refused to join the group that formed the Democratic Party led by President Andrew Jackson.

Y

Yalta Conference: A 1944 meeting between Allied leaders Joseph Stalin, Winston Churchill, and Franklin D. Roosevelt in anticipation of an Allied victory in Europe over the Nazis. The leaders discussed how to manage lands conquered by Germany, and Roosevelt and Churchill urged Stalin to enter the Soviet Union in the war against Japan.

Research and Activity Ideas

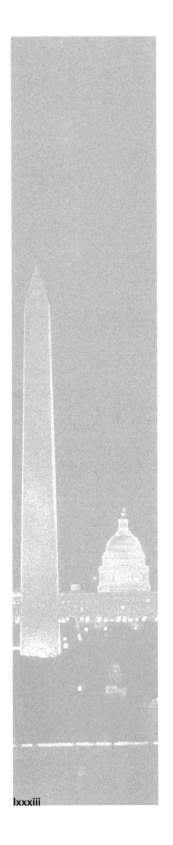

The following research and activity ideas are intended to offer suggestions for complementing social studies and history curricula, to trigger additional ideas for enhancing learning, and to suggest cross-disciplinary projects for library and classroom use.

- The aftermath of the 2000 race between George W. Bush and Al Gore renewed debate over whether the Electoral College system should be abandoned in favor of the popular vote. Research the reasons why the Founding Fathers instituted the Electoral College. Write a paper on arguments for and against the Electoral College, or take one side and have a partner take the other side.

- Several Web sites on presidents are listed in the "Where to Learn More" section. Additional Web sites, linked to presidential libraries and historical sites, are listed at the end of many individual president entries. Using a president of particular interest to you, compare the descriptions of his life and his presidency on the various Web sites. The comparison will show how presidents are appraised by different sources. Pretend you are a media critic. Write a review of the various sites, comparing their different features, the ways they treat the president, and what you find interesting and not useful in each site.

- Plan a debate or a series of debates on important issues in American history. One issue could be the powers of the federal government in relation to the states. That issue can be explored and debated by contrasting the views of a president who took a different view of federal power from the president who preceded him. Such contrasting pairs include John Adams and Thomas Jefferson; James Buchanan and Abraham Lincoln; Herbert Hoover and Franklin D. Roosevelt; and George Bush and Bill Clinton.

- In contemporary times, when a president makes his State of the Union address each year, television networks provide equal time for a member of the opposing party to present his or her party's views. After reading and making notes on one of the speeches in the primary documents section, prepare a response—a speech that takes an opposite view on issues presented by the president.

- Create a timeline of a fifty-year period to parallel the "Timeline of the American Presidents," found on pages xxix–lix. Your timeline might list important inventions, world events, or developments in science and technology. Placing the timelines side by side, consider ways in which the events on your timeline might be connected with events in the presidential timeline.

- Using the resources of your local library, find magazines and newspapers that were published near the time you were born, or pick a date earlier in time. What were some of the big national news stories back then? How did the press view the performance of the president concerning those issues?

- Pretend you are a reporter preparing to interview one of the presidents. Just before your interview is to begin, the president is informed about a major event (select one from the president's entry). You are allowed to follow the president as he plans a course of action. Write an article providing an "insider's view" of the president in action.

- The Congressional cable network C-Span commissioned presidential scholars to rate presidents in ten categories (see http://www.americanpresidents.org/survey/histori-ans/overall.asp). Compare that ranking with other sources that rank presidents in terms of effectiveness. How are the rankings similar and different? What criteria do they use for judging presidents? Consider whether or not you feel the rankings are fair, and write an essay supporting your view.

- Visit a historical site or Web sites devoted to a particular president. Listings for both can often be found in each president's entry. Using biographical information about the president's childhood, his schooling, and his career as president, write a short play in which the president is surrounded by loved ones and aides at a crucial moment during his presidency.

- There were many different kinds of first ladies. Some were politically active (such as Sarah Polk and Eleanor Roosevelt), others believed they should not participate in politics because they were not the one elected to office (such as Bess Truman and Pat Nixon). Compare and contrast those different approaches by profiling several first ladies.

- Research more about a leading opponent of a particular president, perhaps someone he faced in an election. Imagine that the opponent was able to convince voters that he or she should be elected. Write about how history would have been different if the opponent had become president. The focus could be on an election that was very close (such as Rutherford B. Hayes over Samuel Tilden in 1876 or George W. Bush over Al Gore in 2000) or one in which the victor won by a large margin (such as Franklin D. Roosevelt over Alfred Landon in 1936 or Ronald Reagan over Walter Mondale in 1984).

Complete American Presidents Sourcebook

Ulysses S. Grant

Eighteenth president (1869–1877)

Ulysses S. Grant

Born April 27, 1822
Point Pleasant, Ohio
Died July 23, 1885
Mount McGregor, New York

Eighteenth president of the United States
(1869–1877)

Successful Civil War general's popularity
led to two presidential terms

"**L**et us have peace," declared Ulysses S. Grant in a letter in which he accepted the Republican Party nomination for president. The Civil War (1861–65) had ended four years earlier. Outgoing president **Andrew Johnson** (1808–1875; see entry in volume 2) had survived a vote of impeachment (a legislative hearing charging a public official with misconduct while in office). The trial marked the first time a president had been impeached.

Johnson had initiated the policy of Reconstruction (a federally supervised rebuilding of the South) to help bring back into the Union the Southern states that had seceded (separated). But some Republicans wanted to punish the South for having left the Union and having engaged in war. Grant's remark, "Let us have peace," was intended for those who wanted to penalize the Southern states. He wanted all Americans to put the conflict behind them.

But the years of Grant's presidency, 1869 through 1877, proved to be very difficult. Two financial crises left many people bankrupt (financially ruined). Newly emancipated (freed) former slaves faced hostility and threats. Inter-

"One of my superstitions had always been when I started to go anywhere, or to do anything, not to turn back or stop until the thing intended was accomplished."

Ulysses S. Grant

Ulysses S. Grant.
Courtesy of the Library of Congress.

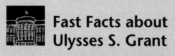

Fast Facts about Ulysses S. Grant

Full name: Hiram Ulysses Simpson Grant

Born: April 27, 1822

Died: July 23, 1885

Burial site: Grant's Tomb, New York, New York

Parents: Jesse Root and Hannah Simpson Grant

Spouse: Julia Boggs Dent (1826–1902; m. 1848)

Children: Frederick Dent (1850–1912); Ulysses S. Jr. (1852–1929); Ellen "Nellie" Wrenshall (1855–1922); Jesse Root (1858–1934)

Religion: Methodist

Education: U.S. Military Academy, West Point (1843)

Occupations: Farmer; real estate agent; soldier

Government positions: Interim secretary of war (under Andrew Johnson)

Political party: Republican

Dates as president: March 4, 1869–March 4, 1873 (first term); March 4, 1873–March 4, 1877

Age upon taking office: 46

national disputes nearly led the United States into war with Great Britain and Spain. The federal government was riddled (spread throughout) with scandal and corruption.

Grant was the Civil War general who led the Union to victory. "One of my superstitions," he wrote later about the crucial Battle of Vicksburg (1862), "had always been when I started to go anywhere, or to do anything, not to turn back or stop until the thing intended was accomplished." Instead of retreating after twice failing to take Vicksburg, Grant found a way to win what became one of the most important battles of the Civil War.

Grant displayed such effort to succeed throughout his life. Only a fair student, he nevertheless was graduated from the West Point Military Academy. He fought because of a sense of duty to his country in the Mexican War (1846–48), a war that he did not support. He was cited for bravery in several key battles. After failing as a farmer and as a real estate agent, Grant began his Civil War service by gathering a group of volunteers, training them, and leading them to the first significant Union victory of the war.

Grant did not fare as well as president, however. His selection of Cabinet officials (presidential advisers) often placed friendship over ability. In war, he had commanded five hundred thousand men, but his presidency was endangered by a few individuals whom he had entrusted with power. He stood firm on financial policies that proved ineffective while the economy grew more and more unstable. A combination of violence against African Americans and pressure from political opportunists led him to take a more

Ulysses S. Grant Timeline

1822: Born in Ohio

1843: Graduates from the U.S. Military Academy in West Point, New York

1846–48 : Serves in the Mexican War; twice cited for bravery in combat

1854: Resigns from military

1861: Civil War begins; Grant rises from commander of a volunteer regiment to the rank of lieutenant general, which until then had been held only by George Washington

1865: Accepts surrender of Confederate general Robert E. Lee, effectively ending the Civil War

1869–77: Serves two terms as eighteenth U.S. president

1869: Financial crisis called Black Friday causes stock market to close on September 24

1872–73: Crédit Mobilier financial scandal hits Grant administration

1873: Another financial crisis—the Panic of 1873—hits the United States

1877: Grant family tours the world, and Grant meets with the heads of states of many European, African, and Asian nations

1880: Grant runs for an unprecedented third term, but loses nomination to James A. Garfield

1885: Grant dies in New York, shortly after completing *Personal Memoirs of U. S. Grant,* which becomes a bestseller

aggressive Reconstruction policy. The war had ended, the slaves had been freed, and business and industry were expanding, but the country was not at peace.

From Hiram to U. S. Grant

The oldest of six children, Grant was originally named Hiram Ulysses Grant. He was commonly called Ulysses while growing up. Grant was born in a two-room log cabin in Point Pleasant, Ohio, on April 27, 1822. His father, Jesse, owned a leather-tanning business and a farm. His mother, Hannah Simpson Grant, was a devoutly religious woman. The family moved to a farm in Georgetown, Ohio, in 1823. Working on the farm while growing up, Grant developed a special talent in training and caring for horses.

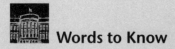 **Words to Know**

Boom and bust: An economic term that describes a cyclical pattern of prosperity ("boom") and decline ("bust") and signifies financial instability.

Carpetbaggers: A term of contempt used by Southerners about agents, humanitarians, politicians, and businessmen who came to the South to assist or to exploit Reconstruction policies. The term suggests that Northerners could stuff everything they owned into a bag made from carpet.

Inflation: An economic term describing a decline in the value of money in relation to the goods and services it will buy. For example, price increases lessen the purchasing power of money.

Kickbacks: When someone representing a group receives an undeclared payment for having arranged a work or supply contract with another firm. The other firm makes a secret payment to influence the awarding of the contract.

Martial law: A state of emergency during which a military group becomes the sole authority in an area and civil laws are set aside.

Reconstruction: A federal policy from 1865 to 1877 in which the national government took an active part in assisting and policing the former Confederate states.

Reparations: Payments for damage caused by acts of hostility.

Secede: Formally withdraw from an organization.

Sidearms: Small weapons such as pistols and knives that are sheathed and holstered (covered and carried) on the body, as opposed to larger weapons like a rifle.

Tribunal: A court of law.

Grant attended the Maysville Seminary in Kentucky when he was fourteen and the Presbyterian Academy in Ripley, Ohio, until age seventeen. He won an appointment to the U.S. Military Academy at West Point in 1839. Grant had been signing his name Ulysses H. Grant by this time, but his sponsor, Congressman Thomas Hamer (1800–1846), mistakenly listed his name as Ulysses S. Grant on documents he submitted to West Point. Hamer, a family friend, probably assumed that Grant's middle name was Simpson—his mother's maiden name and the middle name of Grant's younger brother. Grant decided to keep his new name.

At West Point, Grant displayed excellent skills as a horseman. He was an average student except for a strong showing in mathematics. He hoped to teach math after graduating from the academy in 1843. He was commissioned (given military rank) instead as an officer and stationed near St. Louis, Missouri. His roommate at West Point, Frederick T. Dent (1820–1892), lived in the area. Grant met Dent's sister, Julia (1826–1902; see entry on **Julia Grant** in volume 3), soon after he arrived in Missouri. The two began a romance. They became engaged shortly before Grant was stationed in Louisiana in June 1844.

When the Mexican War broke out in 1846, Grant fought despite his own dislike of the conflict. He called the war "one of the most unjust ever waged by a stronger nation against a weaker nation." He participated in almost all of the major battles during the war and served under two distinguished commanders, **Zachary Taylor** (1784–1850; see entry in volume 2) and **Winfield Scott** (1786–1866; see box in **Martin Van Buren** entry in volume 1). Grant likely learned much from observing the two leaders in action. Both generals related well with men of all ranks, fought valiantly (bravely) and tenaciously (persistently), and respected their opponents. Grant was cited for bravery on several occasions.

Following the war, Grant and Julia were married in St. Louis on August 22, 1848. Julia accompanied her husband to his new assignments: Sacketts Harbor, New York, in the fall of 1848, and Detroit, Michigan, in 1849. She was back in St. Louis in 1850 to give birth to their first child, Frederick. Grant returned to Sacketts Harbor in 1851. Then he was transferred to Fort Vancouver in the Oregon Territory in 1852.

The trip to that fort on the Pacific coast required Grant to sail from New York to Panama, cross land to the Pacific Ocean, and then sail north to Vancouver Island. Julia remained at home and gave birth to the couple's second son. Grant was unhappy in the Northwest and ended up resigning from the army in April 1854. There is speculation that he drank heavily at the time. Historians have debated whether Grant had a persistent alcohol problem that continued during his service in the Civil War.

Hardscrabble civilian becomes military hero

For the next seven years, Grant endured a series of failures. He built a house and cleared land for farming, but he was

Ulysses S. Grant Civil War Timeline

April 12, 1861: Fort Sumter, South Carolina, is attacked by Confederate troops. President Abraham Lincoln issues call for seventy-five thousand volunteers.

April 23, 1861: Grant rejoins the army as a volunteer.

June 17, 1861: Grant is appointed colonel of the Twenty-first Illinois Regiment of Volunteers.

September 1861: Grant establishes headquarters in Cairo, Illinois, in command of the District of Southern Illinois and Southeastern Missouri. He occupies Paducah, Kentucky, giving the Union a strong western foothold.

November 7, 1861: Grant confronts a Confederate force at Belmont, Missouri, scattering his opponents and then withdrawing.

February 1862: Grant captures Fort Henry on the Cumberland River. He leads forces that capture Fort Donelson on the Tennessee River—the first major Union victory of the war. His correspondence to Confederate general Simon Bolivar Buckner—"No terms except an unconditional and immediate surrender can be accepted"—earns him the nickname "Unconditional Surrender" Grant. He

captures thirteen thousand Confederate troops and becomes a Union hero.

April 1862: After being pushed back by a surprise attack, Grant's forces regroup and hold their line in a major and bloody battle at Shiloh, in Virginia. Because of initial confusion under attack, Grant's preparedness for battle is questioned, but he is supported by President Lincoln.

Autumn 1862: Grant enjoys victories at Iuka and Corinth in Mississippi. He is named commander of the Department of Tennessee, October 25, 1862. He is charged with taking Vicksburg, Mississippi—the principal Confederate stronghold on the Mississippi River.

December 1862: Grant's troops are driven back several times by Confederate forces in an attempt to take Vicksburg; he decides to make another try rather than retreat and begin again.

April 1863: After moving his forces through back country to attack from behind Confederate lines, Grant takes Jackson, Mississippi, and assaults and lays siege on Vicksburg.

July 4, 1863: Grant accepts the surrender of Vicksburg (30,000 troops, 15 generals, and 172 cannons). On the same day, Union forces win a major battle at Gettysburg, Pennsylvania.

September 1863: Grant is sent to rescue the Union Army under siege at Chattanooga, Tennessee.

November 1863: Union forces under Grant win three significant battles to take control of Chattanooga, a major east-west railroad junction.

March 1864: Grant is commissioned lieutenant general. As supreme commander of the Union armies, Grant begins coordinating Union armies throughout the Confederacy. Previously in the war, armies acted independently in the western and eastern theaters. Grant uses Union economic advantage to win battles and dig in for long sieges.

May 1864: Grant faces Confederate general Robert E. Lee, commander of the Army of Northern Virginia in the Wilderness Campaign. The campaign results in severe losses on both sides (seventeen thousand for the Union; eleven thousand for the Confederates) and a stalemate. More heavy casualties occur at the Battle of the Bloody Angle. On the North Anna River, Grant's armies force Lee to withdraw to powerful entrenchments south of the river.

June 1864: Grant suffers heavy losses (five thousand to seven thousand men) at the Battle of Cold Harbor. Close to sixty thousand Union soldiers are killed in battle during the spring of 1864. Grant moves over one hundred thousand troops south of the James River before Lee learns of the movement. Grant begins the Petersburg Campaign to cut supply lines between Richmond, Virginia, and the rest of the South. Long war of attrition follows.

Summer 1864/Winter 1865: Elsewhere, Union forces win many battles. General George H. Thomas crushes Confederate forces at Nashville, Tennessee; General Philip H. Sheridan systematically sweeps the Shenandoah Valley of Virginia; General William Tecumseh Sherman marches through Georgia and South Carolina.

April 1865: In the Battle of Five Forks, Grant forces Lee to abandon Petersburg. The Appomattox Campaign follows: Richmond, Virginia, is captured April 3; the Union takes Sayler's Creek; and Lee surrenders at Appomattox Court House, Virginia, April 9, effectively ending the Civil War.

"Council of War" during the Wilderness Campaign in 1864. General Ulysses S. Grant (lower left, leaning over a bench) consults a map held by General George Meade.
Courtesy of the Library of Congress.

unable to support his wife and four children with the farm he called Hardscrabble. (Hardscrabble is usually used as an adjective to refer to barren or poor soil: a hardscrabble piece of land.) He tried and failed at selling real estate. At the time the Civil War broke out in April 1861, Grant was working for his brother in the family's leather goods business in Galena, Illinois.

Grant rejoined the army and rounded up a group of volunteers. He was appointed colonel of the Twenty-first Illinois Regiment of Volunteers. Within a year Grant emerged as a leader in the Union Army. His regiment came face to face with a Confederate force at Belmont, Missouri, in November 1861. They forced a retreat and then retreated themselves.

In February 1862, with the aid of gunboats, forces led by Grant captured Fort Donelson on the Tennessee River—the first major Union victory of the war. Grant wrote a letter to the fort's commander, Confederate general Simon Bolivar Buckner (1823–1914), stating, "No terms except an unconditional and immediate surrender can be accepted." Buckner's

Union general Ulysses S. Grant in front of his tent during the Civil War. *Courtesy of the National Archives and Records Administration.*

unconditional surrender led to the capture of thirteen thousand Confederate troops. Grant became a hero overnight throughout the Union states and was nicknamed "Unconditional Surrender" Grant.

As a military leader, Grant was persistent. He often followed setbacks with clever strategies that led to victory. In April 1862, his forces were hit with a surprise attack at Shiloh, in Virginia. Grant's forces regrouped and won a major and

Robert E. Lee

Robert E. Lee was born into a famous Virginia family on January 19, 1807. Lee's father, Henry "Light-Horse Harry" Lee (1756–1818), was a war hero who fought under General George Washington during the American Revolution (1775–83), then served in Congress and as governor of Virginia. Lee's mother, Ann Hill Carter, came from a respected family that had long held prominent positions in Virginia's government and society. Two of his father's cousins, Richard Henry Lee (1732–1794) and Francis Lightfoot Lee (1734–1797), were among the fifty-six signers of the Declaration of Independence. After his formal education in Alexandria, Virginia, Lee entered the U.S. Military Academy at West Point in 1825. He excelled academically and militarily, and was commissioned into the army's famed Corps of Engineers after his graduation in 1829. Two years later, he married Mary Anne Randolph Custis, great-granddaughter of **Martha Washington** (1731–1802; see entry in volume 1).

Lee first achieved military distinction in the Mexican War (1846–48). Serving under army commander Winfield Scott, Lee made several scouting trips that helped lead to the capture of Mexico City. Wounded in battle, he showed extreme bravery and was promoted from captain to colonel by the war's end in 1848. Four years later, he received the distinguished assignment of superintendent of West Point. He held this post for three years before the War Department transferred him to a cavalry regiment in the Southwest. During the 1850s, violence broke out over the issue of slavery. In October 1859, fiery abolitionist John Brown (1800–1859; see box in **James Buchanan** entry in volume 2) and his antislavery followers seized a government arsenal at Harpers Ferry, Virginia. Lee was ordered to lead a military unit against this rebellion. After Brown refused to surrender, Lee's forces assaulted the building and in three minutes defeated Brown's tiny band.

Brown's raid and the election of Abraham Lincoln in 1860 contributed to outrage in the South that led several states to secede from the Union. In February 1861, these states formed the Confederate States of America; two months later, the Civil War began. Lee thought slavery was a moral evil and secession was unconstitutional, but he believed his first duty was to his home state of Virginia. He refused command of Union forces and resigned from the army on April 20, 1861, two days after Virginia seceded. Lee assumed command of Virginia's military and naval forces and accepted the position of general in the Confederate Army. After mixed success in 1861, Lee was called to the Confederate capital of Richmond, Virginia, on March 2, 1862, to help lead defense of the city against attack by Union general George B.

Robert E. Lee
National Archives and Records Administration.

McClellan (1826–1885). After assuming the overall command, Lee ended McClellan's threat in what came to be known as the Seven Days' battles (June 26–July 2). McClellan then tried to transfer his men to the army of Major General John Pope (1822–1892). Before they had time to combine their forces, Lee attacked Pope at the second battle of Bull Run in Virginia on August 29–30. The Northerners were routed. To threaten Washington, D.C., Lee then marched his men into Maryland. McClellan learned of Lee's plans and met him at Antietam on September 17. The ensuing battle was a draw, but the Union army had succeeded in stopping the Confederate invasion.

Lee spent the next eight months blocking any Union advance on Richmond. After victories in Virginia in December 1862 in the Battle of Fredericksburg and the following May in the Battle of Chancellorsville, Lee took the offensive and moved into Pennsylvania. The Confederates lost to Union forces in a three-day battle at Gettysburg. Lee blamed the loss on himself and offered Confederate president Jefferson Davis (1808–1889; see box in **Abraham Lincoln** entry in volume 2) his resignation. He refused it. Lee did not take part in any major campaigns until he met Union general Ulysses S. Grant the following year at Petersburg, Virginia, just south of Richmond. From June 1864 to April 1865, Grant assaulted the area, but Lee's defenses held. Grant was able to replenish his army with men and supplies, while Lee could not. Eventually, the Confederate lines were too weak to hold off the Union forces. On April 2, 1865, they gave way, and Richmond had to be abandoned. Not wishing to see his men suffer any more, Lee surrendered to Grant at Appomattox Courthouse on April 9.

After the war, Lee became president of Washington College (now Washington and Lee University) in Lexington, Virginia. He earned admirers in both the North and the South with his quiet dignity. He swore renewed allegiance to the United States, but Congress refused to restore his citizenship. Lee died in Lexington, Virginia, on October 12, 1870.

bloody battle. However, his preparedness for battle was questioned because his troops were nearly overrun. Some military leaders suggested to President **Abraham Lincoln** (1809–1865; see entry in volume 2) that Grant should be removed from a leadership role. Lincoln disagreed: "I can't spare this man," the president said. "He fights."

Grant had several other great accomplishments as a military leader (see Grant Civil War timeline box). On July 4, 1863, after eight months of attempting to take Vicksburg, Mississippi—the principal Confederate stronghold on the Mississippi River—Grant achieved a surrender of 30,000 troops, 15 generals, and 172 cannons. On the same day, Union forces won a major battle at Gettysburg, Pennsylvania. In March 1864, Grant was commissioned as lieutenant general, becoming the first man to hold that rank since **George Washington** (1732–1799; see entry in volume 1).

Beginning in May 1864, General Grant faced Confederate general Robert E. Lee (1807–1870; see box), commander of the Army of Northern Virginia. The two armies were engaged for almost a year in Virginia until the Battle of Five Forks on April 1, where Grant's forces overcame Lee's. The Appomattox Campaign followed. Grant captured Richmond, Virginia, on April 3. General Lee, representing the Confederacy, surrendered to Grant at Appomattox Court House on April 9, 1865.

With President Lincoln's approval, the terms of surrender arranged by Grant were respectful. Confederate troops were allowed to keep their sidearms (small weapons carried at the side or waist) and horses. None were taken prisoner, but all had to sign paroles (pledges that they would honor the conditions of their release). These documents stated they were "not to be disturbed by United States authority" so long as they observed the laws in force where they resided. Union rations were shared with hungry Confederate soldiers. An artillery burst (firing of guns) to celebrate the news of surrender was immediately halted by Grant. "We did not want to exult in their surrender," Grant explained later.

Grant elected president

Following the war, Grant toured the South and reported conditions to President Andrew Johnson. Grant favored a

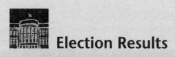 **Election Results**

1868

Presidential / Vice presidential candidates	Popular votes	Presidential electoral votes
Ulysses S. Grant / Schuyler Colfax (Republican)	3,012,833	214
Horatio Seymour / Francis P. Blair Jr. (Democrat)	2,703,249	80

Incumbent president Andrew Johnson, severely weakened politically by his impeachment, received very little support for election at the Democratic convention. Seymour won the nomination on the twenty-second ballot.

1872

Presidential / Vice presidential candidates	Popular votes	Presidential electoral votes
Ulysses S. Grant / Henry Wilson (Republican)	3,597,132	286
Horace Greeley / Benjamin G. Brown (Democratic)	2,834,079	—

Wilson defeated incumbent vice president Colfax for the Republican vice presidential nomination. Democratic presidential nominee Greeley died less than one month after the election; his electoral votes were redistributed to four other men.

moderate policy of Reconstruction that would help restore the war-ravaged South and protect the rights of the newly emancipated former slaves. Meanwhile, President Johnson faced an uproar from Congress when he tried to remove his secretary of war, Edwin M. Stanton (1814–1869), from his Cabinet. Congress demanded the right to vote on the removal. The resulting conflict led to Johnson facing a vote on impeachment (see box in **Andrew Johnson** entry in volume 2).

Johnson appointed Grant to become the new secretary of war, while awaiting approval by Congress. After serving in that position on an interim basis (that is, as a replacement between the old and the new official), Grant decided against continuing. Johnson claimed that Grant betrayed him. Grant insisted that he had planned only to hold the position temporarily. Johnson had hoped to profit from Grant's immense popularity to gain support for his administration.

Republicans nominated Grant as their candidate for the 1868 presidential election. He won the election easily, capturing 214 electoral votes to 80 for his opponent, New York governor Horatio Seymour (1810–1886).

In his inaugural address, Grant called for an end to regional divisiveness (differences of opinion between the North and the South). He supported ratification (formal approval) of the Fifteenth Amendment (see box in **Rutherford B. Hayes** entry in volume 3). The amendment states that no citizen can be denied the right to vote based upon race, color, or previous condition of servitude—that is, whether or not the citizen had been a slave. Grant pledged to reform national policy toward Native Americans. In one of his first presidential actions, he signed the Public Credit Act. This act mandated (officially authorized) that all government debts would be paid in gold.

It was an exciting time in the United States. Western lands were being filled in by settlers, and railroads stretched across the continent. But President Grant soon found the complexities of politics and finance to be much more difficult than waging war. He was not diplomatic as president. He showed poor judgment by surrounding himself with friends who lacked political sophistication. He faced financial crises and government scandals during both of his terms. Meanwhile, the end of the Civil War and slavery did not mean an end to regional divisiveness and racial oppression (the keeping of the former slaves under white control).

From Black Friday to Crédit Mobilier

Among Grant's questionable Cabinet selections were Secretary of the Treasury Alexander T. Stewart (1803–1876), a New York department store tycoon; Secretary of the Navy Adolph E. Borie (1809–1880), a Philadelphia merchant; and Secretary of State Elihu B. Washburne (1816–1887), an old friend of Grant's who had no experience in diplomacy. Fortunately, Stewart was soon replaced by longtime Massachusetts politician George S. Boutwell (1818–1905); Borie was replaced by New Jersey attorney general George Robeson (1829–1897); and Washburne was replaced by Hamilton Fish (1808–1893), an ex-governor and senator of New York who helped Grant win success in international affairs.

Financial matters proved volatile (subject to rapid change). During the Civil War, the government had printed

Ulysses S. Grant Administration

Administration Dates
March 4, 1869–March 4, 1873
March 4, 1873–March 4, 1877

Vice President
Schuyler Colfax (1869–73)
Henry Wilson (1873–75)
None (1875–77)

Cabinet

Secretary of State
Elihu B. Washburne (1869)
Hamilton Fish (1869–77)

Secretary of the Treasury
Alexander T. Stewart (1869)
George S. Boutwell (1869–73)
William A. Richardson (1873–74)
Benjamin H. Bristow (1874–76)
Lot M. Morrill (1876–77)

Secretary of War
John A. Rawlins (1869)
William T. Sherman (1869)
William W. Belknap (1869–76)

Alphonso Taft (1876)
James D. Cameron (1876–77)

Attorney General
Ebenezer R. Hoar (1869–70)
Amos T. Akerman (1870–71)
George H. Williams (1871–75)
Edwards Pierrepont (1875–76)
Alphonso Taft (1876–77)

Secretary of the Navy
Adolph E. Borie (1869)
George M. Robeson (1869–77)

Postmaster General
John A. J. Creswell (1869–74)
James W. Marshall (1874)
Marshall Jewell (1874–76)
James N. Tyner (1876–77)

Secretary of the Interior
Jacob D. Cox (1869–70)
Columbus Delano (1870–75)
Zachariah Chandler (1875–77)

money called "greenbacks" to help farmers and workers pay for necessities. Unlike dollars and coins, greenbacks were not backed by gold reserves (gold the government holds to represent the value of printed money) and their value fluctuated (shifted back and forth). Sometimes a greenback could be worth about the same as a dollar. At other times, it took two greenbacks to equal one dollar.

Grant delayed in addressing the greenback problem. Meanwhile, two wealthy men, Jay Gould (1836–1892) and Jim Fisk (1834–1872), bought up huge amounts of gold, making the precious metal more valuable. The value of green-

Hamilton Fish

As secretary of state, Hamilton Fish distinguished himself in the otherwise scandal-ridden administration of President Ulysses S. Grant. Born August 3, 1808, in New York City, Fish came from a wealthy family. His father was a prominent lawyer and a member of the Federalist Party—the group with which George Washington, **John Adams** (1735–1826; see entry in volume 1), and Alexander Hamilton (1755–1804; see box in **George Washington** entry in volume 1) had been associated. Fish graduated with highest honors from Columbia College in 1827 and was certified as a lawyer in 1830.

Fish entered politics as a member of the Whig Party; he was elected to Congress in 1842 and governor of New York in 1848. His administration expanded the New York canal system and established a statewide framework for public education. In 1851, he was elected to the U.S. Senate. His father had been the member of a dying political party, and so too was Fish: after the Whig Party became hopelessly weak in the early 1850s, Fish joined the Republican Party, which was founded in 1854.

Fish was not known nationally when President Grant appointed him secretary of state in 1869 to replace the inept Elihu Washburne. Fish accepted reluctantly but found the job to his liking and remained for the rest of Grant's two terms. Fish's influence helped rescue Grant's presidency from total failure. Three major foreign policy problems confronted Fish during his tenure. The first was Grant's effort to annex Santo Domingo. Cool toward the project, Fish nevertheless set about loyally to carry out his superior's wishes. A treaty of annexation was concluded, but it was blocked in the Senate. Fish's efforts to settle the *Alabama* claims were more successful. The United States won its claims against Great Britain for having allowed Confederate cruisers, especially the *Alaba-*

backs fell further against the gold-backed dollar, ruining many people and banking institutions that held greenbacks. The gold purchase by Gould and Fisk caused a financial crisis called Black Friday on September 24, 1869. The stock market was forced to close.

President Grant quickly authorized the U.S. government to sell some of its gold reserves to help bring the price of gold back down. Investors who had bought gold at higher prices lost money, but the action helped settle the financial market. Nevertheless, damage had been done to many. Histo-

Hamilton Fish.
Courtesy of the Library of Congress.

the arbitration of the *Alabama* claims and of minor issues between the United States and Canada. The arbitration tribunal awarded the United States $15,500,000 in damages in the *Alabama* case.

An insurrection by Cubans against Spanish authority was in process when Fish took office. In 1873, the *Virginius,* a rebel-owned steamer illegally registered as American was engaged in carrying arms. The ship was captured by the Spanish, and fifty-three crewmen and passengers, including several Americans, were executed as pirates. The incident could have led to war, but Fish negotiated a settlement, which included money for the families of dead Americans and a Spanish promise (never fulfilled) to punish the officer responsible for the executions. Fish retired from public life in 1877 and busied himself in civic and social affairs. He died in New York on September 6, 1893.

ma, to be built and supplied in England, in violation of British neutrality. A commission with representatives from each nation met in Washington, D.C. With Fish leading the way, the commission negotiated the Treaty of Washington (1871), which provided for

rians generally believe that Grant had acted too slowly in addressing the greenback problem.

Grant intended to follow the moderate Republican Reconstruction program, but by 1870 he supported stricter measures. Upset at the lack of progress in race relations in the South, Grant issued a proclamation celebrating the ratification of the Fifteenth Amendment to the Constitution. That proclamation was followed by the Enforcement Act of May 1870. The act authorized the use of federal troops to protect the voting rights of African Americans, who were facing intimidation in the South. Nevertheless, violence against African Americans increased, especially by the Ku Klux Klan, a white supremacist group. The Ku Klux Klan Act of April 1871 was intended to rid the region of organized racial violence.

Radical Republicans, meanwhile, exploited the situation. The president was authorized to declare martial law (a state of emergency during which a military takes over from civil authorities) in areas where violence erupted. Those arrested for violence would be subject to prosecution by federal authorities rather than by state officials. Makeshift courts and governments were set up in several Southern areas. State powers were effectively limited. Northerners who traveled South to take advantage of federal authority were called carpetbaggers by resentful Southerners.

Meanwhile, Grant signed the Indian Appropriation Act in March 1871. The act allowed Native Americans to hold citizenship, provided education and medical programs for them, and began financial drives for food, clothing, and education. Grant's actions on behalf of African Americans and Native Americans represented honest attempts at reform and social improvement, but the nation as a whole was not ready to embrace racial equality.

There were some highlights in Grant's first term. On March 1, 1872, he signed a bill into law that made a Wyoming nature preserve (an area reserved to protect animals and plants) called Yellowstone the country's first national park. The Grant administration also successfully resolved a conflict with Great Britain. The United States demanded reparations (payments) for damage caused during the Civil War by the Confederate warship *Alabama,* which was built in British shipyards. As negotiations for reparations came to a halt, many Americans began calling for war. They felt that Great Britain had tried to undermine the United States by interfering in the Civil War. Grant pressured Great Britain into accepting a neutral international tribunal (court of law) to arbitrate the claims of the two nations. The arbitration ended the threat of war. The United States was awarded over $15 million for damages.

Another area of foreign relations concerned the Dominican Republic and Haiti. The island on which the two nations are located in the West Indies was called Hispaniola.

The island had been switched several times between Spanish and French rule before becoming independent in the mid-eighteenth century. A faction (group) within the Dominican Republic wanted to return to Spanish rule. The Grant administration, with the approval of Congress, promised support to the independent governments of the nation. Grant wanted to take it a step further. He proposed annexing the Dominican Republic (bringing it under the control of the United States). He sent his private secretary, Orville E. Babcock (1835–1884), to arrange a treaty of annexation. Congress and Grant's own Cabinet opposed annexation. The issue was politically dead by 1870, but Grant persisted unsuccessfully through the end of his presidency for the annexation.

As the presidential election of 1872 neared, the taint of scandal began sweeping through the federal government. Scandal, hard economic times, and continued racial and regional divisiveness would be commonplace through Grant's second term. The Crédit Mobilier of America business venture was one of the greatest financial and political scandals of the nineteenth century.

Several Union Pacific Railroad stockholders, including Massachusetts Congressman Oakes Ames (1804–1873), had purchased the Pennsylvania Fiscal Agency in 1864. The new owners changed the agency's name to Crédit Mobilier of America (named after Crédit Mobilier of France). Crédit Mobilier purchased the remaining Union Pacific stock and combined ownership of the two corporations. The Union Pacific had been commissioned by the U.S. government with loans, subsidies (gifts of money), and land grants (gifts of land for public benefit) to complete the railroad from the Midwest to the Pacific coast. The Union Pacific Railroad awarded the contract for the actual construction to Crédit Mobilier. In effect, Union Pacific awarded large amounts of government money to itself as owner of the company. Construction costs reported by Crédit Mobilier and paid to the company were twice as much as actual costs. As a result, company stockholders earned great sums of money in 1867 and 1868.

When an investigation loomed, Congressman Ames tried to stop it by distributing Crédit Mobilier stock among his colleagues in the House of Representatives. Some $33 million was made by those who accepted the bribes. The scandal was exposed during the 1872 presidential campaign. Among those implicated was outgoing vice president Schuyler Colfax (1823–1885) and President Grant's 1872 running mate, Henry Wilson (1812–1875). Many other prominent Republicans were also tainted (negatively marked) by the scandal, which brought to the public's attention the extent of widespread political corruption and unethical business practices. Nevertheless, Grant won reelection in a landslide.

More scandals

The Crédit Mobilier scandal spilled into 1873 and Grant's second term when Congress completed its investigation. Meanwhile, a fresh scandal—the Sanborn Contracts—became news. That uproar implicated Secretary of the Treasury William A. Richardson (1821–1896) in a tax fraud scheme (deceitful plan to avoid paying taxes). In May 1874, the House Ways and Means Committee (a group of legislators who determine the costs and methods for enacting a piece of legislation) moved to declare "severe condemnation of Richardson." Urged to remove Richardson, Grant complied, then promptly appointed him to a judgeship on the U.S. Court of Claims.

Richardson was replaced as secretary of the treasury by Benjamin H. Bristow (1832–1896), who promptly began investigating Internal Revenue Service officials for fraud (deceit) involving collection of taxes on whiskey. Known as the Whiskey Ring, the conspiracy involved more than two hundred people. Among them was Grant's private secretary, Orville E. Babcock. Other scandals involved officials in the Post Office and the Department of the Interior. Secretary of War William W. Belknap (1829–1890) was discovered to have received kickbacks (secret payments) when the government sold off several trading posts to the public. Congress, meanwhile, failed to convict Belknap, reflecting its own problems with corruption. On the final day Congress was in session in 1873, it voted its members a two-year retroactive pay raise (additional money paid for work during that two-year period of time).

Meanwhile, the Grant administration faced another financial crisis, almost four years to the day after Black Friday of 1869. The Panic of 1873 began in September with the failure of a major New York banking firm, Jay Cooke & Company. Economic hard times began again and continued through the remainder of Grant's second term. In January 1875, Grant signed the Specie Resumption Act, which helped stabilize the economy by reducing the number of greenbacks still in circulation. Greenbacks had continued to fluctuate in value, leading to inflation (a decline in the value of money) and loss of spending power for consumers.

The policy of Reconstruction was failing. Many Southerners resented the continued presence of federal troops in their region. Grant stood firm. In his annual address to Congress in 1874, he affirmed that all the laws and provisions of the Constitution would be "enforced with rigor." To counter complaints about federal interference, Grant stated: "Treat the negro [African American] as a citizen and a voter, as he is and must remain," and added, "then we shall have no complaint of sectional interference." Federal troops were sent to Vicksburg, Mississippi, in December 1874 following a mass murder of African Americans.

Racial problems were especially apparent during voting time. White Southerners tended to support Democratic candidates, leading to an erosion of Republican power in the South. Blacks tended to support Republicans. Many blacks were intimidated (discouraged with threats and bullying) from voting. (The winner of the 1876 presidential election—**Rutherford B. Hayes** [1822–1893; see entry in volume 3] had to be determined by a specially appointed electoral commission because of massive voter fraud.) Grant hoped the Civil Rights Act of 1875, which prohibited racial segregation in public housing and transportation, would help improve racial interaction. However, the act was later declared unconstitutional in 1883.

There were positive developments during Grant's second term. Congress passed a bill that decreed equal pay for women and men holding similar jobs in government agencies. As he had with Great Britain during his first term, Grant avoided calls for war against Spain in his second term. The merchant ship *Virginius,* commanded by an American citizen and flying the U.S. flag, was captured by Spanish authorities. All aboard were executed by the Spanish, who claimed that the crew was providing aid to Cubans attempting to liberate their island from Spanish control. The boat was later proved to have been owned by Cubans and was flying the American flag under false pretenses (claims). Meanwhile, Grant secured an apology from the Spanish government in November 1873.

The happiest day of the Grant presidency occurred on May 21, 1874, when Grant's daughter Nellie (1855–1922) was married in an extravagant White House ceremony.

World tour

After leaving office in 1877, Grant and his wife went on an extended world tour. It marked only the third time that a former American president had traveled abroad following his administration. Foreign nations had been unsure how to greet the previous two presidential travelers—**Martin Van Buren** (1782–1862; see entry in volume 1) and **Millard Fillmore** (1800–1874; see entry in volume 2)—but the Grants received state welcomes (formal, official, and usually ceremonious greetings by government representatives) wherever they went. During their travels through Europe, Africa, and Asia, the Grants met with such dignitaries as Queen Victoria (1819–1901) of England, the pope, and the emperor of Japan, Meiji (1852–1912). Many leaders consulted with Grant about situations in their country.

Following their return to America, the Grants settled in New York City. Still a popular figure, Grant was supported for another run at the presidency in 1880. His successor, Rutherford B. Hayes, had promised to serve only one term, and he was unpopular at the end of his presidency anyway. Grant was the early favorite among delegates at the Republican national convention, but he could not secure enough votes to win the nomination. When his opponent, Maine senator James G. Blaine (1830–1893; see box in **Chester A. Arthur** entry in volume 3), threw his support to Ohio congressman **James A. Garfield** (1831–1881; see entry in volume 3), Garfield won the Republican nomination.

Grant remained active over the next few years. He served as president of the Mexican Southern Railroad Company beginning in 1881. After having supported increased trade between the United States and Mexico, he helped negotiate a trade agreement between the two nations in 1883. Never lucky with finances, however, Grant went bankrupt in 1884 after having invested heavily in a New York banking firm that failed.

Deep in debt and ill with throat cancer, Grant followed a suggestion by famous American author Mark Twain (Samuel Clemens, 1835–1910) to write his memoirs (memories; autobiography). Grant completed his memoirs in June 1885. He died the following month, on July 23, at the age of sixty-three. *The Personal Memoirs of U. S. Grant* was a bestseller, providing the money needed to pay off family debts. The book is considered one of the finest military autobiographies ever written.

Grant is buried in New York City's Riverside Park. A monument marks his final resting place. Julia Grant was buried next to him after her death in 1902. The monument bears the inscription, "Let us have peace."

In the final months of his life, Ulysses S. Grant wrote *The Personal Memoirs of U. S. Grant* in order to pay off his debts.
Courtesy of the Library of Congress.

Legacy

Ulysses S. Grant's presidency is not generally ranked among the more successful administrations in American history. Government scandals, economic hardships, and ongoing regional divisiveness are often the most discussed topics of his presidential terms.

Grant's efforts to improve the social situations of African Americans and Native Americans were commendable, but they were eventually obscured by later policies and social behavior. Grant's civil rights legislation was overturned in 1883. Racial segregation (forced separation of people by race) became widespread in American life.

Grant's successor, Rutherford B. Hayes, officially ended the period of Reconstruction in 1877. Shortly after, political power in the South became concentrated among Democrats. Democratic congressmen often voted together on is-

A Selection of Grant Landmarks

Appomattox Court House National Historic Park. Box 218, Appomattox, VA 24552. (540) 352-8987. The historic village where Robert E. Lee surrendered to Ulysses S. Grant has been reconstructed. The McLean House is where the official surrender took place. See http://www.nps.gov/apco/ (accessed on July 21, 2000).

Grant Cottage State Historic Site. Mount McGregor, Box 990, Saratoga Springs, NY 12866. (518) 587-8277. Located in the Adirondack Mountains, Grant lived here during the final weeks of his life while he completed his memoirs. The cottage is preserved as it was at the time of Grant's death. See http://www.artcom.com/museums/vs/gl/12866-82.htm (accessed on July 21, 2000).

Grant Home State Historic Site. 500 Bouthillier St., Galena, IL 61036. (815) 777-3310. The Grant family lived here briefly after the Civil War ended. It sits in the well-preserved historic town of Galena. See http://www.state.il.us/HPA/sites/galenaframe.htm (accessed on July 21, 2000).

Grant's Birthplace. Routes 52E and 322, Point Pleasant, OH 45143. (513) 553-4911. The home in which Grant was born includes the infant Grant's cradle and other family memorabilia. See http://www.ohiohistory.org/places/grantbir/ (accessed on July 21, 2000).

Grant's Boyhood Home. 217 E. Grant St., Georgetown, OH 45121. (513) 378-4222. The house in which Grant lived as a small boy lies in the middle of the historic Georgetown district, which includes schoolhouses attended by the future president.

General Grant National Memorial. Riverside Dr. and 122nd St., New York, NY 10003. (212) 666-1640. Ulysses S. Grant and his wife, Julia, are buried in what is popularly known as Grant's Tomb. See http://www.nps.gov/gegr/ (accessed on July 21, 2000).

Ulysses S. Grant National Historic Site. 7400 Grant Rd., St. Louis, MO 63123. (314) 842–3298. Grant proposed to Julia Dent in this home, called White Haven. They lived here after Grant's first retirement from the army in 1854. See http://www.nps.gov/ulsg/ (accessed on July 21, 2000).

sues, forming a bloc (legislators who act together for a common cause) called "the Solid South" that was influential through the mid-twentieth century.

Government scandals during the Grant administration helped fuel reform in the 1880s that curtailed (lessened) the patronage system. In a patronage system, government officials are appointed based on their support for an elected official rather than because of their skills. Had Grant been less inclined to surround himself with friends, it is likely that his administration would have been less scandalous.

Finally, the financial crises Grant faced were repeated during the next two decades. The cycle of boom and bust—prosperity (good economic conditions) and decline—characterized the American economy until a period of prosperity reigned at the end of the nineteenth century. A period of reform early in the twentieth century brought stability to the economy until the stock market crash of 1929 was followed by the Great Depression (a long period of low economic activity, marked by high levels of unemployment).

Where to Learn More

Archer, Jules. *A House Divided: The Lives of Ulysses S. Grant and Robert E. Lee.* New York: Scholastic, 1995.

Bentley, Bill. *Ulysses S. Grant.* New York: Franklin Watts, 1993.

Cannon, Marian G. *Robert E. Lee.* New York: Franklin Watts, 1993.

Catton, Bruce. *Grant Moves South.* Boston: Little, Brown, 1960.

Catton, Bruce. *Grant Takes Command.* Boston: Little, Brown, 1969.

Frost, Lawrence A. *U. S. Grant Album: A Pictorial Biography of Ulysses S. Grant.* Seattle: Superior, 1966.

Grant, Matthew G. *Ulysses S. Grant: General and President.* Mankato, MN: Creative Education, 1974.

Grant, Ulysses S. *Personal Memoirs of U. S. Grant.* New York: C. L. Webster & Co., 1885. Reprint, New York: Penguin Books, 1999.

Kavanaugh, Jack, and Eugene C. Murdoch. *Robert E. Lee.* New York: Chelsea House, 1994.

Kerby, Mona. *Robert E. Lee: Southern Hero of the Civil War.* Springfield, NJ: Enslow, 1997.

Lee, Fitzhugh. *General Lee: A Biography of Robert E. Lee.* New York: Da Capo Press, 1994.

Mantell, Martin E. *Johnson, Grant, and the Politics of Reconstruction.* New York: Columbia University Press, 1973.

Marrin, Albert. *Unconditional Surrender: U. S. Grant and the Civil War.* New York: Atheneum, 1994.

Marrin, Albert. *Virginia's General: Robert E. Lee and the Civil War.* New York: Atheneum, 1994.

Meyer, Howard N. *Let Us Have Peace.* Collier: New York, 1966.

Nevins, Allan. *Hamilton Fish: The Inner History of the Grant Administration.* New York: Dodd, Mead & Co., 1936. Reprint, New York: F. Ungar Pub. Co., 1957.

O'Brien, Steven. *Ulysses S. Grant.* New York: Chelsea House, 1991.

Rickarby, Laura N. *Ulysses S. Grant and the Strategy of Victory.* Englewood Cliffs, NJ: Silver Burdett Press, 1991.

Simpson, Brooks D. *Let Us Have Peace: Ulysses S. Grant and the Politics of War and Reconstruction, 1861–1868.* Chapel Hill: University of North Carolina Press, 1991.

Thomas, Emory Morton. *Robert E. Lee: A Biography.* New York: W. W. Norton, 1995.

Ulysses Grant Home Page: Civil War General and President. [Online] http://www.mscomm.com/~ulysses/ (accessed on July 21, 2000).

"Ulysses S. Grant." *Cobblestone, the History Magazine for Young People* (October 1995).

Ulysses S. Grant Association. [Online] http://www.lib.siu.edu/projects/usgrant/ (accessed on July 21, 2000).

Ulysses S. Grant Network. [Online] http://saints.css.edu/mkelsey/gppg.html (accessed on July 21, 1999).

Julia Grant

Born February 16, 1826
St. Louis, Missouri
Died December 14, 1902
Washington, D.C.

Soldier's wife loved being the first lady

Julia Dent Grant foresaw great things for the man she called "Ulyss." She kept that faith through difficult times. Their wedding was delayed for four years while **Ulysses S. Grant** (1822–1885; see entry in volume 3) fought in the Mexican War (1846–48). Their early married life was spent in forts in New York and Michigan, far from the easy plantation life in which Julia was raised. Their young children were fatherless while Grant was stationed in the Pacific Northwest—a remote outpost too dangerous for Julia and the children to join him. Then came seven years while Grant struggled, first as a farmer, then as a real estate agent, and then as a clerk in his family's leather goods business.

When the Civil War broke out, Grant was nearly forty. He assembled a group of volunteers, gained a commission, and went off to battle. Great things followed. Grant became the famous, popular, and victorious general of the Civil War (1861–65). He was elected president three years later. After completing his inaugural address (first speech as president), Grant turned to the woman who had always believed he would achieve greatness. "I hope you're satisfied," he said to her.

"The light of [Grant's] glorious flame still reaches out to me, falls upon me, and warms me."

Julia Dent Grant, at the dedication of her husband's tomb

Julia Dent Grant.
Courtesy of the Library of Congress.

Plantation upbringing

The daughter of Frederick and Ellen Dent, Julia was born in 1826 on a plantation near St. Louis, Missouri. She grew up in relative ease, attending a boarding school, mixing with the wealthy families of St. Louis, and enjoying a peaceful life on the plantation.

Grant graduated from the West Point Military Academy in New York in 1843. He became an officer and was stationed at a fort near St. Louis. Grant and Julia first met when he paid a visit to the Dent family home. Their large plantation home was called the White House—the first of two homes Julia would live in with that name. Julia's brother, Frederick T. Dent (1820–1892), had been Grant's roommate at West Point. Grant began paying regular visits to the Dent home, sharing Julia's enjoyment in riding horses. He fell in love with Julia during these visits.

One day he arrived in his horse and buggy just as the Dent family was about to leave to attend a wedding. Grant was invited to join them, and Julia rode with him. When they came to a bridge that was nearly flooded over, Julia grabbed on to Grant's arm and clung to him as they made their way over the weakened structure. "I'll cling to you no matter what happens," Julia informed Grant as they passed over the rickety bridge. Once they had passed over safely and had gone further down the road, Grant said to Julia, "I wonder if you would cling to me all of my life." That was his proposal of marriage. Julia accepted.

Hardscrabble life

Grant and Julia became engaged in 1844, but Grant was soon transferred to a fort in Louisiana, and then to another in Texas. At the time, relations between the United States and Mexico were tense over a border dispute involving Texas. War broke out and Grant served heroically. He did not return to Julia until the war was over in 1848. They were married in St. Louis on August 22, 1848.

Julia accompanied Grant to his new assignment at Sacketts Harbor, New York, in the fall of 1848. She moved with him when he was assigned to Detroit, Michigan, in

1849. Julia returned to St. Louis in 1850 to give birth to their first child, Frederick. Grant was reassigned to Sacketts Harbor in 1851. He was then transferred to Fort Vancouver in the Oregon Territory in 1852.

The trip to that fort on the Pacific coast required Grant to sail from New York to Panama, cross land to the Pacific Ocean, and then sail north to Vancouver Island. The trip was too difficult for Julia and her newborn. She remained at home and gave birth to the couple's second son. Grant, meanwhile, felt miserable in the Northwest and resigned from the army in April 1854.

Grant and Julia were reunited again. Taking possession of land Julia was given by her father, the Grants tried to make a living as farmers on a rough tract Grant called Hardscrabble (a word referring to poor soil). The farm was not a financial success, and Grant became a real estate agent. By 1860, the Grants had four children and had relocated to Galena, Illinois, where Grant worked in his family's leather goods business with his younger brothers.

Greatness later in life

The Civil War began in early April 1861. Within two weeks, Grant had rounded up a group of volunteers and led them in a victorious battle a few months later. He rose rapidly through the Union military ranks, becoming commander of the Department of Tennessee by October 1862. Grant received orders to try to capture Vicksburg, Mississippi, the principal Confederate stronghold on the Mississippi River. After being turned back several times by Confederate forces, Grant decided to make another try rather than retreat and begin again.

Julia Grant visited her husband at several sites during the war whenever it was safe. When they met in April 1863, shortly before Grant was to make a final assault on the Confederate stronghold, Julia Grant immediately asked him, "Why do you not move on Vicksburg?"

Grant was the commander of all Union forces by the war's end in 1865 when he accepted the surrender of Confederate general Robert E. Lee (1807–1870; see box in **Ulysses S.**

Grant entry in volume 3). Three years later, Grant was elected president.

Julia Grant thoroughly enjoyed her time as first lady. She was the hostess of many parties, most of which were lavish. Guests often included industrialists, bankers, military officers, and publishers. Weekly receptions were open to the general public, where it was not uncommon for everyday citizens to mingle with royalty. A high point of the Grants' social occasions was the wedding of their daughter in 1874 during Grant's second term as president. Nellie Grant wed Algernon Sartoris, the nephew of a famous actress, Fanny Kemble (1809–1893).

Julia was so happy in her role as first lady that she wanted Grant to seek a third term in 1876. Grant had lost some popularity by then. His administrations were riddled with corruption. Grant said, "I never wanted to get out of a place as much as I did to get out of the presidency."

World tour and memoirs

Shortly after leaving office, the Grant family embarked on a world tour. They were honored guests wherever they went, treated to parades and banquets. They met with Queen Victoria (1819–1901) of England and with royalty in Russia and Austria. They met with the pope in Rome, toured the Holy Lands of the Middle East, and were provided with a boat to explore the Nile River in Africa by the ruler of Egypt. Passing into Asia, they toured the Taj Mahal in India and enjoyed extravagant receptions in China. The emperor of Japan presented Julia with a set of dining room furniture that she had admired.

Upon returning home in 1880, Grant was courted by Republican supporters to once again seek the presidency. Julia urged him on. Grant was interested, but he refused to make an appearance at the Republican convention that year. His appearance at the convention would likely turn a close vote in his favor. Julia wanted him to go, but Grant felt that such an appearance would be embarrassing. At the convention, Grant supporters could not get enough votes to win the nomination, which eventually went to **James A. Garfield** (1831–1881; see entry in volume 3).

The Grants retired to New York and lived happily for a few years. Suddenly, however, they became bankrupt (financially ruined) when a bank they had invested heavily in failed.

Meanwhile, Grant had been contributing anecdotes (stories) about his Civil War experiences to a magazine. Famous American author Mark Twain (Samuel Clemens; 1835–1910) suggested that he should write his memoirs. He helped Grant get a profitable deal with a publisher. He completed his memoirs just a few weeks before his death in 1885. Grant had been battling throat cancer. *The Personal Memoirs of U. S. Grant* was published the following year and became a tremendous bestseller. Profits from the book paid off the family debts and allowed Julia Grant to live the rest of her life with financial security. She died in New York in 1902.

Where to Learn More

FitzGerald, Christine Maloney. *Julia Dent Grant, 1826–1902.* New York: Children's Press, 1998.

Grant, Julia Dent. *The Personal Memoirs of Julia Dent Grant.* Edited by John Y. Simon. Carbondale: Southern Illinois University Press, 1975. Reprint, 1988.

Grant, Ulysses S. *Personal Memoirs of U. S. Grant* New York: C. L. Webster & Co., 1885. Reprint, New York: Penguin Books, 1999.

Ross, Ishbel. *The General's Wife: The Life of Mrs. Ulysses S. Grant.* New York: Dodd, Mead, 1959.

Grant's Recollection of the Confederate Surrender

Surrender occurred on April 9, 1865; recollections recorded in 1879 and excerpted from *Around the World with General Grant*

The former Union general and U.S. president remembers the day Robert E. Lee surrendered at Appomattox

O n April 9, 1865, Union general **Ulysses S. Grant** (1822–1885; see entry in volume 3) and Confederate general Robert E. Lee (1807–1870; see box in **Ulysses S. Grant** entry in volume 3) met at Appomattox Courthouse in Virginia to discuss the surrender of the Confederacy. The forces of Grant and Lee had been engaged in battle for months. The Confederacy was making its last stand against superior military power and economic support enjoyed by the Union army. When the city of Richmond, Virginia, fell to the Union army, the Civil War was effectively over.

Though the war had been bitterly fought and divided the nation, many key figures were anxious for a respectable peace that would unify the nation. President **Abraham Lincoln** (1809–1865; see entry in volume 2), General Grant, and General Lee were among them. The terms of surrender (see box) demonstrated the shared respect. The following excerpt is from General Grant's recollection of his meeting with General Lee to discuss the terms of surrender. The recollection provides a human side of a historical event, showing two men humbled by the great

"[Lee's] whole bearing was that of a patriotic and gallant soldier, concerned alone for the welfare of his army and his state."

Ulysses S. Grant

and tragic experience of war, rather than exulting in victory or being embittered by defeat.

Things to remember while reading an excerpt from Ulysses S. Grant's recollection of the Confederate surrender:

- Some of the greatest writings on war throughout history show officers and soldiers facing ordinary human concerns. Grant's recollection of his meeting with Lee was one such example. A few years after the book in which this recollection was published (1879), Grant wrote *The Personal Memoirs of U. S. Grant.* The personal, human side of people engaged in war made Grant's *Memoirs* an immediate bestseller and one of the finest military autobiographies ever written.

- The actual discussion of the surrender was short, preceded and followed by small talk. Grant and Lee had met previously when both were fighting in the Mexican War (1846–48).

- Many historians have said that the United States was fortunate that the Confederacy and the Union were represented by Lee and Grant at Appomattox. The two generals had fought desperately against one another for months. But when Lee surrendered, both men showed that they were eager to see an end to hostilities. Grant could have punished Lee's army for its participation in the rebellion against the Union. But instead, Grant drew up generous terms of surrender that eased the pain of the defeated rebels and made it possible for them to return home with some measure of pride and hope. Lee, meanwhile, resisted the temptation to order a campaign of guerrilla warfare that undoubtedly would have brought additional bloodshed and hatred to an already war-weary nation. As historian Bruce Catton commented in *The Civil War*, "In Grant, Lee met a man who was as anxious as himself to see this hardest of wars followed by a good peace. Grant believed that the whole point of the war had been the effort to prove that Northerners and Southerners were and always would be fellow citizens, and the

moment the fighting stopped he believed that they ought to begin behaving that way."

- A key aspect of the surrender agreement was Grant's decision to allow Lee's soldiers to keep their horses. Most of the long and brutal war had been fought in the American South, and much of the area—both urban and rural—had been destroyed. Lee knew that the task of rebuilding premilitary lives would be much more difficult for soldiers if their horses—used for both transportation and farmwork—were taken from them. Grant sensed how strongly Lee felt about this matter. The Union commander's quick decision to allow the Confederate soldiers to keep their horses spared Lee the humiliation of having to beg for this favor.

- In the surrender document that Lee and Grant agreed to, Grant wrote down the terms in pencil and an assistant later made it into an official document. The meeting of

Confederate general Robert E. Lee signs surrender papers as Union general Ulysses S. Grant looks on. *Public domain.*

Official Terms of Confederate Surrender

The following official terms of surrender were presented by Union general Ulysses S. Grant to Confederate general Robert E. Lee.

Head Quarters of the Armies of the United States
Appomattox C.H. Va. Apl 9th 1865
Gen. R. E. Lee
Comd'g C.S.A.

General,

In accordance with the substance of my letter to you of the 8th inst., I propose to receive the surrender of the Army of N. Va. on the following terms to wit;

Rolls of all the officers and men be made in duplicate, one copy to be given to an officer to be designated by me, the other to be retained by such officer or officers as you may designate. The officers to give their individual paroles not to take up arms against the Government of the United States until properly exchanged, and each company or regimental commander to sign a like parole for the men of their commands—

The arms, artillery and public property to be parked and stacked and turned over to the officer appointed by me to receive them. This will not embrace the side arms of the officers nor their private horses or baggage. This done each officer and man will be allowed to return to their homes, not to be disturbed by United States authority as long as they observe their parole and the laws in force where they may reside—

Very Respectfully
U. S. Grant
Lt. Gen

Grant and Lee and the surrender document show two military leaders hoping to put the war behind and reunite the nation.

Excerpt from Ulysses S. Grant's recollection of the Confederate surrender

On the night before Lee's surrender, I had a wretched headache—headaches to which I have been subject, nervous **pros-**

Prostration: Physical or mental exhaustion.

tration, *intense personal suffering. But, suffer or not, I had to keep moving. The object of my campaign was not Richmond, not the defeat of Lee in actual fight, but to remove him and his army out of the contest. You see the war was an enormous strain upon the country. Rich as we were I do not see how we could have endured it another year, even from a financial point of view. So with these views I wrote Lee . . . he does not appear well in that correspondence, not nearly so well as he did in our subsequent interviews, where his whole bearing was that of a patriotic and gallant soldier, concerned alone for the welfare of his army and his state.*

*I received word that Lee would meet me at a point within our lines near [Union commander Philip H.] Sheridan's headquarters. I had to ride quite a distance through a muddy area. I remember now that I was concerned with my personal appearance. I had an old suit on, without my sword, and without any distinguishing mark of rank except the shoulder straps of a Lieutenant-general on a woolen blouse. I was splashed with mud in my long ride. I was afraid Lee might think I meant to show him **studied discourtesy** by so coming—at least I thought so.*

*I went up to the house where Lee was waiting. I found him in a new, splendid uniform, which only recalled my anxiety as to my own clothes while on my way to meet him. I expressed my regret that I was compelled to meet him in so unceremonious a manner, and he replied that the only suit he had available was one which had been sent him by some admirers in Baltimore, and which he then wore for the first time. We spoke of old friends in the army. I remembered having seen Lee in **Mexico.** He was such much higher in rank than myself at the time that I supposed he had no recollection of me. But he said he remembered me very well. We talked about old times and exchanged inquiries about friends.*

*Lee then broached the subject of our meeting. I told him my terms, and Lee, listening attentively, asked me to write them down. I took out my manifold order book and pencil and wrote them down. General Lee put on his glasses and read them over. The conditions **gave the officers** their **side-arms**, private horses, and personal baggage. I said to Lee that I hoped and believed this would be the close of the war; that it was most important that the men should go home and go to work, and the government would not throw any obstacles in the way. Lee answered that it would have the most happy effect, and accepted the terms. I handed over my penciled memorandum to an aide to put into ink, and we resumed*

Studied discourtesy: An intended show of disrespect.

Mexico: A reference to the Mexican War (1846–48) in which both Grant and Lee had served.

Gave the officers: Allowed the officers to keep.

Side-arms: Pistols and other weapons a soldier carries in addition to larger arms, like a rifle.

our conversation about old times and friends in the army. Various officers came in—[James] Longstreet, [John B.] Gordon, [George E.] Pickett, from the South; [Philip H.] Sheridan, [Edward O.] Ord and others from our side. Some were old friends—Longstreet and my-self for instance, and we had a general talk. Lee no doubt expected me to ask for his sword but I did not want his sword. It would only have gone to the Patent Office to be worshipped by the Washington Rebels.

There was a pause, when General Lee said that most of the animals in his cavalry and artillery were owned by the privates, and he would like to know, under the terms, whether they would be regarded as private property or the property of the government. I said that under the terms of surrender they belonged to the government. General Lee read over the letters and said that was so. I then said to the General that I believed and hoped this was the last battle of the war; that I saw the wisdom of these men getting home and to work as soon as possible, and that I would give orders to allow any soldier or officer claiming a horse or mule to take it. General Lee showed some emotion at this—a feeling which I also shared—and said it would have a most happy effect.

*The interview ended, and I gave orders for **rationing** his troops. The next day I met Lee on horseback and we had a long talk. In that conversation I urged upon him the wisdom of ending the war by the surrender of the other armies. I asked him to use his influence with the people of the South—an influence that was supreme—to bring the war to an end. General Lee said that his campaign in Virginia was the last organized resistance which the South was capable of making—that I might have to march a good deal and encounter isolated commands here and there, but there was no longer any army which could make a stand. I told Lee that this fact only made his responsibility greater, and any further war would be a crime.*

I asked him to go among the Southern people and use his influence to have all men under arms surrender to the same terms given to the army of Northern Virginia. He replied that he could not do so without consultation with President [Jefferson] Davis. I was sorry. I saw that the Confederacy had gone beyond the reach of President Davis, and that there was nothing that could be done except what Lee could do to benefit the Southern people. I was anxious to get them home and have our armies go to their homes and fields. But Lee would not move without Davis, and as a matter

Rationing: A portion of food or supplies provided to soldiers. Reflecting the desperate circumstances of the Confederate army, Lee noted that his men had no food rations left, and Grant provided shares from the Union's rations.

| **Complete American Presidents Sourcebook**

of fact at that time, or soon after, Davis was a fugitive in the woods. (Young)

What happened next . . .

The surrender at Appomattox effectively ended the Civil War. While the two generals had arranged a respectful surrender, many in the nation were not as forgiving. President Abraham Lincoln was assassinated within a week by a pro-Confederate extremist named John Wilkes Booth (1838–1865). A group of Northern politicians dominating Congress placed punitive measures on the South, and many former Confederate states were supervised by the federal military for another decade, even after they were readmitted to the Union. Meanwhile, the institution of slavery was abolished by the Thirteenth Amendment (see box in **Andrew Johnson** entry in volume 2) to the U.S. Constitution later in 1865. Other forms of institutionalized racism, including segregation, soon appeared.

General Lee continued to lead a distinguished life, but he was never given back his citizenship—a reflection of the continued bitterness over the war. General Grant was quickly courted as a presidential candidate, and he won the next presidential election, which occurred in 1868. Grant was reelected in 1872 and was nearly nominated again in 1880.

Did you know . . .

General Lee was treated with great respect not only by General Grant, but also by other Union officers who were present at Appomattox. They knew that Lee had been a brilliant commander for the South, and that he had fought for the Confederacy out of loyalty to his home state of Virginia. Even though they had spent the last few years fighting him, they viewed him as an honorable man who deserved courteous treatment.

Where to Learn More

Anderson, Nancy Scott. *The Generals: Ulysses S. Grant and Robert E. Lee.* New York: Knopf, 1988. Reprint, New York: Wings Books, 1994.

Brooks, William Elizabeth. *Grant of Appomattox, A Study of the Man.* Indianapolis: The Bobbs-Merrill Company, 1942. Reprint, Westport, CT: Greenwood Press, 1971.

Grant, Ulysses S. *Personal Memoirs of U. S. Grant.* New York: C. L. Webster & Co., 1885. Reprint, New York: Penguin Books, 1999.

Rickarby, Laura Ann. *Ulysses S. Grant and the Strategy of Victory.* Englewood Cliffs, NJ: Silver Burdett Press, 1991.

Young, John Russell. *Around the World with General Grant.* New York: American News Co., 1879.

Rutherford B. Hayes

Nineteenth president (1877–1881)

Rutherford B. Hayes

**Born October 4, 1822
Delaware, Ohio
Died January 17, 1893
Fremont, Ohio**

**Nineteenth president of the United States
(1877–1881)**

**His presidency signaled the end of one of
the most controversial eras in U.S.
history—Reconstruction**

"My task was to wipe out the color line, to abolish sectionalism. . . . I am forced to admit the experience was a failure."

Rutherford B. Hayes

Rutherford B. Hayes.
Courtesy of the Library of Congress.

The presidential achievements of Rutherford B. Hayes are overshadowed, historically, by accounts of the election of 1876—one of the most disputed presidential elections in American history. Hayes faced conflict throughout his term. Democrats in Congress were combative. Hayes gradually lost support within his own Republican Party as well. Hayes had promised to serve only one term. It was unlikely that he would have been nominated for a second term, even if he wanted to seek reelection.

Still, Hayes provided stability and moderate leadership to an American system rocked by serious problems. Government scandals, political partisanship (placing the concerns of one's group or political party above all other considerations), an unstable economy, and sectionalism (when people place emphasis on policies that would directly benefit their area of the country) had plagued the country since the end of the Civil War (1861–65), a decade before. Hayes maintained conservative fiscal (financial) policies while many called for more radical (extreme) approaches. His methods helped revive what had been a sluggish (slow) economy. Finally, Hayes lobbied for the civil rights of minorities, particularly African Americans and Chinese

Fast Facts about Rutherford B. Hayes

Full name: Rutherford Birchard Hayes

Born: October 4, 1822

Died: January 16, 1893

Burial site: Spiegel Grove State Park, Fremont, Ohio

Parents: Rutherford and Sophia Birchard Hayes

Spouse: Lucy Ware Webb (1831–1889; m. 1852)

Children: Sardis Birchard Austin (1853–1926); James Webb Cook (1856–1935); Rutherford Platt (1858–1927); Joseph Thompson (1861–1863); George Crook (1864–1866); Frances (Fanny) Hayes (1867–1950); Scott Russell (1871–1923); Manning Force (1873–1874)

Religion: Methodist

Education: Kenyon College (1842); Harvard University Law School (1845)

Occupations: Lawyer; soldier

Government positions: U.S. representative from Ohio; Ohio governor

Political party: Republican

Dates as president: March 3, 1877–March 4, 1881

Age upon taking office: 54

Americans, at a time when many white men were fighting to maintain a base of power that was theirs alone.

Such political conflicts reflected the divisiveness (divisions between North and South) still present in the country more than a decade after the Civil War had ended. The antagonism (unfriendly feelings) made it impossible for Hayes to have a successful administration, even though he proved trustworthy and presided over a surging (suddenly increasing) economy. "My task was to wipe out the color line, to abolish sectionalism . . .," Hayes stated in 1878, midway through his term. "I am forced to admit the experience was a failure."

Overcomes childhood illness

Rutherford Birchard Hayes was born in Delaware, Ohio, on October 4, 1822. His family had settled there after moving from Dummerston, Vermont, in 1817. His father, also named Rutherford Hayes, decided to move from Vermont to what was then the American West for new opportunities. Accompanying him to Ohio was his wife, Sophia, their two children, and Sophia's brother, Sardis Birchard.

Hayes's father did well in Ohio over the next five years. He bought land and built a large house, but he died during an epidemic of malaria (an infectious disease transmitted by a mosquito) two months before Rutherford Birchard Hayes was born. Sophia Hayes was left with three children, a farm, and two houses. She leased the farmland and a house in the town of Delaware to have a steady income.

Rutherford B. Hayes Timeline

1822: Born in Ohio

1842: Graduates from Kenyon College

1845: Graduates from Harvard Law School; establishes practice in Fremont (then called East Sandusky), Ohio

1849: Moves law practice to Cincinnati

1861: Begins fighting in Civil War; wounded four times through 1865

1865–67: Serves in U.S. House of Representatives

1868–72: Serves two terms as governor of Ohio

1876–77: Serves third term as governor of Ohio

1876: Trails Samuel J. Tilden in disputed presidential election

1877: Special electoral commission formed containing fifteen members (five representatives, five senators, five Supreme Court justices); disputed electoral votes awarded to Hayes, who is declared the victor on March 2, 1877, only days before the presidential inauguration

1877–81: Serves as nineteenth U.S. president

1881: Retires to Ohio

1893: Dies in Ohio

Hayes was born frail (physically weak). Sophia was very protective of him, even more so following the accidental drowning death of his brother Lorenzo when Hayes was two years old. She kept him isolated as a youngster and gradually taught him to read and write. Hayes began attending private schools by age nine, an education paid for by his uncle Sardis.

Hayes went on to attend Kenyon College in Ohio. He graduated first in his class in 1842. He then moved to Columbus, Ohio, to study law before entering Harvard Law School. After receiving his degree in 1845, Hayes returned to Ohio. He was admitted to the bar (the legal profession) and began a practice in East Sandusky with the help of his uncle, who had become a wealthy banker.

Career as lawyer

Hayes spent at least as much time in pursuing his hobbies—literature and natural science—as he did lawyering with

Words to Know

Abolitionist: One who favors the abolishment of slavery.

Appropriations: Funds authorized for a particular project.

Bar: A term that encompasses all certified lawyers—those who have passed all official requirements (the bar exam) to be certified to practice law.

Bloc: A unified group able to wield power through its size and numbers.

Civil service: A government position.

Compromise of 1850: A group of bills that included allowing Texas to enter the Union as a slave state and California as a free state.

Confederate: Relating to and representing the Southern states that seceded from the United States in the 1860s and fought against the Union during the American Civil War (1861–65).

Dark horse: A term that describes a little-known candidate who shows marginal promise but could finish surprisingly strong.

Electoral College: A body officially responsible for electing the president of the United States. In presidential elections, the candidate who receives the most popular votes in a particular state wins all of that state's electoral votes. Votes are distributed among states in ratios based on population. A candidate must win a majority of electoral votes (over fifty percent) in order to win the presidency.

Enfranchised: Authorized to vote.

Fiscal: Having to do with financial matters.

Gold standard: The economic practice whereby all of the money printed and minted in a nation is based on the amount of gold the nation has stored. (Paper money is printed; coins are minted, or stamped.)

Inflation: An economic term that describes a situation where money loses some of its value, usually because the cost of goods is more expensive.

Partisanship: Placing the concerns of one's group or political party above all other considerations.

Political bosses: Powerful people able to organize support and deliver votes for a political candidate.

Protemperance: Supporting a ban on alcohol manufacturing and consumption.

Reconstruction: A federal policy from 1865 to 1877. The national government took an active part in assisting and policing the former Confederate states.

Riders: Measures added on to legislation. Riders are usually items that might not pass through Congress or will be vetoed by the president if presented alone. Congressmen attempt to attach such items to popular bills, hoping they will "ride" along with the more popular legislation.

Secede: To officially withdraw from an organization.

Sectionalism: The emphasis that people place on policies that would directly benefit their area of the country.

his partner, Ralph P. Buckland. Hayes's most noteworthy accomplishment at the time was assisting in the successful campaign to change the name of the town from East Sandusky to Fremont. He traveled widely in the United States and Canada.

In 1849, Hayes became more ambitious with his career. He moved to Cincinnati, Ohio, a thriving and important western town. He quickly made his reputation there as a lawyer by often presenting shrewd (clever) defenses in the most difficult cases. When he arrived in Cincinnati, he quickly made a call at the home of the Webb family. He had met Lucy Webb (1831–1889; see entry on **Lucy Hayes** in volume 3) several years earlier when she attended school in Delaware, Ohio. She was fifteen back then—"too young to fall in love with," Hayes would recall later in life. He was nine years older than Lucy. When they reunited in Cincinnati, Lucy was an educated and spirited eighteen-year-old woman who was strongly protemperance (in favor of abstaining from alcohol) and abolitionist (supporting the end of slavery). They were married in 1852.

Lucy Webb Hayes's strong abolitionist views influenced "Rud," as she called Hayes, to begin defending runaway slaves who were pursued into the North. Slaveowners could claim their "property" and return with their recaptured slaves to the South, as allowed by the Compromise of 1850, a group of bills that included allowing Texas to enter the Union as a slave state and California as a free state.

Hayes became more politically active. He helped found the Ohio branch of the Republican Party. The party was established nationally in 1854 by attracting members of the former Whig Party as well as the short-lived Free-Soil and American parties. All these parties were against the expansion of slavery into newly settled territories. The party also attracted Northern Democrats with abolitionist sentiments who were at odds with their Southern counterparts over slavery.

Meanwhile, Hayes continued to pursue his interest in books, joining the local Literature Club of Cincinnati. He met many of the most powerful citizens in Cincinnati. He was responsible for arranging guest lectures by notable writers, including American essayist Ralph Waldo Emerson (1803–1882).

In 1858, Hayes was chosen to fill the vacant city solicitor position by the Cincinnati City Council. The next year, he was elected to the position. Hayes supported the candidacy of fellow Republican **Abraham Lincoln** (1809–1865; see entry in volume 2) in his successful election to the presidency in 1860.

Hayes had taken only a mild interest when Southern states began seceding (separating) from the Union following Lincoln's election. However, when Confederate troops (troops from the Southern states that seceded from the United States) attacked Fort Sumter in South Carolina in April 1861, Hayes was inspired into action. He organized about three dozen members of the Literary Club and led them in military drills. As the war spread, Hayes was commissioned (militarily appointed) as major of the Twenty-third Ohio Infantry (foot soldiers).

Civil War hero

Hayes proved to be an able war leader and a brave soldier. Within a year, he showed his courage by leading nine companies of soldiers to safety after they were overwhelmed by a surprise attack by Confederate troops in Parisburg, Virginia. He later commanded a regiment (a military unit of ground troops) in the Battle of South Mountain, which was attacked by Confederate forces under the leadership of General Robert E. Lee (1807–1870; see box in **Ulysses S. Grant** entry in volume 3).

Hayes was severely wounded in the battle and took several weeks to heal. When word of his wounds reached his wife Lucy, she traveled hundreds of miles to be with him despite not knowing the exact location of where he was recuperating. She was a nurse and helped Union soldiers throughout the war, while her children were cared for by her mother. Grateful soldiers commonly referred to her as "Mother Lucy."

Hayes was wounded four times during the war, but he was still fighting at the end. He was leading an expedition against Confederate troops in Lynchburg, Virginia, when the Civil War ended in 1865, with the surrender of General Lee.

Meanwhile, Hayes's popularity in Cincinnati grew with reports of his heroism on the battlefield. While he was still a soldier in 1864, Hayes was nominated as a Republican candidate for Congress. Replying to a request to return home and campaign, he wrote, "I have other business just now. Any man who would leave the army at this time to electioneer [campaign] for Congress ought to be scalped." Even without campaigning, he won the election easily in a district that had been mostly Democratic.

Hayes's first term in Congress was relatively uneventful. He became more active after being reelected for a second term. Hayes supported the Republican policy of Reconstruction (the rebuilding of the South) and chaired (headed) a committee on the Library of Congress, the nation's library. He secured funds to expand the collection of science books in the Library of Congress.

Hayes ran successfully for governor of Ohio in 1867 and served two terms. During his tenure (term of office) the state of Ohio ratified (formally approved) the Fifteenth Amendment (see box) to the Constitution, an amendment that addresses voting rights of former slaves. Ohio State University was established during his tenure as well.

Hayes wanted to retire from public life after his second term, but he was convinced by Republicans in 1872 to again run for Congress. Hayes lost the election, but his presence on the Republican ticket helped President **Ulysses S. Grant** (1822–1885; see entry in volume 3) carry the state.

Hayes then retired from public life. The Hayes family moved to Fremont to live with his uncle, Sardis Birchard. When Birchard died in 1874, he left his substantial wealth to the Hayes family. He left them a mansion as well, Spiegel Grove, that had been completed in 1862.

Called to serve, again

Hayes's retirement was short lived. Even though he lost the congressional race in 1872, the loyalty he showed to embattled president Grant made him appealing to Republi-

 Fifteenth Amendment

The Fifteenth Amendment, ratified on February 3, 1870, was an attempt to bar states from using race as a factor in deciding whether or not to allow citizens the right to vote. "Previous condition of servitude" refers to former slaves.

Section 1. The right of citizens of the United States to vote shall not be denied or abridged by the United States or by any State on account of race, color or previous condition of servitude.

Section 2. The Congress shall have power to enforce this article by appropriate legislation.

Campaign banner used for the 1876 Republican election, featuring presidential candidate Rutherford B. Hayes and vice presidential candidate William A. Wheeler.
Courtesy of the Library of Congress.

cans. He was convinced to run again for governor in 1875. The Republican Party was rapidly losing power in Ohio and was in need of an appealing candidate. Hayes's subsequent victory in Ohio brought him more national recognition among Republicans. He soon became a dark-horse candidate (a candidate who is unknown at the start but can end up winning) the following year, when Republicans met at their national convention to vote on their presidential nominee.

Complete American Presidents Sourcebook

Republicans had held the White House since 1860, but the outgoing Grant administration had been mired (entangled) in corruption (political dishonesty). Maine senator James G. Blaine (1830–1893; see box in **Chester A. Arthur** entry in volume 3) was the likely nominee as the convention began, but he had been implicated in a scandal involving the illegal sales of stocks. Six ballots failed to achieve the necessary majority of delegates for nomination among several candidates. Support turned to Hayes, who had a trustworthy reputation and was a war hero. Ohio also had a high number of electoral votes, meaning that nominating Hayes would likely result in the Republicans "carrying" Ohio (winning the electoral votes in that state). Democrats nominated Samuel J. Tilden (1814–1886; see box), a lawyer and political leader from New York.

Hayes immediately declared that if elected he would not be a candidate for a second term. This stand helped him promote a major campaign issue—restoring a nonpartisan civil service system (government work not controlled by one political party). Many government workers had been pressed into financial support for the Grant administration and by local political bosses, powerful people able to organize voters and to deliver votes for a particular political candidate. Hayes stated that reform of the system "can best be accomplished by an Executive who is under no temptation to use the patronage of his office to promote his own re-election."

The statement reflected the integrity with which Hayes intended to invest into his administration if he were elected president. He proved, indeed, to be a model of integrity. But his actions were greatly overshadowed by a tainted election and by ongoing partisan (political party) and sectional (regional) differences.

The tainted election

The political environment in the United States of the mid-1870s was ripe for controversy. Following the Civil War, federal troops remained stationed in the South to ensure that the laws of the land were carried out. The Republican Party had rallied under President Lincoln in the 1860s to abolish slavery. After the Civil War, the federal policy of Reconstruction was intended to restore the relationship between the for-

Samuel J. Tilden

Samuel Jones Tilden was the Democratic candidate in the most controversial presidential election in American history. An attorney who rose to become governor of New York in the 1870s, Tilden established a reputation as an effective and dedicated reformer. He lost the 1876 presidency to Republican candidate Rutherford B. Hayes in a bitterly-disputed election. Born February 9, 1814, in New Lebanon, New York, Tilden became immersed in the world of politics at a relatively young age. A talented writer, he penned a number of political papers while in his twenties for his friend **Martin Van Buren** (1782–1862; see entry in volume 1), president of the United States from 1837 to 1841. Around this same time, Tilden studied law at the University of the City of New York, and he passed the state bar exam to become a certified lawyer in 1841. He became counsel for the City of New York two years later, and in 1846 he was elected to the New York state legislature.

By the early 1850s, Tilden was firmly entrenched as one of New York City's leading attorneys. He embraced the Democratic Party that his friend Van Buren had helped establish during the 1830s. After the conclusion of the Civil War in 1865, Tilden emerged as a key figure in the Democrats' reorganization efforts. Republicans had rallied behind Abraham Lincoln in the early 1860s, and Congressional Repub-

licans emerged as the nation's strongest political force after Lincoln's assassination. Tilden's unblemished reputation was enhanced in the late 1860s and early 1870s when he and fellow reformer Thomas Nast (1840–1902) crusaded against William "Boss" Tweed (1823–1878) and Tammany Hall, the corrupt Democratic political group that dominated New York City at that time. The notorious Tweed Ring had cheated the city out of millions of dollars over the years. Tilden, Nast, and other reformers were finally able to convict Tweed and send him to prison.

In 1874, Tilden was named the Democratic nominee for New York's governor's office. He won the election and made an immediate impact. One of his most notable achievements was his dismantling of the Canal Ring, a group of politicians and building contractors that had enriched themselves via fraudulent water canal repair agreements. A skilled administrator and determined reformer, Tilden was a popular governor. By the mid-1870s, meanwhile, the Democratic Party had revitalized itself across much of the nation. In the years following the Civil War, Southern Democrats had banded to turn Republicans out of their public offices in the South, and by the mid-1870s only three Southern states were still in Republican hands. Northern Democrats, meanwhile, knew that the public was angry with the corruption-riddled administration

Samuel J. Tilden.
Courtesy of the Library of Congress.

of Ulysses S. Grant, a Republican president elected in 1868 and 1872. Tilden's reformer image and his popularity made the governor of New York an ideal choice to head the Democratic ticket in 1876.

On election night, Tilden won the popular vote and secured 184 uncontested electoral votes, one short of clinching the presidency. Nineteen additional electoral votes, however—from the Republican-held states of South Carolina, Louisiana, and Florida—were claimed by both the Republican and Democratic parties, and a tense standoff ensued as the two sides grappled for possession of the pivotal votes. A few days before the scheduled inauguration of America's new president, a specially-appointed electoral commission finally announced an agreement. The Republicans would get the disputed Electoral College votes, thus pushing Hayes's total just over the number needed to claim victory. In return for handing Hayes the presidency, the Democrats secured promises that the South would receive significant funding for railroads and public works projects and appointment of a Southerner to the president's Cabinet. In addition, Hayes promised to pull the last of the federal troops out of the South (a move that some historians believe would have taken place anyway).

Despite winning the popular vote, Tilden had been denied the presidency of the United States. Mindful of ongoing hostilities between the Southern and Northern regions of the nation, the governor tried to accept the results gracefully. "I can retire to private life with the consciousness that I shall receive from posterity the credit of having been elected to the highest position in the gift of the people, without any of the cares and responsibilities of the office," he said after the agreement was announced. Tilden returned to New York, where he resumed his law practice. A wealthy man at the time of his death in 1886, he left much of his $6 million fortune for the construction of a public library. Tilden's money was combined with the city's Astor and Lenox libraries to form the renowned New York Public Library in 1895.

mer Confederate states and the federal Union, to oversee the transition of the newly freed slaves into citizens, and to help convert the Southern economy from one based on slave labor to one based on paid labor.

During Reconstruction there was an intense national struggle over the shape of government in the postwar South. Republican leadership became increasingly viewed as a federal intrusion (unwelcome presence). Conservative Southern Democrats united to form a political bloc (group united by a common cause) that represented the traditional white, male power of the South. Newly enfranchised (authorized to vote) African Americans sided with the Republican Party, helping it keep a foothold in the South. Troops remained to ensure that federal laws were followed.

The presidential election of 1876 became a dispute that challenged the very workings of the American political system. Vote tallies (counts) in Florida and South Carolina were close and were tainted by claims of fraud (trickery) and intimidation (threats) on the part of Democrats. The Florida State Canvassing Board (a group authorized to count votes) was authorized with the mission to reject returns "that shall be shown, or shall appear to be so irregular, false, or fraudulent that the board shall be unable to determine the vote." The board exercised that power, as did a similar commission in South Carolina. Both revised counts resulted in a majority of votes for Republican candidate Hayes. It was an unsolvable situation. There had indeed been voter intimidation for Democratic candidates, but the election boards were dominated by Republicans.

In Louisiana, the majority of the vote was Democratic, but the results were questioned by the Republican-based State Returning Board (another group organized to count votes). The board had the power to dismiss votes that they believed resulted from violence and fraud. Louisiana ended up sending two different vote counts to Washington, D.C. The original count proved Tilden the winner. A revised count showed a Republican victory.

The number of electoral votes needed for election was 185. Votes excluding those that had come under review in the South and West left Tilden with 184 electoral votes to Hayes's 165. Twenty electoral votes were under dispute—eight from Louisiana, seven from South Carolina, four from Florida, and

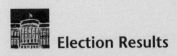

Election Results

1876

Presidential / Vice presidential candidates	Popular votes	Presidential electoral votes
Rutherford B. Hayes / William A. Wheeler (Republican)	4,036,298	185
Samuel J. Tilden / Thomas A. Hendricks (Democratic)	4,300,590	184

Hayes won the Republican nomination on the seventh ballot; U.S. senator James G. Blaine of Maine was the leader on the first six ballots. Despite having fewer popular votes than Democrat Tilden, Hayes won the election after a special electoral commission awarded the twenty disputed electoral votes of Florida, Louisiana, Oregon, and South Carolina to Hayes.

one from Oregon. The disputed votes would determine the victor. The new president was to take office in March of 1877, but no winner had yet been determined by the end of 1876.

After several sessions, Congress on January 29, 1877, established an electoral commission to resolve the issue. The commission consisted of fifteen members—seven Republicans, seven Democrats, and one independent from among five senators, five representatives, and five Supreme Court judges. However, the lone independent, Justice David Davis (1815–1886), was soon elected by the Illinois legislature to fill an open Congressional seat. His replacement on the commission shifted the balance of power to Republicans.

Much haggling (arguing) followed, in which the Republican majority followed a strict partisan (party) line and Democrats consistently disrupted the proceedings. The election dispute was settled shortly before the date the new president was to be inaugurated (formally installed in office). The twenty disputed electoral votes went to Hayes, making him the Electoral College winner, 185 votes to 184. (For more information on the Electoral College, see boxes in **George W. Bush** entry in volume 5.) In a deal often called the Compromise of 1877, the Republican candidate was declared the winner, but Democrats were appeased (pacified), too. They were assured that federal troops would be removed from the South, that a Southern Democrat would be selected to serve in Hayes's Cabinet, and that legislation awarding a federal sub-

Hayes was the first president to have a phone and a typewriter in the White House.

sidy (financial assistance) for the proposed Texas and Pacific railroad would be passed.

During the proceedings of the electoral commission, Hayes quietly awaited the results at home. When the declaration that he was the victor was made on March 2, 1877, Hayes was already on the way to the capital to arrive in time for the inauguration—just in case he won.

"Pacification"

The major themes of Hayes's inaugural address were "permanent pacification of the country" (to bring peace and end divisiveness), the return of self-government to the Southern states, and the need for civil service reform. He was not able to ease political conflicts among Republicans and Democrats. Hayes was effective in ending Reconstruction, reforming the civil service, and strengthening the economy.

In disassembling Reconstruction, Hayes first turned to the situation in the states of South Carolina and Louisiana. Each state had two state governments that were policed by federal troops. After meeting with the rival governors of South Carolina (General Wade Hampton [1818–1902] and Daniel H. Chamberlain [1835–1907]), Hayes withdrew the troops from that state. South Carolina became a single government again.

Federal troops had been stationed in Louisiana to preserve order. That responsibility was turned back to the state and troops were withdrawn. Reconstruction ended as the Southern states regained independence from federal occupation.

In June of 1877, Hayes began acting on civil service reform. He issued an order prohibiting (preventing) government officials from taking part in "the management of political organizations, caucuses, conventions, or election campaigns." The order stated further: "Their right to vote and to express their views on public questions, either openly or through the press is not denied, provided it does not interfere with the discharge of their official duties. No assessment for political purposes on officers or subordinates should be allowed." (Assessment refers to the amount of money a person owes for certain privileges or for taxes.) Those who went against the presidential order were immediately suspended. The most famous case of suspension occurred at the New York Customs House. There, collector **Chester A. Arthur** (1829–1886; see entry in volume 3), who would later become president, was stripped of his responsibilities. He had continued political efforts after the presidential order banning them was issued.

President Hayes's financial policy helped bring the economy out of the doldrums (inactivity) associated with the Panic of 1873 (a downturn in the economy). It also ensured economic stability. Hayes insisted on paying off the national debt. He favored the principle of "sound money," which states that paper money has a single value based on the gold standard. The gold standard means that money is produced based on how much gold the nation has. During the Civil War, the government had printed bank notes, notes promising money to the holder of the note. Bank notes are authorized by banks and are acceptable as money. The particular bank notes printed by the government during the Civil War were called greenbacks. These greenbacks resulted in an increased money supply, which lessened the value of money and caused inflation, an economic situation during which money loses some of its value, usually because the cost of goods is more expensive.

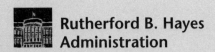

Rutherford B. Hayes Administration

Administration Dates
March 4, 1877–March 4, 1881

Vice President
William Almon Wheeler (1877–81)

Cabinet

Secretary of State
William M. Evarts (1877–81)

Secretary of the Treasury
John Sherman (1877–81)

Secretary of War
George W. McCrary (1877–79)
Alexander Ramsey (1879–81)

Attorney General
Charles Devens (1877–81)

Secretary of the Navy
Richard W. Thompson (1877–80)
Nathan Goff Jr. (1881)

Postmaster General
David M. Key (1877–80)
Horace Maynard (1880–81)

Secretary of the Interior
Carl Schurz (1877–81)

However, Hayes's principles were opposed by Congress, which wanted to make even more money available by coining silver as well as gold. Hayes managed to delay bills allowing the unlimited coinage of silver and refunding of the national debt, but Congress was eventually successful in overriding his vetoes (presidential rejection of legislative bills that prevents or delays a bill becoming law).

As president, Rutherford B. Hayes ended the era of Reconstruction, began civil service reform, and tried to balance the federal budget.
Courtesy of the Library of Congress.

Congress posed other challenges to Hayes. A Democratic majority in 1879 regularly included riders (measures added on to legislation) on basic appropriations bills (bills authorizing funds for a certain project). The Democrats added these riders in an attempt to pass legislation they knew the president would otherwise veto. One such rider prohibited the use of federal troops "to keep the peace at the polls." Hayes agreed that military interference with elections should be prevented, but he insisted that such power might be needed someday. He therefore vetoed the bill. He also defended the supervision of national elections by national authority, as opposed to state authority, to guard against voter fraud and intimidation. He was motivated to maintain measures that could be used in an emergency by news that black voters were being intimidated. The vetoes could not be overcome by Congress. The basic appropriations bills were finally passed without riders.

Hayes was successful on other fronts. In 1880, he gained American approval for a French firm to begin construction of the Panama Canal. In 1823, a policy statement called the Monroe Doctrine (see **James Monroe** primary source entry in volume 1) explained the position of the United States on the activities of European countries in the Western Hemisphere. Since the Monroe Doctrine, the United States had been opposed to European presence in the Americas. Hayes was able to convince Congress to back the building of the canal with the help of the French. The Panama Canal project, however, would take another two decades to get underway (see **Theodore Roosevelt** entry in volume 3).

Hayes vetoed a bill restricting Chinese immigration. Railroad builders had encouraged Chinese immigration for years to help meet labor needs. Some Americans in the 1870s wanted to stop the Chinese population in America from growing larger.

Retirement in Ohio

As Hayes's term came to a quiet close, he was never considered a candidate for reelection. He intended to keep his promise of serving one term, but he had been drawn out of retirement before. Not this time. His public career ended with his retirement from the presidency, and he returned to Spiegel Grove in Fremont, Ohio. Over the next few years, he worked to improve veterans organizations. He served as a trustee of the Peabody Fund for the education of underprivileged children in the South.

After falling ill in Cleveland, Ohio, early in 1893, Hayes returned once more to Fremont, where he died at Spiegel Grove on January 17, 1893. He was buried there next to his wife, Lucy, who had died in 1889.

Legacy

Rutherford B. Hayes effectively ended the era of Reconstruction, returning self-determination to the states of the South. His civil service reforms were continued on by successors, including Chester A. Arthur. Curiously, Arthur had been suspended during the Hayes administration for continuing to use his government finance position for political purposes. Hayes's fiscal conservatism (moderate and cautious financial practice)—balancing the federal budget and regulating the supply of money—proved to have stabilizing effects. His efforts to protect the civil rights of minorities were praiseworthy, but many battles remained to be fought.

The end of Reconstruction and opposition to Republicans solidified Southern Democrats into a bloc that could wield great influence on legislation. The Solid South, as the bloc came to be called, was united and powerful through the mid–twentieth century.

Hayes was the first president to travel to the West Coast of the United States. Over a two-month period in 1880, President Hayes traveled ten thousand miles within the United States, using railroads, stagecoaches, horses, steamers, yachts, ferries, and an army ambulance wagon.

Where to Learn More

Barnard, Harry. *Rutherford B. Hayes and His America*. Indianapolis: Bobbs-Merrill, 1954. Reprint, New York: Russell & Russell, 1967.

Davison, Kenneth E. *The Presidency of Rutherford B. Hayes*. Westport, CT: Greenwood, 1972.

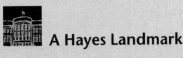 **A Hayes Landmark**

Rutherford B. Hayes Presidential Center. Spiegel Grove, Fremont, OH 43420. (800) 998-7737. Twenty-five-acre estate that includes a museum, the first presidential library, Hayes's house, and the graves of the former president and first lady. See http://www.rbhayes.org/ (accessed on July 24, 2000).

Flick, Alexander C. *Samuel Jones Tilden: A Study in Political Sagacity*. New York: Dodd, Mead & Co., 1939. Reprint, Westport, CT: Greenwood Press, 1973.

Hoogenboom, Ari. *The Presidency of Rutherford B. Hayes*. Lawrence: University Press of Kansas, 1988.

Hoogenboom, Ari. *Rutherford B. Hayes: One of the Good Colonels*. Abilene, TX: McWhiney Foundation Press, 2000.

Hoogenboom, Ari. *Rutherford B. Hayes: Warrior & President*. Lawrence: University Press of Kansas, 1995.

Myers, Elisabeth P. *Rutherford B. Hayes*. Chicago: Reilly & Lee, 1969.

Rutherford B. Hayes Presidential Center. [Online] http://www.rbhayes.org/ (accessed on July 24, 2000).

Woodward, C. Vann. *Reunion and Reaction: The Compromise of 1877 and the End of Reconstruction*. Boston: Little, Brown, 1951. Reprint, New York: Oxford University Press, 1991.

Lucy Hayes

Born August 28, 1831
Chillicothe, Ohio
Died June 25, 1889
Fremont, Ohio

**Popular first lady was nicknamed
"Lemonade Lucy" because she refused to
serve alcohol in the White House**

Lucy Webb Hayes was a spirited woman, but her political activism remained subdued—perhaps a sign of the times. Although her influence on her husband and her personal views on issues remained behind the scenes, she was a visible presence in the cause of education and public service.

As a teenager, Lucy Webb's intellect was so sharp that she was allowed to study in the all-male Wesleyan College in Ohio. Later, the fiercely abolitionist (antislavery) Lucy Webb helped convince lawyer **Rutherford Hayes** (1822–1893; see entry in volume 3) to defend runaway slaves. She married Hayes, bore eight children, and often followed him to the battle sites of the Civil War (1861–65). He commanded troops, and she served as a nurse. Later, as first lady, Lucy Hayes was an active supporter for improved schooling for the less advantaged. She promoted the National Deaf Mute College as well as education for Native Americans, Hispanics, and African Americans. She continued to be involved with these causes throughout her life.

"Woman's mind is as strong as man's—equal in all things and his superior in some."

Lucy Hayes

Lucy Hayes.
*Photograph by C. M. Bell.
Courtesy of the Library of
Congress.*

699

Well schooled

Lucy Webb was born in 1831 in Chillicothe, Ohio, daughter of Dr. James Webb and Maria Cook Webb. Dr. Webb died when Lucy was two years old. He had journeyed to Kentucky to free slaves he had recently inherited. While in Kentucky, he was infected during an epidemic of cholera (an intestinal disease).

When Lucy was entering her teens, her mother relocated the family to Delaware, Ohio, so that Lucy's two older brothers could attend Wesleyan College. During a couple of visits to the school, Lucy greatly impressed instructors at the college with her intellect (ability to think and understand). She was invited to attend classes, thus becoming the first female to study there. Lucy and Rutherford first met at a small and popular swimming hole on the campus. There was a nine-year age difference between fifteen-year-old Lucy and Hayes, a lawyer. Hayes later recalled that he found Lucy "bright-eyed, sunny-hearted, and not quite old enough to fall in love with."

After her brothers graduated, the family relocated to Cincinnati, where the young men could attend medical school. Lucy, meanwhile, completed her education at Wesleyan Female College in Cincinnati, graduating at age eighteen.

At about that time in 1849, Rutherford Hayes had relocated to Cincinnati. After having been an unremarkable lawyer for four years in Fremont, Ohio, he wanted greater opportunities. He found them in Cincinnati, a thriving town of what was then the American West. He also made sure to visit Lucy.

Rutherford Hayes and Lucy Webb began a romance that summer. They attended a wedding together. "Rud," as she called him, found a golden ring in his piece of wedding cake. It was a playful custom of the time that the wedding guest who found a ring in their piece of cake would be the next to be married. Rud gave the ring to Lucy. She returned the favor by putting it on his finger on their wedding day two years later. Hayes wore the ring the rest of his life.

Mother Lucy

The Hayeses were active in the causes of abolition (ending slavery) and temperance (abstinence from—not drinking—alcoholic beverages). With Lucy's encouragement, Hayes soon began defending runaway slaves who fled to the free North and were pursued by their slaveowners.

Over the next twenty years (from 1852 to 1872), Lucy Hayes bore eight children, five of whom survived into adulthood. Lucy's mother helped raise the children, allowing Lucy to take occasional trips with her husband. Hayes was a respected lawyer and an avid Republican. He campaigned for **Abraham Lincoln** (1809–1865; see entry in volume 2) in 1860. He was invited by the new president to ride on part of his journey from Illinois to Washington, D.C., to take office. The Hayeses rode with the Lincolns from Indianapolis to Cincinnati.

When the Civil War broke out in 1861, Hayes became a commander of the Twenty-third Ohio Volunteer Regiment. Lucy often joined her husband after battles while her mother cared for her children. Lucy also accompanied her brother Joe, a doctor, to battle sites. Lucy helped him tend to the wounded and was nicknamed "Mother Lucy" by grateful soldiers. She once undertook a journey of several hundred miles from the Hayes home in Ohio after learning that her husband was recuperating from severe wounds he suffered in a battle in Virginia.

Lucy Hayes and her husband President Rutherford Hayes at the White House.
Reproduced by permission of the Corbis Corporation.

A politician's wife

Rutherford Hayes won election to the House of Representatives in 1864 without even having to campaign—he was still fighting in the war. He served two terms in Congress. Lucy would sit in the gallery wearing a checkered scarf so that Hayes could spot her. Hayes served two terms as governor of Ohio beginning in 1867. As first lady of Ohio, Lucy Hayes visited regularly with orphans and war veterans and was a force for improvement of schools, prisons, and asylums (institutions for the care of the mentally ill). She helped secure state funding for an orphanage for children whose parents were killed in the war.

When Hayes's term as governor ended in 1872, Hayes planned to retire from politics. He and Lucy moved to Fremont to be with his uncle, Sardis Birchard. Birchard died in 1874 and left the Hayeses a substantial fortune and a large estate called Spiegel Grove, of which they grew quite fond. But Hayes was nominated for governor of Ohio in 1875. He won the election and made such an excellent impression that he became the Republican presidential nominee the following year.

The Hayeses occupied the White House for one term, from 1877 to 1881. Lucy Hayes engaged herself in efforts to improve education for disadvantaged students and pushed for completion of the Washington Monument after construction was delayed for lack of funds. White House social occasions were lively and informal. Alcohol was banned from the events for several reasons. For example, President Hayes did not want to offend supporters of temperance, many of whom were Republicans. Lucy Hayes supported the ban on alcohol in respect for her Methodist upbringing. (Methodists believe in individual responsibility and grace freely given by God.) Historically, she is blamed for closing the bar and was given the nickname "Lemonade Lucy."

Lucy Hayes remained behind the scenes politically, even when her husband did not support issues she favored—like women's suffrage. She was known as a good singer. She loved animals. The Hayes White House was home to several dogs, birds, and cats, including a Siamese cat that is believed to have been the first ever brought into the United States. Among many social occasions, the Hayeses celebrated their twenty-fifth wedding anniversary with a White House party in 1877. The annual White House Easter egg hunt was first presided over by Lucy Hayes.

Home in Spiegel Grove

After the Hayes administration ended in 1881, Lucy and Rud returned to Fremont, Ohio. It was the second time they had retired from public life. But this time it was for good.

They remained active in the cause of education. In addition, Lucy continued a role that she began in 1880 as president of the Methodist Woman's Home Missionary Society. The society gave shelter to homeless women. She was active in the cause of education and helping homeless women until her death in 1889. She was buried at Spiegel Grove. Rutherford Hayes died four years later and was entombed next to his wife.

Where to Learn More

Geer, Emily Apt. *First Lady: The Life of Lucy Webb Hayes*. Kent, OH: Kent State University Press, 1984.

Robbins, Neal E. *Rutherford B. Hayes, 19th President of the United States*. Ada, OK: Garrett Educational Corp., 1989.

Scott, George Tressler. *Illinois' Testimonial to Mrs. Rutherford B. Hayes*. Springfield: Illinois State Historical Society, 1953.

Hayes's Speech on the End of Reconstruction

Delivered on September 24, 1877; excerpted from
Speeches of the American Presidents

Before a racially diverse crowd in Atlanta, Georgia, President Hayes announces the end of the federal policy of Reconstruction

Soon after taking office, President **Rutherford B. Hayes** (1822–1893; see entry in volume 3) toured the South. He made many speeches in which he announced his plan to end the federal policy of Reconstruction that followed the end of the Civil War (1861–65). Hayes hoped that Southerners would respond by protecting equal rights guaranteed to all American citizens by the Constitution.

Hayes was a well-reasoned gentleman. He believed that the rightness of his views on equality and fairness could prevail. He wanted to end the post–Civil War era in which the North dominated the South politically, and in which some Southern whites used violence and intimidation to deny constitutional rights of African Americans.

Hayes had won the controversial presidential election of 1876, in which vote tallies in several states were disputed: in some cases, African Americans had been denied their voting rights, and other vote tallies were influenced by the political party in power in a particular area. Hayes hoped to unite the nation by inspiring those divided—Northerners and

"Now, shall we quit fighting?"

Rutherford B. Hayes

Southerners, Republicans and Democrats, blacks and whites—
to respect one another.

Things to remember while reading an excerpt from President Hayes's speech on the end of Reconstruction:

- Hayes wanted to end sectional, political, and racial divisiveness. Appropriately, his speech did not point blame at any one group for problems that had persisted since the end of the Civil War. Instead, he offered his respect to "Republicans, Democrats, colored people, white people, Confederate soldiers, and Union soldiers," and added that he was entitled to their respect as well.

- Hayes acknowledged that peace was not immediate following the Civil War. More than ten years later, however, the time had come, according to Hayes, to quit fighting. He announced his intention to put an end to the section line (regional differences) and the color line (discrimination and intimidation of African Americans).

- Near the end of the excerpt, Hayes addresses the suspicion that the disputed election of 1876 was resolved in his favor with his promise to end Reconstruction. Hayes replied to that accusation in his speech. He insisted that he was compelled to end fighting and differences out of his personal beliefs.

Excerpt from President Hayes's speech on the end of Reconstruction

I suppose that here, as everywhere else, I am in the presence of men of both great political parties. I am speaking, also, in the presence of citizens of both races. I am quite sure that there are before me very many of the brave men who fought in the Confederate army: some, doubtless, of the men who fought in the Union army. And here we are, Republicans, Democrats, colored people, white people, Confederate soldiers, and Union soldiers, all of one mind and one heart today! And why should we not be? What is there to separate us longer? Without any fault of yours or any fault of mine, or of any one of this great audience, slavery existed in this country. It was in the Constitution of the country. The colored man was here, not by his voluntary action. It was the misfortune of his fathers that he was here. I think it is safe to say that it was by the crime of our fathers that he was here. He was here, however, and we of the two sections differed about what should be done with him. As Mr. [Abraham] Lincoln told us in the war, there were prayers on both sides for him. Both sides found in the Bible confirmation of their opinions, and both sides finally undertook to settle the question by that last final means of **arbitration**—force of arms. You here mainly joined the Confederate side, and fought bravely, risked your lives heroically in behalf of your convictions; and can I, can any true man anywhere, fail to respect the man who risks his life for his convictions? And as I accord that respect to you, and believe you to be equally liberal and generous and just, I feel that, as I stand before you as one who fought in the Union army for his convictions, I am entitled to your respect. Now that conflict is over, my friends. . . .

Now, shall we quit fighting? I have been in the habit of telling an anecdote of General [Winfield] Scott and a statesman at Washington, in which the statesman said that as soon as the war was over and the combatants laid down their arms, we should have complete peace. "No," said General Scott, "it will take several years in which all the powers of the general government will be employed in keeping peace between the **belligerent** non-combatants!" Now, I think, we have got through with that and having peace between the soldiers and the noncombatants, that is an end of the war. Is there any reason, then, why we should not be at peace forevermore? We are embarked upon the same voyage, upon the same ship, under the same old flag. Good fortune or ill fortune affects you and your children as well as my people and my children.

Every interest you possess is to be promoted by peace. Here is this great city of Atlanta, gathering to itself from all parts of the country its wealth and business by its railroads; and I say to you that every description of industry and legitimate business needs peace. That is what capital wants. **Discord**, discontent, and dissatisfaction are the enemies of these enterprises. Then, all our interests are for peace. Are we not agreed about that? What do we want for the future? I believe it is the duty of the general government to regard equally and alike the interests and rights of all sections of this country. I am glad that you agree with me about that. I believe, fur-

Arbitration: A means of making a decision after negotiations have failed.

Belligerent: Challenging, threatening.

Discord: Disharmony.

ther, that it is the duty of the government to regard alike and equally the rights and interests of all classes of citizens. That covers the whole matter. That wipes out in the future in our politics the section line forever. Let us wipe out in our politics the color line forever.

And let me say a word upon what has been done. I do not undertake to discuss or defend particular measures. I leave the people with their knowledge of the facts to examine, discuss, and decide for themselves as to them. I speak of general considerations and notions.

What troubles our people at the North, what has troubled them, was that they feared that these colored people, who had been made freemen by the war, would not be safe in their rights and interests in the South unless it was by the interference of the general government. Many good people had that idea. I had given that matter some consideration, and now, my colored friends, who have thought, or who have been told, that I was turning my back upon the men whom I fought for, now, listen! After thinking over it, I believed that your right and interests would be safer if this great mass of intelligent white men were let alone by the general government. And now, my colored friends, let me say another thing. We have been trying it for these six months, and, in my opinion in no six months since the war have there been so few outrages and invasions of your rights, nor you so secure in your rights, persons, and homes, as in the last six months.

Then, my friends, we are all together upon one proposition. We believe, and in this all those who are here agree, in the Union of our fathers, in the old flag of our fathers, the Constitution as it is with all its amendments, and are prepared to see it fully and fairly obeyed and enforced. Now, my friends, I see it stated occasionally that President Hayes has taken the course he has because he was compelled to it. Now, I was compelled to it. I was compelled to it by my sense of duty under my oath of office. What was done by us was done, not merely by force of special circumstances, but because it was just and right to do it.

*Now let us come together. Let each man make up his mind to be a patriot in his own home and place. You may quarrel about the **tariff**, get up a sharp contest about the **currency**, about the removal of state capitals and where they shall go to, but upon the great question of the Union of the states and the rights of all the citizens, we shall agree forevermore. (Podell and Anzovin, pp. 231–32)*

Tariff: A tax placed on imported goods.

Currency: A nation's form of money.

What happened next . . .

The end of Reconstruction was necessary in order for the nation to return to the normal relationship between individual states and the federal government. Unfortunately, the nation was not yet ready. When federal supervision was removed, discrimination and segregation became rampant in most of the South. Republicans—the party of **Abraham Lincoln** (1809–1861; see entry in volume 2)—quickly lost power in the region. Democrats, many representing the concerns of whites only, won elections and formed a solid voting bloc that would persist through the mid-twentieth century.

Halfway through his term, Hayes admitted the failure of his noble pursuits. The president attempted to unite the nation and embrace the laws of the Constitution, but the nation, as a whole, was not prepared to live up to those ideals.

Did you know . . .

- The nation was undergoing great change during the time of Hayes's presidency. The Civil War era was over with the ending of Reconstruction, and industry was expanding, fueled by a steadily improving economy. Hayes began his administration in controversy with the election of 1876 and faced turmoil throughout as he pursued noble causes, including civil service reform and protection for civil rights. The turmoil overshadowed Hayes's effectiveness, and he is not generally considered one of the strongest presidents. But his leadership during a time of confusion should not be underestimated, as the *New York Times* concluded in an obituary on Hayes published on January 18, 1893. "The purity of his private and personal life was never questioned, and during his term of office at Washington there was a distinct elevating of the tone and standard of official life. There is no doubt that his Administrations served a very useful purpose in the transition from sectional antagonism to national harmony, and from the old methods of dealing with the public service as party spoils to the new method of placing ascertained merit and demonstrated fitness above party service or requirements. It was an inevitable consequence that he should lose popularity and political influence in serving these important ends, but the value of his services will nevertheless be permanently recognized."

Where to Learn More

Eckenrode, H. J. *Rutherford B. Hayes: Statesman of Reunion*. Port Washington, NY: Kennikat Press, 1963.

Hayes, Rutherford Birchard. *The Rutherford B. Hayes Papers*. Fremont, OH: Rutherford B. Hayes Presidential Center, 1982.

Podell, Janet, and Steven Anzovin, eds. *Speeches of the American Presidents*. New York: H. W. Wilson Co., 1988.

Simpson, Brooks D. *The Reconstruction Presidents*. Lawrence: University Press of Kansas, 1998.

James A. Garfield

Twentieth president (1881)

James A. Garfield

Born November 19, 1831
Orange, Ohio
Died September 19, 1881
Elberon, New Jersey

Twentieth president of the United States (1881)

Skilled orator and successful politician was never tested as president because he was assassinated only months after his inauguration

"I love agitation and investigation and glory in defending unpopular truth against popular error."

James Garfield

James A. Garfield's presidency lasted only a little more than six months. On July 2, 1881, he was wounded several times by an assassin. Garfield lived for ten more weeks following the shooting, but he never recovered. He died on September 19, 1881.

A supporter of a strong federal government, Garfield wanted to infuse a greater sense of independence and leadership in the presidency. Since the end of the Civil War (1861–65), the presidency had come to be overshadowed by Congress. Garfield was also especially interested in reforming the civil service system, the jobs under the authority of the federal government. At the time, government appointments were dominated by patronage. In a patronage system, elected officials select only their supporters to hold government jobs. Garfield's efforts in this area were carried on by his successor, **Chester A. Arthur** (1829–1886; see entry in volume 3). Arthur signed into law a civil service reform bill (the Pendleton Act) in 1883.

Garfield was an excellent speechmaker who projected a sense of dignity and friendliness. He served in Congress for seventeen years before being elected president. A speech he

James A. Garfield
Courtesy of the Library of Congress.

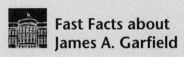

Fast Facts about James A. Garfield

Full name: James Abram Garfield

Born: November 19, 1831

Died: September 19, 1881

Burial site: Lake View Cemetery, Cleveland, Ohio

Parents: Abram and Eliza Ballou Garfield

Spouse: Lucretia Rudolph (1832–1918; m. 1858)

Children: Eliza Arabella (1860–1863); Harry Augustus (1863–1942); James Rudolph (1865–1950); Mary (Mollie; 1867–1947); Irvin McDowell (1870–1951); Abram (1872–1958); Edward Abram (1874–76)

Religion: Disciples of Christ

Education: Williams College (1856)

Occupations: Educator; soldier

Government positions: State senator and U.S. representative from Ohio

Political party: Republican

Dates as president: March 4, 1881–September 19, 1881

Age upon taking office: 49

made in Congress in March 1879 (see **James A. Garfield** primary source entry in volume 3) is considered one of the most eloquent (fluent and persuasive) defenses of the right of the federal government to influence laws above the concerns of individual states. That speech was reprinted and served as campaign information during his successful run for the presidency in 1880.

Garfield was a leader several times over. He was a college president; he commanded Civil War fighting units; he chaired Congressional committees; and he was elected president. Along the way, he managed to overcome a serious illness, dangers of the battlefield, and political scandals (disgraceful political decisions or schemes).

From a log cabin to the White House

James Abram Garfield was born in a log cabin near the town of Orange, near Cleveland, Ohio, on November 19, 1831. He was the youngest of five children born to Abram and Eliza Garfield. Abram died when Garfield was two years old. Eliza worked to support her family. As the children grew up, they divided time between working and attending school. The family joined the Disciples of Christ religious group. The Disciples of Christ were an American Protestant denomination that emerged in the early nineteenth century in Pennsylvania and Kentucky. The group then spread through what is now the midwestern United States. Disciples of Christ rely on the Bible, particularly the New Testament, for guidance in all matters. The vote of the congregation (members of a particular church community who meet to worship together) is often used to resolve issues.

James A. Garfield Timeline

1831: Born in Ohio

1857–61: Serves as president of Hiram College

1859: Serves in Ohio state senate

1861–63: Serves as colonel in Civil War

1863–80: Serves in the U.S. House of Representatives

1877: Member of the fifteen-man electoral commission appointed by Congress to investigate the presidential election of 1876 and to declare a winner

1881: Inaugurated as president, March 4; shot several times by an assassin, July 2; dies in New Jersey on September 19

Garfield enjoyed hunting and reading; he especially liked sea stories. Wanting to become a sailor, he traveled to Cleveland in his teens to sign on for duty on a cargo ship headed for the ocean. He decided against it, however, after being interviewed by a drunken sea captain. Instead, Garfield began working on canal boats and drove a tugboat. But he returned home after catching what was likely malaria, an infectious disease transmitted through the bite of an infected mosquito.

While recovering, Garfield was convinced by his mother to continue his education. He liked to read and attended school at the nearby Western Reserve Eclectic Institute, a school founded by the Disciples of Christ. He moved on to Williams College in Massachusetts, where he excelled in Latin and literature and was known as a strong and excellent athlete. Garfield edited the school magazine and proved to be a fine public speaker, which led him to take part in political debates. On debating, he once said, "I love agitation and investigation and glory in defending unpopular truth against popular error."

Garfield used his public-speaking skills to serve as a traveling preacher for the Disciples of Christ. He returned to the Western Reserve Eclectic Institute as a teacher, another role he enjoyed. The Institute had been renamed Hiram College.

Garfield was a popular instructor and the leader of a literary society. He was so well liked at the school that he won

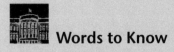

Words to Know

Appropriations: Funds authorized for a particular project.

Civil service: Positions under the authority of the federal government.

Election board: A group authorized to operate elections and count votes.

Pacifist: A person opposed to conflict.

Reconstruction: A federal policy from 1865 to 1877. During this time, the national government took an active part in assisting and policing the former Confederate states following the Civil War (1861–65).

Tariff: A tax placed on imported goods to raise their price and make them less attractive than the goods produced by the nation importing them.

election from his congregation to become the president of Hiram College in 1857 when he was twenty-six years old.

Garfield immediately began introducing improvements to the school. Teachers were required to attend instruction workshops and to hold informal discussion groups with students in addition to class instruction. Classes Garfield taught at the college always overflowed with students.

Garfield became involved in local politics, strongly supporting the abolishment (end) of slavery. He established a local reputation for his speeches and leadership. Garfield was elected to the Ohio state senate in 1859, where he became a vocal supporter of national efforts to end slavery. Garfield, formerly a pacifist (a promoter of peace; someone opposed to conflict), became a supporter in 1861 of the pledge of newly elected president **Abraham Lincoln** (1809–1865; see entry in volume 2) to use federal force to preserve the Union. Garfield had campaigned hard for Lincoln, making over fifty speeches at gatherings in rural areas.

Meanwhile, Garfield married Lucretia Rudolph (1832–1918; see entry on **Lucretia Garfield** in volume 3) on November 11, 1858. "Crete," as he called her, was the daughter of a trustee (a person appointed to act as a director) of Hiram College. She and Garfield had known each other since childhood. They would have seven children, five of whom survived into adulthood.

Garfield began studying law and was certified as an attorney in 1861. From law, he turned his attention to reading books on military strategy and organization as the nation approached the beginning of war.

Book-trained soldier

When the Civil War broke out in 1861, Garfield volunteered for service and was appointed to a position as colonel of the Forty-second Ohio Volunteer Infantry. Many of the volunteers in the unit were former students of Garfield willing to follow him into battle.

Garfield led his unit through a series of skirmishes (small conflicts) in Kentucky, forcing retreats of Confederate soldiers. He took part in several major battles (Middle Creek in January 1862, Shiloh in April 1862). His heroic acts in the Battle of Chickamauga (September 1863) were widely reported back home.

While Garfield was still serving in the Union army, he was elected to the House of Representatives in 1863. His local reputation as a speaker and as a college president, as well as his battlefield exploits, prompted voters in his highly Republican district to elect him even though Garfield did not campaign for the job. Reportedly, President Lincoln encouraged Garfield to accept the position: Lincoln needed more support in Congress at the time than he did on the battlefield.

Skirting disaster and emerging as a leader

Garfield began a distinguished seventeen-year career in Congress. He served as chairman of the Military Affairs committee and established the Reserve Officer Training Corps (ROTC) program on college campuses. He chaired the Banking and Currency committee, giving his support to "hard money"—currency values based on the gold standard. (Using the gold standard, each dollar is backed by a dollar's worth of gold in government reserves.) He chaired the Appropriations committee, which authorized funds for projects. While on the committee, he lobbied (tried to influence legislators) against spending money on projects that would put the country in debt. He was the House minority leader in 1874 when Democrats gained a majority of seats. Along with

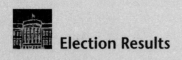

Election Results

1880

Presidential / Vice presidential candidates	Popular votes	Presidential electoral votes
James A. Garfield / Chester A. Arthur (Republican)	4,454,416	214
Winfield Scott Hancock / William H. English (Democratic)	4,444,952	155

After having retired from politics for four years, former president Ulysses S. Grant ran for an unprecedented third term. On the first thirty-five ballots, he failed to receive enough votes to defeat Maine senator James G. Blaine and Secretary of the Treasury John Sherman for the Republican nomination; he lost when the supporters of Blaine and Sherman switched their allegiance to dark horse Garfield.

a firm stand on backing currency with gold, Garfield supported harsher elements of Reconstruction, the federal policy toward the former Confederate states. In particular, he favored the seizure of property owned by those who had served the Confederacy. He advocated expanding and protecting the voting rights of blacks.

Earlier in life, Garfield had managed to avoid disasters: He survived having malaria in his youth during a time when the disease often proved fatal, and despite not having had much military training, he fought in bloody Civil War battles without ever being severely wounded. Likewise, as a politician, Garfield was touched by scandal but not ruined. He was connected with the Crédit Mobilier scandal of the **Ulysses S. Grant** (1822–1885; see entry in volume 3) administration for having accepted stock in what proved to be an illegal business venture. He also represented and accepted legal fees from a company bidding on a government contract for street repairs and improvements in Washington, D.C. In both cases, Garfield's participation is generally viewed as having been minor in nature and dismissed as a lapse in judgment.

Rise in prominence

Garfield distinguished himself on two occasions late in his Congressional career. In 1877, he served on the electoral commission that was formed to decide the disputed presidential election of 1876. In the South, voters had been intimidated (influenced, harassed, or bribed) to favor Democratic candidates, but election boards (groups authorized to operate elections and count votes) were dominated by Republicans. When the boards determined the number of questionable votes and subtracted them from the final count, majorities in three of the disputed states switched from Democratic to Republican candidates. One hundred eighty-five electoral votes were needed for election: Democrat Samuel J. Tilden (1814–1886; see box in **Rutherford B. Hayes** entry in volume 3) had 184 electoral votes to the 165 electoral votes of Republican **Rutherford B. Hayes** (1822–1893; see entry in volume 3). Twenty other electoral votes were contested—eight from Louisiana, seven from South Carolina, four from Florida, and one from Oregon.

As a member of the electoral commission, Garfield plunged into investigative work. He interviewed many people from the areas involved, examined tally sheets that recorded totals from different areas, and visited polling places. The commission eventually agreed with the electoral boards of the disputed states and awarded the remaining twenty electoral votes to Hayes, who was named the winner. The verdict, made three days before the inauguration was set to take place, allowed the nation to proceed, but party bickering (arguing) only increased. A majority of the commission was Republican, and Democrats felt that the majority had simply exercised their power over the will of the people.

The Hayes administration was made weak by conflict in Congress. Democrats were hostile and unreceptive, and Republicans gradually abandoned Hayes for taking a middle

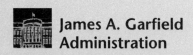 **James A. Garfield Administration**

Administration Dates
March 4, 1881–September 19, 1881

Vice President
Chester A. Arthur (1881)

Cabinet

Secretary of State
James G. Blaine (1881)

Secretary of the Treasury
William Windom (1881)

Secretary of War
Robert Todd Lincoln (1881)

Attorney General
Wayne MacVeagh (1881)

Secretary of the Navy
William H. Hunt (1881)

Postmaster General
Thomas L. James (1881)

Secretary of the Interior
Samuel J. Kirkwood (1881)

ground instead of automatically supporting Republican causes. Garfield was one of the few Republicans who remained supportive of Hayes. When Democrats became the majority party in Congress following the elections of 1878, they sought ways to weaken the influence of the federal government in favor of states' rights. As the House minority leader, Garfield rose in 1879 to make an eloquent defense of the powers of the federal government.

Dark horse

Republicans met for their convention in 1880 to nominate a candidate for president. The party was united on political issues but divided on the issue of patronage. One faction was headed by Roscoe Conkling (1829–1888; see box in **Chester A. Arthur** entry in volume 3), a senator from New York who wanted to ensure that all political appointees—men appointed to political positions—in New York were controlled by their group, nicknamed the Stalwarts (a word meaning "loyal supporters"). Stalwarts supported the nomination of former president **Ulysses S. Grant** (1822–1885; see entry in volume 3). An opposing faction, nicknamed the "Half-Breeds," supported Maine legislator James G. Blaine (1830–1893; see box in **Chester A. Arthur** entry in volume 3). This group insisted that all appointments should be made by the next administration.

Garfield was the campaign manager for a third candidate, John Sherman (1823–1900), secretary of the treasury under Hayes. Hayes, Sherman, and Garfield were all from Ohio. Sherman inspired enough support at the convention to block Grant and Blaine from getting the necessary number of votes for the nomination. Garfield helped as chairman of the convention's rules committee. He introduced a rule that allowed all delegates to vote individually rather than in large state blocks. This rule stopped larger states like New York from dominating the voting for one candidate.

When Garfield nominated Sherman, he gave a rousing speech that received a long round of applause. However, he did not mention Sherman's name until fifteen minutes into the speech. Most of the applause was for Garfield.

The convention voted thirty-five times without any of the three candidates drawing enough support. Finally, Sherman and Blaine dropped their bids for the nomination in favor of Garfield, who won the nomination on the next ballot. To appease New Yorkers and other Stalwarts, Chester A. Arthur, a powerful political leader from New York, was selected as Garfield's running mate.

The general election was a close contest decided by states of the Northeast, where Garfield was favored because the Republican Party supported a high protective tariff (tax on imported goods) favorable to the region. Garfield received just ten thousand more popular votes than the Democratic

Charles J. Guiteau (above) shot President James A. Garfield after being passed over for a government position.
Reproduced by permission of the Corbis Corporation.

nominee, Winfield Scott Hancock (1824–1886). But he triumphed in the Electoral College by winning eastern states and by benefiting when many voters in the West favored small party candidates of regional interest. (For more information on the Electoral College, see boxes in **George W. Bush** entry in volume 5.)

Brief presidency

During his short time as president, Garfield faced two unpleasant issues. The first item was the Star Route case. Western postal officials had secretly planned with stagecoach operators to steal funds, like tax collections, that were to be delivered to Washington, D.C. Garfield quickly assembled a team of government prosecutors to try the case.

The second issue involved patronage. The patronage problem surfaced again as Garfield took office. Garfield selected James G. Blaine to be his secretary of state. He generally passed over men connected with the Stalwart faction of the party. In Congress, where the appointments must be approved, Roscoe Conkling tried to block Garfield's selections. When he failed, Conkling resigned his position in protest.

Garfield pursued legislation to reform the patronage system, but he was not able to follow through. While waiting in a Washington, D.C., train station to begin a trip through New England on the morning of July 2, 1881, Garfield was shot several times by a crazed assassin, Charles J. Guiteau (c. 1840–1882). Guiteau, a religious fanatic, Stalwart supporter, and former civil servant, was angry at having been passed over for a government position. He wanted to kill Garfield "to unite the Republican Party and save the Republic."

The wounded president was taken back to the White House, where surgeons removed bullets from his body. A metal detector—a recent invention by Alexander Graham Bell (1847–1922; see box)—was used to locate the bullets in Garfield's body. However, one bullet remained undetected because of interference: Garfield lay on a bed with metal springs, and the springs disrupted the readings of the metal detector.

An infection caused by the remaining bullet continued to spread. Garfield was never strong enough to leave his

bed. He was moved to Elberton, New Jersey, away from the heat of Washington, D.C., and activities of the White House, to be with his family. Ten weeks after being wounded, Garfield died on September 19, 1881.

In a eulogy (a speech given to praise a recently deceased person) for Garfield, Secretary of State Blaine recalled Garfield's own great speechmaking skills: "He was a preeminently fair and candid man in debate, took no petty advantage, stooped to no unworthy methods, avoided personal allusions, rarely appealed to prejudice, did not seek to inflame passion."

Legacy

With James A. Garfield's death, political support for civil service reform gradually became more serious. After legislation was held up in Congress, Garfield's successor, Chester A. Arthur, helped push a bill through Congress. The Pendleton Act was signed into law by President Arthur in 1883. The

President Garfield was shot on July 2, 1881, in the waiting room of the Baltimore and Ohio Railroad Depot.
Sketches in Frank Leslie's Illustrated Newspaper *by A. Berghaus and C. Upham. Courtesy of the Library of Congress.*

Alexander Graham Bell

Remembered as the inventor of the telephone, Alexander Graham Bell was also an outstanding teacher of the deaf, a prolific inventor of other devices, and a leading figure in the scientific community. He invented the graphophone, the first sound recorder, as well as the photophone, which transmitted speech by light rays. Among his other innovations were the audiometer, a device for the deaf; the induction balance, used to locate metallic objects in the human body; and disc and cylindrical wax recorders for phonographs. The prestigious journal *Science,* which became the official publication of the American Association for the Advancement of Science, was founded primarily through his efforts. Bell was also involved in establishing the National Geographic Society.

Bell was born in Edinburgh, Scotland, to a family of speech educators. His father, Alexander Melville Bell, had invented visible speech, a code of symbols for all spoken sounds that was used in teaching deaf people to speak. Young Bell began studying at Edinburgh University in 1864 and assisted his father at University College in London from 1868 to 1870. During these years, he became deeply interested in the study of sound and the mechanics of speech, which gave him the idea of telegraphing speech. After Bell's two broth-

ers died of tuberculosis, his father took the family to the healthier climate of Canada in 1870. The following year, Bell journeyed to Boston, Massachusetts, to join the staff of the Boston School for the Deaf. In 1872 he opened his own school in Boston for training teachers of the deaf.

Bell's interest in speech and communication led him to research the transmission of sound over wires. In particular, he experimented with the development of the harmonic telegraph, a device that could send multiple messages simultaneously over a single wire. Bell also worked on the transmission of the human voice, experimenting with vibrating membranes and an actual human ear. He was backed financially in his investigations by Gardiner Hubbard (1822–1897) and Thomas Sanders, fathers of two of his deaf pupils. Early in 1874, Bell met Thomas A. Watson (1854–1934), a young machinist at a Boston electrical shop. Watson became Bell's indispensable assistant, bringing to his experiments technical expertise in electrical engineering.

Together, Bell and Watson spent endless hours experimenting. On June 2, 1875, the critical breakthrough on the telephone accidentally came about while they were working on the telegraph. When a stuck reed on Watson's transmitter changed

Alexander Graham Bell.
Public Domain.

an intermittent current into a continuous current, Bell, who had extraordinarily sharp hearing, picked up the sound on his receiver in another room. This event confirmed what Bell had previously suspected: only continuous, varying electrical current can transmit and reconvert continuously varying sound waves. On March 10, 1876, Bell tested a new transmitter. Watson, who was in an adjoining room with a receiver, clearly heard Bell's summons: "Mr. Watson, come here, I want you!" It was the first message transmitted by telephone. The new invention was exhibited at the Philadelphia Centennial Exposition the following June. To-

gether with financial backers Hubbard and Sanders, Bell and Watson formed the Bell Telephone Company in 1877.

After marrying Mabel Hubbard, the daughter of his new partner, Bell sailed to England to promote the telephone. Bell Telephone grew rapidly, making Bell a wealthy man. Upon returning to the United States in 1879, he pursued other interests but also spent much of the next several years defending hundreds of lawsuits over his patents. (All of his patents were finally upheld by the U.S. Supreme Court in 1888.) Pursuing a wide range of interests, Bell worked on air conditioning, an improved strain of sheep (to bear multiple lambs), an early iron lung (an artificial respiration device), and sonar detection of icebergs. In 1881, one of Bell's inventions, a metal detector, was used to locate bullets in President James Garfield's body.

After 1895, Bell turned his attention to aviation. He invented the tetrahedral kite, which is capable of carrying a human being. He helped found the Aerial Experiment Association in 1907. He also designed a hydrofoil boat that set the world water speed record in 1918. Bell, who became a U.S. citizen in 1882, died at his summer home on Cape Breton Island, Nova Scotia, in 1922.

A Selection of Garfield Landmarks

James A. Garfield Birthplace. 4350 S. O. M. Center Rd., Moreland Hills, OH 44022. (440) 248-1188. Although the log cabin in which Garfield was born has long been destroyed, the Moreland Hills Historical Society maintains a charming and scenic trail leading to the original site. Also present are a statue of and information about Garfield.

James A. Garfield Monument. Lake View Cemetery, 12316 Euclid Ave., Cleveland, OH 44106. (216) 421-2687. The assassinated president and his wife are entombed in this stately memorial. See http://www.lakeviewcemetery.com/ (accessed on July 26, 2000).

James A. Garfield National Historic Site. 8095 Mentor Ave., Mentor, OH 44060. (440) 255-8722. Museum and Lawnfield, Garfield's recently renovated thirty-room house, are located on this site. See http://www.nps.gov/jaga/ (accessed on July 26, 2000).

act established the Civil Service Commission, an agency that reviews political appointments to ensure that they are based on merit rather than handed out as political favors. A system based on merit looks at the candidate's qualifications for the job: education, experience, and personal integrity.

An era of political reform began. The Republican Party was gradually transformed from a collection of political factions to a more united party by the 1890s. Although Garfield's term was too brief to evaluate, he was a forerunner of the more powerful presidents who were elected in the 1890s and on through World War I (1914–18).

Where to Learn More

Brisbin, James S. *From the Tow-Path to the White House: The Early Life and Public Career of James A. Garfield.* Philadelphia: Hubbard Bros., 1880.

Doenecke, Justus D. *The Presidencies of James A. Garfield and Chester A. Arthur.* Lawrence: University Press of Kansas, 1981.

Grosvenor, Edwin S. *Alexander Graham Bell: The Life and Times of the Man Who Invented the Telephone.* New York: Harry Abrams, 1997.

Lillegard, Dee. *James A. Garfield: Twentieth President of the United States.* Chicago: Children's Press, 1987.

McElroy, Richard L. *James A. Garfield: His Life & Times: A Pictorial History.* Canton, OH: Daring Books, 1986.

Peskin, Allan. *Garfield: A Biography.* Kent, Ohio: Kent State University Press, 1999.

Severn, Bill. *Teacher, Soldier, President: The Life of James A. Garfield.* New York: I. Washburn, 1964.

Smith, Theodore Clarke. *The Life and Letters of James Abram Garfield.* New Haven: Yale University Press, 1925. Reprint, Hamden, CT: Archon Books, 1968.

Lucretia Garfield

Born April 19, 1832
Hiram, Ohio
Died March 13, 1918
South Pasadena, California

Endured the deaths of two children, marriage troubles, political pressure, and her husband's assassination

It was fitting that Lucretia Rudolph and **James A. Garfield** (1831–1881; see entry in volume 3) first met as youngsters in school. They both loved reading and later became teachers. Exchanging letters helped them through many separations: Garfield spent periods away from home as a Civil War commander and as a politician. "Crete," as Garfield called Lucretia, remained behind at home in Ohio raising their children. The family later maintained two homes: one in Washington, D.C., where Garfield served in Congress for seventeen years before becoming president, and the other in Ohio.

When she was a young schoolteacher, Lucretia challenged the system where she was automatically paid less for similar work than her male counterparts. The public never saw that independent-thinking side of her. Wives of politicians during the nineteenth century were expected to keep their opinions to themselves. Garfield agreed with that belief, but Lucretia preferred to stay out of the public eye anyway. The letters she exchanged with her husband reveal a progressive-minded woman who likely kept her own views to herself for the sake of social propriety (the standards a society sets for behavior).

"[Lucretia] grows up to every new emergency with fine tact and faultless taste."

James Garfield

Lucretia Garfield.
Courtesy of the Library of Congress.

Lucretia was most widely known to the public for the grace she displayed during the difficult period following the assassination of her husband. She herself had been ill at the time, but she nursed him while he tried to recover from bullet wounds.

Raised on religion and learning

Lucretia Rudolph was born on April 19, 1832, in Hiram, Ohio. Her father, Zebulon, was a leading citizen of the town and in the Disciples of Christ religious group. Lucretia attended local schools and also enjoyed a fine education at home. In her teens, she attended Western Reserve Eclectic Institute, a school of higher learning founded by the Disciples of Christ. The group was an American Protestant denomination that emerged in the early nineteenth century on the frontiers of Pennsylvania and Kentucky. Most issues in each local church are decided on by a vote of the congregation.

Lucretia first met James Garfield at school when they were children. Garfield lived in a nearby town, but he left early in his teens for Cleveland. Inspired by sea stories, he tried to become a crew member on a ship heading out for an ocean voyage. After a disappointing interview with a drunken sea captain, Garfield decided instead to work on canal boats. However, he contracted a slight case of malaria, an infectious disease transmitted by mosquitoes, and returned home to recover. His mother convinced him that he ought to finish school, and Garfield enrolled at the Western Reserve Eclectic Institute. There he renewed his friendship with Lucretia.

Both Garfield and Lucretia were excellent public speakers. Lucretia became a schoolteacher, and Garfield went off to college in Massachusetts. They corresponded frequently. He had fallen in love with another woman in Massachusetts, but he returned to Ohio to teach at the Institute, which had been renamed Hiram College. Garfield then resumed his romance with Lucretia. They married in 1858.

Meanwhile, Garfield's career blossomed. He was so popular as a professor at Hiram College that he was elected president of the institution. (The school was founded by the Disciples of Christ.) When the Civil War (1861–65) began in 1861, Garfield was made a colonel. He headed a group of volunteers, many of whom had been former students of his willing to follow their leader into battle.

By 1863, Garfield was a war hero, and his exploits were widely known in his native area. He was already a popular speaker, having campaigned vigorously for **Abraham Lincoln** (1809–1865; see entry in volume 2), who won the presidential election of 1860. Garfield was elected to the House of Representatives in 1863. Lucretia remained in Ohio after Garfield returned from battle and headed out to Washington, D.C. The couple's relationship was strained when Garfield had an extramarital affair with a widow from New York. Then, after the Garfields drew close together again, they suffered the death of their three-year-old daughter.

When they relocated to Washington, D.C., the Garfields met regularly with a literary society, a group that met to discuss books they had read, often hosting the gathering in their home. Lucretia Garfield was fond of small dinners and conversation, a preference she maintained when her husband was elected president in 1880. Rather than having large-scale parties or formal dinners, the Garfields made a habit of having twice-weekly receptions at which they could dine and talk with friends and politicians in a more personal setting. The schedule of small receptions ended soon, however.

New emergencies

Garfield had once noted that Lucretia "grows up to every new emergency with fine tact and faultless taste." He was commenting on how she endured the deaths of two children, their marital problems, and everyday political pressures as Garfield battled with political opponents. A new series of emergencies began shortly after Garfield took the office of president.

In May 1881, just weeks after Garfield's inauguration, Lucretia fell ill with symptoms of malaria and exhaustion. She was taken to regain her health and strength in Long Branch, a seaside town in New Jersey.

On the morning of July 2, 1881, Garfield waited for a train that would take him to New England and a stop to visit the first lady. He never boarded the train. In the station, he was shot several times. The fallen president was rushed back to the White House for emergency care. Lucretia Garfield, still frail and exhausted, returned to Washington by special train. She was at her husband's side during the three months while he fought for his life. An outpouring of sympathy and respect from the nation helped her during that period.

Garfield was moved to Elberton, New Jersey, so the whole family could be with him in a more private setting than the White House. But the president never recovered. He died from his wounds on September 19, 1881, ten weeks after the shooting.

The images of Lucretia Garfield and her children at the funeral services appeared very moving to the nation. She was described as having coped during the difficult time with dignity and strength, despite her own weakened health. One daughter, Caroline, shed a long, slow tear during the service—an image described in newspaper reports throughout the country.

Following the funeral, the Garfield family returned to their farm in Ohio. Lucretia Garfield lived another thirty-six years, mostly in private. She supervised the preservation of her husband's papers and correspondences—among the largest of any president. Her correspondences and diaries are also among the collection. They reveal a woman who had a strong sense of independence that she kept to herself for the sake of social propriety and her husband's career.

She lived to see her children grow up and become successful. Harry, the eldest, was a lawyer and a professor and later became president of Williams College, a school his father had attended. James was a lawyer and politician who served as secretary of the interior under president **Theodore Roosevelt** (1858–1919; see entry in volume 3). Irwin was a lawyer; Abram was an architect; and the youngest, Mollie, married Joseph S. Brown (1858–1941), who had been her father's private secretary while he was president.

Lucretia Garfield died on March 13, 1918. She was buried in the tomb of the Garfield Monument in Cleveland, Ohio, next to her husband.

Where to Learn More

Peskin, Allan. *Garfield: A Biography.* Kent, OH: Kent State University Press, 1999.

Shaw, John, ed. *Crete and James: Personal Letters of Lucretia and James Garfield.* East Lansing: Michigan State University Press, 1994.

Garfield's "Revolution Against the Constitution" Speech

Delivered on March 29, 1879; excerpted from
Speeches of the American Presidents

Representative Garfield chastises his fellow congressmen for attempting to control the federal government

Following the end of Reconstruction in 1877, Democrats made large gains in congressional elections in the South. Northern Republicans had been responsible for Reconstruction programs that undermined the powers of individual Southern states—partly to protect the rights of recently freed slaves, and partly to maintain influence over the national government: no Democrat was elected president from 1860 through 1884.

A Democratic majority gained control of the House of Representatives in 1878. They wanted to remove the last example of Reconstruction and return full constitutional power to Southern states. Nevertheless, the federal government continued to supervise elections in the South because of widespread evidence that African American voters were being intimidated from voting—through laws enacted to discriminate against them, and often through violence.

James A. Garfield (1831–1881; see entry in volume 3), a Republican congressman from Ohio, had served on the special committee that investigated voter fraud during the 1876 presidential election, in which **Rutherford B. Hayes**

"No view I have ever taken has entered more deeply and more seriously into my conviction than this, that the House has today resolved to enter upon a revolution against the Constitution and government of the United States."

James A. Garfield

(1822–1893; see entry in volume 3) was the victor. Garfield had interviewed many people as part of his investigation. He found evidence supporting many instances of fraud. That led him to continue supporting federal supervision of elections in the South.

A Democratic majority in the House of Representatives in 1879 consistently included riders (additions of unrelated items to major legislation) on basic appropriations bills—legislation that provided funding for government programs. Riders were their attempts to pass legislation they knew the president would otherwise veto. One such rider prohibited the use of federal troops to supervise elections. Since that rider was attached to an important funding bill, Congress either had to pass the entire piece of legislation or deny important funding to government programs.

Garfield viewed the situation as unconstitutional. Usually a dignified speaker, he made an impassioned speech before Congress, declaring that Democrats supporting the rider were attempting to revolt against the federal government. He accused congressmen of "resolv[ing] to enter upon a revolution against the Constitution and government of the United States."

Things to remember while reading an excerpt from James A. Garfield's "Revolution Against the Constitution" speech:

- Early in the address, Garfield took pains to fully review and explain the problem of riders that threatened to delay military funding. Some congressmen were willing to compromise and allow the riders, even if they disagreed with them. Garfield was not willing to compromise.

- In the middle portion of the excerpt, Garfield explained his reason for speaking out against the riders. He asserted that the riders' supporters were attempting to hold the federal government hostage: the supporters would not allow the federal government to function unless their demands were met. Garfield declared that position unconstitutional. He further claimed that Congress was attempting to revolt, and compared the present situation to the beginning of the Civil War (1861–65). After **Abraham Lincoln** (1809–1865; see entry in volume 2) was elected president in 1860, several Southern states quit the Union because Lincoln planned to use federal powers to curtail slavery. Similarly, congressmen supporting the riders were willing to compromise the constitutional process of Congress to ensure that their views—represented by the riders—were enacted.

- Garfield completed his speech by again asserting that supporters of the riders were engaging in an unconstitutional act. By defining those actions as unconstitutional, Garfield presented his case as a defense of the federal government.

Excerpt from James A. Garfield's "Revolution Against the Constitution" speech

*Mr. Chairman, I have no hope of being able to convey to the members of this House my own conviction of the very great gravity and solemnity of the crisis which this **decision of the chair** and of the Committee of the Whole has brought upon this country. I wish I could be proved a false prophet in reference to the result of this action. I wish I could be overwhelmed with the proof that I am utterly mistaken in my views. But no view I have ever taken has entered more deeply and more seriously into my conviction than this, that the House has today resolved to enter upon a revolution against the Constitution and government of the United States. I do not know that this intention exists in the minds of half the representatives who occupy the **other side of this hall**; I hope it does not; I am ready to believe it does not exist to any great extent; but I affirm that the consequence of the programme just adopted, if persisted in, will be nothing less than the total subversion of this government. Let me in the outset state, as carefully as I may, the precise situation.*

*At the last session, all our ordinary legislative work was done in accordance with the usages of the House of Senate, except the passage of two bills. Two of the twelve great **appropriation** bills for the support of the government were agreed to in both houses as to every*

Decision of the chair: "The chair" is short for chairman, in this case the House Majority Leader who directs debate on issues. Garfield had been overruled by the chair during an earlier debate.

Other side of this hall: In Congress, it is common for representatives of the two parties to sit on opposite ends of the floor; thus, Republican Garfield is referring here to Democrats.

Appropriations: Funding for a particular program.

matter of detail concerning the appropriations proper. We were assured by the committees of conference in both bodies that there would be no difficulty in adjusting all differences in reference to the amounts of money to be appropriated and the objects of their appropriation. But the House of Representatives proposed three measures of distinctly independent legislation; one upon the army appropriation bill, and two upon the legislative appropriation bill. The three grouped together are briefly these: first, the substantial modification of certain sections of the law relating to the use of the army; second, the repeal of the jurors' test oath; and third, the repeal of the laws regulating elections of members of Congress. These three propositions of legislation were insisted upon by the House, but the Senate refused to adopt them. So far it was an ordinary proceeding, one which occurs frequently in all legislative bodies. The Senate said to us through their conferees, "We are ready to pass the appropriation bills; but we are unwilling to pass as riders the three legislative measures you ask us to pass." Thereupon the House, through its conference committee, made the following declaration,—and in order that I may do exact justice, I read from the speech . . . on the report of the second conference committee on the Legislative, Executive, and Judicial Appropriation Bill:—

"The Democratic conferees on the part of the House seemed determined that unless those rights were secured to the people"—alluding to the three points I have named—"in the bills sent to the Senate, they would refuse, under their constitutional right, to make appropriations to carry on the government, if the dominant majority in the Senate insisted upon the maintenance of these laws and refused to consent to their repeal."

Then, after stating that, if the position they had taken compelled an extra session, the new Congress would offer the repealing bills separately, and forecasting what would happen when the new House should be under no necessity of coercing the Senate, he said:—

"If, however, the president of the United States, in the exercise of the power vested in him, should see fit to veto the bills thus presented to him, . . . then I have no doubt those same amendments will be again made part of the appropriation bills, and it will be for the president to determine whether he will block the wheels of government and refuse to accept necessary appropriations rather than allow the representatives of the people to repeal **odious** laws which they regard as **subversive** of their rights and privileges. . . . Whether that course is right or wrong, it will be adopted, and I have no doubt adhered to, no matter what happens with the appropriation bills."

Odious: Severely unlikeable.

Subversive: Destructive.

*That was the proposition made by the Democracy in Congress at the close of the **Congress now dead.***

Another distinguished senator, Mr. [Allen G.] Thurman, of Ohio—and I may properly refer to senators of a Congress not now in existence—reviewing the situation, declared in still more succinct terms: "We claim the right, which the House of Commons in England established after two centuries of contest, to say that we will not grant the money of the people unless there is a redress of grievances. . . ."

*The question, Mr. Chairman, may be asked, Why make any special resistance to certain repealing clauses in this bill, which a good many gentlemen on this side declared at the last session that they cared but little about, and regarded as of very little practical importance, because for years there had been no actual use for any part of the laws proposed to be repealed, and they had no expectation there would be any? It may be asked, Why make any controversy on either side? So far as we are concerned, Mr. Chairman, I desire to say this. We recognize the other side as accomplished **parliamentarians** and strategists, who have adopted with skill and **adroitness** their plan of assault. You have placed in the front one of the least objectionable of your measures; but your whole programme has been announced, and we reply to your whole order of battle. The logic of your position compels us to meet you as promptly on the skirmish line as afterward when our intrenchments are assailed; and therefore, at the outset, we plant our case upon the general ground where we have chosen to defend it. . . .*

*Up to this hour our **sovereign** has never failed us. There had never been such a refusal to exercise those primary functions of sovereignty as either to endanger or cripple the government; nor have the majority of the representatives of that sovereign, in either house of Congress, ever before announced their purpose to use their voluntary powers for its destruction. And now, for the first time in our history—and I will add, for the first time for at least two centuries in the history of any English-speaking nation—it is suggested and threatened that these voluntary powers of Congress shall be used for the destruction of the government. I want it distinctly understood that the proposition which I read at the beginning of my remarks, and which is the programme announced to the American people today, is this: that if this House cannot have its own way in certain matters not connected with appropriations, it will so use or refrain from using its voluntary powers as to destroy the government.*

Congress now dead: Previous (forty-fourth) Congress, that ended March 3, 1877.

Parliamentarians: Individuals experienced in serving in a legislative body.

Adroitness: Cleverness.

Sovereign: A supreme authority; Garfield's reference is to the Constitution.

Now, Mr. Chairman, it has been said on the other side, that, when a demand for the **redress** of grievances is made, the authority that runs the risk of stopping and destroying the government is the one that resists the redress. Not so. If gentlemen will do me the honor to follow my thought for a moment more, I trust I shall make this denial good.

Our theory of law is free **consent.** That is the granite foundation of our whole superstructure. Nothing in this republic can be law without consent—the free consent of the House, the free consent of the Senate, the free consent of the executive, or, if he refuse it, the free consent of **two thirds of these bodies.** Will any man deny that? Will any man challenge a letter of the statement that free consent is the foundation of all our institutions? And yet the programme announced two weeks ago was, that, if the Senate refused to consent to the demand of the House, the government should stop. And the proposition was then, and the proposition is now, that, although there is not a Senate to be coerced, there is still a third independent branch of the legislative power of the government whose consent is to be coerced at the peril of the destruction of this government; that is, if the president, in the discharge of his duty, shall exercise his plain constitutional right to refuse his consent to this proposed legislation, the Congress will so use its voluntary powers as to destroy the government. This is the proposition which we confront; and we denounced it as revolution.

It makes no difference, Mr. Chairman, what the issue is. If it were the simplest and most inoffensive proposition in the world, yet if you demand, as a measure of coercion, that it shall be adopted against the free consent prescribed in the Constitution, every fair-minded man in America is bound to resist you as much as though his own life depended upon his resistance. Let it be understood that I am not arguing the merits of any one of the three amendments. I am discussing the proposed method of legislation; and I declare that it is against the Constitution of our country. It is revolutionary to the core, and is destructive of the fundamental principle of American liberty, the free consent of all the powers that unite to make laws. In opening this debate, I challenge all comers to show a single instance in our history where this consent has been thus coerced. This is the great, the paramount issue, which dwarfs all others into insignificance.

I now turn aside from the line of my argument, for a moment, to say that it is not a little surprising that our friends on the other side should have gone into this great contest on so weak a cause as

Redress: Removal.

Consent: Agreement.

Two thirds of these bodies: Garfield is referring to the fact that the Senate and the House can override a presidential veto if two-thirds of the members of each legislature agree to do so.

Complete American Presidents Sourcebook

the one embraced in the pending amendment to this bill. *[French novelist]* Victor Hugo said, in his description of the battle of **Waterloo**, that the struggle of the two armies was like the wrestling of two giants, when a chip under the heel of either might determine the victory. It may be that this amendment is the chip under your heel, or it may be that it is the chip on our shoulder; as a chip, it is of small account to you or to us; but when it represents the integrity of the Constitution, and is assailed by revolution, we fight for it. . . .

And now, Mr. Chairman, I ask the **forbearance** of gentlemen on the other side while I offer a suggestion, which I make with reluctance. They will bear me witness that I have, in many ways, shown my desire that the wounds of the war should be healed; that the grass which has grown green over the graves of the dead of both armies might symbolize the returning spring of friendship and peace between citizens who were lately in arms against each other. But I am compelled by the conduct of the other side to refer to a chapter of our recent history.

The last act of Democratic domination in this Capitol, eighteen years ago, was striking and dramatic, perhaps heroic. Then the Democratic Party said to the Republicans, "If you elect the man of your choice president of the United States, we will shoot your government to death"; but the People of this country, refusing to be coerced by threats or violence, voted as they pleased, and lawfully elected Abraham Lincoln president. Then your leaders, though holding a majority in the other branch of Congress, were heroic enough to withdraw from their seats and fling down the gage of mortal battle. We called it rebellion; but we recognized it as courageous and manly to avow your purpose, take all the risks, and fight it out in the open field. Notwithstanding your utmost efforts to destroy it, the government was saved. . . . And now lawfully, in the exercise of our right as representatives, we take up the gage you have this day thrown down, and appeal again to our common sovereign to determine whether you shall be permitted to destroy the principle of free consent in legislation under the threat of starving the government to death.

We are ready to pass these bills for the support of the government at any hour when you will offer them in the ordinary way, by the methods prescribed by the Constitution. If you offer your other propositions as separate measures, we will meet you in the fraternal spirit of fair debate and will discuss their merits. Some of your measures many of us will vote for in separate bills. But you shall not coerce any independent branch of this government, even by the threat

Waterloo: A decisive battle that stopped the French emperor Napoleon from conquering Europe.

Forbearance: Patience.

James A. Garfield: "Revolution Against the Constitution" Speech   741

of starvation, to surrender its lawful powers until the question has been appealed to the sovereign and decided in your favor. On this ground we plant ourselves, and here we will stand to the end. (Podell and Anzovin, pp. 242–47)

What happened next . . .

Garfield's speech proved decisive, as he rallied all Republicans and some Democrats to back his position. The basic appropriations bills were finally passed without riders. His impassioned speech helped him become the Republican candidate for the presidential election of 1880. His speech before Congress was reprinted and distributed as part of his campaign literature during his successful run for the presidency in 1880.

Garfield showed promise as being an independent and powerful president, but he was assassinated in 1881 after only a few months in office. Since the 1865 assassination of President Lincoln, Congress had come to dominate the federal government. Garfield might have become the first president to reassert the firm authority of the executive branch of the U.S. government. Instead, he helped restore the power of the presidency by setting in motion a trend of executive leadership that was broadened by presidents **Grover Cleveland** (1837–1908; see entry in volume 3), from 1885 to 1889 and 1893 to 1897, and **William McKinley** (1843–1901; see entry in volume 3), from 1897 to 1901.

Did you know . . .

- Garfield did almost no campaigning during the presidential election of 1880. He did not seek the Republican nomination; he emerged as the nominee only after thirty-six rounds of voting had failed to provide the necessary support for one of three candidates. Garfield's name was placed in nomination on the thirty-seventh ballot, and he won the nomination. Garfield did not actively campaign for president. Instead, he remained at home and spoke to interested voters and reporters on his front porch. He received less than ten thousand more popular votes than his opponent, Winfield S. Hancock (1824–1886).

Where to Learn More

Bates, Richard O. *The Gentleman from Ohio: An Introduction to Garfield.* Durham, NC: Moore Publishing Co., 1973.

Booraem, Hendrik. *The Road to Respectability: James A. Garfield and His World, 1844–1852.* Lewisburg, PA: Bucknell University Press, 1988.

Peskin, Allan. *Garfield: A Biography.* Kent, OH: Kent State University Press, 1999.

Podell, Janet, and Steven Anzovin, eds. *Speeches of the American Presidents.* New York: H. W. Wilson Co., 1988.

Chester A. Arthur

Twenty-first president (1881–1885)

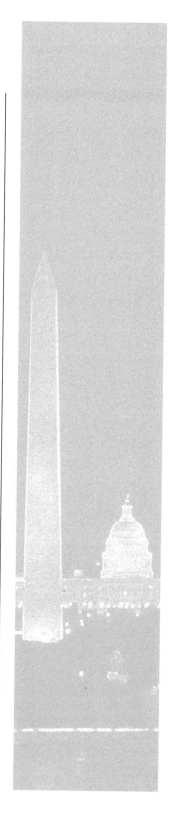

Chester A. Arthur

Born October 5, 1829
Fairfield, Vermont
Died November 18, 1886
New York, New York

Twenty-first president of the United States
(1881–1885)

Former political boss helped enact civil
service reform

Chester A. Arthur.
Courtesy of the Library of
Congress.

A fancy dresser, an expert on fine food and wine, and a cheery conversationalist, Chester A. Arthur was nicknamed "the Elegant Arthur" and "the Gentleman Boss." A boss, in political terms, refers to a powerful person able to organize support and deliver votes for a political candidate. Arthur was a boss in the New York political machine called the Stalwarts (a word meaning "loyal supporters"). During the post–Civil War era from 1865 to 1880, the Stalwarts controlled the state Republican Party and had influence nationally.

Arthur, in fact, was nominated as a vice presidential candidate in an effort to please the Stalwarts. Their candidate for the 1880 presidential election, former president **Ulysses S. Grant** (1822–1885; see entry in volume 3), was passed over at the Republican convention in favor of **James A. Garfield** (1831–1881; see entry in volume 3), who represented other groups in the party. Arthur was chosen as his running mate to ensure that Stalwarts would unite behind the presidential ticket and to help the party win eastern states in the Electoral College, a body of representatives officially responsible for electing the president of the United States. The strategy worked.

"All personal considerations and political views must be merged in the national sorrow. I am an American among millions grieving for their wounded chief [President James Garfield]."

Chester Arthur

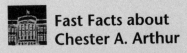

Fast Facts about Chester A. Arthur

Full name: Chester Alan Arthur

Born: October 5, 1829

Died: November 18, 1886

Burial site: Rural Cemetery, Albany, New York

Parents: William and Malvina Stone Arthur

Spouse: Ellen Lewis Herndon (1837–1880; m. 1859)

Children: William Lewis Herndon (1860–1863); Chester Alan Jr. (1864–1937); Ellen Herndon (1871–1915)

Religion: Episcopalian

Education: Union College (B.A., 1848; M.A., 1851)

Occupations: Educator; attorney

Government positions: Vice president under James A. Garfield

Political party: Republican

Dates as president: September 20, 1881–March 4, 1885

Age upon taking office: 51

Arthur's career had benefited greatly from the patronage system. In a patronage system, elected officials appoint their supporters to civil service (government) jobs. President Garfield wanted to reform that practice because it placed party loyalty above government service. Garfield's efforts ended when he was assassinated just a few months after taking office. When Arthur succeeded him as president, everyone expected that civil service reform would be ignored by the Gentleman Boss.

Arthur surprised everyone by pushing for and achieving much needed reform. It cost him support from his party, but Arthur proved to be a fairly effective president without much Congressional backing. His small-scale victories were early signs that national political reform was underway and that America could rise above partisanship (placing the concerns of a certain political group or party above all other considerations).

Rural youth

Chester Alan Arthur was born in Fairfield, Vermont, on October 5, 1829, the eldest of the seven children of William and Malvina Stone Arthur. William Arthur was an Irish-born Baptist minister and schoolteacher who had a quick temper and difficulty maintaining positions in Baptist congregations. The family moved frequently among towns in Northern Vermont and New York. Some political opponents would later claim that Arthur was born further north, in Canada, which would make him ineligible (not qualified) to serve as president.

Chester A. Arthur Timeline

1829: Born in Vermont

1844: Holds first political job, as a crier—a boy who stands on street corners and shouts out the name and qualifications of a candidate running for office

1848: Graduates from Union College

1854: Certified as a lawyer

1860–63: Named chief of the state military of New York, an honorary position that becomes important with the beginning of the Civil War

1868: Named collector of the New York Customs House

1877: Fired from Customs House position by President Rutherford B. Hayes

1880: Nominated as surprise vice presidential candidate to James Garfield

1881: Assumes presidency following the assassination of Garfield

1881–85: Serves as twenty-first U.S. president

1886: Dies in New York

The family settled in the Saratoga County area of New York in 1839. Although Arthur would grow to be a true man of the city, concerned with fashion, culture, and urban issues, he would often return to the country to pursue his boyhood hobby of fishing. Arthur especially enjoyed fishing for salmon.

At age fifteen in 1844, Arthur had his first political job: He received a few pennies to serve as a crier—a boy who stands on street corners and shouts out the name and qualifications of a candidate running for office. He shouted out his support for Whig Party presidential candidate Henry Clay (1777–1852; see box in **John Quincy Adams** entry in volume 1) on that first occasion. (The Whig Party was a political party that existed from about 1836 to 1852.)

In 1848, Arthur graduated from Union College—then one of the finest schools in the East—located in Schenectady, New York. He taught school and studied law after college. He was principal of North Pownal Academy in Bennington, Vermont, in 1851, when James A. Garfield taught there for one semester. In 1853, Arthur moved to New York City to study in a law office. He passed the bar examination to enter the legal profession and was certified as a lawyer in 1854.

Words to Know

Adjourn: To end a session where a group meets until sessions resume at a later scheduled date.

Appropriations: Funds authorized for a particular project.

Bar: A term that encompasses all certified lawyers—those who have passed all official requirements (the bar exam) to be certified as lawyers.

Electoral College: A body officially responsible for electing the president of the United States. In presidential elections, the candidate who receives the most popular votes in a particular state wins all of that state's electoral votes. Votes are distributed among states in ratios based on population. A candidate must win a majority of electoral votes (over fifty percent) in order to win the presidency.

Grass roots: A term that describes political activity that begins with small groups of people acting without the influence of large and powerful groups.

Kansas-Nebraska Act: A United States law authorizing the creation of the states of Kansas and Nebraska and specifying that the inhabitants of the territories should decide whether or not to allow slaveholding.

Partisanship: Placing the concerns of one's group or political party above all other considerations.

Patronage system: Also called spoils system; a system where elected officials appoint their supporters to civil service (government) jobs.

Political machine: An organized political group whose members are generally under the control of the leader of the group.

Power broker: A person able to control votes or individuals.

Whig Party: A political party that existed roughly from 1836 to 1852. Made up of different factions from the former Democratic-Republican Party, Whig members had refused to join the group led by President Andrew Jackson that formed the Democratic Party.

In New York, Arthur quickly established his reputation as a fine lawyer. Involved in several civil rights cases, Arthur successfully represented Lizzie Jennings, an African American woman who sued the city of New York for the right to ride on city streetcars. The suit was successful, and African Americans were no longer forbidden to use the city's streetcars.

Arthur's interest in civil rights led him to become further involved in politics. He joined with those protesting the

Kansas-Nebraska Act of 1854 that would allow those states to decide on whether or not to permit slavery when they entered the Union. The Republican Party was formed around that time to oppose expansion of slave territory. Arthur was active at the convention in which the New York Republican Party was established. He supported the candidacy of John Frémont (1813–1890; see box in **James K. Polk** entry in volume 2), the first Republican presidential candidate, in 1856. He also supported the successful election to the presidency of **Abraham Lincoln** (1809–1865; see entry in volume 2) in 1860.

Arthur left New York for a brief period to try his luck in opening a law practice out west. Shortly after his return he began courting Ellen Lewis Herndon (1837–1880; see entry on **Ellen Arthur** in volume 3), the sister of a friend of his. She came from a wealthy family and shared his taste for fashionable clothing and entertainment. They were married in 1859. The Arthurs would have three children, two of whom grew to adulthood.

In 1860, Arthur was named by New York governor Edwin D. Morgan (1811–1883) as engineer in chief of the State Military. The position was honorary (that is, it was a position of respect but without power or payment), but Arthur was in charge of supervising the state's military operations. When the Civil War (1861–65) broke out in 1861, Arthur's position took on great importance. He was in charge of recruiting soldiers and ensuring that they were fully equipped for battle. By 1863, the fighting force from New York reached over two hundred thousand men.

Arthur was relieved from the position in 1863 when a Democrat became governor of New York. Thus, Arthur won and then lost the position because of patronage—a system in which elected officials appoint friends and supporters to government positions. Arthur returned to his law practice, but the patronage system soon turned again in his favor. Senator Roscoe Conkling (1829–1888; see box) of New York selected Arthur to build and run his state political machine. (A political machine is an organized political group whose members are generally under the control of the leader of the group.)

Arthur organized voters and recommended Conkling supporters for government jobs. The New York political machine of Conkling's became very powerful by 1868 and

Roscoe Conkling

Born on October 30, 1829, in Albany, New York, Roscoe Conkling attended Mount Washington Collegiate Institute and studied law. He became a lawyer and rose quickly to the position of district attorney of Albany. Becoming a powerful figure in the new Republican Party (founded in 1854), he moved to Utica, New York, and was elected the city's mayor. In 1858, he was elected to the House of Representatives, where he served from 1859 to 1863 and 1865 to 1867. A staunch supporter of Thaddeus Stevens (1792-1868; see box in **Andrew Johnson** entry in volume 2) and the Radical Republicans, Conkling sat on the committee that drafted the Radical program of Reconstruction meant to punish Southern states following the Civil War.

By 1867, Conkling controlled the New York state Republican organization. He was elected to the Senate and became a devoted follower of President Ulysses S. Grant, who served as chief executive from 1869 to 1877. Conkling was able to place supporters in the New York Customs House, which collected a majority of the nation's taxes on imported goods. Conkling used the operation to build a strong party organization called the "Stalwarts" that provided jobs and involved workers in donations of time and money to the Republican Party. President Grant offered to make him chief justice of the Supreme Court in 1873, and President Chester A. Arthur, one of Conkling's leading supporters, offered him a seat on the Court a decade later. But he rejected both.

Roscoe Conkling. *Photograph by Mathew Brady. Courtesy of the Library of Congress.*

Conkling had a brilliant, quick mind in debate and saved his most scathing remarks for reformers who sought to eliminate political patronage through civil service reform. Conkling worked hard in 1880 to have Grant elected to the presidency for a third time, but Republicans nominated James A. Garfield of Ohio. Conkling battled with President Garfield over the patronage issue. In an attempt to rebuff him, Conkling resigned his Senate seat: he planned to be reelected to show up Garfield and demonstrate his personal power in New York. But Garfield was assassinated by a madman claiming to be a "Stalwart," and the shocked New York Legislature refused to elect Conkling back to the Senate seat he had vacated. Conkling retired to a lucrative legal practice and to fashionable New York City society. He died in New York City on April 18, 1888.

helped elect New York resident and Civil War general Ulysses S. Grant to the presidency.

To the victors go the spoils

Arthur was greatly rewarded for delivering votes for Grant. He was named collector of the New York Customs House, a huge operation employing over one thousand workers responsible for collecting almost seventy percent of all taxes on imported goods. All the staff, which included many more employees than were actually needed, were Republicans who spent a good portion of their work hours on party causes. Through this political machine Arthur became a leader of a Republican faction called "the Stalwarts," who offered full support for all Republican policies and could deliver thousands and thousands of votes.

The system Arthur established was not illegal at the time. Employees did not directly benefit financially, other than performing little work for good pay. Part of their wages was donated to the Republican Party—a legal maneuver at the time, but a corrupt practice.

The patronage system was among the many scandals of the Grant administration. By the 1876 presidential election, the scandals were so widespread that Republicans faced the possibility of losing control of the White House after having won the previous four national elections. Republican nominee **Rutherford B. Hayes** (1822–1893; see entry in volume 3) helped prevent defeat in the controversial election of 1876 by promising to reform the civil service system.

Shortly after taking office, Hayes began taking action. He focused on the high-profile Customs House practices. Stating that Arthur had used his position inappropriately, President Hayes asked Arthur to quit. Arthur, however, had the support of Roscoe Conkling, a powerful senator who promised a Senate challenge to Hayes's action. Hayes waited until the Senate adjourned (ended its session) for the summer and then fired Arthur.

Arthur returned to his law practice and managed to restore his reputation. He was still a major power broker when the next election came around. (A power broker is a

Campaign poster for 1880
Republican Party
candidates—James A.
Garfield for president and
Chester A. Arthur for vice
president.

*Reproduced by permission of
the Corbis Corporation.*

person able to control votes or individuals.) Hayes had
promised to serve only one term, but by 1880 he was not
popular enough to run for reelection anyway.

The Stalwart faction of the Republican Party nominated ex-president Grant as its candidate, while another faction,
called "the Half-Breeds," nominated Maine senator James G.
Blaine (1830–1893; see box). The Half-Breeds embraced a
wider variety of views on issues than the Stalwarts, and they
based their center of power in Washington, D.C. A third candidate, Secretary of the Treasury John Sherman (1823–1900),
was backed by the strong Ohio-based Republican Party led by
Congressman James A. Garfield. Outgoing president Hayes
was also from Ohio.

After thirty-five rounds of voting, no candidate
emerged with the necessary number of delegates to win the
nomination. Sherman and Blaine decided to drop their bids
in favor of James Garfield, an eight-term congressman who

After President Garfield died, Vice President Arthur (second from right) was sworn is as president by New York Supreme Court justice John R. Brady at Arthur's home in New York City. *From* Frank Leslie's Illustrated Newspaper. *Courtesy of the Library of Congress.*

had served as Sherman's campaign manager and was a respected political figure. Garfield won the nomination. To pacify the Stalwart faction and to ensure that Republicans could win in eastern states, the convention chose Arthur, who had never held elected office before, as the vice presidential candidate. The ploy worked: Garfield won the election by fewer than ten thousand votes, but he won all the important eastern states for a sure victory in the Electoral College. (For more information on the Electoral College, see boxes in **George W. Bush** entry in volume 5.)

James G. Blaine

James Gillespie Blaine was among the most powerful American politicians of the second half of the nineteenth century. He served twice as secretary of state and was a presidential candidate on several occasions. He was born January 31, 1830, in West Brownsville, Pennsylvania. His father, Ephraim Lyon Blaine, was a lawyer and a county clerk. Blaine graduated from local Washington and Jefferson College in 1847. He took a teaching position at the Western Military Institute in Georgetown, Kentucky. While working there from 1848 to 1851, he courted Harriet Stanwood, a teacher at a nearby woman's seminary. They married on June 30, 1850, and would have seven children.

Blaine had a growing interest in politics, inspired by Whig Party leader Henry Clay, an influential senator from Kentucky. Leaving Kentucky in late 1851, Blaine taught at the Pennsylvania Institute for the Blind from 1852 to 1854. He also pursued legal studies while in Philadelphia. Through his wife's family connections and his own activism on behalf of the Whig Party, Blaine was asked in 1853 to fill a vacancy for an editor position of the *Kennebec Journal*, a Whig newspaper in Augusta, Maine. By November 1854, he was managing the paper.

The Whig Party dissolved around this time and Blaine became active with the new Republican Party. He was elected to the Maine legislature in 1858 and was re-elected three times. In 1862, he was elected to the U.S. House of Representatives. Known as "Blaine from Maine," he spent thirteen years in the House and served as its Speaker between 1869 and 1875. He was a moderate on Reconstruction, endorsed black suffrage (voting rights), and favored protection of civil rights in the South, standing against more aggressive action toward the region favored by the powerful Congressional group called the Radical Republicans.

As a moderate, Blaine became a leader of a group nicknamed the "Half-Breeds." Republican "half-breeds" contrasted with Republican "Stalwarts," who formed a more united and unwavering loyalty to issues of interest to northern businessmen. Blaine and Roscoe Conkling, a representative from New York, often clashed on issues. Conkling helped undermine Blaine's presidential chances in 1876 and 1880. In 1876, Blaine moved to the Senate. He had been the leading candidate for the Republican presidential nomination that year, but a controversy arose over whether Blaine had acted corruptly in helping to save a land grant for an Arkansas railroad in 1869. The facts on the case were allegedly contained in a packet of documents known as the Mulligan Letters, named for the man who possessed them. The letters came into Blaine's hands, he read from them to the House, and his friends said that he had vindicated himself. Enemies charged that the papers proved his guilt. Republican dele-

James G. Blaine.
Courtesy of the Library of Congress.

gates at the party's national convention that year decided that Blaine was too controversial to win the presidency, and they turned instead to Rutherford B. Hayes of Ohio.

After Hayes served a single term, the race to be the Republican nominee for president in 1880 was wide open. The Stalwart faction favored former president Ulysses S. Grant. Blaine led opposition to Grant. Congressman James A. Garfield of Ohio became the compromise nominee. After Garfield won narrowly in the national election, he asked Blaine to be his secretary of state. In his brief tenure at the State Department, Blaine pursued his concern for a canal across Central America, improved relations with South American nations, and expanded trade. Following Garfield's assassination in the summer of 1881, President

Chester A. Arthur, a longtime Stalwart, received Blaine's resignation.

Blaine received the Republican nomination for president on the first ballot in 1884. He lost in a bitter campaign to Grover Cleveland, governor of New York. Over the next four years Blaine led opposition to Cleveland's policy of low tariff rates. Blaine stayed out of the presidential race of 1888 and strongly supported the Republican Party's nominee, **Benjamin Harrison** (1833–1901; see entry in volume 3). After Harrison defeated Cleveland, Blaine was again named secretary of state.

As a member of the Harrison Cabinet, Blaine faced quite a few important diplomatic issues, including a conflict with Great Britain over fishing rights and the fur trade along the Pacific coast. He convened the first Pan-American Conference, a meeting among nations of the Americas, in Washington in 1889; fought for annexation of Hawaii; and pushed for broader presidential power in trade agreements. Blaine resigned as secretary of state shortly before the Republican convention of 1892. It is not clear whether Blaine was actually a candidate for the presidency, but the incumbent Harrison easily controlled the convention and was renominated on the first ballot. Blaine made one speech for the Republicans in the 1892 campaign, a race Harrison lost to Grover Cleveland, but he was ill with Bright's disease, a kidney ailment. He died on January 27, 1893, at the age of sixty-two.

Arthur Becomes President

Chester A. Arthur became president of the United States following the death of James A. Garfield. (See Garfield entry for election results from the Garfield/Arthur campaign.) This marked the fourth time in U.S. history that a vice president became president following the death of his predecessor. In 1884, Arthur attempted to be elected as president on his own, but lost the Republican nomination to James G. Blaine.

Death amid victory

Arthur's sudden rise to national prominence came while he was in mourning. In January 1880, his wife Ellen caught a cold while waiting outside on a snowy evening for a carriage to arrive after having attended a benefit concert in New York. The cold quickly turned into pneumonia, a disease of the lungs caused by a virus or bacteria. She died on January 12, 1880, months before Arthur's national triumphs. "Honors to me now are not what they once were," he remarked.

At the inauguration (formal ceremony installing him as president) in March 1881, President Garfield announced his intention to fulfill his campaign pledge of reforming the civil service system. An earlier attempt at reform and ending political patronage had been started by Garfield's predecessor, Rutherford B. Hayes, but had stalled in Congress.

Garfield lost support for his efforts when his Cabinet selections leaned heavily to Half-Breeds, as did the majority of his other political appointments. Garfield was selecting the men he felt comfortable with, but Stalwart leader Roscoe Conkling and his fellow New Yorker Thomas Platt (1833–1910) resigned from the Senate in protest. As a show of strength, Conkling and Platt went before the New York state legislature to have themselves reappointed to their seats—the point of their resignations having been made. Arthur joined them.

While Arthur and the two ex-senators were in New York, President Garfield was to take a trip to New England. As he waited for his train to arrive in a Washington, D.C., station, Garfield was shot several times by Charles J. Guiteau (c. 1840–1882), a deranged (mentally unbalanced) Stalwart supporter and former civil servant who was upset at having been passed over by Garfield. Reportedly, Guiteau had cried out, "I am a Stalwart and now Arthur is president!" before shooting Garfield.

Arthur rushed back to Washington as the president was returned to the White House to recuperate. Garfield

never did recover. After ten weeks, as the nation worried about the president's health and the future course of the nation, Garfield died on September 19, 1881. Arthur was sworn in as president the next day.

Many expected that Arthur would serve as a puppet— a person whose behavior and decisions are determined by others—for Stalwart causes. Arthur emerged as his own man, instead. Meanwhile, Stalwarts began losing support after the assassination, and Conkling and Platt were not reappointed to their Senate seats by the New York legislature. During Garfield's long disabled period, Arthur became determined to steer his own course.

Do the right thing

Arthur had benefited from the spoils system (another word for the patronage system), but he acted quickly to contin-

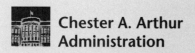

Chester A. Arthur Administration

Administration Dates
September 20, 1881–March 4, 1885

Vice President
None (1881–85)

Cabinet

Secretary of State
James G. Blaine (1881)
Frederick T. Frelinghuysen (1881–85)

Secretary of the Treasury
William Windom (1881)
Charles J. Folger (1881–84)
Walter Q. Gresham (1884)
Hugh McCulloch (1884–85)

Secretary of War
Robert Todd Lincoln (1881–85)

Attorney General
Wayne MacVeagh (1881)
Benjamin H. Brewster (1882–85)

Secretary of the Navy
William H. Hunt (1881–82)
William E. Chandler (1882–85)

Postmaster General
Thomas L. James (1881–82)
Timothy O. Howe (1882–83)
Walter Q. Gresham (1883–84)
Frank Hatton (1884–85)

Secretary of the Interior
Samuel J. Kirkwood (1881–82)
Henry M. Teller (1882–85)

ue the reforms promised by Hayes and Garfield. He supported the trial against postal workers in the Star Route Fraud case that Garfield's administration had begun prosecuting, and he pushed for civil service reform legislation. The Star Route trial, which involved western postal officials who conspired with stagecoach companies to steal money collected by the government, produced no convictions (no one was found guilty). But the trial helped fuel overwhelming public sentiment for cleaning up government corruption.

Arthur pushed for civil service legislation in 1882, but he was ignored by Congress. In 1883, he tried again, this time with the public solidly supporting him. Dorman B. Eaton (1823–1899), president of the grass-roots (locally begun) National Civil Service Reform League, drafted legislation that was sponsored by Senator George H. Pendleton (1825–1889) of Ohio. The Pendleton Civil Service Reform Act passed Congress and was signed into law by President Arthur in 1883. The Act established the Civil Service Commission, an organization that oversees federal appointments, administers competitive tests, and ensures that appointees do not actively participate in partisan affairs while an employee of the government. Eaton was named chairman of the commission.

In doing the right thing, Arthur lost support among some Republican Party members. The Pendleton Act was the most noteworthy event of his administration. Unfortunately, the act resulted in a lack of support that hindered Arthur's other efforts and ensured that the Republican Party would look elsewhere for a candidate for the 1884 presidential election.

Arthur is not generally ranked among the most effective presidents. However, he proved stronger than most had expected. Intending to keep the government out of debt, for example, Arthur vetoed (rejected) several appropriations bills (legislation that sets money aside for a project); however, his vetoes were overridden by Congress. He vetoed legislation that would limit Chinese immigration and deny citizenship to recent Chinese arrivals for twenty years. That veto was also overridden, but Arthur won a small victory by having the citizenship wait reduced to ten years. Arthur supported appropriations for building new naval ships, thus improving the U.S. Navy. A decade later, the U.S. Navy emerged as a major international naval force.

None of those measures won back support from his party, and Arthur quietly finished his term. White House occasions, meanwhile, were festive and elegant. Arthur had brought a personal chef and a butler along with him to Washington, D.C. He was the first president to have a valet, a male attendant whose job is to look after his employer's personal needs. He hired designer Charles Lewis Tiffany (1812–1902) to redecorate the White House. (Tiffany was a noted American merchant who established a fancy goods store in New York City.) He had new plumbing, a new bathroom, and the first elevator installed in the White House. He loved to entertain and hated to leave a party. Dinner guests would often stay past midnight at White House social gatherings.

In one of his final acts as president, Arthur dedicated the newly completed Washington Monument on February 27, 1885. Arthur was ill with Bright's disease, a kidney ailment, when he left office in 1885. He resumed his law practice in New York City, but he never again enjoyed good health. He died of the kidney illness on November 18, 1886.

Legacy

Often overlooked in listings of the most effective presidents, Chester A. Arthur proved to be a more able and fairer administrator than his background suggested that he would be. The Pendleton Act, which he signed into law, re-

A Selection of Arthur Landmarks

Albany Rural Cemetery. Cemetery Ave., Menands, NY 12204. (518) 463-7017. Gravesite of President and Mrs. Arthur.

Chester A. Arthur State Historic Site. Route 36, Fairfield, VT 05455. (802) 828-3226. Replication of two-room house in which Arthur was born. See http://www.state.vt.us/dca/historic/hp_sites.htm#arthur (accessed on July 26, 2000).

formed the civil service system and remains in effect in the twenty-first century. Arthur's support of the legislation cost him the base of support that carried him to the White House, but it brought much needed and lasting improvement to the American political system.

Arthur's support for fairer treatment of Chinese immigrants won a small measure of success and helped the United States maintain diplomatic relations with China. Like his earlier success in winning the rights for blacks to use New York streetcars, the small victory helped the cause of civil rights. Finally, Arthur's support for the appropriations bill that added new ships to the U.S. Navy was a significant early step toward the United States becoming a major naval power. Just over a decade later, the United States achieved a quick and decisive victory in the Spanish-American War (1896).

Arthur presided over a dying era. The New York political machine, of which he had been a major player, lost its momentum (driving force) while he was in office. Arthur helped assist in its downfall. The end of Stalwart influence was assured when Democrat **Grover Cleveland** (1837–1908; see entry in volume 3) was elected governor of New York during Arthur's term. Significantly, the reform-minded Cleveland followed Arthur as president, breaking a Republican stronghold on the White House that had existed in presidential elections since 1860. In addition, Cleveland defeated a Half-Breed, Blaine, in the election of 1884, effectively weakening that powerful wing of the Republican Party as well. The Republican Party would regroup and unify in the 1890s without the spoils system.

Where to Learn More

Crapol, Edward P. *James G. Blaine: Architect of Empire.* Wilmington, DE: Scholarly Resources, 2000.

Doenecke, Justus D. *The Presidencies of James A. Garfield and Chester A. Arthur.* Lawrence: University Press of Kansas, 1981.

Howe, George Frederick. *Chester A. Arthur: A Quarter-Century of Machine Politics.* New York: Dodd, Mead and Co., 1934. Reprint, New York: F. Ungar Pub. Co., 1957.

Jordan, David M. *Roscoe Conkling of New York: Voice in the Senate.* Ithaca, NY: Cornell University Press, 1971.

Levin, Peter R. *Seven by Chance: Accidental Presidents.* New York: Farrar, Straus and Co., 1948.

Poole, Susan D. *Chester A. Arthur, The President Who Reformed.* Reseda, CA: M. Bloomfield, 1977.

Reeves, Thomas C. *Gentleman Boss: The Life of Chester Alan Arthur.* New York: Alfred A. Knopf, 1975. Reprint, Newtown, CT: American Political Biography Press, 1991.

Simon, Charnan. *Chester A. Arthur: Twenty-first President of the United States.* Chicago: Children's Press, 1989.

Stevens, Rita. *Chester A. Arthur, 21st President of the United States.* Ada, OK: Garrett Educational Corp., 1989.

Ellen Arthur

Born August 30, 1837
Culpeper, Virginia
Died January 12, 1880
New York, New York

Dying before her devoted husband was elected vice president, Ellen Arthur was honored in memory during her husband's years in the White House

When Vice President **Chester A. Arthur** (1829–1886; see entry in volume 3) assumed the presidency after the assassination of **James Garfield** (1831–1881; see entry in volume 3), he was a widower. Ellen Lewis Herndon Arthur had died the previous year after contracting pneumonia, a lung infection caused by a virus or bacteria. The Arthurs had enjoyed an elegant lifestyle of dinner parties, shopping sprees, and cultural events.

As president, Arthur did his best to maintain some of their practices. He brought along his own chef and butler to the White House. He hired designers to redecorate the rooms and grounds, to make them, he said, look less like "barracks" (plain buildings used to house soldiers). Each morning, he placed a fresh flower near the portrait of his beloved wife, whom he had affectionately called Nell.

Singer in the church choir

Nell was born Ellen Lewis Herndon on August 30, 1837, in Culpeper, Virginia, the only child of Elizabeth Hans-

"Honors to me now are not what they once were [since the death of his wife]."

Chester Arthur

Ellen Arthur.
Courtesy of the Library of Congress.

brough and William Lewis Herndon. The Herndon family could trace their roots back to the twelfth century and William I (1143–1214), king of Scotland. Ellen's father was a naval officer. The family moved to Washington, D.C., when he was assigned to help his brother-in-law Lieutenant Matthew Fontaine Maury (1806–1873) establish the Naval Observatory.

Young Ellen had a lovely contralto voice, the lowest female singing voice. She joined the choir at St. John's Episcopal Church on Lafayette Square. She was a member of the choir for several years before the family moved to New York City while she was in her late teens.

In New York, she was introduced by her cousin, Dabney Herndon, to Chester Alan Arthur in 1856. "Chet" was a young lawyer beginning to make a name for himself as a defense attorney in civil rights cases. He was active in local and national politics as a member of the recently formed Republican Party. Chet and Nell began a romance, but tragedy struck the following year when Ellen's father died at sea. William Herndon was caught in a storm off Cape Hatteras, North Carolina, and went down with his ship.

Chester helped Ellen through her period of mourning. Gradually, they began attending social and cultural activities around New York City and occasionally retreated to the countryside. Arthur was raised around Saratoga Springs in northern New York and liked to return to the natural surroundings to fish for salmon. The couple was married on October 25, 1859.

Arthur's career began to prosper shortly after marriage. In 1860, he was named to an honorary (unpaid) position, engineer in chief of the State Military. The position became essential when the Civil War broke out in 1861. He was in charge of recruiting soldiers and ensuring they were fully equipped for battle. By 1863, the fighting force from New York reached over two hundred thousand men. After the war, Arthur became a major figure in the New York Republican Party, organizing support for Senator Roscoe Conkling (1829–1888; see box in **Chester A. Arthur** entry in volume 3). Arthur received the desirable assignment of collector at the New York Customs House in 1868.

Meanwhile, the Arthurs were raising a family. Their first child, a boy named after Ellen's father, died at age two. A second boy, Chester Jr., was born in 1864, and the couple had a daughter, Ellen, in 1871. The Arthurs purchased a large home in New York City and had it elegantly decorated. Arthur often bought his wife jewelry made by famous designer Charles Lewis Tiffany (1812–1902), and they were active in New York social circles.

Arthur lost his Customs House position in 1877 for having used it to help support the Republican Party. He returned to his law practice and remained an important force in the party as a leader of the Stalwarts, a powerful faction based in New York. When Ohioan James A. Garfield was the surprise nominee for president at the Republican convention in 1880, he selected Arthur as his running mate to ensure that the ticket would receive full support from the Stalwart faction. By then, Arthur was a widower.

On the evening of January 10, 1880, Ellen Arthur attended a benefit concert in New York City. She caught cold while waiting for her carriage, and her health rapidly deteriorated into pneumonia. Arthur, who was at the state capitol in Albany, rushed home to be at her side, but she was already unconscious by the time he arrived. She died on January 12, 1880. She was only forty-two years old. "Honors to me now are not what they once were," Arthur said, following his nomination as vice president.

Tribute to a singer

Arthur had loved to hear Ellen sing. When he arrived in Washington, D.C., the town where Ellen was raised, to begin his term as vice president, he paid a visit to the church where Ellen used to sing in the choir. He presented a stained-glass window to the parish in his wife's memory. The glass depicted angels of the Resurrection, the Christian concept of the rising of the dead for the Last Judgment. Upon becoming president, Arthur requested that the window be placed in a location where he could see it at night from the White House with the lights of the church shining through.

Arthur paid other tributes to Ellen, including a daily practice of placing fresh flowers by her portrait. At White House dinners, a place next to Arthur was always set aside in memory of his wife.

White House elegance

Arthur had the White House redecorated. He supervised the work in his spare time. Meanwhile, he asked his sister, Mary McElroy (1841–1917), to handle White House hostess duties for larger occasions. After having supported reform-minded ideas in her youth, Mary had become a more conservative woman. She had married a minister and focused on raising a family. In her early forties when Arthur became president, she temporarily left her family from fall to spring for the following four years to organize formal gatherings and to assist her brother.

Where to Learn More

Boller, Paul F. *Presidential Wives*. New York: Oxford University Press, 1998.

Joseph, Paul. *Chester Arthur*. Edina, MN: Abdo and Daughters Publishers, 1999.

Arthur's First Annual Address to Congress

Delivered on December 6, 1881; excerpted from
Archives of the West: 1877–1887 **(Web site)**

Acknowledging the U.S. government's "sorry history" of relations with Native Americans, President Arthur introduces a new plan for the late nineteenth century

In his first annual address to Congress, President **Chester A. Arthur** (1830–1886; see entry in volume 3) acknowledged that the U.S. government's relations with Native Americans had been "a cause of trouble and embarrassment" since the beginning of the nation. At the time he spoke, Native Americans were seriously endangered as a people. War and disease had severely reduced their number. Land where the nomadic (roaming) Plains tribes hunted was being rapidly settled by whites, who were defended by the U.S. military in a series of wars on the the Plains (from Montana to Texas). These battles raged during much of the last half of the twentieth century on the final area of frontier within the continental United States.

By the time the United States was founded with ratification of the Constitution in 1789, Americans were journeying beyond the thirteen states to settle in present-day Ohio, Kentucky, and Tennessee—areas where various Native American nations were still strong. A series of battles over the land concluded in 1795 with the Treaty of Greenville, which designated land as either "Indian Territory" or white settlement. During the administration of President **Thomas Jefferson**

> "We have to deal with the appalling fact that though thousands of lives have been sacrificed and hundreds of millions of dollars expended in the attempt to solve the Indian problem, it has until within the past few years seemed scarcely nearer a solution than it was half a century ago."
>
> *Chester A. Arthur*

(1743–1826; see entry in volume 1) from 1801 to 1809, a program was developed to try through religious groups to integrate Native Americans into U.S. society. While that program was failing to take hold, further land concessions were gained by the United States from Native Americans in Indiana and the Great Lakes region during the period that ended with the War of 1812 (1812–15). The Black Hawk War of 1832 effectively pushed Native Americans west of the Mississippi River in the present-day Midwest. The Indian Removal Act of 1830 empowered President **Andrew Jackson** (1767–1845; see entry in volume 1) to move Native Americans in southern states across the Mississippi River to what was then "Indian Territory" (mostly present-day Oklahoma).

As the United States gained western territory to form the present-day continental United States during the late 1840s, Americans began crossing into the Plains and the Rocky Mountains in larger numbers. Railroads stretched to those areas following the Civil War (1861–65). During the administration of **Ulysses S. Grant** (1822–1885; see entry in volume 3) in the early 1870s, the U.S. government abandoned the process of making treaties with Native American tribes because the treaties often failed. Instead, Congress began to pass legislation that affected all Native Americans. Native Americans then became dependent on the U.S. government for their protection.

Things to remember while reading an excerpt from President Arthur's first annual address to Congress:

- The period when Arthur spoke was particularly crucial for Native Americans in their battle for survival. The Plains Indian Wars gradually weakened the last Native American strongholds. Native Americans were able to stem the tide on occasion, as in the Battle of Little Big Horn ("Custer's Last Stand") in 1876, but those victories were few. The year after Little Big Horn, for example, the great warrior Chief Joseph (c. 1840–1904) surrendered with his famous declaration, "I will fight no more, forever."

- President Arthur struck a compromising note in his speech, trying to win support by not pointing blame.

Like President Thomas Jefferson, Arthur believed that attempting to integrate Native Americans into American society was their best hope for survival. In the speech, he presented three ways to bring that about: extend the rights guaranteed to American citizens to Native Americans; enhance Native American property rights; and support education for Native American youths.

Excerpt from President Arthur's first annual address to Congress

Prominent among the matters which challenge the attention of Congress at its present session is the management of our Indian affairs. While this question has been a cause of trouble and embarrassment from the infancy of the Government, it is but recently that any effort has been made for its solution at once serious, determined, consistent, and promising success.

It has been easier to resort to convenient makeshifts for tiding over temporary difficulties than to grapple with the great permanent problem, and accordingly the easier course has almost invariably been pursued.

*It was natural, at a time when the national territory seemed almost **illimitable** and contained many millions of acres far outside the bounds of civilized settlements, that a policy should have been initiated which more than **aught** else has been the fruitful source of our Indian complications.*

*I refer, of course, to the policy of dealing with the various Indian tribes as separate nationalities, of **relegating** them by treaty stipulations to the occupancy of immense reservations in the West, and of encouraging them to live a savage life, undisturbed by any earnest and well-directed efforts to bring them under the influences of civilization.*

The unsatisfactory results which have sprung from this policy are becoming apparent to all.

As the white settlements have crowded the borders of the reservations, the Indians, sometimes contentedly and sometimes against

Illimitable: Without limits.

Aught: Anything.

Relegating: Assigning.

their will, have been transferred to other hunting grounds, from which they have again been dislodged whenever their new-found homes have been desired by the adventurous settlers.

These removals and the frontier collisions by which they have often been preceded have led to frequent and disastrous conflicts between the races.

It is profitless to discuss here which of them has been chiefly responsible for the disturbances whose recital occupies so large a space upon the pages of our history.

We have to deal with the appalling fact that though thousands of lives have been sacrificed and hundreds of millions of dollars ex-pended in the attempt to solve the Indian problem, it has until within the past few years seemed scarcely nearer a solution than it was half a century ago. But the Government has of late been cautiously but steadily feeling its way to the adoption of a policy which has already produced gratifying results, and which, in my judgment, is likely, if Congress and the Executive accord in its support, to relieve us ere long from the difficulties which have hitherto beset us.

For the success of the efforts now making to introduce among the Indians the customs and pursuits of civilized life and gradually to absorb them into the mass of our citizens, sharing their rights and holden to their responsibilities, there is imperative need for legislative action.

My suggestions in that regard will be chiefly such as have been already called to the attention of Congress and have received to some extent its consideration.

First. I recommend the passage of an act making the laws of the various States and Territories applicable to the Indian reservations within their borders and extending the laws of the State of Arkansas to the portion of the Indian Territory not occupied by the Five Civilized Tribes.

The Indian should receive the protection of the law. He should be allowed to maintain in court his rights of person and property. He has repeatedly begged for this privilege. Its exercise would be very valuable to him in his progress toward civilization.

Second. Of even greater importance is a measure which has been frequently recommended by my predecessors in office, and in furtherance of which several bills have been from time to time introduced in both Houses of Congress. The enactment of a general law

Expended: Spent.

Ere: Before.

Hitherto: Previously.

Five Civilized Tribes: A group of five tribes that formed systems of government and economy similar to those of the United States and Western European nations. The five tribes—Cherokee, Chickasaw, Choctaw, Creek, and Seminole—established a headquarters in Muskogee, Oklahoma.

*permitting the **allotment in severalty,** to such Indians, at least, as desire it, of a reasonable quantity of land secured to them by patent, and for their own protection made inalienable for twenty or twenty-five years, is demanded for their present welfare and their permanent advancement.*

*In return for such considerate action on the part of the Government, there is reason to believe that the Indians in large numbers would be persuaded to sever their tribal relations and to engage at once in agricultural pursuits. Many of them realize the fact that their hunting days are over and that it is now for their best interests to conform their manner of life to the new order of things. By no greater inducement than the assurance of permanent title to the soil can they be led to engage in the occupation of **tilling** it.*

*The **well-attested** reports of their increasing interest in **husbandry** justify the hope and belief that the enactment of such a statute as I recommend would be at once attended with gratifying results. A resort to the allotment system would have a direct and powerful influence in dissolving the tribal bond, which is so prominent a feature of savage life, and which tends so strongly to perpetuate it.*

Third. I advise a liberal appropriation for the support of Indian schools, because of my confident belief that such a course is consistent with the wisest economy. . . . (Archives of the West: 1877–1887 [Web site])

Allotment in severalty: Dispersal among individuals.

Tilling: Cultivating.

Well-attested: Authentic.

Husbandry: The act of raising farm animals and crops.

What happened next . . .

Arthur represented the concerns of Americans who wanted to take humanitarian actions on behalf of Native Americans. Not much progress on Native American affairs occurred during Arthur's term. His three-part policy based on land ownership, citizenship, and education provided a model for future action. Unfortunately, none of those actions helped. The lives of Native Americans worsened as the century progressed.

Congress introduced a plan to simultaneously protect Native Americans and undermine tribal structures. The Dawes

Act (or General Allotment Act), went into effect in 1887. Under this Act, tribal-owned land was parceled in 160-acre allotments on an individual basis to Native American Indian families. The remaining land was to be sold, with proceeds going to the tribe that owned it. The Dawes Act was a disaster. Native Americans lost "surplus" land to white speculators and settlers, and many Native American families ended up losing their allotted land as well. The poorest of groups in North America became poorer.

A majority of Native Americans continued to resist the idea of integrating into American culture. The slaughter of Sioux men, women, and children on December 29, 1890, at Wounded Knee, South Dakota, was the last major battle in a series of wars that ranged on the Plains from Montana to Texas since the 1860s. Native Americans reached their lowest population numbers shortly after the turn of the twentieth century.

Did you know . . .

- One part of Arthur's three-part proposal for integrating the Native Americans became reality over forty years later. In June 1924, the U.S. Congress granted Native Americans U.S. citizenship.

Where to Learn More

Doenecke, Justus D. *The Presidencies of James A. Garfield and Chester A. Arthur.* Lawrence: Regents Press of Kansas, 1981.

Levin, Peter R. *Seven by Chance: Accidental Presidents.* New York: Farrar, Straus and Co., 1948.

PBS Online. "Indian Policy Reform: Extract from President Chester Arthur's First Annual Message to Congress." *Archives of the West: 1877–1887.* [Online] http://www.pbs.org/weta/thewest/wpages/wpgs670/indpol.htm (accessed on July 28, 2000).

Grover Cleveland

Twenty-second president (1885–1889)
Twenty-fourth president (1893–1897)

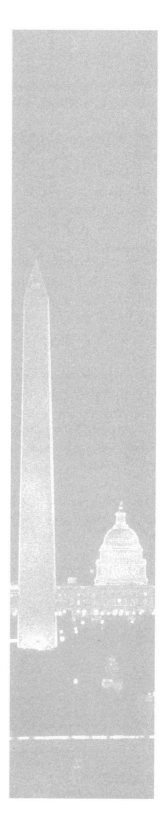

Grover Cleveland

Born March 18, 1837
Caldwell, New Jersey
Died June 24, 1908
Princeton, New Jersey

Twenty-second and twenty-fourth
president of the United States
(1885–1889, 1893–1897)

Demonstrated his dedication to honesty
and integrity throughout his two terms as
president regardless of the political
consequences

G rover Cleveland is the only president to have served nonconsecutive (unconnected) terms. He was elected president in 1884, lost his bid for reelection in 1888, and won again in 1892. His shifting political fortunes reflected the state of the nation. Americans faced an unstable economy despite the continued growth of industry and railroads. Many businessmen were growing extremely wealthy, while farmers and laborers struggled against steadily increasing prices for such basic necessities as food and clothing. National politics had been dominated for years by patronage (selecting people for government jobs based on their support for an elected official rather than on their qualifications), partisanship (putting the concerns of a political group or party above all other concerns), and scandals. The United States was growing increasingly involved in international affairs and schemes.

Cleveland is admired not so much for what he did about such problems as for what he did not do. For example, Cleveland maintained conservative (traditional) economic policies despite the desire by many for more radical (extreme; new and risky) programs. He resisted attempts to raise tariff

"A public office is a public trust."

Grover Cleveland

Grover Cleveland.
Courtesy of the Library of Congress.

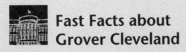

Fast Facts about Grover Cleveland

Full name: Stephen Grover Cleveland

Born: March 18, 1837

Died: June 24, 1908

Burial site: Princeton Cemetery, Princeton, New Jersey

Parents: Richard and Anne Neal Cleveland

Spouse: Frances Folsom (1864–1947; m. 1886)

Children: Oscar Folsom (1874–?; Cleveland claimed paternal responsibility for this child, named after his law partner and future father-in-law; the mother later gave him up for adoption); Ruth (1891–1904); Esther (1893–1980); Marion (1895–1977); Richard Folsom (1897–1974); Francis Grover (1903–1995)

Religion: Presbyterian

Education: High school

Occupation: Lawyer

Government positions: Erie County, New York, sheriff; Buffalo, New York, mayor; New York governor

Political party: Democratic

Dates as president: March 4, 1885–March 4, 1889 (first term); March 4, 1893–March 4, 1897 (second term)

Age upon taking office: 47

rates (rates of taxes on imports) and to increase the supply of money. In foreign affairs, Cleveland countered attempts to expand American influence and possession of lands beyond the continental United States. (The continental United States refers to the states whose borders touch each other, so present-day Hawaii and Alaska are not included. At the beginning of Cleveland's first term in 1885, the number of states in the Union was thirty-eight; at the end of his second term in 1892, the number was forty-five.) In Washington, D.C., he frustrated attempts by some members of his own Democratic Party to get important government jobs. He insisted that job applicants have skills and qualifications for the job rather than rely on their political background.

Cleveland's reputation rests with the integrity that he displayed as chief executive. He maintained those qualities even as his support eroded because he refused to back down on his principles in favor of more popular policies. His actions reflected his statement, "A public office is a public trust." He is considered as having been a strong president for his independence and leadership.

Finding success in Buffalo

Stephen Grover Cleveland was born in Caldwell, New Jersey, on March 18, 1837. He was the fifth of nine children of Richard Falley Cleveland (1804–1853) and Anne Neal Cleveland (1806–1882). Richard Cleveland was a Presbyterian minister who moved his family to Fayetteville, New York, in

Grover Cleveland Timeline

1837: Born in New Jersey

1870–73: Serves as sheriff of Erie County, New York

1881–82: Serves as mayor of Buffalo, New York

1883–85: Serves as governor of New York

1885–89: Serves as twenty-second U.S. president (first term)

1888: Loses bid for reelection to Benjamin Harrison

1893–97: Serves as twenty-fourth U.S. president (second term), becoming the first chief executive to serve nonconsecutive terms

1893: Financial crisis hits the United States

1908: Dies in New Jersey

1841. There, he became district secretary of the American Home Mission Society. Richard Cleveland died in 1853, when Grover was sixteen. The family's financial resources were soon drained. Cleveland abandoned his plans for college in favor of working to help support the family. He taught at a school for the blind in New York City for a short period. Then, he decided to head west for better opportunities.

Cleveland stopped in Buffalo, New York, where his uncle, Lewis F. Allen, owned a cattle ranch. The stop proved fortunate for Cleveland. He was hired to do bookkeeping for his uncle's ranch. During his spare time, Cleveland studied law. He passed the bar (examination to enter the legal profession) in 1859 and set up a law practice that soon began thriving. During this time, he also became active in politics as a Democrat.

When the Civil War (1861–65) broke out, Cleveland was pressed into service, but he hired a man to replace him. Such arrangements were legal under the Federal Conscription Act. Cleveland was still supporting his family at the time. Meanwhile, Cleveland served for a brief period as assistant district attorney of Erie County, New York. He then returned to private practice and his law firm prospered.

Cleveland was elected county sheriff in 1870. He was well thought of for fighting crime and corruption in that po-

Words to Know

Annex: To add to an existing organization.

Bar: A term that encompasses all certified lawyers—those who have passed all official requirements (the bar exam) to be certified as lawyers.

Electoral votes: The votes a presidential candidate receives for having won a majority of the popular vote in a state. Electoral votes are distributed among states in ratios based on population. A candidate must win a majority of electoral votes (over fifty percent) in order to win the presidency.

Graft: Misuse of a public position to gain profit or advantages.

Imperialism: The process of expanding the authority of one government over other nations and groups of people.

Inflation: An economic term describing a decline in the value of money in relation to the goods and services it will buy.

Legal tender: Bills or coin designated with value.

Manifest Destiny: The belief that American expansionism is inevitable and divinely ordained.

Monroe Doctrine: A policy statement issued during the presidency of James Monroe (1817–25) that explained the position of the United States on the activities of European powers in the western hemisphere; of major significance was the stand of the United States against European intervention in the affairs of the Americas.

Neutrality: The decision of a nation not to take sides in a dispute.

Partisanship: Placing the concerns of one's group or political party above all other considerations.

Patronage: When people are selected for jobs based on their support for an elected official instead of their qualifications.

Pendleton Civil Service Reform Act: A congressional act signed into law by President Arthur that established the Civil Service Commission, an organization that oversees federal appointments and ensures that appointees do not actively participate in party politics while holding a federal job.

Political machine: A powerful group able to organize support and deliver votes for a political candidate.

Populism: An agricultural movement of rural areas between the Mississippi River and the Rocky Mountains of the late nineteenth century that united the interests of farmers and laborers. In 1891, the movement formed a national political party, the People's Party, whose members were called Populists.

Radical: Risky, more extreme.

Tariff: A protective tax placed on imported goods to raise their price and make them less attractive than goods produced by the nation importing them.

DRINK TO YOUR FAVORITES.

sition and in his private law practice. Cleveland was so well respected that he was elected mayor of Buffalo in 1881. After noticing that many contracts awarded by the city to local businesses benefited elected officials, Cleveland began exposing graft (misuse of a public position to gain profit or advantages). He was nicknamed the "veto mayor" for refusing to pass many contracts and bills that would benefit city leaders at the expense of taxpayers. He saved the city over $1 million during his first year in office.

Cleveland's reputation spread quickly during a time of public reaction to political patronage and scandal. New York politics had been under the influence of U.S. senator Roscoe Conkling (1829–1888; see box in **Chester A. Arthur** entry in volume 3) and future president **Chester A. Arthur** (1829–1886; see entry in volume 3), who ran Conkling's political machine. (A political machine is a powerful group able to organize support and deliver votes for a political candidate.) Conkling and Arthur provided government jobs for

Caricatures (exaggerated drawings) of the candidates in the presidential campaign of 1884: (left to right in each illustration) Republican nominees James G. Blaine (president) and John A. Logan (vice president) and Democrat nominees Thomas A. Hendricks (vice president) and Grover Cleveland (president). *Courtesy of the Library of Congress.*

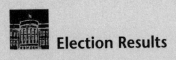

Election Results

1884

Presidential / Vice presidential candidates	Popular votes	Presidential electoral votes
Grover Cleveland / Thomas A. Hendricks (Democratic)	4,874,986	219
James G. Blaine / John A. Logan (Republican)	4,851,981	182

Incumbent president Chester A. Arthur finished second in the Republican nomination voting.

1892

Presidential / Vice presidential candidates	Popular votes	Presidential electoral votes
Grover Cleveland / Adlai E. Stevenson (Democratic)	5,556,918	277
Benjamin Harrison / Whitelaw Reid (Republican)	5,176,108	145
James B. Weaver / James G. Field (Populist)	1,041,028	22

Incumbent president Harrison was defeated by Cleveland, four years after Harrison defeated then-incumbent president Cleveland (see Harrison entry for 1888 election results). This marked the only time in U.S. history that a president served two nonconsecutive terms.

their supporters. These supporters in turn worked for Republican causes while being paid by the government. By the time Arthur became vice president of the United States in 1881, however, the political machine had begun to lose power. When Arthur became president in 1881 following the assassination of **James A. Garfield** (1831–1881; see entry in volume 3), he surprised many by continuing Garfield's plans for civil service reform. The reforms led to the end of the New York Republican political machine by 1883.

During the downfall of the state political machine, Cleveland became an attractive candidate for governor of New York in 1882. With popular sentiment (feeling) clearly favoring government reform, Cleveland won the election. He continued to fight corruption as governor.

For the 1884 presidential election, Republicans chose James G. Blaine (1830–1893; see box in **Chester A. Arthur** entry in volume 3) as their candidate. Blaine was a powerful national figure, but he was the wrong kind of candidate for a public that was tired of government corruption. Blaine had been said to be involved in a shady deal with railroad officials. He was also head of a political machine operating from Washington, D.C.

Cleveland was a popular alternative for Democrats: He had a spotless public record, and he could win New York, the state with the largest number of electoral votes. (Electoral votes are the votes a presidential candidate receives for winning the majority of the people's votes in a state.) Those qualities and an anti-Blaine faction (a group that disliked Blaine) within the Republican Party helped win the presidential election for Cleveland. New York proved highly important: Cleveland accumulated thirty-seven more electoral votes than Blaine, thirty-six of which came by winning in New York. He won New York by less than one percent—he received about one thousand more votes than Blaine of about one million votes cast.

The presidential campaign of 1884 was ugly. Blaine's ties with railroad officials and political machines were used against him. His campaign manager made a slur against Irish Catholics that cost the candidate thousands of votes. But Blaine's shortcomings were temporarily ignored when it was revealed that the bachelor Cleveland had fathered a child. That Cleveland had bought his way out of duty in the Civil War became another issue. Cleveland readily acknowledged the truth of both charges. He noted that he helped support the child he had fathered. He explained that his legal strategy for avoiding military service had allowed him to support his family. His willingness to be honest proved assuring to many voters.

Prevention is the best medicine

As president, Cleveland delivered what he promised during the campaign. His Cabinet (presidential advisors) included businessmen who supported lower tariff rates—against the wishes of many Democrats. He included Southerners in his administration. All previous presidents since the Civil War had been Northerners. They rarely offered positions to those Southerners who had supported the Confederacy (the Southern states that separated from the United States during the 1860s) during the Civil War.

Cleveland began a fight against corruption that extended even to government pensions (money received because of disability or for past service). At the time, Civil War veterans who did not qualify for certain disability pensions could petition their local representative to introduce a "pension bill" that would grant money to that particular veteran. Many had taken advantage of the process to make fraudulent (false) claims. Cleveland carefully examined each pension bill before him and ended up rejecting over two hundred bills that he believed were unnecessary. Civil War veterans associations were outraged.

Cleveland's political appointments, which he attempted to base on merit instead of political party, were continually questioned by Congress. The policy of executive privilege, which allows the president to keep certain papers private, was made solid during Cleveland's term. He repeatedly refused to turn over to Congress files concerning his appointments. He wanted to protect his ability to make decisions without having Congress continuously looking closely at his decision-making process.

For the most part, Cleveland was a "preventative president." Rather than aggressively enacting policies, he tried to improve and protect those already in place. In his political appointments, for example, he used as his guide the Pendleton Civil Service Reform Act, an act that President Arthur had signed into law in 1883. Although Cleveland vetoed many pension requests, he supported those already in place.

The late 1880s was an extreme period of change in American history. Big businesses were overpowering smaller ones, and railroads and industries grew prosperous while workers and farmers struggled to survive. Responding to the need to monitor the pricing practices of railroad companies, Cleveland supported the establishment of the Interstate Commerce Commission. This government group was authorized to ensure that railroad rates were reasonable and just.

To protect the rights of Native Americans, Cleveland supported the Dawes Act of 1887. This legislation encouraged Native Americans to move from a tribal culture to become private citizens by allowing individuals to buy lots on tribal lands. Almost five hundred thousand acres of tribal land had been offered for sale to any interested buyer during the administration

Grover Cleveland Administrations

Administration Dates
March 4, 1885–March 4, 1889
March 4, 1893–March 4, 1897

Vice President
Thomas A. Hendricks (1885)
None (1885–89)
Adlai E. Stevenson (1893–97)

Cabinet

Secretary of State
Thomas F. Bayard Sr. (1885–89)
Walter Q. Gresham (1893–95)
Richard Olney (1895–97)

Secretary of the Treasury
Daniel Manning (1885–87)
Charles S. Fairchild (1887–89)
John G. Carlisle (1893–97)

Secretary of War
William C. Endicott (1885–89)
Daniel S. Lamont (1893–97)

Attorney General
Augustus H. Garland (1885–89)
Richard Olney (1893–95)
Judson Harmon (1895–97)

Secretary of the Navy
William C. Whitney (1885–89)
Hilary A. Herbert (1893–97)

Postmaster General
William F. Vilas (1885–88)
Donald M. Dickinson (1888–89)
Wilson S. Bissel (1893–95)
William L. Wilson (1895–97)

Secretary of the Interior
Lucius Q. C. Lamar (1885–88)
William F. Vilas (1888–89)
Hoke Smith (1893–96)
David R. Francis (1896–97)

Secretary of Agriculture
Norman J. Colman (1889)
Julius S. Morton (1893–97)

of Cleveland's predecessor, Chester A. Arthur. Much of that land was returned to Native Americans under Cleveland.

Cleveland was not so forward-thinking in the area of women's rights. On that issue, he disagreed with his sister, Rose Elizabeth "Libbie" Cleveland (1846–1918). She served as the White House hostess during his first year in office, while he was still a bachelor. Libbie Cleveland was a proponent for equal rights between the sexes and for women's voting rights. Her views were shared by other women activists, including Susan B. Anthony (1820–1906; see box) and Elizabeth Cady Stanton (1815–1902). Between 1881 and 1886, Anthony and Stanton published three volumes of the *History of Woman Suffrage,* a collection of writings about the movement's struggle.

Susan B. Anthony

Born on February 5, 1820, in a New England farmhouse, Susan Brownell Anthony was the daughter of Lucy Read Anthony and Daniel Anthony, a cottonmill owner. Her father instilled in his children the ideas of self-reliance and self-discipline. She was raised a Quaker, a religion founded on the belief that places of organized worship are not necessary for a person to experience God. Quakers do not believe in armed conflict or slavery, and they were among the first groups to practice full equality between men and women. Other American women did not experience the freedom and respect Anthony did while growing up. She worked to change that disparity by becoming a leader in the crusade for women's rights.

After having completed her schooling at the age of seventeen, Anthony began teaching in schools in rural New York state. Teaching wages for men and women differed greatly: Anthony's weekly salary was equal to one-fifth of that received by her male colleagues. When she protested this inequality, she lost her job. She then secured a better position as principal of the Girls' Department at an academy in Rochester, New York. In 1849, after having taught for over ten years, Anthony found her spirit drained and her professional future bleak. She focused her energies on social improvements and joined the local temperance (anti-alcohol) society. After she

was denied the chance to speak at a Sons of Temperance meeting because she was a woman, she founded the Daughters of Temperance, the first women's temperance organization. She began writing temperance articles for the *Lily,* the first woman-owned newspaper in the United States. Through the paper's editor, Amelia Bloomer (1818–1894), Anthony met women involved in the abolitionist movement and in the recently formed woman suffrage (voting rights) movement.

At a temperance meeting in 1851, Anthony met women's rights leader Elizabeth Cady Stanton. They formed a deep personal friendship and a political bond that would last for the rest of their lives. From this point on, Anthony worked tirelessly for the women's suffrage movement. She lectured on women's rights and organized a series of state and national conventions on the issue. She collected signatures for a petition to grant women the right to vote and to own property. Her hard work helped. In 1860, the New York state legislature passed the Married Women's Property Act. It allowed women to enter into contracts and to control their own earnings and property. During the Civil War (1861–65), Anthony and most other members of the women's movement worked toward the emancipation of the slaves. In 1863, she helped form the Women's Loyal League, which supported the policies of

Susan B. Anthony.
Courtesy of the Library of Congress.

President **Abraham Lincoln** (1809–1865; see entry in volume 2). After the war, Anthony and others tried to link women's suffrage with that of the freed slaves. They were unsuccessful.

Anthony and Stanton formed their own organization, the National Woman Suffrage Association. The Fourteenth Amendment (see box in **Andrew Johnson** entry in volume 2), adopted in 1868, had declared that all people born in the United States were citizens and that no legal privileges could be denied to any citizen. Anthony decided to challenge this amendment. Saying that women were citizens and the amendment did not restrict the privilege of voting to men, she registered to vote in Rochester, on November 1, 1872. Four days later, she and fifteen other women voted in the presidential election. All sixteen women were arrested three weeks later, but only Anthony was brought before a court. Her trial, *United States v. Susan B. Anthony,* began on June 17, 1873. The presiding judge opposed women's suffrage and wrote his decision before the trial had started. Refusing to let Anthony testify, he ordered the jury to find her guilty, then sentenced her to pay a $100 fine. She refused, but no further action was taken against her.

Anthony continued to campaign for women's rights. Between 1881 and 1886, she and Stanton published three volumes of the *History of Woman Suffrage,* a collection of writings about the movement's struggle. In 1890, they strengthened the suffrage cause by forming the larger National American Woman Suffrage Association. Through Anthony's determined work, many professional fields became open to women by the end of the nineteenth century. Nevertheless, at the time of her death in Rochester, on March 13, 1906, only four states—Wyoming, Colorado, Idaho, and Utah—had granted suffrage to women. But her crusade carried on, and in 1920, Congress adopted the Nineteenth Amendment, finally giving women throughout America the right to vote.

During Cleveland's first term, the federal government had large budget surpluses (more money was coming in through tax collection than was being spent). Some politicians wanted to spend the excess money on projects that would benefit their home states and, thus, enhance their popularity. Cleveland recognized that the surpluses were a result of high tariff rates.

High tariffs were favored by manufacturers because the taxes added to the cost of foreign goods. Consumers, especially those in poorer regions of the country, were hurt by high tariffs, which added to costs of basic necessities, like clothing. Cleveland spent his entire annual address to Congress in 1887 arguing for tariff reduction. When Congress failed to address the issue, tariffs became a major topic of the 1888 election between Cleveland and his Republican opponent, **Benjamin Harrison** (1833–1901; see entry in volume 3).

Meanwhile, the Cleveland presidency was brightened when he became the first chief executive to be married in the White House. His bride, Frances Folsom (1864–1947; see entry on **Frances Cleveland** in volume 3), was the daughter of Cleveland's former law partner, Oscar Folsom. Cleveland had looked after Folsom's wife, Emma, and their daughter, Frances, after Oscar's death in 1875. At Frances's birth, Cleveland bought the Folsoms a baby carriage as a gift.

When Frances and Emma visited the White House in the spring of 1885, Cleveland and "Frank," as he called her, became secretly engaged. They were married the following June in the White House.

Changing fortunes

Cleveland bet his reelection on the tariff issue. His Republican opponent for the 1888 election, Benjamin Harrison, took the opposing view on the issue: His support for high tariffs made him popular among businessmen. In addition, Harrison was a Civil War hero, making him appealing to veterans of that war, and he was promoted to the public as less of an "Indian supporter." Cleveland received over 100,000 more popular votes than Harrison, but he lost in the Electoral College, 233 to 168. (For more information on the Electoral College, see boxes in **George W. Bush** entry in volume 5.)

Cleveland returned to his law practice in New York after leaving the White House. He spent time fishing off Cape Cod, Massachusetts, and occasionally commenting on issues of the day. He came out strongly against bimetallism, a policy where two precious metals are used to give value to legal tender (bills or coin assigned a certain value). Gold was the single precious metal used as the basis for the value of money in the United States, but there were people during the latter half of the nineteenth century who wanted to include silver as well. Those in favor of silver were generally farmers who lived in western and southern states. They argued that "free silver" would allow the United States to print more money that people could earn and use to buy much needed goods—like food and clothing—that many could not afford. Those against including silver believed that increasing the money supply would lead to inflation, an economic decline in the value of money.

The Harrison administration reversed several policies of Cleveland's administration. U.S. senator **William McKinley** (1843–1901; see entry in volume 3) of Ohio sponsored the McKinley Tariff Act of 1890 which led to higher tariffs, and Harrison eagerly signed into law new pension benefits for veterans and their widows and families. When a revolt in Hawaii led by private American citizens toppled the island's leader, Queen Liliuokalani (lih-LEE-uh-woh-kuh-LON-ee; 1838–1917), Harrison actively sought to annex the island (add it to the United States). Cleveland opposed the action. (See **Grover Cleveland** and **Benjamin Harrison** primary source entries in volume 3).

As the presidential election of 1892 drew near, the nation was divided on many issues. Once again, Democrats turned to Cleveland as their nominee (person chosen as a candidate). Because the McKinley Tariff proved unpopular and Harrison was an uninspiring leader, Democrats believed Cleveland could beat Harrison this time.

The presidential campaign that year was somber. First lady **Caroline Harrison** (1832–1892; see entry in volume 3) had fallen ill. President Harrison refused to leave her to campaign. Cleveland paid his respect by refusing to campaign as well. Cleveland won the popular vote again, this time by over four hundred thousand votes. He won in the Electoral College, 277 to 145. James B. Weaver (1833–1912; see box in **Benjamin Harrison** entry in volume 3), a member of the

Populist Party, which united the interests of farmers and laborers and favored bimetallism, won twenty-two electoral votes in western states.

"His Obstinacy"

Cleveland's second term was made difficult from the beginning. The economy took a nosedive: Over five hundred banks failed in 1893, major railroads went bankrupt, millions of workers became unemployed, and thousands of others went on strike. Cleveland continued to show integrity with his decisions, but his actions, however well reasoned, often proved unpopular. Because he refused to change his views, Cleveland was nicknamed "His Obstinacy."

The financial crisis that began soon after he took office in 1893 remained for much of his second term. In retrospect, historians and economists often blame high tariff rates and overexpansion of the nation's railroads for the country's economic problems. Still, Congress passed an even higher tariff rate during Cleveland's second term. With businesses solidly backing the tariff, Cleveland faced the prospect of having his veto overridden in Congress. He neither signed nor vetoed the legislation, and after ten days it became law.

Overexpansion of railroads led to losses of jobs and reduction of pay, a situation that affected many other industries as well. When the workers who manufactured Pullman train cars went on strike in 1894, they were supported by the American Railway Union. As the nation's railroads came to a halt, Cleveland sent in federal troops to break the strike. Several other incidents of labor unrest troubled the country.

Meanwhile, Cleveland had to confront foreign policy issues as well. He had been disturbed by the American-led revolt in Hawaii in 1891 that overthrew the island's monarchy and established a civil government. Five days after taking office for his second term, Cleveland withdrew a treaty that would have led to annexation of the island. Although Cleveland officially recognized the Republic of Hawaii that had negotiated the treaty, he refused to go forward with annexation. Cleveland viewed the events in Hawaii as an example of imperialism on the part of the United States. (Imperialism is the policy of expansion that favors one government's authority over other nations and groups of people.)

Cleveland twice invoked the Monroe Doctrine (see **James Monroe** primary source entry in volume 1). The doctrine, a policy statement issued in 1823 during the presidency of **James Monroe** (1758–1831; see entry in volume 1), declared the position of the United States against European activity in the Western Hemisphere. Cleveland used the doctrine to help Venezuela and Cuba, respectively, as they battled against European colonizers. A border dispute between Venezuela and British Guiana was eventually settled, but during Cuba's struggle for independence from Spain, Cuba received only diplomatic support from the United States. Cleveland maintained American neutrality (he refused to take sides) while Spanish forces subdued Cuban revolutionaries.

Finally, Cleveland resisted efforts by groups of people who favored printing more currency and adding silver to the nation's reserves. More money would have been available to consumers, but it would have led to inflation. When the nation's gold reserves, which are used to back the value of money, became alarmingly low, Cleveland negotiated with wealthy industrialist J. P. Morgan (1837–1913; see box) to help purchase more gold. The policy proved helpful, but it frustrated many Americans: Morgan grew wealthier, while many people were having problems buying the necessities of life.

Cleveland was unpopular as his term came to a close. Democrats turned to William Jennings Bryan (1860–1925; see box in **William McKinley** entry in volume 3), who supported more radical approaches to fiscal policy. Bryan became their candidate in the 1896 election.

Back to where he began

When Cleveland retired from office in 1897, he returned with his wife and three children to New Jersey, where he had been born sixty years before. The Clevelands would have two more children. Cleveland remained politically active as a member of the Anti-Imperialism League, a group that opposed the United States maintaining the possessions—Cuba, Puerto Rico, and the Philippines—that it won during the Spanish-American War in 1898. Some supporters wanted

J. P. Morgan

As an investment banker, railroad baron, and founder of U.S. Steel Corporation, the nation's first billion-dollar company, J. P. Morgan was deeply involved and influential during a period of aggressive economic growth and industrialism in the United States. He was born John Pierpont Morgan on April 17, 1837, in Hartford, Connecticut, to Junius and Sarah Morgan. His mother came from a preacher's family in Boston, Massachusetts. Morgan's father owned part of a large trading company, and then became partner and later successor to banker George Peabody (1795–1869), an American who made his career in London, England. Junius settled there in 1854 and lived there the rest of his life.

J. P. Morgan was educated in New England and Europe. Seriously ill as a teenager, he had a long and successful recovery in the Azores (a group of islands in the north Atlantic). At age twenty, he began his career as a clerk in a New York bank. Two years later, while traveling in the Caribbean to study the sugar and cotton markets, he bought, without authorization, a cargo of unwanted coffee using his employer's money. The employer complained but accepted the profit of the several thousand dollars he earned by selling the coffee to New Orleans retailers. In 1860, Morgan set up his own company. He had plenty of business from his father in London and also took advantage of many opportunities to buy and sell in the booming commercial city of New York. In 1861, he married Amelia Sturges, who died of tuberculosis (a lung disease) a year later.

Forming a business called J. P. Morgan and Company, Bankers, Morgan traded in gold and on one occasion bought obsolete arms from the federal government in the East and then sold them to General John Charles Frémont (1813–1890; see box in **James K. Polk** entry in volume 2) in the West at an enormous profit. By age twenty-seven, Morgan was a leading financier in the nation's largest city. He helped raise money for the wounded and widowed during the Civil War (1861–65) and worked to establish and enlarge the Young Men's Christian Association (YMCA), an organization devoted to improving the lives of young men. In 1865, he married Frances Tracy, with whom he would have four children. In the summer of 1869, Morgan and his wife rode the new transcontinental railroad to Utah and to California, where they toured extensively by stagecoach and horseback. Returning east, Morgan accepted a new partnership with the powerful Drexels of Philadelphia. He would be a full partner and would head their New York office under the title of Drexel, Morgan, and Company.

Morgan wanted to ensure that railroads were efficiently managed so that stockholders (the owners of a company) and bondholders (those who lend money

J. P. Morgan.
Reproduced by permission of Archive Photos.

to companies) would be properly rewarded for their investments. He helped establish the practice of bringing to railroads large, integrated systems, in which a single corporation controlled main lines and feeders to operate without competition. He brought in other major banking houses, in the United States and abroad, to organize syndicates (a group of companies working together to complete a financial transaction) to help protect investments during times of financial crisis.

Morgan was involved in the finances of the federal government on four major occasions. With other leading bankers, he helped refinance the federal debt under President **Ulysses S. Grant** (1822–1885; see entry in volume 3). In the

summer of 1877, Morgan lent the U.S. Army money to pay its troops after Congress had adjourned without setting aside the funds. Since the army was not authorized to borrow, Morgan paid out more than $2 million at his own risk; Congress, however, repaid the banker. Much more effort was required to save the U.S. Treasury's gold reserve in the depression of 1893. A combination of laws had forced the Treasury to sell gold until it was on the brink of bankruptcy. The Panic of 1893 had generated a flight of moving gold to Europe. To save the situation, Morgan formed a syndicate of American and European bankers to lend gold to the government at acceptable rates and to stop the flow of gold out of the country.

Morgan's greatest triumphs and defeats came at the end of his life. In 1901, he formed the U.S. Steel Corporation, the world's first billion-dollar corporation. Morgan then turned to a merger of the Northern Pacific railroad with its regional rival, the Great Northern. President **Theodore Roosevelt** (1858–1919; see entry in volume 3) ordered an antitrust prosecution, contending that the combination of the two railroads would be too powerful and in violation of antitrust law. The government won the lawsuit in 1904, and the merger fell apart. Morgan, however, was called on in 1907 to lead yet another syndicate of bankers to prevent a financial panic. He died in 1913.

A Selection of Cleveland Landmarks

Grover Cleveland Birthplace State Historic Site. 207 Bloomfield Ave., Caldwell, NJ 07006. (973) 226-1810. Museum and birthplace of the twenty-second and twenty-fourth U.S. president. See http://caldwellnj.com/grover.htm (accessed on July 28, 2000).

Princeton Cemetery. 29 Greenview Ave., Princeton, NJ 08542-3316. (609) 924-1369. Burial site of President and Mrs. Cleveland. See http://www.princetonol.com/patron/cemetery.html (accessed on July 28, 2000).

Cleveland to run again for president in 1904, but he discouraged the idea.

Cleveland lived until June 24, 1908. By that time, he had won back respect as having been an honest and independent politician. During his last years, he was a trustee of Princeton University. (A trustee is a person appointed to help direct the affairs of an institution.) He became friends with the university president, **Woodrow Wilson** (1856–1924; see entry in volume 4), who would later become president of the United States in 1913. Cleveland's last words were fitting: "I have tried so hard to do right!"

Legacy

Grover Cleveland's courageous stands against higher tariffs, American expansionism, and radical economic policies, as well as his honesty, helped provide stability to a troubled nation on the edge of the modern world. Electricity and skyscrapers were becoming commonplace. Power struggles between business and labor—management and unions—were often bitter. That Cleveland remained independent—trying hard to do right, often instead of taking more popular stands—was his finest quality. After almost five decades in which Congress often dominated national politics, Cleveland was the first in a succession of strong presidents who reinstated forceful executive leadership to the nation.

Nevertheless, many of his policies were overturned by his successor, William McKinley. McKinley reinstated high tariff rates before gradually easing them to lower levels in order to further international trade. Cleveland's antiexpansionist views were overwhelmed during McKinley's presidency, which saw the fulfillment of American expansion and the idea of manifest destiny, the belief that American expansionism was meant to happen. McKinley reintroduced the annexation of Hawaii. Following victory in the Spanish-American War, the United States took possession of Cuba, Puerto Rico, and the Philippines.

Cleveland's fiscal policies were generally maintained by McKinley. He, too, was against bimetallism. The economy recovered early in McKinley's presidency. As people went back to work and enjoyed more spending power, McKinley's popularity rose. As chief executive, McKinley was the firm leader of the nation, enjoying the power and independence that Cleveland had brought back to the office of president.

Where to Learn More

Brodsky, Alyn. *Grover Cleveland: A Study in Character.* New York: St. Martin's Press, 2000.

Collins, David R. *Grover Cleveland: 22nd and 24th President of the United States.* Ada, OK: Garrett Educational Corp., 1988.

Forbes, John D. *J. P. Morgan, Jr., 1867–1943.* Charlottesville: University Press of Virginia, 1981.

Jackson, Stanley. *J. P. Morgan: A Biography.* New York: Stein and Day, 1983.

Nevins, Allan. *Grover Cleveland: A Study in Courage.* New York: Dodd, Mead & Co., 1932.

Sherr, Lynn. *Failure Is Impossible: Susan B. Anthony in Her Own Words.* New York: Times Books, 1995.

Weisberg, Barbara. *Susan B. Anthony.* New York: Chelsea House, 1988.

Welch, Richard E., Jr. *The Presidencies of Grover Cleveland.* Lawrence: University Press of Kansas, 1988.

Frances Cleveland

Born July 21, 1864
Buffalo, New York
Died October 29, 1947
Baltimore, Maryland

Married in the White House, she maintained confidence in her husband despite diminishing popularity

When bachelor president **Grover Cleveland** (1837–1908; see entry in volume 3) entertained widow Emma Folsom and her daughter, Frances, in the White House shortly after he became president, gossip swirled about a possible romance. Rumors continued even as the Folsoms left for a European vacation during that summer of 1885. Cleveland, meanwhile, grew impatient with the gossip: "I don't see why the papers keep marrying me to old ladies," the confirmed bachelor reportedly said to an aide.

When the Folsoms returned to the United States in May 1886, reporters were waiting for their ship, which was due to arrive in New York. The reporters wanted to pursue the romance angle. Cleveland's White House secretary, meanwhile, chartered a boat and met the ship out in the harbor. The Folsoms were helped on to the boat, which then sped away to a harbor safe from nosy reporters.

Meanwhile, Cleveland arrived in New York to attend Memorial Day festivities. He watched a parade. Inspired by news of a possible presidential romance, a marching band suddenly began playing a wedding march and then a popular

"I want you to take good care of all the furniture. I want to find everything just as it is now when we come back again."

Frances Cleveland, to a White House caretaker, following the end of her husband's first term

Frances Cleveland.
Courtesy of the Library of Congress.

song, "He's Going to Marry Yum-Yum." The next morning, newspapers ran stories about Emma Folsom, who was rumored as the president's bride-to-be. Later that day, the official announcement came that the forty-nine-year-old president was indeed engaged. However, he was not marrying the woman targeted by those who spread rumors. Instead, he was marrying her daughter, twenty-two-year-old Frances Folsom, whom he affectionately called "Frank." They had become secretly engaged before the Folsoms' European vacation.

On June 2, 1886, President Cleveland became the first chief executive to be married in the White House. Outside the White House grounds, the group of reporters that had been waiting on New York docks was joined by a throng of peers from all over the country. The mob of journalists followed the newlywed Clevelands on their Maryland honeymoon, where Cleveland complained that he could get no freedom from the press. After the couple returned to Washington, D.C., Cleveland wrote a letter that was published in the *New York Evening Post.* In the letter, he referred to snooping reporters as "a colossal impertinence."

Carriage, love, and marriage

Cleveland had known Frances since her birth in 1864. He gave her parents a carriage as a gift for their newborn baby. Cleveland and Oscar Folsom, Frances's father, were law partners in Buffalo, New York. When Oscar died in a horse and buggy accident in 1875, Cleveland administered the Folsom estate. He helped ensure that Emma and Frances would live comfortably, and he helped support Frances's education.

Cleveland was elected mayor of Buffalo in 1881 and governor of New York in 1882. He and Frances wrote letters to each other at that time. She had recently begun studying at Wells College in New York. Cleveland was elected president in 1884. When the couple married in 1886, Frances Cleveland became the youngest-ever first lady at the age of twenty-two.

Prior to marrying, the president said to his sister, Rose Elizabeth Cleveland (1846–1918), that "a good wife loves her husband and her country with no desire to run either." During the wedding ceremony, however, he had traditional wed-

ding vows altered to omit the word "obey." (Cleveland's sister served as White House hostess during the period between Cleveland's inauguration in 1885 and his wedding in June 1886. Strongly independent, "Libbie" Cleveland was a proponent for equal rights between the sexes and for women's voting rights. She was a teacher at a girl's school and a respected writer of essays on literature.)

Famous American composer John Philip Sousa (1854–1932) conducted the U.S. Marine Band, which played at the wedding reception. (Sousa's fame would increase within the next dozen years after writing such well-known marches as "Semper Fidelis" [1888] and "The Stars and Stripes Forever" [1897].) The Cleveland wedding was a small ceremony attended only by Cabinet officials (presidential advisors) and a few close friends of the Clevelands. The train of Frances Cleveland's wedding dress was nearly as long as the receiving line, the line that formed as the newlyweds greeted guests.

President Grover Cleveland was the first president to be married in the White House when he married Frances Folsom on June 2, 1886. *Courtesy of the Library of Congress.*

Popular first lady

Vivacious and attractive, Frances Cleveland was a popular first lady. She was soon more popular than her husband. A flock of journalists followed the Clevelands, as much to report on events involving the first lady as to provide information on the Cleveland administration. There were rumors that the Clevelands were having marital difficulties during the presidential campaign of 1888, but the first lady denied such reports.

Cleveland lost the election of 1888. As the couple was leaving the White House shortly before the inauguration of **Benjamin Harrison** (1833–1901; see entry in volume 3), Frances Cleveland spoke to a caretaker. She told him, "I want you to take good care of all the furniture," and added, "I want to find everything just as it is now when we come back again." The Clevelands were, indeed, back in the White House following the presidential election of 1892.

In her role as first lady, Frances Cleveland held two receptions each week. She made sure that one reception was open to the public and held on Saturday afternoon, when women with jobs were free to attend. At one reception, she personally greeted over eight thousand guests.

A long and happy life

After the president's defeat in 1888, the Clevelands lived in New York City, where their first child, Ruth (1891–1904), was born. Frances Cleveland, meanwhile, had remained so popular that she was often pictured with candidate Cleveland on his campaign posters for the 1892 election. Much of her time during the president's second term was spent caring for the couple's children, two of whom were born while the Clevelands were in the White House. Esther (1893–1980) was born in 1893, and Marion in 1895. A son, Richard (1897–1974), was born shortly after the Clevelands left the White House in 1897. Their youngest child, Francis Grover (1903–1995), was born in 1903 in Princeton, New Jersey, where the couple retired.

The Clevelands often entertained the faculty members and students of Princeton University. They became friends with **Woodrow Wilson** (1856–1924; see entry in volume 4), the president of Princeton at the time. Wilson would be elected president of the United States in 1912. Cleveland occasionally wrote articles on political matters and was approached about running for president in 1904. He declined. Cleveland's health began failing soon after. He died in 1908 at age seventy-two. His widow, Frances, was forty-four.

Frances continued to live in Princeton and was involved in fundraising activities for several schools, including the school she had attended, Wells College. In 1913, she married Thomas J. Preston Jr., an archaeology professor at Princeton. She lived a long and happy life, dying at age eighty-three in 1947. Shortly before her death, she attended a White House luncheon arranged by President **Harry S. Truman** (1884–1972; see entry in volume 4) and was introduced to World War II hero **Dwight D. Eisenhower** (1890–1969; see entry in volume 4), who would follow Truman as president. After learning that Frances had lived in Washington, D.C., many years before, Eisenhower asked her where in town she had resided. "In the White House," she responded.

Where to Learn More

Boller, Paul F. *Presidential Wives.* New York: Oxford University Press, 1998.

Sinnott, Susan. *Frances Folsom Cleveland, 1864–1947.* New York: Children's Press, 1998.

Cleveland's Message to Congress Opposing the Annexation of Hawaii

Delivered on December 18, 1893; excerpted from
The Annals of America

President Cleveland rescinds a treaty to annex the Hawaiian Islands because the native monarchy was overthrown by American citizens

In 1892, the monarchy that ruled Hawaii was overthrown by a group led by American businessmen. This led to a new constitutional government. That government negotiated a treaty of annexation with the United States. President **Benjamin Harrison** (1833–1901; see entry in volume 3) presented the treaty to the U.S. Senate for ratification in February 1893 (see **Benjamin Harrison** primary source entry in volume 3).

Before the treaty could be approved, President Harrison's term of office expired in March 1893. He was succeeded by **Grover Cleveland** (1837–1908; see entry in volume 3), who opposed the treaty. Cleveland was among those Americans who warned against American imperialism—actions by a stronger nation to dominate a weaker one. Cleveland withdrew the treaty from the Senate and supported efforts to return Hawaii's deposed monarch, Queen Liliuokalani (lih-LEE-uh-woh-kuh-LON-ee; 1838–1917), to the throne. Cleveland officially described his reasons for withdrawing the treaty during his annual message to Congress in December 1893.

". . . the United States, in aiming to maintain itself as one of the most enlightened nations, would do its citizens gross injustice if it applied to its international relations any other than a high standard of honor and morality."

Grover Cleveland

Things to remember while reading an excerpt from President Cleveland's message to Congress opposing the annexation of Hawaii:

- America was restless during the 1880s and 1890s, as reflected in several political developments. President Cleveland, for example, had won election in 1884, lost in 1888, and was elected again in 1892—becoming the only president to serve nonconsecutive terms. He was favored by those who opposed high tariff rates (taxes placed on imported goods) and those who were concerned that the United States was becoming an imperialist nation—attempting to take advantage of weaker nations. Cleveland was respected as president, but many of his policies, including lower tariff rates and anti-annexation sentiments toward Hawaii, were overturned by his successor, **William McKinley** (1843–1901; see entry in volume 3).

- The following excerpt focuses on Cleveland's reasons for withdrawing the treaty. He explained that the treaty was negotiated after the Hawaiian monarchy was deposed by a group primarily led by Americans. Cleveland wanted to investigate whether their actions were illegal. During the course of his address, he suggested that the American-led revolt was carefully planned.

Excerpt from President Cleveland's message to Congress opposing the annexation of Hawaii

*When the present administration entered upon its duties, the Senate had under consideration a treaty providing for the annexation of the Hawaiian Islands to the territory of the United States. Surely under our Constitution and laws the enlargement of our limits is a manifestation of the highest attribute of **sovereignty**, and if entered upon as an executive act, all things relating to the transaction should be clear and free from suspicion. Additional importance attached to this particular treaty of annexation because it contemplated a departure from unbroken American tradition in providing for the addition to our territory of islands of the sea more than two thousand miles removed from our nearest coast. . . .*

Sovereignty: Authority.

I conceived it to be my duty, therefore, to withdraw the treaty from the Senate for examination, and meanwhile to cause an accurate, full, and impartial investigation to be made of the facts attending the **subversion** *of the constitutional government of Hawaii and the installment in its place of the Provisional Government. . . .*

As I apprehend the situation, we are brought face to face with the following conditions:

> The lawful government of Hawaii was overthrown without the drawing of a sword or the firing of a shot by a process every step of which, it may safely be asserted, is directly traceable to and dependent for its success upon the agency of the United States acting through its diplomatic and naval representatives.

But for the notorious **predilections** *of the United States minister for annexation, the Committee of Safety, which should be called the Committee of Annexation, would never have existed.*

> But for the landing of the United States forces upon false **pretexts** respecting the danger to life and property, the committee would never have exposed themselves to the pains and penalties of treason by undertaking the subversion of the queen's government.

> But for the presence of the United States forces in the immediate vicinity and in position to afford all needed protection and support, the committee would not have proclaimed the Provisional Government from the steps of the government building.

> And, finally, but for the lawless occupation of Honolulu under false pretexts by the United States forces, and but for Minister [John L.] Stevens' [U.S. minister to the Hawaiian Islands in 1889] recognition of the Provisional Government when the United States forces were its sole support and constituted its only military strength, the queen and her government would never have yielded to the Provisional Government, even for a time and for the sole purpose of submitting her case to the enlightened justice of the United States.

Believing, therefore, that the United States could not, under the circumstances disclosed, annex the islands without justly incurring the **imputation** *of acquiring them by unjustifiable methods, I shall not again submit the treaty of annexation to the Senate for its consideration, and in the instructions to Minister [Albert S.] Willis [U.S. minister to the Hawaiian Islands from 1893 to 1897], a copy of which accompanies this message, I have directed him to so inform the Provisional Government.*

But in the present instance our duty does not, in my opinion, end with refusing to **consummate** *this questionable transaction. It*

Subversion: Undermine.

Predilections: Preferences.

Pretexts: Claims.

Imputation: Burden.

Consummate: Bring to conclusion.

has been the boast of our government that it seeks to do justice in all things without regard to the strength or weakness of those with whom it deals. I mistake the American people if they favor the **odious** doctrine that there is no such thing as international morality; that there is one law for a strong nation and another for a weak one, and that even by indirection a strong power may **with impunity despoil** a weak one of its territory.

By an act of war, committed with the participation of a diplomatic representative of the United States and without authority of Congress, the government of a feeble but friendly and confiding people has been overthrown. A substantial wrong has thus been done which a due regard for our national character as well as the rights of the injured people requires we should endeavor to repair. The Provisional Government has not assumed a **republican** or other constitutional form, but has remained a mere executive council or **oligarchy**, set up without the **assent** of the people. It has not sought to find a permanent basis of popular support and has given no evidence of an intention to do so. Indeed, the representatives of that government assert that the people of Hawaii are unfit for popular government and frankly avow that they can be best ruled by arbitrary or **despotic** power.

The law of nations is founded upon reason and justice, and the rules of conduct governing individual relations between citizens or subjects of a civilized state are equally applicable as between enlightened nations. The considerations that international law is without a court for its enforcement and that obedience to its commands practically depends upon good faith instead of upon the mandate of a superior **tribunal** only give additional sanction to the law itself and brand any deliberate infraction of it not merely as a wrong but as a disgrace. A man of true honor protects the unwritten word which binds his conscience more scrupulously, if possible, than he does the bond a breach of which subjects him to legal liabilities, and the United States, in aiming to maintain itself as one of the most enlightened nations, would do its citizens gross injustice if it applied to its international relations any other than a high standard of honor and morality.

On that ground the United States cannot properly be put in the position of **countenancing** a wrong after its commission any more than in that of consenting to it in advance. On that ground it cannot allow itself to refuse to redress an injury inflicted through an abuse of power by officers clothed with its authority and wearing its

Odious: Detested.

With impunity: Without punishment.

Despoil: Rob.

Republican: A form of government in which political authorities are elected by citizens.

Oligarchy: Government in which a small group exercises control for their own benefit.

Assent: Agreement.

Despotic: Absolute.

Tribunal: Court of law.

Countenancing: Acknowledging.

| **Complete American Presidents Sourcebook**

*uniform; and on the same ground, if a feeble but friendly state is in danger of being robbed of its independence and its sovereignty by a misuse of the name and power of the United States, the United States cannot fail to vindicate its honor and its sense of justice by an earnest effort to make all possible **reparation.***

*These principles apply to the present case with irresistible force when the special conditions of the queen's surrender of her sovereignty are recalled. She surrendered, not to the Provisional Government but to the United States. She surrendered, not absolutely and permanently but temporarily and conditionally until such time as the facts could be considered by the United States. Furthermore, the Provisional Government **acquiesced** in her surrender in that manner and on those terms, not only by tacit consent but through the positive acts of some members of the government who urged her peaceable submission, not merely to avoid bloodshed but because she could place implicit reliance upon the justice of the United States and that the whole subject would be finally considered at Washington. (Adler, pp. 480–82)*

Reparation: Compensation.

Acquiesced: Passively accepted.

What happened next . . .

By the time Cleveland withdrew the treaty, revolutionaries in Hawaii were firmly in power and refused to yield to Cleveland's pressures for a return to monarchy. Realizing that annexation was being delayed, the revolutionaries began to establish an independent republic. On May 30, 1894, they held a constitutional convention in Honolulu, and on July 4 the constitution creating the new Republic of Hawaii took effect.

Cleveland was successful in making Americans consider whether the nation should continue to pursue foreign relations that bordered on being imperialistic. Many Americans, however, were more concerned about increasing and benefiting from international trade. The anti-imperialist views of Cleveland and fellow Democrat William Jennings Bryan (1860–1925; see box in **William McKinley** entry in volume 3) were not as well received as the more aggressive international approach of Republican presidents Benjamin Harrison and William McKinley. In March 1897, McKinley succeeded Cleveland as president. In 1898, both houses of Congress approved a joint resolution to annex Hawaii. A joint resolution is different than a treaty: resolutions require only a majority vote in both houses of Congress, while a treaty requires two-thirds ratification by the Senate. President McKinley signed the resolution on July 7, 1898, and the formal transfer of Hawaiian sovereignty to the United States took place in Honolulu on August 12, 1898. On June 14, 1900, Hawaii became a U.S. territory, making all its citizens U.S. citizens.

Since the arrival of whites to Hawaii in the late eighteenth century, natives of the island lost their religion, land, and traditions; with the overthrow of the monarchy, they lost their independence. That was the situation Cleveland had hoped to avoid.

Did you know . . .

- The Hawaiian Islands were originally settled by Polynesians sometime between A.D. 400 and 1000. In 1768, English voyager Captain James Cook (1728–1779) was the first European to reach the island. Hawaii was a U.S. territory when Japanese airplanes bombed the U.S. naval base at Pearl Harbor in 1941, which led the United States to enter World War II (1939–45). Hawaii, which is made up of eight islands—Hawaii, Kahoolawe, Kauai, Lanai, Maui, Molokai, Niihau, and Oahu—became a state in 1959.

Where to Learn More

Adler, Mortimer J., ed. *The Annals of America. Volume 1: Great Issues in American Life: A Conspectus.* Chicago: Encyclopedia Britannica, 1968.

Gillis, James Andrew. *The Hawaiian Incident: An Examination of Mr. Cleveland's Attitude Toward the Revolution of 1893.* Boston: Lee and Shepard, 1897. Reprint, Freeport, NY: Books for Libraries Press, 1970.

Hollingsworth, Joseph R. *The Whirligig of Politics: The Democracy of Cleveland and Bryan.* Chicago: University of Chicago Press, 1963.

Hugins, Roland. *Grover Cleveland: A Study in Political Courage.* Washington, DC: The Anchor-Lee Publishing Company, 1922.

Benjamin Harrison

Twenty-third president (1889–1893)

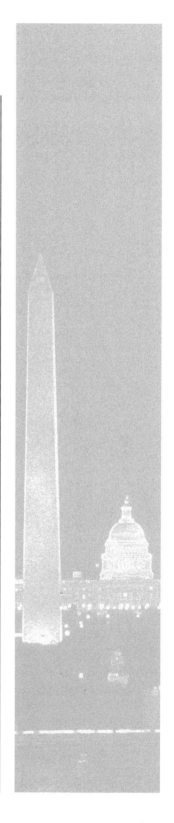

Benjamin Harrison

Born August 20, 1833
North Bend, Ohio
Died March 13, 1901
Indianapolis, Indiana

Twenty-third president of the United States
(1889–1893)

"Centennial president" pursued U.S. interests abroad and helped establish the United States as a power in world politics

"The law, the will of the majority [of Americans] . . . is the only king to which we bow."

Benjamin Harrison

Benjamin Harrison was a soft-spoken man who patiently went about his business as a lawyer and as a politician. There were no major events during his presidential administration (1889–93), but he signed into law several important economic measures and sought to expand the Union. Montana, North Dakota, South Dakota, Washington, Idaho, and Wyoming became states during his presidency, and he supported measures that helped several other territories—Utah, Oklahoma, and Hawaii—enter the Union after he left office. At the beginning of Harrison's term in 1889, the number of states in the Union was thirty-eight; when he left office in 1891, the number was forty-four.

The most difficult challenges Harrison faced as president occurred in foreign relations. The governments of the United States and Great Britain argued over fishing rights in the Bering Straits around the Alaska Territory. Anti-Italian sentiments in New Orleans caused a major diplomatic crisis between the United States and Italy. The United States confronted Chile over the deaths of two American sailors in that nation. After the monarchy of Queen Liliuokalani (lih-LEE-

Benjamin Harrison.
Courtesy of the Library of Congress.

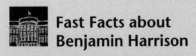

Fast Facts about Benjamin Harrison

Full name: Benjamin Harrison

Born: August 20, 1833

Died: March 13, 1901

Burial site: Crown Hill Cemetery, Indianapolis, Indiana

Parents: John and Elizabeth Irwin Harrison

Spouse: Caroline Lavinia Scott (1832–1892; m. 1853); Mary Scott Lord Dimmick (1858–1948; m. 1896)

Children: Russell Benjamin (1854–1936); Mary Scott (1858–1930); unnamed girl (died at birth in 1861); Elizabeth (1897–1955)

Religion: Presbyterian

Education: Miami University (B.A., 1852)

Occupation: Lawyer

Government positions: U.S. senator from Indiana

Political party: Republican

Dates as president: March 4, 1889–March 4, 1893

Age upon taking office: 55

uh-woh-kuh-LON-ee; 1838–1917) of Hawaii was overturned in a revolution led by Americans, Harrison attempted to annex the island (add it to the United States).

Harrison was an effective president but not a powerful or an inspiring one. Like many administrations of the period from 1865 to 1896, Harrison's was continually challenged by congressional actions, whereas the general public was more interested in regional concerns. Harrison received one hundred thousand fewer votes than his Democratic opponent, incumbent president Democrat **Grover Cleveland** (1837–1908; see entry in volume 3), in the 1888 presidential election. But Harrison won most of the large states for a sure victory in the Electoral College (233 to 168), a body of representatives officially responsible for electing the president by casting their state's electoral votes. (For more information on the Electoral College, see boxes in **George W. Bush** entry in volume 5.)

After failing to win reelection in 1892, Harrison returned to his law practice and served as an attorney in important international trials. He wrote a book, *This Country of Ours,* that explains how the federal government operates.

Little Ben and the family tree

It is not surprising that Benjamin Harrison became involved in politics. His grandfather, **William Henry Harrison** (1773–1841; see entry in volume 2), was elected president in 1840, when young Ben was seven years old. Ben's great-

Benjamin Harrison Timeline

1776: Benjamin Harrison's great-grandfather, also named Benjamin Harrison, is one of the signers of the Declaration of Independence

1833: Benjamin Harrison is born in Ohio

1840: William Henry Harrison, Benjamin's grandfather, is elected president when young Ben is seven years old

1854: Benjamin Harrison opens law practice in Indianapolis

1862: Begins fighting in Civil War (1861–65); finishes the war as brigadier general

1876: Loses Indiana governor's race

1881–87: Serves in U.S. Senate

1888: Defeats incumbent Grover Cleveland to become the "centennial president," elected to office one hundred years after George Washington became the first U.S. president

1889–93: Serves as twenty-third U.S. president

1892: Loses presidential election to former president Cleveland

1901: Dies in Indiana

grandfather, also named Benjamin Harrison (1726–1791), was one of the signers of the Declaration of Independence and later served as governor of Virginia. A Harrison ancestor named Thomas served as an official for Oliver Cromwell (1599–1658), a leader of the English Revolution (1640–60) that overthrew the monarchy of King Charles I (1600–1649); Thomas Harrison was later beheaded for his involvement in the revolution, and his descendants fled to America. Ben's father, John (1804–1878), was elected to Congress in 1854, when Harrison was twenty-one years old.

Benjamin Harrison was born on his grandfather's farm in North Bend, Ohio, on August 20, 1833, the second of the six children of John and Elizabeth Harrison. He was raised on his parents' four-hundred-acre farm nearby. Harrison performed chores as a youngster, attended school, and spent his spare time swimming and hunting. He moved on to Farmer's College near Cincinnati, Ohio, and then transferred to the University of Miami in Ohio, where he graduated in 1852. He was an excellent student and participated in debates. Harrison became deeply religious around this time and considered becoming a Presbyterian minister. He eventually chose to study law instead.

Words to Know

Annex: To add on to an existing thing; annexing a territory, for example, means that a nation officially adds another territory to its possessions.

Arbitration: When a neutral third party settles an issue involving two opposing sides.

Bar: A term that encompasses all certified lawyers—those who have passed all official requirements (the bar exam) to be certified as lawyers.

Confederate: Relating to and representing the Southern states that seceded from the United States in the 1860s and fought against the Union during the American Civil War (1861–65).

Dark horse: A term that describes a little-known candidate who shows marginal promise but could finish surprisingly strong.

Electoral College: A body officially responsible for electing the president of the United States. In presidential elections, the candidate who receives the most popular votes in a particular state wins all of that state's electoral votes. Votes are distributed among states in ratios based on population. A candidate must win a majority of electoral votes (over fifty percent) in order to win the presidency.

Military tribunal: A court presided over by military officials to try cases in an area under a state of war.

Reparations: Payments for damage caused by acts of hostility.

Populism: An agricultural movement of rural areas between the Mississippi River and the Rocky Mountains of the late nineteenth century that united the interests of farmers and laborers. In 1891, the movement formed a national political party, the People's Party, whose members were called Populists. Populist ideals remained popular even when the party faded early in the twentieth century.

Tariffs: Taxes placed on imported goods to raise their prices and make them less attractive to consumers than goods produced in the home country.

In 1853, Harrison married Caroline Livinia Scott (1832–1892; see entry on **Caroline Harrison** in volume 3). They had been friends for several years and fell in love while they both attended school in Oxford, Ohio; he was a student at the University of Miami, and she attended the Oxford Female Institute. Her father, a Presbyterian minister, presided over the wedding ceremony. The couple would have three children, one of whom died at birth.

When the Civil War broke out, Benjamin Harrison joined the army as a colonel. *Courtesy, Library of Congress.*

Benjamin Harrison's father, John, has the distinction of being the only man in U.S. history to be the son of one president and the father of another.

Harrison was admitted to the bar (the legal profession) in 1854. He decided to open a law office in Indianapolis, Indiana. He and Caroline would maintain a home there for the rest of their lives.

Harrison gradually developed a distinguished law practice. As a lawyer, he was known for his careful, polite, and persistent cross-examinations of witnesses. He became involved in presidential politics as a Republican—campaigning locally for John C. Frémont (1813–1890; see box in **James K. Polk** entry in volume 2) in 1856 and **Abraham Lincoln** (1809–1865; see entry in volume 2) in 1860. He became city attorney for Indianapolis. In 1858, he was elected secretary of the Republican State Central Committee.

In 1862, during the Civil War (1861–65), Harrison was commissioned as a colonel and charged with recruiting and preparing soldiers to fight in the Seventieth Indiana Volunteer Infantry. Short and stocky, Harrison was nicknamed "Little Ben" by his soldiers, who respected his seriousness and determination. After fighting successfully in a few small battles in Kentucky, Harrison's group came under the leadership of General William Tecumseh Sherman (1820–1891). Harrison took part in the key battles of Atlanta and Peach Tree Creek. He was cited "for ability and manifest energy and gallantry in command of brigades." By the end of the war in 1865, he attained the rank of brigadier general.

"Kid Glove" Harrison overcomes defeat

After the war ended in 1865, Harrison returned to Indianapolis and resumed his law practice and his involvement in Republican politics. He was selected as the defense lawyer in 1871 when the government was sued for $100,000 by Lambdin Milligan. Milligan was a Southern civilian and secret member of a Confederate group supporting the states that had separated from the United States. Accused by Federal troops of inciting (stirring up) a rebellion, he was tried before a military tribunal, found guilty, and sentenced to death. (A military tribunal is a court headed by military officials.) His case was eventually heard by the Supreme Court, which overturned the conviction. The Court ruled that the case should have been tried in a civil court rather than by a tribunal of Federal forces occupying the South.

By the end of the Civil War, Benjamin Harrison had been promoted to brigadier general. Pictured with Harrison (far left) are fellow Civil War commanders (left to right): General William T. Ward, Colonel Daniel Dustin, and General William Cogswell.
Photograph by Mathew Brady. Reproduced by permission of the Corbis Corporation.

In the subsequent civil case, Harrison made the convincing argument that the tribunal had acted in good faith and was performing a normal procedure. The jury ruled in favor of Milligan, but his compensation (money received) for damages was set at only $5.

Harrison's professional career prospered. He became a more powerful force within the Republican Party, even though he kept losing when he ran for office. He tried but failed to win the Republican nomination for governor of Indiana in 1872. In 1876, he lost the gubernatorial (governor's) election to James D. "Blue Jeans" Williams (1808–1880), a farmer who got his nickname for the plain clothes he wore. Harrison's mild nature led his opponents to nickname him "Kid Glove Harrison."

Nevertheless, Harrison emerged as leader of the state Republican Party. In 1879, President **Rutherford B. Hayes** (1822–1893; see entry in volume 3) appointed Harrison to head of the Mississippi River Commission. Harrison was responsible for developing economic activity along the river, a position that gave him exposure in several states. At the 1880 Republican convention, Harrison was one of the early supporters of **James A. Garfield** (1831–1881; see entry in volume 3), who emerged as the convention's dark-horse nominee (a little-known candidate), even though he was not one of the three leading contenders when the convention began.

Harrison won his first election when the Indiana legislature voted him to the U.S. Senate in 1881. During his tenure (term of office) as senator, he supported many of the same causes that he would later champion as president: statehood for the Dakota territory (the measure failed); creation of a civil government for the Alaska territory (a step towards statehood); support for civil rights (regulating the power of railroads to remove settlers and Native Americans from land adjacent to railroads); backing high tariffs to protect American businesses; and supporting the expansion of government pensions and providing additional benefits to Civil War veterans. In an 1886 speech on the Senate floor, he shamed Democrats by coming to the defense of a poor widow who was fired from her post office position in a small Illinois town. She had been replaced by a Democratic Party supporter.

Harrison lost his reelection bid to the Senate in 1887. The Indiana legislature, which was responsible for electing the state's U.S. senators, favored his Democratic counterpart by one vote. But Harrison remained a nationally known figure for his family background and the integrity he had displayed in Congress. He was popular with Civil War veterans and well respected in key Electoral College states of the Midwest.

Republican official H. T. Michner began a quiet, behind-the-scenes campaign to have Harrison nominated as the Republican presidential candidate for the 1888 election. Harrison won the nomination and campaigned effectively against his Democratic opponent, Grover Cleveland. His support for high tariffs and his appeal to Civil War veterans (Cleveland had not fought in the war) helped him carry large states of the East and Midwest. The result was an Electoral College victory (233 votes to 168), even though Cleveland received over one hundred thousand more popular votes.

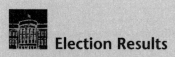

Election Results

1888

Presidential / Vice presidential candidates	Popular votes	Presidential electoral votes
Benjamin Harrison / Levi P. Morton (Republican)	5,444,337	233
Grover Cleveland / Allen G. Thurman (Democratic)	5,540,309	168

Former secretary of the Treasury John Sherman was the early leader in the race for the Republican nomination. Harrison went from fifth place on the first ballot to his victory on the eighth ballot. On the Democratic side, former Ohio senator Thurman was chosen as the incumbent president Cleveland's running mate; Cleveland's previous running mate, Thomas A. Hendricks, had died during his first year as vice president.

A "legal deal"

Harrison had promised a "legal deal" in his campaign for the presidency. It had been common for incoming presidents to reward their party supporters with government jobs, but Harrison proved to be more independent. Two future presidents, **Theodore Roosevelt** (1858–1919; see entry in volume 3) and **William Howard Taft** (1857–1930; see entry in volume 3) held federal positions during Harrison's tenure, as did many lawyers. However, in bypassing some Republican supporters, Harrison lost support from his own party in Congress. The situation grew worse when a Democratic majority was elected to the House of Representatives in 1890.

Still, Harrison was effective working with Congress in several areas. The McKinley Tariff, which placed high taxes on many imported goods, was signed into law in 1890. The Sherman Antitrust Act, which made it illegal for large corporations to force out competing, smaller businesses from a particular market, was also passed that year. Harrison's continued support for Civil War veterans led to the authorization of government funds for disabled veterans even if their injuries occurred after the war. Harrison pushed for several other pensions (money received because of disability or for past service) to be enacted.

Harrison faced a series of international disputes. A conflict with Great Britain over fishing rights in the Bering Sea was eventually settled in arbitration (a process in which two opposing parties in a dispute submit their points of view to a neutral

President Benjamin Harrison speaks from a grandstand.
Reproduced by permission of the Corbis Corporation.

third party to settle the issue). When American sailors were injured in an unprovoked attack in Chile, Harrison threatened to end diplomatic relations with that country. The dispute was quickly settled by an apology and reparations (payments for damage caused by acts of war) from the Chilean government. Harrison also faced a crisis with Italy. A case concerning Italian-based organized crime in New Orleans escalated into violence: A policeman was killed, and then eleven Italians were murdered by an angry mob. In an apologetic letter to the Italian government, Harrison denounced the lynching (an execution without a trial and due process of law). To answer the Italian government's insistence that the federal government should prosecute the offenders, the letter carefully explained that the case would be subject to state legal procedures, rather than federal jurisdiction, as mandated by the Constitution.

In Hawaii, meanwhile, Americans began a revolt against the native leader Queen Liliuokalani, who had begun to take measures against the growing American business influence on the Hawaiian Islands. Seeking to extend American naval bases, Harrison did nothing when a revolution overthrew the queen and resulted in an American-led civil government. Harrison backed the new government. He signed a treaty with them and proposed the annexation of Hawaii.

Harrison was viewed as an honest but dull politician, never quite able to rally great enthusiasm for his causes. The 1892 presidential election, which again pitted Harrison and Cleveland, was somber: Harrison's wife Caroline was gravely ill. The president refused to campaign, choosing to remain with his wife. Cleveland showed his respect by refusing to campaign as well. Caroline died shortly before the election.

The only real excitement of the campaign occurred in western states, where Populist candidate James B. Weaver (1833–1912; see box) was enthusiastically supported by farmers and settlers. (Populism was a rural political movement that united the interests of farmers and laborers; see box.) Meanwhile, Harrison's chances were hurt by labor unrest—several strikes occurred throughout the country—and by predictions of an economic downturn. Cleveland had attracted over 100,000 more votes than Harrison in 1888; in 1892, the difference grew to over 400,000 popular votes, and Cleveland won election handily with 277 electoral votes to Harrison's 149 votes. Weaver, the well-liked Populist of the West, captured twenty-two electoral votes.

An active aftermath

Harrison mourned the death of his wife through the remainder of his term. He returned to the Indianapolis home

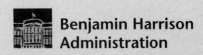

Benjamin Harrison Administration

Administration Dates
March 4, 1889–March 4, 1893

Vice President
Levi P. Morton (1889–93)

Cabinet

Secretary of State
James G. Blaine (1889–92)
John W. Foster (1892–93)

Secretary of the Treasury
William Windom (1889–91)
Charles Foster (1891–93)

Secretary of War
Redfield Proctor (1889–91)
Stephen B. Elkins (1891–93)

Attorney General
William H. H. Miller (1889–93)

Secretary of the Navy
Benjamin F. Tracy (1889–93)

Postmaster General
John Wanamaker (1889–93)

Secretary of the Interior
John W. Noble (1889–93)

Secretary of Agriculture
Jeremiah M. Rusk (1889–93)

What's in a Nickname?

Benjamin Harrison is considered to have been one of the dullest presidents. His low key demeanor did not exactly inspire lively nicknames: His Civil War troops called him "Little Ben" (he was only five feet six inches tall), political opponents in Indiana called him "Kid Glove Harrison" (for his mild nature), and he was known as the "centennial president" for taking office one hundred years after George Washington.

On the other hand, Harrison's grandfather, William Henry Harrison, the nation's ninth president, was known as a more charismatic, vigorous individual. As a famous general, he defeated Chief Tecumseh, then ran for president with the famous nickname "Tippecanoe." The public's fond memories of Grandfather Harrison often annoyed Grandson Harrison. According to *The American President* (Philip B. Kunhardt Jr., Philip B. Kunhardt III, and Peter W. Kunhardt, 1999), Benjamin Harrison sought to distance himself from his famous grandfather. "My ambition is for quietness rather than for publicity," he said. "I want it understood that I am the grandson of nobody."

that they had shared for almost forty years, but he was soon active again. He lectured on Constitutional law at Stanford University and wrote a book, *This Country of Ours,* that was published in 1897. Meanwhile, he remarried in 1896 and fathered a daughter the following year, at age sixty-five. His second wife, Mary Scott Lord Dimmick (1858–1948), was a niece of Caroline Harrison. The new Mrs. Harrison had been widowed in 1882, less than three months after she was married. In 1899, former president Harrison helped represent the nation of Venezuela in a border dispute, and he was appointed to the international court of arbitration at The Hague (in the Netherlands) the following year. After falling ill, Harrison returned home again to Indianapolis, where he died on March 13, 1901.

Legacy

Benjamin Harrison's most noteworthy accomplishments rest in avoiding or settling several international disputes. After years of isolationism, the United States was finding itself increasingly involved in international conflicts, which continued after Harrison's presidency. Harrison foresaw the trend: He supported appropriations bills to expand the fleet of the navy, and his interest in annexing Hawaii was at least partly due to its prime location for naval operations in the Pacific Ocean.

Grover Cleveland, Harrison's successor, withdrew the annexation treaty from Congress, but Cleveland's successor, William McKinley, reintroduced the measure. Hawaii officially became a U.S. territory in 1900. McKinley also presided during the Spanish-American War (1896) when

The Emergence of Populism

The concerns of farmers were largely ignored in the post–Civil War (1861–65) era as industry brought prosperity to America. Agricultural prices sagged during the 1870s and 1880s, and Eastern, urban-based trusts dominated distribution of farm products. In the South and West, where agriculture remained the backbone of the economy, the problem was especially critical. Out of these frustrations, a political movement emerged to challenge the established Democratic and Republican parties. The People's Party, better known as the Populist Party, became powerful in those regions during the 1880s and 1890s. Farmers were joined by urban laborers, who shared their problems as consumers making wages that could barely pay for basic necessities.

Populists wanted to increase the money supply, which would circulate more money among farmers and laborers. Among programs that were later adopted, Populists called for an income tax that would shift the burden of taxation from land to income; an eight-hour work day for wage earners; and the popular election of U.S. senators (senators were elected by the state governments in those days). The Populist movement gained enough strength to elect numerous candidates to statewide and national offices, and by 1892 the Populists mounted a presidential campaign with General James B. Weaver of Iowa as their leader.

The Populists' platform in 1892 called for free and unlimited coinage of silver and government ownership of the railroad and telegraph industries. Weaver polled over one million votes and carried four states, placing third behind winner Grover Cleveland and President Benjamin Harrison. The presidential campaign divided the working people along racial lines. Southern blacks lined up with the Populists, while western and southern white farmers clung to the Democratic Party, fearful of losing what little political clout they had. The solid black vote for the Populists and a continuing cycle of poverty in the South led to a backlash by whites, who enacted Jim Crow laws that placed voting restrictions aimed at black citizens.

The Populist movement grew stronger during an economic depression from 1893 to 1896. When 1896 Democratic presidential candidate William Jennings Bryan embraced the unlimited coinage of silver in his famous "Cross of Gold" speech ("You shall not press down upon the brow of labor this crown of thorns, you shall not crucify mankind upon a cross of gold," he said to Republicans who supported a currency backed only by gold), Populists jumped on the Bryan bandwagon. In a close race, Bryan, the champion of the Democrats and Populists, lost to Republican **William McKinley** (1843–1901; see entry in volume 3). It was to be the last major effort of Populism and the agrarian movement against industrialism.

James B. Weaver

James Baird Weaver was born on June 12, 1833, in Dayton, Ohio. His family soon moved to Iowa, and Weaver attended country schools while growing up. At age twenty, he journeyed to California during the great gold rush years, but he returned without success. Weaver entered and graduated from Cincinnati Law School in a single year; then he opened a law practice in Bloomfield, Iowa, in 1856.

Weaver became involved in local politics as a Republican opposed to the expansion of slavery into new territories. During the Civil War, he volunteered as an officer and participated in the bloody battles at Ft. Donelson, Shiloh, and Corinth, where he assumed field command when his superior officers were mortally wounded. He was soon promoted to major. By the time he returned to Iowa in 1864, he was a breveted (honorary) brigadier general and was known subsequently as "General" Weaver.

Weaver became a district attorney in 1866. Between 1867 and 1873, while holding the appointive position of assessor of revenue for the federal government, he found himself at odds with the Republican leadership over currency policies and the subsidization of railroads. Weaver wanted the currency expanded to meet the needs of common people. Weaver joined the Greenback Party, which favored his views on monetary reform. He was elected to Congress in 1878, ran for president in 1880, lost the congressional election in

James B. Weaver.
Courtesy of the Library of Congress.

1882, but won two additional terms after 1884 as a candidate for this minor party.

Weaver joined a group called the Farmers' Alliance, which championed his views on money matters. He played a major role in bringing that organization into the Populist Party. As the Populist Party's candidate for president in 1892, he received over one million popular votes and twenty-two votes in the Electoral College. Four years later, he brought about a merger with the Democrats behind William Jennings Bryan's unsuccessful presidential campaign. This terminated the Populist crusade, and Weaver's career as a national politician was over. He later served as mayor of Colfax, his Iowa hometown. Weaver died in Des Moines, Iowa, on February 6, 1912.

America emerged as a major international naval power.

The economy took a downturn shortly after Harrison left office. Many blamed high tariff rates, excessive government spending (especially on pensions Harrison approved), and a devaluation of currency (a decline in the value of money), all of which can be traced to policies Harrison supported. Still, the high tariff rate established in 1890 was authored by William McKinley; the tariff issue did not hurt him when he ran for president in 1896. A good portion of increased government spending under Harrison went for good causes—pensions and improvement of the U.S. Navy. The devaluation of the currency arose because of widespread public support for printing more money, backed by increased mining of silver.

Benjamin Harrison's second wife, Mary Harrison. She was the niece of Harrison's first wife, Caroline, and helped with the social functions of the White House while her aunt was ailing.
Courtesy of the Library of Congress.

Harrison is often referred to as the "centennial president" because he was elected one hundred years after the first U.S. president, **George Washington** (1732–1799; see entry in volume 1). The nation was in a period of transition while Harrison was in office. His family roots stretched back to the beginnings of the Republic, and Harrison was among the last leaders of that old order. A new century was close at hand, and the beginning of the modern presidency is often set by historians at 1896 with the administration of William McKinley.

Where to Learn More

Harrison, Benjamin. *Public Papers and Addresses of Benjamin Harrison, Twenty-third President of the United States, March 4, 1889, to March 4, 1893*. Washington, DC: Government Printing Office, 1893.

Harrison, Benjamin. *This Country of Ours*. Chicago: Reilly & Lee Books, 1969.

Myers, Elisabeth P. *Benjamin Harrison*. Chicago: H. Regnery Co., 1952. Newtown, CT: American Political Biography Press, 1997.

A Selection of Harrison Landmarks

Crown Hill Cemetery. 700 West 38th St., Indianapolis, IN 46208. (317) 925-8231. Burial site of President Harrison and his wives. See http://www.crownhill.org/cemetery/index.html (accessed on August 2, 2000).

President Benjamin Harrison Home. 1230 North Delaware St., Indianapolis, IN 46202-2598. (317) 631-1898. The home in which Harrison lived from 1875 until his death in 1901 (except for his presidential years) contains exhibits, a museum, and a research library. See http://www.surf-ici.com/harrison/default.htm (accessed on August 2, 2000).

Sievers, Harry J. *Benjamin Harrison: Hoosier President: The White House and After, 1889–1901*. Indianapolis: Bobbs-Merrill Co., 1968. Reprint, Newtown, CT: American Political Biography Press, 1997.

Socolofsky, Homer E., and Allan B. Spetter. *The Presidency of Benjamin Harrison*. Lawrence: University Press of Kansas, 1987.

Stevens, Rita. *Benjamin Harrison, 23rd President of the United States*. Ada, OK: Garrett Educational Corp., 1989.

Caroline Harrison

Born October 1, 1832
Oxford, Ohio
Died October 25, 1892
Washington, D.C.

Used her sense of history and artistic talent in renovating the White House and became the first president of the Daughters of the American Revolution

An accomplished pianist and painter, Caroline "Carrie" Harrison blended her interest in the arts with the growing sense of national history that accompanied her husband's presidential administration. **Benjamin Harrison** (1833–1901; see entry in volume 3) was called the "centennial president," having taken office one hundred years after the first American president, **George Washington** (1732–1799; see entry in volume 1).

Carrie Harrison supported the founding of the Daughters of the American Revolution, a group that helps preserve items and places of historical significance, and served as the group's first president. She applied the group's historical service to the White House: Among other accomplishments, she designed the china pattern used for place settings during the Harrison presidency and gathered examples of dinnerware from past administrations. The china collection has since grown into one of the more visually informative displays on exhibit at the White House.

The White House had undergone alternating periods of grandeur and neglect. It was described as "barracks" just ten years earlier by President **Chester A. Arthur** (1829–1886;

"We have within ourselves the only element of destruction; our foes are from within, not from without. Our hope is in unity and self-sacrifice."

Caroline Harrison, address to the DAR's First Continental Congress

Caroline Harrison
Courtesy of the Library of Congress.

see entry in volume 3), who introduced many improvements. Under Carrie Harrison's direction, the White House was transformed into its modern status as a stately manor filled with historically significant artifacts and artworks. As the nation moved into a second century of Constitutional government, an especially appropriate symbol of progress was introduced to the White House when Carrie Harrison supervised the installation of electricity.

Artistic background

Caroline Lavinia Scott was born on October 1, 1832, in Oxford, Ohio. She was the second daughter of John W. Scott, a Presbyterian minister, and Mary Potts Neal Scott. Reverend Scott was founder of the Oxford Female Institute, where Carrie later studied. After graduating, she briefly taught piano classes at the Institute. Her father was a longtime professor at Miami University in Oxford. He taught there at the time of Caroline's birth and he was there eighteen years later teaching the physical sciences when Benjamin Harrison arrived.

Harrison was a junior, recently transferred from Farmer's College in Cincinnati. He had met Caroline previously. Benjamin Harrison was a serious young man who was becoming more deeply religious and who excelled in the study of Latin, Greek, and the natural sciences. Caroline was more lively and interested in the arts and dancing. They graduated from their respective schools in 1852, became engaged, and were married in 1853.

The Harrisons moved to Indianapolis in 1854, where Benjamin began a law practice. Harrison came from a distinguished family that included grandfather **William Henry Harrison** (1773–1841; see entry in volume 2), the ninth president of the United States. The Harrison name was well known in Indiana for his grandfather's exploits in leading troops that defeated Native Americans in the famous Battle of Tippecanoe in 1811. Benjamin and Caroline lived modestly as he established his practice and became involved in politics as a supporter of Republican Party presidential candidates John C. Frémont (1813–1890; see box in **James K. Polk** entry in volume 2) in 1856 and **Abraham Lincoln** (1809–1865; see entry in volume 2) in 1860.

Harrison served in the Civil War (1861–65) while Caroline raised their two children in Indianapolis. He returned to Indianapolis after the war and resumed his law practice. Harrison became a distinguished lawyer over the next decade and became a leader in the Republican Party. Nevertheless, he twice failed in bids to be elected governor of Indiana. He was elected to the U.S. Senate in 1881 and served through 1887, when he lost a bid for reelection. But Harrison remained a nationally known figure for his family background and the integrity he had displayed in Congress. He was nominated as the Republican presidential candidate for the 1888 election and won a close contest.

Active first lady

The Harrison White House was extremely active. The couple was joined by their son and daughter and their families. Benjamin Harrison was seven years old when his grandfather was elected president; now he was the president and his grandchildren roamed the White House grounds. Caroline's father, sister, and a niece also lived in the mansion, forming a large extended family that enlivened White House dinners and parties.

Carrie Harrison was active with local charities and with her public role as president of the Daughters of the American Revolution. She was involved in fundraising, helping gain financial support for a new medical school at Johns Hopkins University. She plunged into that cause after being assured that the medical school at Johns Hopkins would accept female applicants.

In addition to painting china, designing dinnerware patterns, and establishing the White House china collection, Carrie Harrison was involved in White House improvements. She supervised the installation of electricity and also worked with an architect on plans to enlarge the mansion. Wanting to create more office space for the president and administration officials, as well as more living space (the quarters were cramped with so many Harrison family members around), she proposed building two wings that would give the White House a U-shaped appearance. One wing would be devoted entirely to office space, while the other wing would be devoted to a museum. However, the plans were never approved by Congress. Before Carrie Harrison could pursue them further, she was struck down by a serious illness during the winter of 1891.

Carrie Harrison never recovered from what was diagnosed as tuberculosis (a communicable disease that mainly affects the lungs). Her husband was nominated to run for a second term in 1892, but his thoughts and feelings were focused on his stricken wife. Harrison refused to leave her side to campaign. In respect toward his action and to honor the first lady, Harrison's opponent, **Grover Cleveland** (1837–1908; see entry in volume 3), also refused to campaign. On October 25, 1892, shortly before election day, Caroline Harrison died. Mary Harrison McKee, the Harrison's daughter, fulfilled hostess duties for the remainder of her father's term.

Where to Learn More

Boller, Paul F. *Presidential Wives*. New York: Oxford University Press, 1998.

Melick, Arden Davis. *Wives of the Presidents*. Maplewood, NJ: Hammond, 1985.

Harrison's Message to the Senate Supporting the Annexation of Hawaii

Delivered on February 15, 1893; excerpted from
The Annals of America

*President Harrison announces his support
for the annexation of Hawaii*

During the latter part of the nineteenth century, American and European business leaders in Hawaii struggled against native rulers King Kalakaua (1836–1891), who led from 1874 to his death in 1891, and his sister, Queen Liliuokalani (lih-LEE-uh-woh-kuh-LON-ee; 1838–1917), who succeeded him. By 1887, a group of American and other white business leaders had established an armed militia and were successful in developing a new constitution that limited royal powers. The "Bayonet Constitution," as it was called, based the right to vote on wealth, a provision that disenfranchised about three-fourths of the native Hawaiian voters. European and American males could vote, even if they were not Hawaiian citizens, but Asian immigrants were excluded.

Queen Liliuokalani attempted to regain some of the power of the monarchy when she took the throne in 1891. She opposed efforts of the white business community to have Hawaii annexed (added) to the United States. When the queen attempted to impose a new constitution in January 1893, powerful white leaders occupied the government office building in Honolulu and overthrew the monarchy. The

"I think [annexation] . . . will be highly promotive of the best interests of the Hawaiian people and is the only one that will adequately secure the interests of the United States."

Benjamin Harrison

rebels were helped by the official U.S. representative in Hawaii, who ordered troops from a U.S. warship to land in Honolulu to protect American lives and property. The rebels proclaimed a provisional government headed by Sanford B. Dole (1844–1926), the son of an American missionary.

Two days after taking over, the new government sent representatives to Washington to negotiate a treaty of annexation. A treaty was signed in February. On February 15, 1893, President **Benjamin Harrison** (1833–1901; see entry in volume 3) sent a message to the Senate and presented the treaty for ratification.

Things to remember while reading an excerpt from President Harrison's message to the Senate supporting the annexation of Hawaii:

- Annexation of Hawaii was a controversial issue. Because U.S. citizens had assisted in the fall of the Hawaiian monarchy and the establishment of a new government, some Americans did not want the treaty negotiated by President Harrison to be ratified. One such American opposed to the treaty was President **Grover Cleveland** (1837–1908; see entry in volume 3). When he succeeded Harrison, he withdrew the treaty of annexation (see **Grover Cleveland** primary source entry in volume 3).

- President Harrison is careful in the message to claim that the overthrow of the Hawaiian monarchy was not promoted by the U.S. government.

- President Harrison provides two choices for U.S. action on Hawaii. The first option would make Hawaii a "protectorate," in which the islands would be protected by the United States, but would not have political power. Annexation, which would give Hawaiians the opportunity to petition for statehood and become U.S. citizens, is the second option Harrison proposes, and which he supports.

Excerpt from President Harrison's message to Congress supporting the annexation of Hawaii

It has been the policy of the administration not only to respect but to encourage the continuance of an independent government in the Hawaiian Islands so long as it afforded suitable guarantees for the protection of life and property and maintained a stability and strength that gave adequate security against the domination of any other power. The moral support of this government has continually manifested itself in the most friendly diplomatic relations and in many acts of courtesy to the Hawaiian rulers.

The overthrow of the monarchy was not in any way promoted by this government, but had its origin in what seems to have been a reactionary and revolutionary policy on the part of Queen Lili-uokalani, which put in serious peril not only the large and **preponderating** interests of the United States in the islands but all foreign interests, and, indeed, the decent administration of civil affairs and the peace of the islands. It is quite evident that the monarchy had become **effete** and the queen's government so weak and inadequate as to be the prey of designing and unscrupulous persons. The restoration of Queen Liliuokalani to her throne is undesirable, if not impossible, and unless actively supported by the United States would be accompanied by serious disaster and the disorganization of all business interests. The influence and interest of the United States in the islands must be increased and not diminished.

Only two courses are now open—one, the establishment of a **protectorate** by the United States, and the other **annexation**, full and complete. I think the latter-course, which has been adopted in the treaty, will be highly promotive of the best interests of the Hawaiian people and is the only one that will adequately secure the interests of the United States. These interests are not wholly selfish. It is essential that none of the other great powers shall secure these islands. Such a possession would not consist with our safety and with the peace of the world. This view of the situation is so apparent and conclusive that no protest has been heard from any government against proceedings looking to annexation. Every foreign representative at Honolulu promptly acknowledged the **Provisional Govern-**

Preponderating: Dominating.

Effete: Weak and less vital.

Protectorate: When one nation serves as authority over another one and provides protection from other nations.

Annexation: Addition to an existing organization.

Provisional Government: An interim government.

ment, and I think there is a general concurrence in the opinion that the deposed queen ought not to be restored. (Adler, pp. 470-71)

What happened next . . .

The issue of the annexation of Hawaii occurred very late in Harrison's presidency. In fact, by the time his administration had negotiated the treaty of annexation and transmitted it to the Senate, Harrison had already been defeated in a reelection bid. His presidential term expired three weeks after the treaty was sent to the Senate.

Grover Cleveland, Harrison's successor as president, withdrew the treaty of annexation. He wanted an investigation of the overthrow of the Hawaiian government to be conducted to ensure the negotiated treaty was legal. Under the guidelines of the Constitution, the president is responsible for negotiating a treaty, and the Senate votes on whether or not to ratify the agreement (two-thirds of the senators must vote in support of a treaty in order for it to be ratified). Cleveland never reintroduced the treaty to the Senate. His successor, President **William McKinley** (1843–1901; see entry in volume 3), supported annexation of Hawaii, as did a majority of the American people. The annexation of Hawaii became official in July 1898 following a joint resolution of Congress. Hawaii became a U.S. territory in 1900 and the fiftieth state in 1959.

Did you know . . .

- Some historians call the time Benjamin Harrison served as president "The Period of No Decision." The country was undergoing rapid change toward a predominantly industrial economy, and political power was split among urban and rural areas, businessmen and workers. Harrison defeated President Grover Cleveland in the election of 1888, only to lose to Cleveland in 1892. Harrison signed the treaty of annexation of Hawaii and presented it to the Senate in February 1893, only to watch Cleveland withdraw the treaty a few weeks later. Voters were equally divided on many issues, making it difficult for politicians to establish power through clear majorities.

Where to Learn More

Adler, Mortimer J., ed. *The Annals of America. Volume 1: Great Issues in American Life: A Conspectus.* Chicago: Encyclopedia Britannica, 1968.

Sievers, Harry J. *Benjamin Harrison: Hoosier President: The White House and After, 1889–1901.* Indianapolis: Bobbs-Merrill Co., 1968. Reprint, Newtown, CT: American Political Biography Press, 1997.

Socolofsky, Homer E., and Allan B. Spetter. *The Presidency of Benjamin Harrison.* Lawrence: University Press of Kansas, 1987.

William McKinley

Twenty-fifth president (1897–1901)

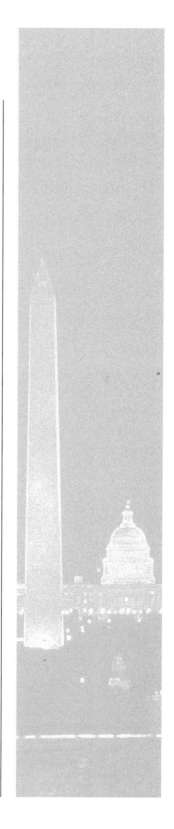

William McKinley

Born January 29, 1843
Niles, Ohio
Died September 14, 1901
Buffalo, New York

Twenty-fifth president of the United States (1897–1901)

Supported U.S. business and committed the United States to a course of territorial and economic expansion that made the country a player in the international marketplace

William McKinley was a popular president. He led the nation during the emergence of the United States into its modern position as a global economic and military power.

Businesses did well, jobs were abundant, and the booming economy grew even stronger as the United States became more heavily involved in international trade. During McKinley's presidency, the United States quickly and decisively won the Spanish-American War (1898).

Debate continues, however, about McKinley's effectiveness as president. He intended to address several key issues during his second term. But his opportunity was cut short with his assassination in 1901.

Throughout his political career—as a congressman, as governor of Ohio, and as president—McKinley promoted business interests. Taking a cautious approach, he supported the protection of American business and industry by taxing imported goods to keep their prices high. He preferred to allow home businesses to manufacture and sell their wares without government controls.

"We have good money, we have ample revenues, we have unquestioned national credit, but what we want is new markets. . . ."

William McKinley

William McKinley.
Courtesy of the Library of Congress.

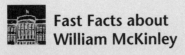

Fast Facts about William McKinley

Full name: William McKinley Jr.

Born: January 29, 1843

Died: September 14, 1901

Burial site: McKinley National Memorial, Westlawn Cemetery, Canton, Ohio

Parents: William and Nancy Campbell Allison McKinley

Spouse: Ida Saxton (1847–1907; m. 1871)

Children: Katherine (1871–1876); Ida (1873–1873)

Religion: Methodist

Education: Attended Allegheny College

Occupations: Soldier; lawyer

Government positions: U.S. representative from Ohio; Ohio governor

Political party: Republican

Dates as president: March 4, 1897–March 4, 1901 (first term); March 4, 1901–September 14, 1901 (second term)

Age upon taking office: 54

As president, McKinley also urged a cautious and diplomatic approach toward the increasing tensions between the United States and Spain over Cuba, which was still a Spanish colony during the 1890s. When Cubans began rebelling against Spanish rule over their island, Americans supported their cause. The support was first fueled by sometimes sensationalistic (strongly emotional and graphically detailed) newspaper accounts of Spanish oppression (unjust and harsh rule) of Cubans, and then by the suspicious and unexplained explosion of an American ship in a Cuban harbor. The events led McKinley to ask Congress to declare war on Spain in April 1898.

American forces won important battles in Cuba and other Spanish colonies, including Puerto Rico and the Philippines. The war lasted only four months. With victory, the United States for the first time in history took possession of land beyond the North America mainland.

The success of the economy, the war, and American expansionism (the intent of a nation to enlarge its size or add to its possessions) helped McKinley win reelection in 1900 against his Democratic counterpart William Jennings Bryan (1860–1925; see box), whom McKinley had also defeated in 1896. Shortly after his second inauguration, McKinley undertook a transcontinental tour to reach out to the American people. But the tour proved to be tragic. Early on, in California, first lady **Ida McKinley** (1847–1907; see entry in volume 3) fell ill. Near the end of the tour, President McKinley was assassinated in Buffalo, New York. Many Americans paid their respects as the train bearing the president's casket made its way from

William McKinley Timeline

1843: Born in Ohio

1861: Civil War begins with firing on Fort Sumter; McKinley enlists in the Twenty-third Ohio Voluntary Regiment under the command of future president Rutherford B. Hayes

1865: Civil War ends; McKinley leaves the military, having been honored several times for bravery and having reached the rank of brevet major

1877–84, 1885–91: Serves in the U.S. House of Representatives

1890: Authors the McKinley Tariff Act; loses election and his seat in the U.S. House of Representatives

1893–97: Serves as Ohio governor

1897–1901: Serves as twenty-fifth U.S. president; seeks to revive a stagnant economy

1898: Economy booming; battleship *Maine* explodes in Havana Harbor, killing 266 American soldiers; McKinley asks for and receives from Congress a Declaration of War on Spain; Spanish-American War lasts four months, with the United States winning and gaining control of Cuba, Puerto Rico, and the Philippines

1900: McKinley's Open Door policy to China is threatened by revolutionary group called the Boxers who want to drive all foreigners out of China; U.S. Marines join forces with other Western nations to end the Boxer Rebellion; McKinley is reelected

1901: McKinley undertakes an ill-fated cross-country tour following his second inauguration; first lady becomes ill while in California, and McKinley is assassinated in Buffalo, New York

Buffalo to Washington, D.C., and then to Canton, Ohio, where McKinley was buried.

Civil War hero

William McKinley was born in Niles, Ohio, in 1843, the seventh of nine children. Both of his great-grandfathers fought in the Revolutionary War (1775–83). His paternal grandfather (his father's father) settled in Niles and opened up an iron foundry. When McKinley was nine, he and his younger siblings and their mother moved to Poland, Ohio, where they could attend better schools. McKinley's father, William (1807–1892), remained in Niles to run the foundry.

Anarchist: One against any form of government.

Annex: To incorporate an outside territory within the domain of a nation.

Boxer Rebellion: A violent campaign by a group of Chinese nationalists in 1900 who were intent on ridding their country of foreign influences.

Confederate: Relating to and representing the Southern states that ceded from the United States in the 1860s and fought the Union during the American Civil War (1861–65).

Expansionism: The policy of a nation that plans to enlarge its size or gain possession of other lands.

Gerrymandered: When a congressional district is rezoned following a census; the party in power changes the bound-aries to include more people likely to support the party in power.

Imperialist: One who favors expanding the authority of the government over other nations and groups of people.

Industrialist: An owner or a manager of a large manufacturing firm.

Inflation: An economic term describing a decline in the value of money in relation to the goods and services it will buy. For example, price increases lessen the purchasing power of money.

Insurrections: Armed rebellions against a recognized authority.

Internationalism: Interest and participation in events involving other countries.

Isolationism: A national policy of avoiding pacts, treaties, and other official agree-

While attending school at the Poland Academy, McKinley was a rather shy student. With encouragement from his mother and teachers, he overcame his shyness and soon developed a great talent for public speaking. He took an active role in the school's debate club and became president of a local debating group.

McKinley was close to his mother, Nancy (1809–1897). She was devoutly religious in the Methodist faith and hoped her son would become a minister. She believed that a life of virtue (goodness, moral excellence) led to wealth and that vice (offensive acts, immoral behavior) led to poverty—views that influenced McKinley throughout his life. In his midteens, McKinley decided against the ministry, however, choosing instead to pursue studies at Allegheny College in

ments with other nations in order to remain neutral.

Laissez faire: A French term (roughly translated as "allow to do") commonly used to describe noninterference by government in the affairs of business and the economy.

Legal tender: Bills or coin that have designated value.

Monopoly: A business sector controlled by one company.

Open Door Policy: A program introduced by President William McKinley to extend trade and relations with China, opening up a vast new market.

Oppression: Abuse of power by one party against another.

Platform: A declaration of policies that a candidate or political party intends to follow if elected.

Reciprocity: A mutual exchange of different items to attain equal value.

Sensationalistic: A style of reporting intended to arouse a strong emotional response from readers by emphasizing graphic details and claims of frightful and shocking behavior.

Tariffs: Taxes imposed by the government on imported goods to keep their prices as high or higher than the same goods produced in America.

Trusts: A legal combination of firms and businesses formed to dominate a business sector and squash competition.

Pennsylvania, across the border from Ohio. But an illness and a lack of money interrupted his education. McKinley returned home to Poland in 1860. He worked as a postal clerk and a part-time schoolteacher, saving money and planning to return to college.

When the Civil War (1861–65) broke out, eighteen-year-old McKinley enlisted with the Twenty-third Voluntary Ohio Regiment. The regiment, which was sent to western Virginia to battle Confederate forces of the Southern states that had separated from the United States during the 1860s, was led by Major **Rutherford B. Hayes** (1822–1893; see entry in volume 3). Hayes would later become the nineteenth president of the United States.

McKinley quickly showed his bravery in battle by delivering supplies and food to soldiers while under heavy fire. He soon rose to the rank of second lieutenant on the battlefield and served as an officer on Hayes's staff. Near the end of the war, he distinguished himself (conducted himself well and became well known) in several battles (Opequan, Cedar Creek, and Fisher's Hill).

After considering whether or not to remain in the military when the war ended, McKinley chose to return home to Ohio in 1865 and resume his schooling. Major McKinley, as he liked to be called—based on his last military rank—studied law at the offices of Charles E. Glidden, a county judge in Youngstown, Ohio, and then at Albany College. In 1867, he passed the bar exam (a test prospective lawyers must score well on to be officially certified to practice law) and opened an office in Canton, Ohio.

McKinley soon became active in politics. He supported his former commander, Rutherford B. Hayes, during his campaign for governor; Hayes won the election in 1867. The following year McKinley was involved on the local level, helping Republican **Ulysses S. Grant** (1822–1885; see entry in volume 3) carry Ohio in his election to the presidency. McKinley himself ran for the local office of prosecuting attorney and was elected in 1869.

Happiness and grief

During this time, McKinley met Ida Saxton, daughter of an influential Canton banker. She was full of life and very fashion-conscious. Ida had recently taken a job at her father's bank in order to become a more responsible young woman. There, she and McKinley first became friends. They married in 1871.

Everything was going well for the newlyweds, who had their first child, Katherine (1871–1876), the following year. But health problems and tragedy soon followed.

Ida was ill during her pregnancy with the couple's second child, and the situation grew worse when Ida's mother died. Ida was grief-stricken. In 1873, Baby Ida was born premature and died four-and-a-half months after birth. Then, in 1875, daughter Katherine came down with typhoid fever (a highly infectious bacterial infection); she died a few weeks later. Ida would never again fully recover her physical or mental health. She suffered occasional episodes of epileptic seizures (convulsive attacks caused by a nervous system disorder) and depression. In between, she made great efforts to be a spirited public figure during her husband's official appearances.

Saddened by the deaths of his daughters and the illnesses of his wife, McKinley plunged further into work to help him deal with those difficult times. His local reputation, based on his engaging speeches, spread wide enough for him to consider running for the U.S. Congress. He was elected to the House of Representatives in 1876. Fellow Ohioan Hayes was elected president the same year.

McKinley was reelected through 1890, except for one term when his district was gerrymandered (when boundaries are changed after a census to include more people likely to support the party in power). As a young congressman, McKinley was immediately faced with two issues that would have a lasting effect on his political career—bimetallism and tariffs.

Defining issues

Bimetallism is a policy of using two precious metals to give value to legal tender (bills or coin assigned a certain value). Gold was the single precious metal used to base the value of money in the United States, but there were people during the last half of the nineteenth century who wanted to include silver as well as gold. Those who wanted to include silver were generally farmers who lived in western and southern states. They argued that "free silver" would allow the United States to print more money that people could earn and use to buy much needed goods—like food and clothing—that many could not afford. Those against including silver were generally bankers and industrialists of the eastern states. They believed that increasing the money supply would lead to inflation, a decline in the value of money in relation to the goods and services it will buy.

Although his fellow Republicans and President Hayes were against bimetallism, McKinley noted that the people he represented in his Ohio congressional district generally favored including silver in the monetary standard. He voted for a limited inclusion of silver. Then, after President Hayes vetoed (rejected) the measure, McKinley voted with the Democratic majority to override the veto.

McKinley then turned to another major issue—tariffs. Tariffs are taxes imposed by the government on imported goods to keep their prices as high or higher than the same goods produced in America. For example, a pair of shoes might be cheaper to produce in a foreign country because of lower costs to make those shoes. When the shoes are imported into the United States, they can be sold at a lower price than American shoes can be sold. As consumers purchase the lower-cost shoes, American-made shoes are left unsold; the American shoe business, then, becomes less profitable and workers are laid off.

McKinley consistently backed high tariffs as a congressman to protect American businesses. His long-standing support of tariffs reached its high point with the McKinley Tariff Act of 1890, which created new highs on imported goods except for a few isolated items. In order to win enough support from fellow congressmen for his bill, McKinley again in 1890 voted for increased but limited coinage of silver.

Defeat leads to new opportunities

The McKinley Tariff Act contributed to McKinley's loss of his congressional seat in the election of 1890. The tariff created higher prices on goods, which protected American businesses but meant that people had to pay more for many items. Angry consumers voted against congressional incumbents (people currently holding office) that year because of the higher prices they were paying.

McKinley did not let the defeat stop him. He ran for governor of Ohio the next year, relying on his excellent speech-making skills and his pro-business platform (political point of view to be followed if elected) as he undertook a vigorous campaign. He won the election and was easily reelected two years later. McKinley's popularity increased during a time when the country was facing hard times and falling into an economic depression in 1893.

McKinley impressed fellow Republicans at their 1892 convention, where many party members argued heatedly over whom the party should nominate for president. He was even mentioned as a possible presidential candidate. Then, in

Republican Party presidential campaign poster for William McKinley. *Reproduced by permission of Corbis.*

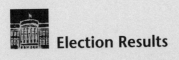 **Election Results**

1896

Presidential / Vice presidential candidates	Popular votes	Presidential electoral votes
William McKinley / Garret A. Hobart (Republican)	7,104,779	271
William Jennings Bryan / Arthur Sewall (Democrat)	6,509,052	176

Bryan was also the People's (Populist) Party presidential nominee; that party's vice presidential nominee was Georgia politician Thomas E. Watson.

1900

Presidential / Vice presidential candidates	Popular votes	Presidential electoral votes
William McKinley / Theodore Roosevelt (Republican)	7,207,923	292
William Jennings Bryan / Adlai E. Stevenson (Democratic)	6,358,138	155

Bryan was also the presidential nominee of the People's (Populist) and Imperialist parties. Roosevelt's selection as Republican vice presidential nominee was necessitated by the death of Hobart in 1899.

1896, McKinley was backed by wealthy Ohio industrialist Mark Hanna (1837–1904). (An industrialist is the owner or manager of a large manufacturing business.) Hanna had great financial resources and excellent organizational skills. He left his business in order to run the McKinley campaign.

McKinley won the Republican nomination. His opponent in the presidential election was William Jennings Bryan, who was nominated both by the Democratic Party and the People's Party, or the Populists. The Populists represented people of the West and the South hit hard by the depression, those suspicious of powerful banking institutions of the East, and supporters of bimetallism.

Two familiar issues—bimetallism and tariffs—helped propel the McKinley campaign. Bryan proposed several options to reform the economy, such as increasing the use of silver as a currency (monetary) standard. McKinley abruptly switched his position on bimetallism. By announcing that he favored only the gold standard, McKinley won overwhelming support from the business community. Coupled with his con-

Complete American Presidents Sourcebook

tinued strong stand on tariffs, McKinley was offering a cautious but clear message on how to regain prosperity for the nation. Bryan, meanwhile, was increasingly portrayed as a man with wild economic ideas that could further damage the economy. McKinley won a close election.

Presiding in prosperity

Beginning with his inaugural address (his first speech as president; see **William McKinley** primary source entry in volume 3) and his appointment of several successful businessmen to Cabinet (advisory) posts, McKinley tackled issues relating to the economy. Helped by good timing—the economy was finally beginning to show signs of improvement—McKinley and a supportive Congress enacted a few carefully chosen tariffs to protect American industry. Many raw materials, such as iron ore, were not taxed with a tariff; manufacturers could buy the raw goods cheaply to help keep down their cost for producing goods. Meanwhile, the administration promoted a generous business climate, and the Alaskan Gold Rush in the final years of the nineteenth century made more of the precious mineral available. The gold rush also effectively killed the bimetallism issue. Prosperity returned, and McKinley's popularity grew.

McKinley favored a *laissez-faire* approach to the economy, in which the government does not intervene in business affairs. This approach helped stimulate growth and investment, but it also allowed for the proliferation of trusts—corporate monopolies formed to dominate a business sector; that is, to control a certain section of business. (A monopoly is the exclusive control of a good or a service by a business.) Unwilling to disrupt the booming (prosperous) economy, McKinley hesitated to address this unfair, and later illegal, business practice.

Meanwhile, just offshore of the United States, trouble had been brewing for several years. Cuba was still ruled as a colony by Spain, as it had been for centuries, and many Cubans wanted to establish their own government. A rebellion in 1894 had failed, and tensions soon heated again. American newspapers began reporting on Spanish oppression: Many Cubans were herded into internment camps, and thousands

"Remember the Maine!" was the American battle cry during the Spanish-American War, referring to the mysterious explosion that killed 266 men on the battlehip anchored in Havana Harbor. Over 70 years later, in 1969, the U.S. Navy determined that a defective boiler had caused the explosion on the Maine.

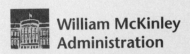

William McKinley Administration

Administration Dates
March 4, 1897–March 4, 1901
March 4, 1901–September 14, 1901

Vice President
Garret A. Hobart (1897–99)
None (1899–1901)
Theodore Roosevelt (1901)

Cabinet

Secretary of State
John Sherman (1897–98)
William R. Day (1898)
John M. Hay (1898–1901)

Secretary of the Treasury
Lyman J. Gage (1897–1901)

Secretary of War
Russell A. Alger (1897–99)
Elihu Root (1899–1901)

Attorney General
Joseph McKenna (1897–98)
John W. Griggs (1898–1901)
Philander C. Knox (1901)

Secretary of the Navy
John D. Long (1897–1901)

Postmaster General
James A. Gary (1897–98)
Charles E. Smith (1898–1901)

Secretary of the Interior
Cornelius N. Bliss (1897–99)
Ethan A. Hitchcock (1899–1901)

Secretary of Agriculture
James Wilson (1897–1901)

died there from malnutrition (lack of food) and disease. Some news stories, however, were sensationalistic and meant to sell newspapers. "Yellow journalism"—a term that describes sensationalistic reporting that strains the bounds of truth in order to attract attention and sell newspapers—was becoming more common. A bitter rivalry between newspaper magnates William Randolph Hearst (1863–1951; see box) and Joseph Pulitzer (1847–1911; see box) was raging.

Sentiment in America began to move toward military intervention in Cuba, but President McKinley urged caution and diplomacy. In retrospect (looking backward), some historians have argued that he moved too cautiously. Two events in February 1898 led him to change course. The *New York Journal,* a newspaper owned by Hearst, reprinted a letter alleged to have been written by Spain's minister to Washington in which he described McKinley as weak. The following week, a mysterious explosion destroyed the U.S.S. *Maine,* killing all 266 sailors aboard. The ship had recently been sent to Cuba and was anchored in Havana Harbor. McKinley continued to urge caution until results of an official investigation into the explosion were released, but popular sentiment continued to grow for intervention. McKinley responded in April by asking Congress to declare war on Spain.

The Spanish-American War lasted little more than four months, with the United States winning crucial naval battles in Spanish possessions, including Cuba, Puerto Rico, and the

Philippines. The swiftness of the victory, as well as newspaper stories and images such as **Theodore Roosevelt** (1858–1919; see entry in volume 3) leading his group of "rough riders" up San Juan Hill in Cuba, increased McKinley's standing.

The victory over Spain created an unprecedented event (an event that had never happened before): For the first time, the United States was in possession of lands not part of the North America mainland. McKinley soon began supporting expansion as well in international trade. Among several initiatives (new legislative measures), he introduced the Open Door Policy to extend trade and relations with China, opening up a vast new market.

This expansionism became an issue in the election of 1900, when William Jennings Bryan, again the Democratic nominee, portrayed McKinley as an imperialist, a person who believes in acquiring or dominating other lands. He also called McKinley a tool of big business, noting that many

After a mysterious explosion, the U.S.S. *Maine* sank in Havana Harbor. Its sinking was the spark that ignited the Spanish-American War.
Courtesy of the U.S. Army Military History Institute.

Joseph Pulitzer

Born in Budapest, Hungary, in April 1847, Joseph Pulitzer was the son of a successful grain-trader. At age seventeen, he emigrated to America and soon enlisted in the Union cavalry near the end of the Civil War (1861–65). After the war, he settled in a largely German area of St. Louis, Missouri. Pulitzer worked as a mule tender, waiter, and driver before landing a job as a reporter for a German-language newspaper. A short time later, he was nominated for the state legislature by Republicans. His candidacy was considered a joke because he was nominated in a Democratic district. Pulitzer, however, ran seriously and won. In the legislature, he fought against corruption, and in one wild dispute shot an adversary in the leg. He escaped punishment with a fine, which was paid by friends.

Industrious and ambitious, Pulitzer bought the *St. Louis Post* for about $3,000 in 1872, then bought a German-language paper that was connected with the large Associated Press syndicate and sold it for a large profit. In 1878, Pulitzer purchased the decaying *St. Louis Dispatch* at an auction and combined it with the *Post*. Aided by his brilliant editor in chief, John A. Cockerill, Pulitzer launched crusades against lotteries, gambling, and tax dodging, mounted drives for cleaning and repairing streets, and sought to make St. Louis more civic-minded. The *Post-Dispatch* became a success. In 1883, Pulitzer, then thirty-six, purchased the *New York World* for $346,000 from financier Jay Gould (1836–1892), who was losing $40,000 a year on the paper. Pulitzer made the down payment from *Post-Dispatch* profits and made all later payments out of profits from the *World*. During the 1880s, Pulitzer's eyes began to fail. He went blind in 1889. During his battle for supremacy with William Randolph Hearst,

trusts had developed under McKinley's administration and that the nation's finances continued to be dominated by bankers and industrialists of the East.

The new internationalism—interest and participation in events involving other countries—also created new problems. Rebels in the Philippines, no more interested in being ruled by America as they had been by Spain, began insurrections (armed rebellions against a government). Over the next several years, McKinley sent over seventy thousand troops to maintain order and protect American interests in the Philippines; battles raged there through 1902, when the rebellion was finally put down. Meanwhile, as another example of the

Joseph Pulitzer.
Courtesy of the Library of Congress.

publisher of the *New York Journal,* Pulitzer had to rely on secretaries to be his eyes.

In New York, he pledged the *World* would "expose all fraud and sham, fight all public evils and abuses" and "battle for the people with earnest sincerity." He concentrated on lively human-interest stories, scandal, and sensational material. Pulitzer's *World* was a strong supporter of common people and was frequently pro-union during strikes in an era of labor unrest. In the early part of his career, Pulitzer was opposed to large headlines and other attention-grabbing graphics. During the 1890s, in a circulation contest between the newspaper empires of Pulitzer and Hearst, Pulitzer's newspaper went to larger headline type and fantastic art, and indulged in sensationalism.

Pulitzer died aboard his yacht in the harbor at Charleston, South Carolina, on October 29, 1911. In his will, he provided $2 million for the establishment of a school of journalism at Columbia University. Also, by the terms of his will, the prizes bearing his name were established in 1915.

United States moving from isolationism (a policy of avoiding involvement with other countries) to expansionism, McKinley agreed that the United States should annex Hawaii (add it as a possession of the United States). In stating his reasons for this action, McKinley used the popular term "Manifest Destiny"—an idea stressing that American expansionism is inevitable and "divinely ordained" (arranged by God).

Triumph and tragedy

While the economy continued to boom, unrest in foreign lands became a major concern for McKinley. Rebellions in

William Randolph Hearst

William Randolph Hearst was born April 29, 1863, in San Francisco, California. His father George was a wealthy mine-owner. Hearst was energetic from an early age and enjoyed private tutoring and travel. In 1879, he attended a private preparatory school in Concord, New Hampshire. A disruptive student, he was asked to leave that school the following year. After returning home for more private tutoring, Hearst was admitted to Harvard University. He took charge of the school's fading newspaper, the *Harvard Lampoon,* serving as editor and writer, selling advertising, and soliciting subscriptions from students, and made it profitable. His work on the *Lampoon* was his major achievement at Harvard before he was banished from the university in 1885 for playing pranks.

Meanwhile, his millionaire father had become interested in politics. He supported Democratic Party candidates and the newspaper that took up their cause, the *San Francisco Examiner.* After the paper could not repay loans he had provided, George Hearst took it over in 1880. In 1886, he was appointed to complete the term left by the death of U.S. senator John F. Miller (1831–1886), then was elected to his own six-year term. William Randolph Hearst had been working as a reporter for the *New York World* beginning in 1886 and soon returned to San Francisco to run the *Examiner,* where he quickly became publisher. Hearst revived a dying newspaper. He hired top reporters, including noted author Ambrose Bierce (1842–1914?). He wanted the *Examiner* to be the first newspaper to report an event and to report the event more sensationally than any other newspaper. His idea was that the newspaper should be exciting to read. Hearst personally took charge of a front page column. The *Examiner* staff searched for sensational news items and wrote the news articles as lively and recklessly as possible. The newspaper was soon accused of practicing yellow journalism, that is, of exaggerating and playing up violence and scandal stories to increase sales.

Hearst agreed to direct the *Examiner* to support Democratic candidates in return for a share of campaign money. Hearst used the *Examiner* and, later, other papers, to champion Democratic candidates and smear their opponents. So successful were his methods that the *Examiner* began to prosper, and Hearst thought of starting a similar paper in the East. In 1895, he acquired the *New York Morning Journal* and a year later added the *New York Evening Journal.* Hearst moved to New York and devoted much of his time to these newspapers.

While Hearst was in New York, difficulties between the United States and Spain eventually erupted into war in 1898. He campaigned for war through his newspapers and even engineered a daring res-

William Randolph Hearst.
Courtesy of the Library of Congress.

cue of a Cuban girl held in a Spanish prison. At the same time, a newspaper war with Joseph Pulitzer's *New York World* began. The *World* investigated the *Journal's* rescue story and reported that the conditions it described were a sham, but readers continued to read Hearst's *Journal.*

In 1898, a vessel, the U.S.S. *Maine,* anchored in Havana Harbor, was sunk in a mysterious explosion. Investigators thought the explosion came from outside the battleship, perhaps from a mine or bomb set off by the Spanish; 260 were killed. "Remember the *Maine!*" became a battle cry, especially in the Hearst papers. President McKinley called for the Spanish to leave Cuba. Spain responded by declaring war on the United States. Hearst's papers continued with their sensational articles, encouraged war with Spain, and even offered a $50,000 reward to solve the mystery of who was responsible for the explosion on the *Maine.*

Hearst was determined that his *New York Journal* reporters would be first to publish accounts of the battles of the Spanish-American War. Hearst gathered reporters, artists, writers, and a printing press, and sailed to war. With Hearst as the key reporter, the Hearst team stayed close to the battle lines, so close that they were accused of drawing enemy artillery fire on American troops.

The Spanish-American War greatly increased Hearst's influence in the publishing industry. He built a publishing empire that included dozens of newspapers and magazines, including *Cosmopolitan, Good Housekeeping,* and *Harper's Bazaar.* In 1903, he was elected to the House of Representatives, where he served for four years. He later ran unsuccessfully for mayor of New York City and governor of New York.

Hearst opposed American involvement in both world wars; the *New York Tribune* portrayed him as a snake named Hearsssst. Hearst newspapers eventually campaigned for an all-out effort to win World War II (1939–45) against the Japanese after the bombing of Pearl Harbor, but his previous antiwar stances had damaged his reputation. Hearst died on August 14, 1951.

William Jennings Bryan

Three-time presidential nominee William Jennings Bryan was a famed speechmaker and an influential figure in America from the 1890s through the 1920s. His father was a school superintendent and a politician. The family lived on a five-hundred-acre farm near Salem, Illinois. William Jennings Bryan was born there on March 19, 1860. The entire family worked on the farm and were very religious.

In 1872, Bryan's father ran unsuccessfully for a seat in the U.S. Congress. Already a gifted speaker, William campaigned for his father. After graduating from high school, Bryan went to Whipple Academy to prepare for Illinois College. Bryan was a good student and an active debater. His powerful voice and well-researched speeches covered positions he would fight for throughout his life. After graduating in 1881, Bryan entered Chicago's Union College of Law.

In 1883, Bryan joined a law firm in Jacksonville, Illinois. In 1884, he married Mary Baird; the two would have two children. In 1887, the Bryans moved to Lincoln, Nebraska, where the Republican Party was dominant. But Bryan thought Democrats had a chance in districts that included large cities. His theory proved accurate when in 1890 he was elected to the U.S. Congress.

Bryan favored income tax changes and also spoke out against gold being the only standard for the country's money. He said he would support anything that would promote free citizens, just laws, and an economical government. When a depression began in 1893, Bryan proposed to help the economy by taking U.S. currency off the gold standard. Many countries guaranteed the value of their money by keeping reserves of gold. Others kept reserves of both gold and silver to guarantee their paper money. With two different standards, some countries had a difficult time trading with others. Bryan argued that there was not enough gold in the world to support all the money of the world and that the United States should accept both gold and silver as guarantees. He was certain trade would improve and prosperity would return.

Bryan served two terms in the U.S. House. He lost in an 1894 bid for a U.S. Senate seat. He was then nominated for president of the United States three times—in 1896, 1900, and 1908—and defeated three times. Although he never held elective office again, Bryan was still recognized as the Democratic Party leader. His continued pleas for the average person and battles against trusts and tariffs earned him the nickname the Great Commoner. Bryan went on to serve as secretary of state for **Woodrow Wilson** (1856–1924; see entry in volume 4) from 1913 to 1915.

As a lifelong fundamentalist who believed the Bible to be completely accurate, Bryan spoke out against evolution

William Jennings Bryan.
Courtesy of the Library of Congress.

(which holds that present forms of living things have arisen over time from other life forms). In 1925, the state of Tennessee arrested Dayton high school teacher John T. Scopes, who was accused of using a textbook in his classroom that described evolution, a violation of state law. In the subsequent trial, prominent attorney Clarence Darrow (1857–1938) was the defense lawyer and Bryan helped the prosecution.

Bryan's opening presentation made it clear that he was on a crusade for fundamentalist Christianity. Darrow, on the other hand, was prepared to fight for freedom of speech and thought in schools. Bryan spoke out to the media as well as in courts and used every opportunity to make headlines. He even offered $100 to any sci-

entist who would admit to being a descendent of apes. When a scientist made the admission, Bryan paid up and used the event to ridicule both him and the theory of evolution.

Witnesses were summoned, scientists explained their theory of evolution, and ministers defended their religious positions. On the trial's ninth day, Darrow called Bryan to the witness stand. Through careful questioning, Darrow led Bryan to admit that some Bible stories are illustrations rather than fact. About Jonah and the whale, for example, Darrow wondered whether Bryan really believed that a man could be swallowed by a big fish and live inside for three days? The prosecution lost ground. On the eleventh day, Bryan was scheduled to make his closing arguments. He was capable of preaching and using wit, sarcasm, and false reasoning to persuade any audience, which is what he intended to do. But Darrow expected this. Darrow believed he had already won his point on the right of teachers to present new and challenging ideas. So Darrow rose to tell the court that his client was, in fact, guilty as charged and asked that the case be closed. The judge agreed. Scopes was found guilty of violating Tennessee's antievolution law and fined $100. Bryan lost the opportunity to give his great closing, a speech that some estimated would have been six hours in length. On July 25, 1925, five days after the trial ended, a weary Bryan died in his sleep.

In 1899, McKinley became the first president to ride in an automobile—a Stanley Steamer.

the Philippines were followed by those in China, where McKinley's Open Door policy was threatened by the Boxer Rebellion. The West—Europe and the Western Hemisphere—used the term Boxers to describe a group of Chinese nationalists who called themselves Righteous and Harmonious Fists. The Boxers were intent on ridding their country of foreign influences. When they began a violent campaign against foreigners, U.S. marines were sent in to fight alongside troops from other Western nations. The Boxers were overcome in August 1900, just a couple of months before the U.S. presidential election.

McKinley chose the popular Theodore Roosevelt, then governor of New York, as his running mate. Garret Hobart (1844–1899), his original vice president, had died shortly before the end of his first term. As Bryan stormed the country in search of votes, McKinley remained in Canton, Ohio, where he met delegates from around the country on his front porch and promised continued prosperity—"a full dinner bucket" for everyone. Reelected by a large margin, McKinley planned to address several pressing issues during his second term: He wanted to further U.S. involvement in international trade after years of isolationism, and he was concerned about the growing influence of corporate monopolies.

Following his second inauguration, McKinley decided to embark on a transcontinental (cross-country) tour to meet and hear from Americans across the land. The scheduled six-week tour would turn tragic. Early on, in California, Ida McKinley fell ill. She had been frail since the deaths of her daughters almost thirty years before.

In September, McKinley made an address in Buffalo, New York, at the Pan-American Exposition. As an indication of the direction he planned for his second term, McKinley announced in his speech his decision to abandon the protectionism of high tariffs in favor of free trade. He stressed the term "reciprocity," a trading balance achieved by nations by transacting items of equal value. For example, sugar was a popular import into the United States. Instead of regulating imported sugar by using the tariff, the United States would export items of similar value in trade agreements with sugar-exporting countries.

The day following his speech at the Exposition, McKinley stood before a long line of people. He greeted them,

shook hands, and spoke with them briefly. Leon Czolgosz (1873–1901), a mentally disturbed man and an admitted anarchist (someone who believes that all forms of government should be abolished), was in the line with a gun hidden beneath a handkerchief that was wrapped around his hand. McKinley extended his hand to Czolgosz, and Czolgosz shot the president. A crowd immediately tackled and began beating Czolgosz, but they were held back after the fallen president cried out, "Don't let them harm him."

The wounded president was rushed to the Exposition's emergency hospital and treated, then he was moved to a private residence. He seemed to be recovering, but gangrene—a form of infection that was incurable at the time—set in. In the early morning hours of September 14, a week after the shooting, McKinley whispered his final words: "Good-bye all, good-bye. It is God's way. His will be done."

McKinley's body was placed in a casket and taken to Washington, D.C., for a state funeral, then moved to Canton,

Ohio, where he was laid to rest. Americans lined the route to say farewell to the popular president.

Legacy

William McKinley is often called the first modern president. Several policies and events that occurred during his administration came to characterize the United States of the twentieth century. For example, the United States moved from isolationism to become a world economic and military power. America began adopting free-trade policies, as opposed to the policies of isolationism and protective tariffs that had been common during most of the nineteenth century.

McKinley's interpretation of the powers of the presidency and his use of the powers were much more expansive than those of the presidents immediately before him. He called a special session of Congress to pass a tariff act early in his presidency. During the Spanish-American War, he functioned as the nation's chief diplomat: First, he tried to avoid war through diplomacy; when that failed he directed the war effort; and following American victory, McKinley personally supervised negotiations for the peace treaty. These are all examples of power characteristic of the modern presidency.

Although McKinley's effort to increase business competition in the United States by identifying and breaking trusts and monopolies was cut short by his assassination, his intentions were vigorously pursued by his vice president, Theodore Roosevelt. Roosevelt became known as a "trustbuster" after he assumed the office of president in 1901 and was reelected in 1904. McKinley's support for the single gold standard, coupled with the Alaska Gold Rush, put an end to the bimetallism issue, although bimetallism again won a small measure of support during the Great Depression (1929–41) of the 1930s.

McKinley reacted cautiously to the changing business and social climate, and some historians argue that he did little to influence the changes. The economy, they contend, was already improving when he became president, and big business took advantage of his policies by forming trusts that squeezed out smaller businesses. On the international front, tensions with Spain over Cuba had been brewing for years,

| **Complete American Presidents Sourcebook**

and McKinley took decisive action only after the explosion on the *Maine*.

Nevertheless, the United States of today began taking shape during McKinley's administration, partly through his changing positions on bimetallism and tariffs. International trade began flourishing, and the American military became a stronger international presence. During his first campaign for the presidency, McKinley promised a cautious approach that favored business growth, and he certainly delivered on that promise.

Where to Learn More

"Assassination." *A Souvenir of the Pan-American Exposition.* [Online] http://intotem.buffnet.net/bhw/panamex/ (accessed on August 14, 2000).

Cherny, Robert W. *A Righteous Cause: The Life of William Jennings Bryan.* Boston: Little, Brown, 1985. Reprint, Norman: University of Oklahoma Press, 1994.

Collins, David R. *William McKinley: 25th President of the United States.* Ada, OK: Garrett Educational Corp., 1990.

Dobson, John M. *Reticent Expansionism: The Foreign Policy of William McKinley.* Pittsburgh: Duquesne University Press, 1988.

Glad, Paul W. *McKinley, Bryan and the People.* New York: Lippincott, 1964. Reprint, Chicago: I. R. Dee, 1991.

Gould, Lewis L. *The Presidency of William McKinley.* Lawrence: The Regents Press of Kansas, 1980.

Kent, Zachary. *William McKinley: Twenty-Fifth President of the United States.* Chicago: Children's Press, 1988.

Leech, Margaret. *In the Days of McKinley.* New York: Harper, 1959. Reprint, Westport, CT: Greenwood Press, 1975.

Library of Congress. "The Last Days of a President: Films of McKinley and the Pan-American Exposition, 1901." *American Memory.* [Online] http://lcweb2.loc.gov/papr/mckhome.html (accessed on August 14, 2000).

Morgan, H. Wayne. *William McKinley and His America.* Syracuse: Syracuse University Press, 1963.

Nasaw, David. *The Chief: The Life of William Randolph Hearst.* Boston: Houghton Mifflin, 2000.

Offner, John L. *An Unwanted War: The Diplomacy of the United States and Spain Over Cuba, 1895–1898.* Chapel Hill: University of North Carolina Press, 1992.

A young boy in a sailor uniform stands by the flag-draped mourning portrait of the late President William McKinley.

Courtesy of the Library of Congress.

A Selection of McKinley Landmarks

McKinley National Memorial and Museum. 800 McKinley Monument Dr., NW, Canton, OH 44701. (330) 455-7043. President McKinley, his wife, and two children are laid to rest in one of the largest memorials of a U.S. president. On the grounds is a museum with McKinley memorabilia, as well as a science museum and planetarium. See http://mckinleymuseum.org/cgi-bin/mckinley/exhibits.cgi?memorial:adults (accessed on August 3, 2000).

National McKinley Birthplace Memorial. 46 N. Main St., Niles, OH 44446. (330) 652-1704. A small library of McKinley artifacts is opposite Niles' public library. The Library has planned to build a replica of McKinley's birthplace home. See http://www.mckinley.lib.oh.us/memorial.htm (accessed on August 3, 2000).

Saxton-McKinley House / National First Ladies' Library. 331 S. Market Ave., Canton, OH 44702. (330) 452-0876. Ida Saxton McKinley lived in this house as a girl; she and her husband occupied it from 1878 to 1891. In June 1998, the house became the headquarters of the new National First Ladies' Library. See http://www.firstladies.org/ (accessed on August 3, 2000).

Ohio State University Department of History. *The Era of William McKinley.* [Online] http://www.cohums.ohio-state.edu/history/projects/McKinley/ (accessed on August 14, 2000).

Springen, Donald K. *William Jennings Bryan: Orator of Small-town America.* New York: Greenwood Press, 1991.

Swanberg, W. A. *Citizen Hearst: A Biography of William Randolph Hearst.* New York: Scribner, 1961. Reprint, New York: Galahad Books, 1996.

Whitelaw, Nancy. *Joseph Pulitzer and the New York World.* Princeton, NJ: Princeton University Press, 1966. Reprint, Greensboro, NC: Morgan Reynolds, 2000.

Ida McKinley

Born June 8, 1847
Canton, Ohio
Died May 26, 1907
Canton, Ohio

Despite personal tragedy and illness, the Belle of Canton made a valiant effort to fulfill her role as first lady

A s a young woman, Ida McKinley was known as the Belle of Canton, Ohio, because of her lively attitude and her family's wealth and social position. Her fashionable appearance and attractiveness—tufts of reddish brown hair around her delicate facial features—contributed to the nickname. Active in local theater and community affairs, she was also independent-minded and self-reliant, taking a job in her father's bank at a time when it was rare for a woman to be in a public business position. But before she turned thirty, Ida McKinley suffered health problems and personal tragedies. She spent the rest of her life in a semi-invalid condition, occasionally able to appear in public but in need of constant care.

"My wife—be careful . . . how you tell her—oh, be careful."

William McKinley, after being shot

Vibrant youth

Ida Saxton was born in Canton in 1847. Her father was a wealthy banker and community leader. The large house in which the Saxton family lived is still in excellent condition over a century later and forms part of the National First Ladies' Library complex in Canton.

Ida McKinley.
Courtesy of the Library of Congress.

Ida attended private school in Cleveland and later graduated from Miss Eastman's Seminary, a finishing school in Media, Pennsylvania, where she was an excellent student. Upon returning to Canton, Ida became involved in community affairs, including fundraising to build a new Presbyterian Church for the congregation (church community) to which her family belonged. She participated in local theater, including a performance at Schaefer's Opera House in Canton, where she was voted the most popular actress.

At about this time, in 1868, Ida first encountered **William McKinley** (1843–1901; see entry in volume 3), a young lawyer active in Republican politics. They were introduced by his sister, Anna, who was the principal of Canton's West Grammar School. Ida and William did not immediately become friends, for they moved in different social circles. Twenty-one-year-old Ida was part of Canton's social elite, the richer and more powerful members of society. Ida was regularly invited to exclusive masquerade (costume) parties and debutante balls (dances at which a young woman is introduced to the elite social circle). The twenty-five-year-old McKinley, a decorated Civil War veteran who liked to be called "Major" after the military rank he had attained, was a lawyer just getting started in his career.

Later that year, Ida and her sister Mary, along with a chaperone (older female companion), traveled to Europe for an extended vacation of sightseeing and shopping. When the sisters returned home, Ida took a job at her father's bank. She started as a teller interacting with the general public, but soon worked her way up to cashier and handled larger business transactions. It was so rare for a woman to work in such a position in those days that many friends of the Saxtons thought the family was going through financial difficulties. Not so, replied Ida's father, James Saxton. He and his daughter both wanted her to be self-reliant.

Ida continued to have a passing acquaintance with William McKinley—they passed each other several times on Sunday mornings as they walked to their respective churches. Ida was Presbyterian, and McKinley was a Methodist who taught Sunday school classes. William had an account at the Stark County Bank where Ida worked; they first began a relationship there. William seemed to be at the bank regularly, at least in part because of his growing success as a lawyer. He was elected prosecuting attorney of Stark County, and he and Ida became engaged shortly after he took office early in 1869.

Losses

William and Ida McKinley were married in 1871 in an extravagant ceremony attended by over a thousand people. Their ceremony was the first to be performed in the new Presbyterian church for which Ida McKinley had helped raise funds. Their happy life as newlyweds was made more joyous when their first child, Katherine (1871–1876), was born on Christmas Day in 1871. But Ida McKinley began having health problems while pregnant with the couple's second child. Ida McKinley suffered from phlebitis (a painful swelling of a vein) and from epileptic seizures (convulsive attacks caused by epilepsy, a disorder of the nervous system). Ida's frail health was further complicated when her mother died. Deeply grieving, she fell into depression. The couple's second child, Ida, was born premature in April 1873 and was never fully healthy, dying four months later. Three years later, young Katie came down with typhoid fever (an infectious bacterial infection) and died.

Even while presiding over the country, William McKinley took the time to attend to his fragile wife, Ida.

Courtesy of the Library of Congress.

The ordeals left Ida McKinley physically and emotionally drained. In constant need of attention for her health, she became semi-invalid, only occasionally able to attend social functions. She would never again regain full physical or mental health. Still, Ida McKinley made efforts at meeting the demands of being a public figure, because her husband won election to Congress and then served as governor of Ohio before being elected president in 1896. McKinley was always attentive to her needs and concerned for her health. He was never far from her for more than a few days.

Newspapers were respectful to Ida McKinley as first lady and remained quiet about her fainting spells. In fact, many details concerning her health were only revealed later, after McKinley was assassinated and Ida McKinley had returned home to Canton.

Coping in public

Ida McKinley spent most days of her adult life in a rocking chair, where she passed time by knitting, crocheting, and reading. For those official functions she could attend, she was always fashionably dressed and often met guests while seated in a velvet chair to ease the strain of social interaction. She would occasionally hold a bouquet of flowers, which would discourage the many guests from attempting to shake her hand and possibly sap her strength and energy. At dinners she always sat next to her husband, who would monitor her health and look for signs of an oncoming seizure. The president carried a large handkerchief, which he would use to shield the first lady from sight if she should happen to suffer a seizure. The seating arrangement of having her by his side was maintained even when it went against official protocol (forms of ceremony followed in the presence of important people; for example, at state dinners the president is supposed to be seated with fellow heads of state and dignitaries, with wives and other officials seated separately).

Following McKinley's reelection in 1900, the president decided to take a transcontinental (cross-country) tour to promote new policies, including his tougher stand against business trusts that dominated some markets. During McKinley's campaign tours and political travels, Ida McKinley usually remained at home, but for the transcontinental tour she made an effort to travel with her husband. However, she fell ill at one of the first stops in California and had to be rushed away from the scene for treatment.

Ida McKinley was not with her husband when he stopped in Buffalo, New York, later that year to speak at the Pan-Am Exposition. The day after the speech, the president greeted a long line of people at the exposition. In that line, a man named Leon Czolgosz (1873–1901) stood with a gun hidden beneath a handkerchief and shot the president after

McKinley extended his hand in greeting. As the president fell and gasped for life, he was heard to say to his secretary, George B. Cortelyou (1862–1940), "My wife—be careful . . . how you tell her—oh, be careful."

McKinley never recovered from the wounds and died a week later. His body was taken by train to Washington, D.C., for a state funeral, and then Ida McKinley accompanied her husband's casket on a train from Washington, D.C., back home to Canton.

Mrs. McKinley lived the remainder of her life under the care of her sister. She died in 1907 and was entombed next to her husband and their two daughters in the McKinley Memorial Mausoleum in Canton.

Where to Learn More

Gould, Lewis, ed. *American First Ladies: Their Lives and Their Legacy.* New York: Garland, 1996.

Leech, Margaret. *In the Days of McKinley.* New York: Harper, 1959. Reprint, Westport, CT: Greenwood Press, 1975.

McKinley's First Inaugural Address

Delivered on March 4, 1897; excerpted from
***Bartleby.com* (Web site)**

The first "modern president" presents his vision on the eve of renewed national prosperity

Tariffs (taxes on imported goods) have been an issue of contention since the earliest days of the United States. The issue was particularly controversial during the nineteenth century. Tariffs are used to raise tax revenue for the government and to protect domestic businesses from foreign competition. Some nations can afford to manufacture products more cheaply than others, or have greater access to resources or materials. The products, resources, or materials sell at lower costs than those of other nations. In such cases, a nation like the United States imposes tariffs on lower-cost, imported goods, making them less attractive to consumers, who then buy similar goods produced in their own country.

During the 1820s and 1830s, the government imposed tariffs to help protect emerging American industries. Those tariffs were generally beneficial to the more industrialized North. People living in rural areas, especially in the South and in new states outside of New England, had to pay higher prices for goods because of the tariffs. During the administration of President **Andrew Jackson** (1767–1845; see entry in volume 1), the state of South Carolina rebelled against tariffs.

> "The credit of the Government, the integrity of its currency, and the inviolability of its obligations must be preserved. This was the commanding verdict of the people, and it will not be unheeded."
>
> *William McKinley*

The state attempted to nullify (reject) new tariffs and threatened to secede from the Union over the issue. President Jackson, otherwise a champion of states' rights, threatened military action if the state defied the laws of the land.

After steady growth through the 1840s and 1850s, American industry boomed following the Civil War (1861–65). Tariffs were used to protect emerging industries. Again, those tariffs benefited industrialized areas. In addition to facing a shifting population from rural to urban areas, farmers faced higher prices for goods they needed (including clothes and equipment). Heated debate over tariffs was characteristic of the last few decades of the century. Those opposed to tariffs rallied successfully behind **Grover Cleveland** (1837–1908; see entry in volume 3) for president in the 1884 and 1892 elections. **Benjamin Harrison** (1833–1901; see entry in volume 3) and **William McKinley** (1843–1901; see entry in volume 3), supporters of tariffs, won in 1888 and 1896, respectively.

As a congressman, McKinley authored a sweeping tariff act (called the McKinley Tariff of 1890). The tariff contributed to an economic downturn that plagued the United States in the early 1890s. Nevertheless, McKinley enjoyed the backing of businesses and urban areas and won the presidential election of 1896 over William Jennings Bryan (1860–1925; see box in **William McKinley** entry in volume 3), who was anti-tariff and supported the causes of rural folks.

Things to remember while reading an excerpt from President McKinley's first inaugural address:

- At the time McKinley took office, the United States was just beginning to emerge from economic hard times that began in 1893. In his inaugural address, McKinley wanted to provide clear indications of how he was going to deal with the weak economy. He used the word "economy" (which can be defined as thrifty and efficient) to define his administration's approach: he wanted the government to spend less and pay off its debts.

- Not surprisingly, McKinley also announced his intention of raising tariff rates on some goods. McKinley had been a supporter of the use of tariffs since the mid-1870s, when he first entered Congress. As president, he wanted to use the revenue the government received from tariffs to help pay off the national debt.

- McKinley mentioned his support for reciprocity (an arrangement that brings equal value in trade to parties involved), which was part of the McKinley Tariff Act of 1890. Under reciprocity agreements, a trade imbalance with another nation could be addressed directly by the president. For example, a nation trading sugar to the United States for a more valuable product would trade a much larger amount of sugar in order to equal the value of what they were receiving in trade. McKinley had planned to emphasize reciprocal trade agreements during his second term in office. However, he was assassinated only months after his second inaugural.

- In the final paragraph of the excerpt, McKinley addresses the need for Americans to continue to support rights guaranteed by the Constitution. During the 1890s, a continuing cycle of poverty in the South and increasing strength among black voters led to a backlash by whites, who enacted Jim Crow laws (laws targeted against blacks meant to deny their voting rights).

Excerpt from President McKinley's first inaugural address

*The **credit** of the Government, the integrity of its currency, and the inviolability of its **obligations** must be preserved. This was the commanding verdict of the people, and it will not be unheeded.*

Economy is demanded in every branch of the Government at all times, but especially in periods, like the present, of depression in business and distress among the people. The severest economy must be observed in all public expenditures, and extravagance stopped wherever it is found, and prevented wherever in the future it may be developed. If the revenues are to remain as now, the only relief that can come must be from decreased expenditures. But the present

Credit: Financial standing.

Obligations: Money owed.

*must not become the permanent condition of the Government. It has been our uniform practice to **retire**, not increase our outstanding obligations, and this policy must again be resumed and vigorously enforced. Our revenues should always be large enough to meet with ease and promptness not only our current needs and the **principal** and **interest** of the public debt, but to make proper and liberal provision for that most deserving body of public creditors, the soldiers and sailors and the widows and orphans who are the pensioners of the United States. . . .*

*The best way for the Government to maintain its credit is to pay as it goes—not by resorting to loans, but by keeping out of debt—through an adequate income secured by a system of taxation, external or internal, or both. It is the settled policy of the Government, pursued from the beginning and practiced by all parties and Administrations, to raise the bulk of our revenue from taxes upon foreign productions entering the United States for sale and consumption, and avoiding, for the most part, every form of direct taxation, except in time of war. The country is clearly opposed to any needless additions to the subject of internal taxation, and is committed by its latest popular utterance to the system of tariff taxation. There can be no misunderstanding, either, about the principle upon which this tariff taxation shall be levied. Nothing has ever been made plainer at a general election than that the controlling principle in the raising of revenue from duties on imports is zealous care for American interests and American labor. The people have declared that such legislation should be had as will give ample protection and encouragement to the industries and the development of our country. It is, therefore, earnestly hoped and expected that Congress will, at the earliest practicable moment, enact revenue legislation that shall be fair, reasonable, conservative, and just, and which, while supplying sufficient revenue for public purposes, will still be signally beneficial and helpful to every section and every enterprise of the people. To this policy we are all, of whatever party, firmly bound by the voice of the people—a power vastly more potential than the expression of any political platform. The paramount duty of Congress is to stop deficiencies by the restoration of that protective legislation which has always been the firmest prop of the Treasury. The passage of such a law or laws would strengthen the credit of the Government both at home and abroad, and go far toward stopping the drain upon the **gold reserve** held for the redemption of our currency, which has been heavy and well-nigh constant for several years.*

Retire: Pay off, in financial terms.

Principal: Money remaining to be paid on a loan.

Interest: The additional cost of not paying off a loan immediately.

Gold reserve: The practice of storing precious metal gold to protect the value of currency (for example, $1 of gold for every dollar bill).

*In the revision of the tariff especial attention should be given to the re-enactment and extension of the **reciprocity principle** of the law of 1890, under which so great a stimulus was given to our foreign trade in new and advantageous markets for our surplus agricultural and manufactured products. The brief trial given this legislation amply justifies a further experiment and additional discretionary power in the making of commercial treaties, the end in view always to be the opening up of new markets for the products of our country, by granting concessions to the products of other lands that we need and cannot produce ourselves, and which do not involve any loss of labor to our own people, but tend to increase their employment.*

The depression of the past four years has fallen with especial severity upon the great body of toilers of the country, and upon none more than the holders of small farms. Agriculture has languished and labor suffered. The revival of manufacturing will be a relief to both. No portion of our population is more devoted to the institution of free government nor more loyal in their support, while none bears more cheerfully or fully its proper share in the maintenance of the Government or is better entitled to its wise and liberal care and protection. Legislation helpful to producers is beneficial to all. The depressed condition of industry on the farm and in the mine and factory has lessened the ability of the people to meet the demands upon them, and they rightfully expect that not only a system of revenue shall be established that will secure the largest income with the least burden, but that every means will be taken to decrease, rather than increase, our public expenditures. Business conditions are not the most promising. It will take time to restore the prosperity of former years. If we cannot promptly attain it, we can resolutely turn our faces in that direction and aid its return by friendly legislation. However troublesome the situation may appear, Congress will not, I am sure, be found lacking in disposition or ability to relieve it as far as legislation can do so. The restoration of confidence and the revival of business, which men of all parties so much desire, depend more largely upon the prompt, energetic, and intelligent action of Congress than upon any other single agency affecting the situation.

It is inspiring, too, to remember that no great emergency in the one hundred and eight years of our eventful national life has ever arisen that has not been met with wisdom and courage by the American people, with fidelity to their best interests and highest destiny, and to the honor of the American name. These years of glorious history have exalted mankind and advanced the cause of freedom throughout the world, and immeasurably strengthened the

Reciprocity principle: A trade agreement where more items of lesser value are traded for fewer items of higher value until the value of trading is equal for both sides.

precious free institutions which we enjoy. The people love and will sustain these institutions. The great essential to our happiness and prosperity is that we adhere to the principles upon which the Government was established and insist upon their faithful observance. Equality of rights must prevail, and our laws be always and everywhere respected and obeyed. We may have failed in the discharge of our full duty as citizens of the great Republic, but it is consoling and encouraging to realize that free speech, a free press, free thought, free schools, the free and unmolested right of religious liberty and worship, and free and fair elections are dearer and more universally enjoyed to-day than ever before. These guaranties must be sacredly preserved and wisely strengthened. (Bartleby.com [Web site])

What happened next . . .

The economy of the United States rebounded, and President McKinley's popularity soared. The following year, the United States emerged victorious in the Spanish-American War (1898) and took possession of former Spanish colonies in the Caribbean and the Pacific oceans. American military strength had grown along with the surging economy.

There were problems as well. Americans debated about whether they should maintain control over areas won from Spain. At home, living conditions in many cities were bad, despite the improved economy. Segregation and voter intimidation became more rampant in the South, and Native Americans were facing a crisis for survival (their population would soon reach an all-time low). Large businesses were dominating smaller ones. McKinley was prepared to address the problems when he won reelection in 1900. However, he was assassinated months into his second term. Vice President **Theodore Roosevelt** (1858–1919; see entry in volume 3) would become known as the "trust-buster" for leading the government to investigate and punish large corporations that engaged in unfair business practices.

During McKinley's administration, the United States transformed into its modern identity as an economic, industrial, and military giant. How much McKinley's policies actually contributed to that transformation is debatable, but he was certainly influential. Beginning with his election in 1896, Republicans held the presidency for twenty-eight of the next thirty-six years (they won seven of nine presidential elections). The economic policies advocated by McKinley were echoed by each of those later Republican presidents.

Did you know . . .

- There were three important issues in the presidential campaign of 1896—tariffs, bimetallism (the policy of having two precious metals to back the value of money), and American expansionism. The nation was divided on the issues, and candidates William McKinley and William Jennings Bryan had opposing views on each issue. McKinley won the election and established himself as the most powerful president since **Abraham Lincoln** (1809–1865; see entry in volume 2). The nation may have been divided on the three issues in 1896, but by the time McKinley ran again in 1900, the nation backed him with the largest margin of victory in the popular vote up to that time. During McKinley's first term, the Dingley Tariff (1897) called for higher rates; the United States won the Spanish-American War (1898) and took possession of several of Spain's former colonies; and the Gold Standard Act (1900) declared the gold dollar as the sole standard of currency.

Where to Learn More

Damiani, Brian P. *Advocates of Empire: William McKinley, the Senate, and American Expansion, 1898–1899.* New York: Garland, 1987.

Gould, Lewis L. *The Presidency of William McKinley.* Lawrence: Regents Press of Kansas, 1980.

Morgan, H. Wayne. *William McKinley and His America.* Syracuse: Syracuse University Press, 1963.

"William McKinley: First Inaugural Address." *Bartleby.com.* [Online] http://www.bartleby.com/124/pres40.html (accessed on August 4, 2000).

Theodore Roosevelt

Twenty-sixth president (1901–1909)

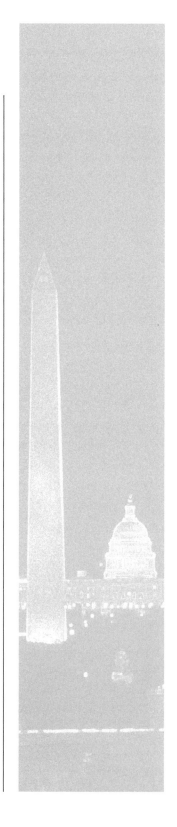

Theodore Roosevelt

Born October 27, 1858
New York, New York
Died January 6, 1919
Long Island, New York

Twenty-sixth president of the United States
(1901–1909)

Popularized the Progressive movement,
led the United States in playing a greater
role in world affairs, and was a pioneer
in conservation

O ne of the most popular, controversial, and important presidents, Theodore Roosevelt was a hearty, dynamic leader. His administration introduced much-needed monitoring of business with an established set of guidelines. His foreign policy aimed to make the United States a more significant force in international affairs as well as the guardian of the Western Hemisphere.

Roosevelt was full of personal contradictions (opposites). Born to a wealthy family, he used the power of elected office to protect the general public against powerful institutions. He was a sickly child who grew into a strong and vigorous man. He was the first president to confront problems associated with industrialization (the use of machinery for making goods), while at the same time he became famous for his ground-breaking efforts at conserving natural resources. A fearless and heroic military leader, Roosevelt also received the Nobel Peace Prize. Along with his love for physical activity and outdoor life, Roosevelt was a man of impressive intellectual achievement. He was the author of more than thirty books.

"Get action. Do things . . . take a place wherever you are and be somebody; get action."

Theodore Roosevelt

Theodore Roosevelt.
Courtesy of the Library of Congress.

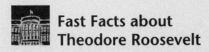

Fast Facts about Theodore Roosevelt

Full name: Theodore Roosevelt

Born: October 27, 1858

Died: January 6, 1919

Burial site: Young's Memorial Cemetery, Oyster Bay, New York

Parents: Theodore and Martha Bulloch Roosevelt

Spouse: Alice Hathaway Lee (1861–1884; m. 1880); Edith Kermit Carow (1861–1948; m. 1886)

Children: Alice Lee (1884–1980); Theodore Jr. (1887–1944); Kermit (1889–1943); Ethel Carow (1891–1977); Archibald Bulloch (1894–1979); Quentin (1897–1918)

Religion: Dutch Reformed

Education: Harvard University (B.A., 1880)

Occupations: Rancher; soldier; author

Government positions: New York state assemblyman; New York City police commissioner; New York governor; assistant U.S. secretary of the Navy and vice president under William McKinley

Political party: Republican

Dates as president: September 14, 1901–March 4, 1905 (first term); March 4, 1905–March 4, 1909 (second term)

Age upon taking office: 42

Force of will

Born October 27, 1858, in New York City, Theodore Roosevelt was the second of four children of Theodore Sr. (1831–1878)—a merchant, banker, and philanthropist (a person, generally wealthy, who donates money)—and Martha Bulloch Roosevelt (1834–1884), who came from a prominent Georgia family. Her brothers fought for the Confederacy, the Southern states that separated from the United States during the Civil War (1861–65). Later, as Roosevelt developed a fascination with military history, he took great pride in the wartime service of his Southern relatives, even though he and his father were staunch Unionists, those who supported the preservation of the United States and the North during the Civil War.

The Roosevelt children were schooled at home by private tutors. Although he was nearsighted, Teedy (as Roosevelt was called) learned to read very early and was interested in a wide variety of subjects, especially American history and literature. He developed a love of nature and became an expert on birds, flowers, and animals. By the time he was fifteen, Roosevelt had traveled throughout Europe, Africa, and the Middle East. During his teens in 1872 and 1873, he lived with a family in Dresden, Germany, and learned the German language.

In addition to nearsightedness, Roosevelt suffered from asthma as a child and was frequently ill. His father cautioned him that, although he was eagerly training his mind, the

Theodore Roosevelt Timeline

1858: Born in New York

1877: *The Summer Birds of the Adirondacks in Franklin County, New York,* the first of over thirty books written by Roosevelt, is published privately; his first major publication, *The History of the Naval War of 1812,* is published in 1882

1882–84: Serves as New York state assemblyman

1884–86: Builds and lives on Elkhorn Ranch in the Dakota Territory

1889–95: Serves on U.S. Civil Service Commission

1895–97: Serves as police commissioner of New York City

1897–98: Serves as assistant secretary of the Navy

1898: Volunteers for service during the Spanish-American War; as a lieutenant colonel in the First U.S. Volunteer Cavalry, he forms a squadron called the "Rough Riders," whose exploits are well publicized by newspapers

1899–1900: Serves as New York governor

1901: Serves as vice president under William McKinley; assumes the presidency following McKinley's assassination

1901–9: Serves as twenty-sixth U.S. president

1909–10: Leads an African safari, collects more than five hundred different birds and animals, and writes *African Game Trails;* tours Europe

1912: Finishes second in the presidential election (to Woodrow Wilson) as a third-party candidate, outpolling incumbent president William Howard Taft

1919: Dies in New York

weakness of his body might hold him back in the future. Young Theodore started a training program to improve his physical fitness: He learned to ride and hunt, he took up boxing and swimming, he played sports, and he hiked and camped in the wilderness. With this emphasis on physical activity, Roosevelt developed robust good health and an outstanding physical condition.

Before graduating from Harvard University in 1880, Roosevelt had already published two books on birds. He began research for another book, a naval history of the War of 1812 (1812–15) between Great Britain and the United States. Published in 1882, the book drew little public interest, but it was a respected scholarly study that became required

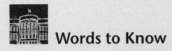

Words to Know

Annexing: Adding a new state or possession to the existing United States of America.

"Big stick" foreign policy: Theodore Roosevelt's theory that in diplomatic efforts, it was wise to "speak softly and carry a big stick," meaning that one should attempt peaceful solutions while at the same time being prepared to back up the talk with action when necessary.

Civil Service: All nonmilitary personnel employed by the federal government.

Industrialization: The use of machinery for manufacturing goods.

Isthmus: A narrow tract of land between two large and separate bodies of water.

Monroe Doctrine: A policy statement issued during the presidency of James Monroe (1817–25) that explained the position of the United States on the activities of European powers in the Western Hemisphere. Of major significance was the stand of the United States against European intervention in the affairs of the Americas.

Muckrakers: A circle of investigative reporters during Theodore Roosevelt's term in office who exposed the seamier (unwholesome) side of American life. These reporters thoroughly researched their stories and based their reports on provable facts.

Populism: An agricultural movement of rural areas between the Mississippi River and the Rocky Mountains of the late nineteenth century that united the interests of farmers and laborers. In 1891, the

reading at the Naval War College. The U.S. Navy ordered that one copy be made available on every ship in its fleet.

In 1878, Roosevelt met Alice Hathaway Lee (1861–1884) and fell in love with her. They married several months after his graduation from Harvard, honeymooned in England (where he did research for his naval history project), and settled in New York City.

Political career begins

Roosevelt enrolled in law classes at Columbia University in New York City, but he did not enjoy attending class as much as researching and writing. Feeling a sense of duty to his fellow citizens, Roosevelt ran for public office. In 1881, at

movement formed a national political party, the People's Party, whose members were called Populists. Populist ideals remained popular even when the party faded early in the twentieth century.

Primary elections: Elections held to determine which of several candidates from a particular political party will represent that party in a general election.

Progressive "Bull Moose" Party: Party in which Theodore Roosevelt ran as a third-party candidate in 1912. He came in second to incumbent president William Howard Taft, but lost to New Jersey governor Woodrow Wilson.

Progressivism: A movement that began late in the nineteenth century whose followers pursued social, economic, and government reform. Generally located in urban areas, Progressivists ranged from individuals seeking to improve local living conditions to radicals who pursued sweeping changes in the American political and economic system.

Regulation: Monitoring business with an established set of guidelines.

Roosevelt Corollary: An addition that Theodore Roosevelt made to the Monroe Doctrine that declared that if any country in the Western Hemisphere acted irresponsibly and caused a European country to intervene in its affairs, the United States would consider that action as a threat to its interests.

Trusts: A business combination formed to reduce competition and control prices.

the age of twenty-three, he was elected to the New York state assembly in Albany.

Roosevelt quickly won the respect of his fellow legislators: He revealed abuses of power by a corrupt judge, and he supported laws that began regulating workshops that had horrible conditions—many of the workshops employed child labor. After being named Republican minority leader, he developed a reputation for working effectively with members of both political parties.

Roosevelt was serving his third term in the state assembly when tragedy struck. Alice Lee Roosevelt died of kidney failure on February 14, 1884, following the birth of the couple's daughter. She was named Alice in honor of her mother. On that same day, Roosevelt's mother died of typhoid fever

Alice Roosevelt, Roosevelt's first wife, died in 1884 when Roosevelt was still a New York state assemblyman. *Courtesy of the Library of Congress.*

(a highly infectious disease transmitted by contaminated food or water). Grief-stricken, Roosevelt continued to work, while Roosevelt's older sister, Anna (known as "Bamie"; 1855–1931), cared for baby Alice (1884–1980).

Home on the range

In 1883, Roosevelt traveled throughout the western United States. Inspired by the wide-open frontier, bountiful animal life, and freedom of the range, Roosevelt used some of his family inheritance to buy land in the Dakota Territory. He built the Elkhorn Ranch and lived there from 1884 until 1886, writing western history and operating a cattle ranch. He enjoyed the western lifestyle, wearing buckskin (strong leather) shirts, sporting a gun belt with a pearl-handled revolver, and spending most of his time with his cowboy work crews. Roosevelt hunted big game (large animals), observed wildlife and plants, and worked on several books of natural history and biography.

Roosevelt returned to New York City for a visit during this period. He fell in love with Edith Kermit Carow (1861–1948; see entry on **Edith Roosevelt** in volume 3), a woman he had known for most of his life. When they became engaged, he moved back east to Sagamore Hill, a home he had built at Oyster Bay, Long Island. He soon returned to politics. Roosevelt became the Republican candidate for mayor of New York City, but lost badly, finishing third in the election.

Discouraged by his poor showing, Roosevelt and Edith traveled to Europe. They were married in London on December 2, 1886. When they returned to the United States, the Roosevelts set up residence at Sagamore Hill, which would be their family home for the rest of their lives. They raised five children in addition to Alice, Roosevelt's daughter from his first marriage.

Roosevelt supported **Benjamin Harrison** (1833–1901; see entry in volume 3) in the presidential election of 1888 and was appointed to the U.S. Civil Service Commission in Washington following Harrison's victory. (The Civil Service consists of all nonmilitary personnel employed by the federal government.) In that position, he fought against the patronage system, in which government jobs went to those who demonstrated party loyalty. He believed jobs should go to the most qualified individuals. He also aggressively weeded out fraud (deceit or corruption for personal gain), rewrote Civil Service examinations to make them more fair, and opened more jobs to women. At the time, Roosevelt's actions were considered radical (extreme, risky), but he quickly earned a growing reputation as a reformer.

Reformer and Rough Rider

Roosevelt returned to New York City in 1895 to accept the post of police commissioner. During this period, people

Known as an adventurer and nature lover, Theodore Roosevelt is shown here riding a moose—a bit unusual for most people, but not for Roosevelt. *Reproduced by permission of the Corbis Corporation.*

began expressing frustration over abuses of power by politicians and the huge profits of corporations. People demanded more accountability from government and business. Many farmers and laborers in rural areas of the West and South supported a political movement called populism that supported their interests, whereas those in urban areas wanting social, economic, and government reform turned to progressivism. So began the era of the reformer.

As police commissioner, Roosevelt exposed police corruption—particularly the actions of officers who accepted money to overlook criminal activities. He enforced laws that regulated establishments where alcoholic beverages were served and began prosecution of landlords who treated tenants unfairly. In the process, Roosevelt made enemies throughout city government, but his national reputation was boosted and he learned a great deal about issues that mattered to common people.

Roosevelt openly desired a career in national politics. Through his study and his writing, he developed firm ideas on how the country should be run. He recognized that military strength, especially a strong navy, was vital for national survival and the key to enforcing foreign policy. Therefore, when Ohio governor **William McKinley** (1843–1901; see entry in volume 3) was elected president in 1896, Roosevelt talked his friends in Washington, D.C., into pressuring McKinley to appoint him assistant secretary of the Navy. In 1897, McKinley agreed.

As assistant naval secretary, Roosevelt began helping to prepare the Navy for a possible war with Spain. For some time, Spain had been trying to suppress a movement for independence in Cuba, a Spanish colony in the Caribbean Sea just south of Florida. Some Cubans had started a revolution in 1895, hoping to free their country, but Spanish authorities remained in power and established prison camps to hold revolutionaries. American journalists began exposing the terrible conditions of those camps. Some reports were exaggerated, reflecting a sensationalistic (strongly emotional and graphically detailed) reporting style popular at the time that was called "yellow journalism." (For more on yellow journalism, see William Randolph Hearst and Joseph Pulitzer boxes in **William McKinley** entry in volume 3.)

In 1897, the United States sent the battleship *Maine* to the port of Havana, Cuba's capital, to protect American citizens and property. On February 15, 1898, the *Maine* sank after being ripped by a mysterious explosion that killed 260 American sailors. Although no cause for the explosion was determined, sabotage (destructive action by an enemy agent) was suspected and widely reported, and many Americans called for war. (Over seventy years later, in 1969, the U.S. Navy determined that a defective boiler had caused the explosion on the *Maine*.)

Roosevelt was in charge while the secretary of the Navy was out of town. He instructed Commodore George Dewey (1837–1917), the commander of the Navy's Asian fleet, to sail for Hong Kong and prepare for action in the Philippines, a group of islands in the Pacific that were controlled by Spain. Wanting to see European influence in the Caribbean come to an end, Roosevelt was anxious for war with Spain. In April 1898, President McKinley approved a congressional resolution calling for the immediate withdrawal of Spanish forces from Cuba. Several days later, the Spanish officially refused and declared war on the United States. The next day, the U.S. Congress voted for its own declaration of war on Spain. Commodore Dewey attacked and quickly defeated the Spanish fleet at Manila Bay in the Philippines.

Roosevelt had served for three years in the National Guard, attaining the rank of captain, and wanted to take part in combat. When war was declared, he resigned his position as assistant secretary of the Navy to serve as a lieutenant colonel in the First U.S. Volunteer Cavalry. He organized his own unit,

Theodore Roosevelt in his Rough Riders uniform.
Courtesy of the Library of Congress.

"Teedy," "Teddy," and "T.R." are among the nicknames Theodore Roosevelt had during his lifetime. As a boy, he accepted the name Teedy, but as a man he disliked being called Teddy. He preferred T.R., which is how he is often referred to in histories and biographies.

the "Rough Riders," and recruited volunteers from his circle of friends, from socialites (men of high society) and cowboys. Very shortly, the Rough Riders found themselves in Cuba.

The unit performed heroically in the war. Since Cuba was so close to the United States, newspapers were able to report on developments daily. Roosevelt, already well known nationally because of his various high-profile reform efforts, made a good story. Reporters began referring to him as "Teddy." His fearless leadership of the Rough Riders was well documented. Promoted to colonel, he led a wild charge up Kettle Hill in the battle for San Juan and became an instant hero to the nation. When the war ended after three months with a Spanish surrender, Roosevelt gained more publicity and popularity for his efforts to get the soldiers home as quickly as possible.

Pesky governor made vice president

In the summer of 1898, Roosevelt accepted a Republican invitation to run for governor of New York. Campaigning tirelessly and taking every opportunity to remind voters of his recent war record, Roosevelt won by a narrow margin. Roosevelt soon became a popular and respected governor: he dismantled a system in which many civil servants received jobs through the patronage system; he attacked large corporations that charged excessive prices for goods and services; he supported pro-labor legislation, increased teachers' salaries, and led support for a bill that outlawed racial discrimination in public schools; and he pursued preservation of state forests and wildlife.

Roosevelt's success as governor, his increasing popularity, and especially his tendency to attack powerful businesses and politicians of both major parties, began to annoy senior New York senator Thomas Collier Platt (1833–1910). "Boss" Platt, as he was known, wanted to get rid of the young governor. He convinced several Republican Party officials to support Roosevelt for vice president on the ticket with President McKinley in the election of 1900. The vice presidency had been vacant since the death of Garret Hobart (1844–1899).

Although he was at first reluctant to become vice president, a position without any real political power, Roo-

sevelt campaigned with typical vigor and helped McKinley win reelection by a landslide. But only six months into his second term, McKinley was shot by an assassin in Buffalo, New York, on September 6, 1901. He died eight days later. Theodore Roosevelt was sworn in as the twenty-sixth president of the United States; at age forty-two, Roosevelt became the youngest man to become president. (No one younger has held that office since then.)

Theodore Roosevelt speaks at a public gathering in Evanston, Illinois, during a western tour in the early 1900s.
Reproduced by permission of Archive Photos.

Roosevelt Becomes President

Theodore Roosevelt became president of the United States following the death of William McKinley. (See McKinley entry for election results from the McKinley/Roosevelt campaign.) This marked the fifth time in U.S. history that a vice president became president following the death of his predecessor. Roosevelt's victory in 1904 marked the first time that a former vice president finishing his predecessor's term was elected as president on his own in the next election.

"Trustbuster"

Roosevelt's approach to the presidency surprised no one who had been following his political career. After carefully building momentum and support during his first few months in office, he pursued his policies with the same aggressiveness that characterized his cavalry charges in Cuba. Viewing himself as the representative of the common people, he believed the federal government should resolve disputes between forces of business and labor.

Pursuing reform of those business practices that benefited a few wealthy individuals and corporations, Roosevelt brought more regulation to big business. As a result, he gained a reputation as a "trustbuster." Some businesses that created similar products or provided similar services linked to form trusts—a business combination formed to reduce competition and control prices. Since a trust controls a particular market sector (that is, a particular division of trade or commerce), it does not face competition over the prices it demands for goods and services. Small and new companies cannot survive in business sectors dominated by trusts.

Unlike some of the more radical reformers, Roosevelt did not want to dissolve all big companies, just those that he thought were exploiting their financial power at the sake of the public good. Roosevelt influenced Congress to pass several measures that helped the federal government enforce existing antitrust laws. During the term Roosevelt completed as successor to President McKinley and the next term when Roosevelt was elected on his own, the Department of Justice launched forty-three lawsuits against trusts and won several important judicial decisions. Among the victories was a suit against the Northern Securities Company, a group of several railroad companies run as though they were one company. That arrangement had allowed them to reduce competition and control prices.

In his first annual address to Congress in 1901 (see **Theodore Roosevelt** primary source entry in volume 3), Roosevelt argued that since many trusts were involved in goods and services vital to public welfare, they ought to disclose their financial records and business practices to the public they served. Roosevelt persuaded Congress to create the Bureau of Corporations, which had the power to investigate big companies.

In 1902, Roosevelt had the federal government intervene in a coal strike, convincing both sides to accept the ruling of an independent committee appointed by the president. This is considered the first significant pro-labor move by any U.S. president. Such actions were part of a program Roosevelt called the "Square Deal," intended to show that no one, rich or poor, would be given special treatment under his administration.

That same year, Roosevelt named Oliver Wendell Holmes (1841–1935; see box) to the U.S. Supreme Court. Holmes went on to become one of the most significant justices in the history of the Court. Roosevelt believed Holmes would support his efforts to break up large corporations, but Holmes insisted on judging each case by his own standards. Selecting Holmes to the court, where he served with distinction for over two decades, was one of several outstanding legacies of Roosevelt's presidency.

The "big stick" foreign policy

Roosevelt's military service had enhanced his national reputation, and he was known to favor expansion of American interests abroad. However, his foreign policy while president was surprisingly modest. He often said that in diplomatic efforts, it was wise to "speak softly and carry a big stick," meaning that one should attempt peaceful solutions while at the same time being prepared to back up the talk with action when necessary.

Unlike some Americans of the time, Roosevelt did not favor American domination of the Caribbean. For example, he opposed annexing Cuba and other islands. Still, he wanted European powers to continue to decrease their influence in Latin America. His foreign policy in that area came to be known as the Roosevelt Corollary to the Monroe Doctrine (see **James Monroe** primary source entry in volume 1). The Monroe Doctrine was a policy statement issued during the presidency of **James Monroe** (1758–1831; see entry in vol-

Oliver Wendell Holmes Jr.

Oliver Wendell Holmes Jr. was born in Boston, Massachusetts, on March 8, 1841. At age sixteen, Holmes began attending Harvard University. He wrote articles for student publications and complained of the school's unwillingness to accept new ideas. One such idea was the theory of evolution, first published in 1859 by English naturalist Charles Darwin (1809–1882). Holmes was fascinated by the scientific reasoning Darwin used to arrive at his idea that humans and other animals had evolved from earlier forms of life.

Holmes served in the Civil War (1861–65) for three years before enrolling at Harvard Law School in 1864. In 1866, he began his career as a lawyer and also wrote and taught law. In 1881, Holmes published *The Common Law,* in which he argued that laws should not be unchanging rules that are simply passed on from generation to generation, but should change and develop through the ages. Holmes thus applied Darwin's ideas to the history of law.

In 1882, Holmes was named to the Massachusetts Supreme Court, where he served for twenty years. In the late 1800s, the nation faced increasing tensions between workers and their employers. The tensions resulted from growth brought about by the Industrial Revolution, as large corporations with thousands of employees sprang up for the first time. Following Holmes's theories in *The Common Law,* new laws had to be made and old laws had to be interpreted in new ways.

In 1902, President Theodore Roosevelt named Holmes to the U.S. Supreme Court. Roosevelt believed Holmes would support his political goals. In particular, Roosevelt was "trust-busting"—trying to break up large corporations that held monopolies and were controlling important industries. In Massachusetts, some of Holmes's opinions seemed sympathetic to Roosevelt's aims. But in Holmes's first trust-busting case as a U.S. Supreme Court justice, he angered Roosevelt by disagreeing with the government. Holmes insisted on judging each case by his own standards, rather than by anyone's political aims.

Holmes's independent views and eloquent language led to his being called the Great Dissenter. In fact, though, his dissents (disagreeing against a majority opinion) only amounted to about three percent of the cases he heard. But his elegant writing style and clear logic made his opinions stand out more than those of other justices. In *Lochner v. New York* (1905), for example, the Court declared unconstitutional a New York law establishing a sixty-hour work week for bakers, saying that it limited the economic freedom of bakery owners. Remaining true to his idea of a living law that changes to follow the needs of society, Holmes wrote that the Constitution is not intended to embody a particular economic theory but to defend the rights of people with widely differing views.

Oliver Wendell Holmes Jr.
Courtesy of the Library of Congress.

When the United States entered World War I in 1917, Congress passed laws to prevent antiwar activists from spreading their views, which were thought to be dangerous to the war effort. The Federal Espionage Act of 1917 set stiff penalties for interfering with recruiting efforts. An amendment to the act also set penalties for disloyal language about the government, the war effort, or such symbols as the flag or the Constitution. After the war ended, several such cases came before the Supreme Court. Freedom of speech was the main issue. The Court's decisions—and Holmes's contributions—influenced how the issue would be viewed for the rest of the century. During the war, Socialist Party secretary Charles Schenck had been arrested under the Espionage Act. He was convicted of trying to cause insubordination (disregard for authority) in the army and for interfering with the draft by sending leaflets to drafted men urging them to oppose the draft and the war. The Supreme Court unanimously upheld Schenck's conviction. Holmes wrote that in ordinary times Schenck's leaflets would be protected under the First Amendment, which guarantees freedom of speech. Yet, as Holmes had written in *The Common Law,* the character of every act depends upon the circumstances in which it is done. War, Holmes wrote, changed the circumstances of Schenck's acts, giving the state the right to limit them. Said Holmes: "The most stringent protection of free speech would not protect a man in falsely shouting fire in a theatre and causing a panic. . . . The question in every case is whether the words used are used in circumstances and are of such a nature as to create a clear and present danger that they will bring about the substantive evils which Congress has the right to prevent." Both the "fire in a theatre" scenario and the phrase "clear and present danger" have become commonplace in considering how the law applies in certain cases.

After thirty years on the Supreme Court, Holmes retired in 1932. He died in Washington, D.C., on March 5, 1935, just three days short of his ninety-fourth birthday.

During Roosevelt's presidency, eminent writer and scholar Booker T. Washington (1856–1915) became the first African American invited to dine at the White House.

ume 1). The doctrine explained the position of the United States against involvement of the European powers in the affairs of the countries in the Western Hemisphere. The Roosevelt Corollary (corollary, meaning an addition to something already proved) declared that if any country in the Western Hemisphere acted irresponsibly and caused a European country to intervene in its affairs, the United States would consider that action as a threat to its interests.

Roosevelt's most controversial stand as president involved the Central American country of Panama, then a part of Colombia. Recognizing Panama's strategic importance in the commerce of the Western Hemisphere, he was greatly interested in a French company's plans to build a canal across the isthmus of Panama. (An isthmus is a narrow piece of land between two large and separate bodies of water. The isthmus of Panama separates the Atlantic and Pacific oceans.) Early in 1903, Roosevelt arranged to buy out the rights to construct the canal from the French firm.

When the Colombian government rejected Roosevelt's offer to build the canal, the president encouraged anti-Colombian forces in Panama to start a revolution, which began on November 3, 1903. Three days later, the government of the United States officially recognized Panama as an independent country. At the request of the new Panamanian government, U.S. naval ships arrived to prevent Colombian armed forces from suppressing the revolution. The new government of Panama granted the United States full control of a strip of land ten miles wide, all the way across the isthmus, to construct the Panama Canal. Although the canal was not completed during his presidency, Roosevelt took a personal interest in the construction project and visited Panama in 1906.

Second term

Since Roosevelt assumed office on the death of his predecessor, he was anxious to prove that he could get elected on his own. In 1904, he won his party's nomination for president and ran with U.S. senator Charles W. Fairbanks (1852–1918) of Ohio as his running mate. They were pitted against Democratic presidential nominee Alton B. Parker (1852–1926), a conservative judge from New York, and Henry G. Davis (1823–1916), an eighty-year-old former U.S. senator

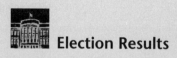

Election Results

1904

Presidential / Vice presidential candidates	Popular votes	Presidential electoral votes
Theodore Roosevelt / Charles W. Fairbanks (Republican)	7,623,486	336
Alton B. Parker / Henry G. Davis (Democratic)	5,077,911	140

from West Virginia. Roosevelt received the greatest margin of popular votes up to that time—over a million-and-a-half—and easily won in the Electoral College, 336 votes to 140. (For more information on the Electoral College, see boxes in **George W. Bush** entry in volume 5.)

Roosevelt continued to pursue business reform. Attacking high prices for railroad transportation, he supported the Hepburn Act of 1906. This law gave the Interstate Commerce Commission the authority to set railroad rates. Another key piece of legislation backed by the president was the Pure Food and Drug Bill, also passed in 1906. The bill set health standards for food and regulated medicine. Roosevelt had begun lobbying for reform of the meat-packing industry as far back as 1899, when he criticized the badly processed meat that had been sent to his soldiers in Cuba. The American people became aware of unsanitary (dirty, unhealthy) conditions in meat-packing plants with the publication of *The Jungle* (1906), a book by American novelist and journalist Upton Sinclair (1878–1968) that exposed those conditions in horrifying detail. Such legislation further enhanced Roosevelt's image as the moral voice of the people.

Meanwhile, Roosevelt continued his "Big Stick" policy in foreign affairs. Ships were rapidly increasing speed and firepower (the ability to fire weapons) and were becoming much more important as instruments of foreign policy. When Japanese forces defeated Russia in a series of naval battles in 1904 and 1905, the president thought it best to help calm things down. Since Japan was not in a strong economic position at the time, authorities of that nation eagerly accepted Roosevelt's offer to have the United States negotiate a peace treaty. The Treaty of

Upton Sinclair and the Muckrakers

American novelist and journalist Upton Sinclair (1878–1968) was best known for his book *The Jungle,* which exposed unsanitary conditions in American meat-packing plants in 1901. During the first decade of the twentieth century, Sinclair was associated with a circle of investigative reporters called "muckrakers," because they exposed the seamier (unwholesome) side of American life. Muckrakers are considered to have been excellent reporters who thoroughly researched their stories and based their reports on provable facts. Nevertheless, President Roosevelt lumped those writers with more sensationalistic journalists who wrote stories without presenting evidence to back their claims.

The term "muckraker," was, in fact, coined by President Roosevelt in a col-

orful speech he gave on April 15, 1906 (see **Theodore Roosevelt** primary source entry in volume 3). Quoting from *Pilgrim's Progress* by John Bunyan, he labeled journalists who focused their reporting on the seamier side of American life as "the Man with the Muckrake, the man who could look no way but downward." He referred to those who wanted radical changes in government and business as the "lunatic fringe." The socially committed writers— Sinclair, Lincoln Steffens (1866–1936), Ida Tarbell (1857–1944), and Ray Stannard Baker (1870–1946), among others—who based their reports on significant evidence, enthusiastically adopted Roosevelt's scornful description and are linked by literary historians with the muckraking movement of 1900 to 1912.

Portsmouth ended the war between the Russians and the Japanese, known as the Russo-Japanese War. The treaty was considered one of Roosevelt's greatest foreign-policy achievements, and in 1906 it earned him the Nobel Peace Prize.

Conservation

One of the most significant themes of Roosevelt's presidency is the emphasis he placed on the conservation of the country's natural resources. At a time when most people believed clean air, water, forests, and animals would be plentiful forever, Roosevelt recognized how fragile the ecology was against ever-expanding industrialization.

One of Roosevelt's advisors in this area, Gifford Pinchot (1865–1946), was a university-trained naturalist who be-

Theodore Roosevelt Administration

lieved in the scientific management of undeveloped land. Roosevelt used the 1891 Forest Reserve Act to increase federal-owned land from forty million acres when he took office to more than two hundred million acres by the time he left the presidency. He appointed Pinchot as head of the new U.S. Forest Service to administer those federal lands.

With the assistance of Pinchot and other conservationists, Roosevelt brought under government control many irrigation and dam projects as well as forest, seashore, and

Theodore Roosevelt (left) and noted conservationist John Muir in Yosemite Valley, California.
Reproduced by permission of the Corbis Corporation.

wilderness areas. For the first time, private companies—like utilities and coal mining and lumber industries—were subjected to federal regulations in protected areas and required special permission to operate there. (Utilities are public service companies, such as gas, electric, and water companies.)

By the end of his second term in office, Roosevelt had doubled the number of national parks, created fifty-one wildlife refuges, and proclaimed eighteen national monuments. Among the national treasures that would be forever safeguarded were Yellowstone National Park and the Grand Canyon National Monument (now a national park).

After the presidency

Roosevelt had pledged not to seek reelection in 1908. Reluctantly, he kept his promise and left the White House in 1909 after the inauguration of **William Howard Taft** (1857–1930; see entry in volume 3), a close friend and advisor who had served as Roosevelt's secretary of war. Roosevelt was only fifty-one and was determined to continue to lead what he called "the strenuous life." Shortly after leaving office, he led an African safari (a hunting expedition), sponsored by the Smithsonian Institution, to collect more than five hundred different birds and animals. While in Africa, he wrote his first post-presidency book, *African Game Trails*. Following the safari, Roosevelt and his family toured Europe, where the former president met with heads of state, reviewed troops, made speeches, and lectured at universities.

Roosevelt returned from his travels in June 1910 still very popular with the public. President Taft had not carried out Roosevelt's programs as expected. Taft had disagreed with some of the sweeping conservation laws that had been passed under Roosevelt, and he forced Gifford Pinchot to resign as head of

Gifford Pinchot, the first chief of the U.S. Forest Service.
Courtesy of the Library of Congress.

The Teddy Bear toy is linked with President Roosevelt. While hunting one day, he tracked a bear but refused to shoot it when he discovered that it was small. Reports of the incident were followed by cartoons, a book of stories called The Adventures of the Roosevelt Bears, *and then a stuffed animal.*

the Forest Service. Taft angered many progressive Republicans by backing the party's old-line (most traditional) conservatives in Congress, and he angered the public by backing legislation that raised taxes. Progressive Republicans were soon pressuring Roosevelt to run for the presidency again in 1912.

Roosevelt was content to spend time with his family as well as to travel, study, and write. But he eventually entered the race against Taft and beat the president in several states that held primary elections (elections to determine which candidate from a political party will represent that party in a general election). At the Republican Party's national convention in Chicago, however, Taft's supporters were able to win the battle for delegates. Outraged Roosevelt backers stormed out of the convention hall. They urged Roosevelt to consider running as a third-party candidate.

Six weeks after the convention, Roosevelt's supporters formed the Progressive "Bull Moose" Party and made him their candidate for the election. While making a speech in Milwaukee, Wisconsin, on October 14, 1912, Roosevelt was wounded in an assassination attempt. The bullet just missed his right lung, but it did not stop Roosevelt, who finished his speech before going to the hospital.

Unfortunately for the Republicans, Roosevelt's Bull Moose candidacy split the party's support. New Jersey governor **Woodrow Wilson** (1856–1924; see entry in volume 4)— the Democratic candidate—won by a landslide, taking 435 electoral votes. Roosevelt won over Taft by more than half-a-million votes.

Following defeat in the 1912 election, Roosevelt again left the country. He led an expedition to explore an unmapped river in Brazil—the River of Doubt (now called the Roosevelt River)—and collect animal specimens for the Museum of Natural History in New York City. It proved a much more difficult journey than his African adventure some years earlier, and Roosevelt contracted a malarial fever (a disease transmitted by the bite of an infected mosquito) that at one point threatened his life. He recovered and published one of his most popular books, *Through the Brazilian Wilderness*; but it is said the illness may have contributed to his death.

The outbreak of World War I (1914–18) gave Roosevelt a new cause. The sinking of the British passenger ship

Lusitania by a German submarine convinced Roosevelt that the United States should prepare to enter the conflict. President Wilson, however, did not ask Congress for a declaration of war until 1917. Ever the man of action, Roosevelt requested an army command in Europe, but he was turned down by Wilson's secretary of war, Newton D. Baker (1871–1937). Roosevelt continued making speeches in favor of a strong national defense and constant military preparedness. After the armistice in 1918, Roosevelt publicly ridiculed Wilson's programs for postwar Europe.

Meanwhile, recurring trouble with the malaria he contracted in South America, combined with the death of his youngest son, Quentin (1897–1919), in air combat in Europe, had sapped Roosevelt's strength. He was hospitalized for a time with rheumatism, a disabling condition of the joints and muscles, and had lost the hearing in one ear. Roosevelt died at home in Oyster Bay in his sleep on January 6, 1919. He was buried unceremoniously, according to his wishes, with no eulogy (funeral speech) or military honors, at Sagamore Hill, the home he had built in 1884. At the time of his death, Vice President Thomas R. Marshall (1854–1925) said, "Death had to take him sleeping, for if Roosevelt had been awake, there would have been a fight."

Always the adventurer, Roosevelt was the first president to fly in an airplane. He flew in 1910, after leaving office, but during his presidency the government bought its first plane—from the Wright brothers for $25,000—and the U.S. Air Force was born.

Legacy

Theodore Roosevelt is consistently listed among the most effective presidents. He quickly and forcefully led the government to address problems of the time: Much needed reforms attacked unfair business practices, unhealthy food processing, and questionable medicines. Recognizing that the great expansion of business and industry had far exceeded the commerce laws addressed by the Constitution, he broadened federal powers to oversee interstate commerce (the selling of goods from state to state).

Roosevelt also proved to be fair and balanced. Ignoring radicals who called for more vigorous pursuit of business reform, he ensured that careful investigations were completed before the government pursued lawsuits against trusts. By being the first president to recognize the rights of labor in disputes with management, he helped instill a more balanced

A Selection of Roosevelt Landmarks

North Creek Railway Depot Museum. Box 156, North Creek, NY 12853-0156. (518) 251-3661. Site where Vice President Roosevelt learned that President McKinley had died. The old train station has been renovated and contains a museum that includes exhibits about Roosevelt's fateful train ride. See http://www.northcreekraildepot.org/ (accessed on August 3, 2000).

Rough Riders Memorial and City Museum. 725 Grand Ave., Las Vegas, NM 87701. (505) 425-8726. Museum is home to artifacts of Theodore Roosevelt's famed Rough Riders, the largest contingent of which was from New Mexico. See http://arco-iris. com/teddy/index.htm (accessed on August 3, 2000).

Sagamore Hill National Historic Site. 20 Sagamore Hill Rd., Oyster Bay, NY 11771-1807. (516) 922-4447. Home of Theodore Roosevelt from 1886 until his death in 1919. The Old Orchard Museum—in a house built by the president's eldest son—contains Roosevelt exhibits. See http://www.nps.gov/sahi/home.htm (accessed on August 4, 2000).

Theodore Roosevelt Bird Sanctuary and Trailside Museum. East Main St., Oyster Bay, NY 11771. (516) 922-3200. A memorial to the outdoors-loving Roosevelt, who is buried in nearby Youngs Memorial Cemetery. See http://www.516web.com/museum/trs-menu.htm (accessed on August 3, 2000).

Theodore Roosevelt Birthplace National Historic Site. 28 E. 20th St., New York, NY 10003. (212) 260-1616. Home is a 1923 reconstruction of the house (built in 1858) that Roosevelt lived in during his first fourteen years of life. See http://www.nps.gov/thrb/ (accessed on August 4, 2000).

Theodore Roosevelt Inaugural National Historic Site. 641 Delaware Ave., Buffalo, NY 14202. (716) 884-0095. Small museum in the house where Theodore Roosevelt was sworn in as president, following the death of William McKinley. See http://www.nps. gov/thri/ (accessed on August 4, 2000).

Theodore Roosevelt National Park. P.O. Box 7, Medora, ND 58645-0007. (701) 842-2333, north unit; (701) 623-4466, south unit. A thirty-thousand-acre living memorial to conservationist Theodore Roosevelt sits in the North Dakota Badlands. Featured on the site are the Maltese Cross Cabin, where Roosevelt stayed when he was in North Dakota, and Roosevelt's Elkhorn Ranch. See http://www.nps.gov/thro/home.htm (accessed on August 4, 2000).

negotiating process for wages and benefits. His conservation efforts were the first large-scale effort to preserve and protect natural resources.

Roosevelt's foreign policy placed the United States at the forefront of international diplomacy backed by a strong military. He achieved great success—winning the Nobel Peace Prize for helping end the Russo-Japanese War—but his aggressiveness in this area also created problems. The Roosevelt Corollary to the Monroe Doctrine further enhanced the role of the United States as leader and protector of the Western Hemisphere, but U.S. relations with Latin America became strained following intervention against Colombia to help create and defend the new nation of Panama. Relations of the United States with several Latin American countries remained uneasy for the next few decades.

After Roosevelt, Republican leaders became less reform-minded toward business. William Howard Taft, Roosevelt's successor, proved more successful as a trustbuster, but he also set up a more pro-business administration. More reforms followed when Democrat Woodrow Wilson became president in 1912, and then three Republican administrations of the 1920s followed the principle that government should intervene as little as possible in the affairs of business. Their cautious approach to government was opposite of Roosevelt, who once expressed his credo (guiding idea) as "Get action, do things."

Where to Learn More

Brands, H. W. *T. R: The Last Romantic.* New York: Basic Books, 1997.

Burton, David H. *Theodore Roosevelt.* New York: Twayne Publishers, 1972.

Chessman, G. Wallace. *Theodore Roosevelt and the Politics of Power.* Edited by Oscar Handlin. Boston: Little Brown, 1969. Reprint, Boston: G. K. Hall, 1976.

Cutright, Paul R. *Theodore Roosevelt: The Making of a Conservationist.* Urbana: University of Illinois Press, 1985.

Dinunzio, Mario R., ed. *Theodore Roosevelt: An American Mind: A Selection from His Writings.* New York: St. Martin's Press, 1994.

Gable, John A. *Theodore Roosevelt Cyclopedia* Rev. ed. Westport, CT: Meckler, 1989.

Garraty, John A. *Theodore Roosevelt: The Strenuous Life.* New York: American Heritage, 1967.

Holmes, Oliver Wendell. *The Common Law.* Boston: Little, Brown, 1881. Reprint, New York: Dover, 1991.

Library of Congress. "Theodore Roosevelt Papers at the Library of Congress: 1759–1919." *American Memory.* [Online] http://lcweb2.loc.gov/ammem/trhtml/trhome.html (accessed on August 14, 2000).

New York State. *Theodore Roosevelt: "A Great New Yorker."* [Online] http://www.trthegreatnewyorker.com/ (accessed on August 14, 2000).

Public Broadcasting System. "TR, The Story of Theodore Roosevelt." *The American Experience.* [Online] http://www.pbs.org/wgbh/amex/tr/ (accessed on August 14, 2000).

Roosevelt, Theodore. *African Game Trails, An Account of the African Wanderings of an American Hunter-Naturalist.* New York: Scribner, 1910. Reprint, Birmingham, AL: Palladium Press, 1999.

Roosevelt, Theodore. *The Naval War of 1812; or, The History of the United States Navy During the Last War with Great Britain.* New York: Putnam's, 1882. Reprint, New York: Modern Library, 1999.

Roosevelt, Theodore. *The Rough Riders.* New York: Scribner, 1899. Reprint, New York: Modern Library, 1999.

Roosevelt, Theodore. *Theodore Roosevelt: An Autobiography.* New York: Macmillan, 1913. Reprint, New York: Da Capo Press, 1985.

Roosevelt, Theodore. *Through the Brazilian Wilderness.* New York: Scribner, 1914. Reprint, New York: Cooper Square Press, 2000.

Schullery, Paul. *Wilderness Writings.* Salt Lake City: Peregrine Smith Books, 1986.

Theodore Roosevelt Association. [Online] http://www.theodoreroosevelt.org/ (accessed on August 14, 2000).

Theodore Roosevelt Tribute Site. [Online] http://users.metro2000.net/~stabbott/tr.htm#menu (accessed on August , 2000).

White, G. Edward. *Oliver Wendell Holmes: Sage of the Supreme Court.* New York: Oxford University Press, 2000.

Edith Roosevelt

Born August 6, 1861
Norwich, Connecticut
Died September 30, 1948
Long Island, New York

Promoted the arts, oversaw the successful remodeling of the White House, assisted and advised her husband, and efficiently managed the household

E dith Roosevelt knew her husband, **Theodore Roosevelt** (1858–1919; see entry in volume 3), since childhood. They had not seen each other for many years when their paths crossed again when they were in their twenties in the mid-1880s. At the time, Roosevelt was a recent widower with a young daughter, Alice. After a year-long engagement, the couple married in 1886. They took up residence in the White House when Roosevelt, who had been vice president, assumed the office of president after the death of President **William McKinley** (1843–1901; see entry in volume 3) in 1901.

Edith Roosevelt presided over a very active household. She was determined to maintain as normal a life as possible for her children and did her best to shield them from public attention. At the same time, she was a charming first lady who enthusiastically took a leading position in the social life of Washington, D.C. She was the first president's wife to employ a full-time social secretary of her own.

"[Edith Roosevelt was] one of the strongest-minded and strongest-willed presidential wives who ever lived in the White House"

Life *magazine*

Edith Roosevelt.
Courtesy of the Library of Congress.

New York society

The daughter of Charles and Gertrude Tyler Carow, Edith Kermit Carow was born in Norwich, Connecticut, in 1861. She grew up in New York City and enjoyed a childhood of wealth and privilege. One of her best friends, Corinne Roosevelt (1861–1933)—younger sister of Theodore—came from another wealthy family.

Edith and Theodore became friends. They traveled in the same social circles, corresponded when he went to Europe with his family as a teenager, and there was speculation that their friendship might one day become a romance. But they lost touch with each other when he left for Harvard University in 1876.

In his junior year, Theodore met and fell in love with Alice Hathaway Lee (1861–1884), another young woman from a prominent eastern family. They were married in 1880, honeymooned in England, and then set up residence in New York City, where he began studying law at Columbia University. Roosevelt quickly tired of his law studies, and in 1881 he was elected to the New York state assembly in Albany.

In 1884, Alice Roosevelt died shortly after giving birth to a daughter, Alice Lee Roosevelt (1884–1980), named in her honor. Theodore Roosevelt, distraught after the death of both his wife and mother on the same day, went to live on a ranch in the Dakota Territory. During a trip to New York in the fall of 1885, he ran into Edith Carow at his sister's house. They began seeing each other again and were secretly engaged in November 1885.

Homemaker

Edith and Theodore Roosevelt were married in London, England, on December 2, 1886. They settled at Sagamore Hill, the house Roosevelt had built at Oyster Bay, Long Island, New York. Even though Edith had a reputation for being somewhat aloof, their marriage would prove to be an extremely happy one. They would have five children—four boys and a girl—in addition to caring for Alice, Roosevelt's daughter from his first marriage.

Since Theodore's life in politics consumed a large share of his time, Edith ran the household. She managed the finances, disciplined the children, and planned the couple's social life. She was not always comfortable with her husband's love of danger—his active duty during the Spanish-American War in 1898 as a Rough Rider or his big-game hunting trips. But she accepted this part of his nature and handled family matters efficiently in his absences.

First lady

In September 1901, Theodore Roosevelt became president after William McKinley died from an assassin's bullet. The Roosevelts moved into the White House and Theodore immediately began the busy duties of the presidency.

With six children, ranging from an infant to a teenager, as well as dozens of pets, the family turned the White House into a noisy family home. Edith Roosevelt managed the most famous residence in the country with the same efficiency she showed at Sagamore Hill. She won the devotion of the household staff with her kindness, and she hosted many lavish dinner parties and receptions.

Edith read widely, studied a variety of subjects, and prepared carefully for her role as first lady. She was able to converse on almost any topic, and she greatly impressed everyone who met her with her intelligence, grace, and wit. She hired a full-time social secretary to assist her with meetings and state functions. In 1906, she arranged the most regal wedding ever held at the White House for Alice, then twenty-two years old. Two years later, she presided over an elaborate coming-out party for seventeen-year-old Ethel.

In addition to arranging social events, she also took an active role in her husband's work. She handled mail, reviewed his speeches, and marked stories in newspapers for him to read. Many people felt that Edith was instrumental in balancing her husband's impulsiveness: They believed she often saved him from making rash errors in public by using her caution and thoughtfulness to keep him in check.

Life after the White House

When Roosevelt left the White House in 1909, he was still a relatively young man and in no mood for retirement.

He stayed involved in politics, even making another bid for the presidency in 1912. He took trips to the wilderness of Africa and South America. When the United States entered World War I (1914–18) in 1917, he made headlines with his opinions on the war. Through it all, Edith remained the rock of the family: She ran the household, supported her husband even when she did not agree with his direction, and guided him as best she could.

After Roosevelt's death in 1919, Edith traveled through Europe and Asia for a while. Back home at Sagamore Hill, she did a great deal of work for her church and for charitable organizations, and she was active in the Women's Republican Club. She became a popular spokesperson for the Republican Party, giving speeches in favor of local and national candidates. When **Franklin D. Roosevelt** (1882–1945; see entry in volume 4), a distant cousin of Theodore's, became president on the Democratic ticket, Edith soundly denounced him and became a vocal critic of his "New Deal" policies.

Edith Roosevelt died on September 30, 1948, at the age of eighty-seven. An editorial in *Life* magazine at the time called her "one of the strongest-minded and strongest-willed presidential wives who ever lived in the White House."

Where to Learn More

Caroli, Betty Boyd. *The Roosevelt Women.* New York: Basic Books, 1998.

Morris, Sylvia Jukes. *Edith Kermit Roosevelt: Portrait of a First Lady.* New York: Coward, McCann & Geoghegan, 1980. Reprint, New York: Vintage Books, 1990.

Renehan, Edward J., Jr. *The Lion's Pride: Theodore Roosevelt and His Family in Peace and War.* New York: Oxford University Press, 1998.

Roosevelt's First Annual Address to Congress

Delivered on December 3, 1901; excerpted from
The American Presidency: Selected Resources,
An Informal Reference Guide **(Web site)**

The "trust buster" announces his modest plan for business regulation

> "In the interest of the whole people, the nation should, without interfering with the power of the states in the matter itself, also assume power of supervision and regulation over all corporations doing an interstate business."
>
> *Theodore Roosevelt*

During the second half of the nineteenth century, the United States emerged as a major industrial nation. Industrialization involves a population movement from rural to urban areas and a shift from producing goods at home or in small shops to manufacturing them in factories. By the 1890s, industries were enjoying large profits and employing millions of people. There were drawbacks as well. Cities grew crowded and dirty, and there was an ever widening gap between wealthy industrialists and workers. Large businesses began overwhelming smaller ones.

Some businesses that created similar products or provided similar services combined to form trusts—a business combination formed to reduce competition and control prices. Trusts dominated such commodities as oil and coal, beef and sugar, and railroads. By 1900, there were over two hundred trusts operating in the United States. Since a trust dominates a particular market sector, it does not face competition over the prices it demands for goods and services. It became extremely difficult for small and new companies to survive in business sectors dominated by trusts.

President **William McKinley** (1843–1901; see entry in volume 3) did much to encourage business growth during his first term in office, from 1897 to 1901. He noted the ever-increasing power of trusts and planned to address the issue during his second term, which began in March 1901. However, McKinley was assassinated in September of that year. His successor, Vice President **Theodore Roosevelt** (1858–1919; see entry in volume 3), became an active "trust-buster" upon assuming the office of president.

Since Roosevelt was already known as a reformer, people were anxious to see what he would do. They expected that he would be more aggressive than President McKinley, who wanted businesses to be relatively free of government regulation. Some were calling for swift action against trusts. Their passions were aroused in part by a form of journalism that arose near the turn of the century. From sensationalistic reporting called "yellow journalism" to more carefully researched stories, journalists regularly exposed corruption, unhealthy living and working conditions, and business dominance by trusts.

Roosevelt addressed the issue of trusts as part of his first annual address to Congress in December 1901. He recognized that business combinations were legal. He wanted to ensure that they engaged in fair business practices. Since trusts controlled goods and services vital to public welfare—such as food, energy, and transportation—Roosevelt argued that they ought to disclose their financial records and business practices to the public they served. That principle helped start momentum for trust busting.

Things to remember while reading an excerpt from President Roosevelt's first annual address to Congress:

- Roosevelt acknowledged positive and negative effects of industrialization. He spoke of the enormous progress that had been made and the better paying jobs that had resulted from industrialization. Roosevelt also noted that the nation faced very serious social problems and that a few businesses and individuals had gained an enormous amount of wealth. He warned against some of the more radical solutions to those problems while pointing out the many benefits and general prosperity that industrialization had helped to realize for many Americans. Roosevelt was being careful. While he was trying to persuade Congress and the general public about excessive influence of some trusts, he also wanted to avoid language that might antagonize powerful business forces and their supporters. Roosevelt was trying to build momentum for reform at this point in his early presidency (he had been in office less than three months).

- After having indicated that he would not support more radical approaches to the nation's problems, Roosevelt turned his attention specifically to trusts. He outlined ways in which trusts had developed, then he began to note ways in which their practices could be harmful. Still, Roosevelt called for a moderately aggressive approach. He stated that trusts should not be prohibited, but they should be subject to public scrutiny.

- Early in his address on trusts, Roosevelt stated that old laws that guided the relationship between government and business were no longer sufficient. The nation had changed greatly since the Constitution was adopted in 1789. The Constitution placed much of the responsibility on individual states for monitoring business developments. By the beginning of the twentieth century, however, many large businesses operated in several states.

- Since such interstate actions were subject to federal jurisdiction, Roosevelt wanted Congress to decide whether or not the federal government had the constitutional right to impose strict regulations on business. If Congress decided against federal supervision of businesses, he suggested that a constitutional amendment should be introduced that would give the federal government that right.

Excerpt from President Roosevelt's first annual address to Congress

The tremendous and highly complex industrial development which went on with ever accelerated rapidity during the latter half of the nineteenth century brings us face to face, at the beginning of the twentieth, with very serious social problems. The old laws, and the old customs which had almost the binding force of law, were once quite sufficient to **regulate** *the accumulation and distribution of wealth. Since the industrial changes which have so enormously increased the productive power of mankind, they are no longer sufficient.*

The growth of cities has gone on beyond comparison faster than the growth of the country, and the upbuilding of the great industrial centers has meant a startling increase, not merely in the **aggregate** *of wealth, but in the number of very large individual, and especially of very large corporate, fortunes. The creation of these great corporate fortunes has not been due to the* **tariff** *nor to any other governmental action, but to natural causes in the business world, operating in other countries as they operate in our own.*

The process has aroused much antagonism, a great part of which is wholly without warrant. It is not true that as the rich have grown richer the poor have grown poorer. On the contrary, never before has the average man, the wage-worker, the farmer, the small trader, been so well off as in this country and at the present time. There have been abuses connected with the accumulation of wealth; yet it remains true that a fortune accumulated in legitimate business can be accumulated by the person specially benefitted only on condition of **conferring** *immense incidental benefits upon others. Successful enterprise, of the type which benefits all mankind, can only exist if the conditions are such as to offer great prizes as the rewards of success.*

The captains of industry who have driven the railway systems across this continent, who have built up our commerce, who have developed our **manufactures**, *have on the whole done great good to our people. Without them the material development of which we are so justly proud could never have taken place. Moreover, we should recognize the immense importance to this material development of leaving as unhampered as is compatible with the public good the*

Regulate: Monitor by establishing a set of guidelines.

Aggregate: Sum total.

Tariff: A tax placed on imported goods to raise their price and make them less attractive to consumers than goods produced by the nation importing them.

Conferring: Bestowing.

Manufactures: Items manufactured.

strong and forceful men upon whom the success of business operations inevitably rests. . . .

*America has only just begun to assume that commanding position in the international business world which we believe will more and more be hers. It is of the utmost importance that this position be not jeopardized, especially at a time when the overflowing abundance of our own natural resources and the skill, business energy, and mechanical aptitude of our people make foreign markets essential. Under such conditions it would be most unwise to cramp or to **fetter** the youthful strength of our nation.*

Moreover, it cannot too often be pointed out that to strike with ignorant violence at the interest of one set of men almost inevitably endangers the interests of all. The fundamental rule in our national life—the rule which underlies all others—is that, on the whole, and in times of adversity some will suffer far more than others; but speaking generally, a period of good times means that all, share more or less in them, and in periods of hard times all feel the stress in them to a greater or lesser degree. . . .

There is widespread conviction in the minds of the American people that the great corporations known as trusts are in certain of their features and tendencies hurtful to the general welfare. This springs from no spirit of envy or uncharitableness, nor lack of pride in the great industrial achievements that have placed this country at the head of the nations struggling for commercial supremacy. It does not rest upon a lack of intelligent appreciation of the necessity of meeting changing and changed conditions of trade with new methods, nor upon ignorance of the fact that combination of capital in the effort to accomplish great things is necessary when the world's progress demands that great things be done. It is based upon sincere conviction that combination and concentration should be, not prohibited, but supervised and within reasonable limits controlled; and in my judgment this conviction is right.

*It is no limitation upon property rights or freedom of contract to require that when men receive from government the privilege of doing business under **corporate** form, which frees them from individual responsibility, and enables them to call into their enterprises the capital of the public, they shall do so upon absolutely truthful representations as to the value of the property in which the capital is to be invested. Corporations engaged in interstate commerce should be regulated if they are found to exercise a **license** working to the public injury. It should be as much the aim of those who seek for*

Fetter: Confine.

Corporate: Relating to a corporation. When a business becomes incorporated, it obtains legal rights and liabilities similar to those enjoyed by citizens (including legal protection and the obligation to report income and pay necessary taxes).

License: Permission to act.

Theodore Roosevelt: First Annual Address to Congress   913

social betterment to rid the business world of crimes of cunning as to rid the entire body politic of crimes of violence. Great corporations exist only because they are created and safeguarded by our institutions; and it is therefore our right and our duty to see that they work in harmony with these institutions.

The first essential in determining how to deal with the great industrial combinations is knowledge of the facts—publicity. In the interest of the public, the government should have the right to inspect and examine the workings of the great corporations engaged in interstate business. Publicity is the only sure remedy which we can now invoke. What further remedies are needed in the way of governmental regulation, or taxation, can only be determined after publicity has been obtained, by process of law, and in the course of administration. The first requisite is knowledge, full and complete—knowledge which may be made public to the world.

Artificial bodies, such as corporations and joint stock or other associations, depending upon any **statutory law** for their existence or privileges, should be subject to proper governmental supervision, and full and accurate information as to their operations should be made public regularly at reasonable intervals.

The large corporations, commonly called trusts, though organized in one state, always do business in many states, often doing very little business in the state where they are incorporated. There is utter lack of uniformity in the state laws about them; and as no state has any exclusive interest in or power over their acts, it has in practice proved impossible to get adequate regulation through state action.

Therefore, in the interest of the whole people, the nation should, without interfering with the power of the states in the matter itself, also assume power of supervision and regulation over all corporations doing an interstate business. This is especially true where the corporation derives a portion of its wealth from the existence of some **monopolistic** element or tendency in its business. There would be no hardship in such supervision; banks are subject to it, and in their case it is now accepted as a simple matter of course. Indeed, it is probable that supervision of corporations by the national government need not go so far as is now the case with the supervision exercised over them by so conservative a state as Massachusetts, in order to produce excellent results.

When the Constitution was adopted, at the end of the eighteenth century, no human wisdom could foretell the sweeping

Statutory law: A law that is enforced by the legislative branch of government.

Monopolistic: Like a monopoly; a monopoly occurs when one business completely dominates a business service or commodity.

Complete American Presidents Sourcebook

changes, alike in industrial and political conditions, which were to take place by the beginning of the twentieth century. At that time it was accepted as a matter of course that the several states were the proper authorities to regulate, so far as was then necessary, the comparatively insignificant and strictly localized corporate bodies of the day. The conditions are now wholly different and wholly different action is called for. I believe that a law can be framed which will enable the national government to exercise control along the lines above indicated, profiting by the experience gained through the passage and administration of the Interstate Commerce Act. If, however, the judgment of the Congress is that it lacks the constitutional power to pass such an act, then a constitutional amendment should be submitted to confer the power. (The American Presidency: Selected Resources, An Informal Reference Guide *[Web site]*)

What happened next . . .

During Roosevelt's first term (in which he was completing the term of President McKinley) he influenced Congress to pass several measures that helped the federal government to enforce existing antitrust laws. The Department of Justice then proceeded to initiate some forty-three different lawsuits against trusts, and won several important judicial decisions. For example, the Northern Securities Company was a group of several railroad companies run as though they were one company. That arrangement allowed them to reduce competition and control prices. The government sued Northern Securities for violating the Sherman Antitrust Act of 1890, which outlawed such mergers.

Roosevelt's trust-busting practices were carried on by his successor, **William Howard Taft** (1857–1930; see entry in volume 3), who served as president from March 1909 to March 1913. Taft had served as Roosevelt's secretary of war. The Taft administration broke the Standard Oil Company's dominance of the energy industry.

In addition to trust-busting, Roosevelt's presidency was distinguished by other examples of reform led by the federal government. The Pure Food and Drug Act (1906), for example, prohibited the manufacture of unsafe foods or drugs. In 1905, Roosevelt urged "government supervision and regulation of charges by the railroads." The Hepburn Act of 1906 authorized the Interstate Commerce Commission to determine rates for rail transport.

Did you know . . .

- Roosevelt is often portrayed as a vigorous leader of reform, but he was reluctant to expand government regulation of business. He proceeded cautiously while facts were gathered concerning individual business practices that might be in need of reform. Only when evidence of being guilty of unfair practices was established did he direct the government to proceed vigorously.

Where to Learn More

"Annual Message: Theodore Roosevelt." *The American Presidency: Selected Resources, An Informal Reference Guide* (Web site). [Online] http://www.interlink-cafe.com/uspresidents/1901.htm (accessed on August 7, 2000).

Beach, James C. *Theodore Roosevelt: Man of Action.* Champaign, IL: Garrard Press, 1960. Reprint, New York: Chelsea Juniors, 1991.

Beale, Howard K. *Theodore Roosevelt and the Rise of America to World Power.* Baltimore: Johns Hopkins University Press, 1956. Reprint, Baltimore: Johns Hopkins University Press, 1984.

Harbaugh, William H. *Power and Responsibility: The Life and Times of Theodore Roosevelt.* New York: Farrar, Straus and Cudahy, 1961. Reprint, Newtown, CT: American Political Biography Press, 1997.

Markham, Lois. *Theodore Roosevelt.* New York: Chelsea House, 1985.

Roosevelt's "The Man with the Muck Rake" Speech

Delivered on April 15, 1906; excerpted from
Speech Communication @ Texas A&M University **(Web site)**

A reformer president chastises journalists who focus on the seamier side of American life

President **Theodore Roosevelt** (1858–1919; see entry in volume 3) had a reputation as a reformer—one who exposes corruption and injustice and fights for fairness. There were many reform crusades by individuals or groups at the turn of the century. It was during this period when exposé journalism first became widely popular in the United States. Exposé journalism refers to investigative reporting of a person or organization suspected of wrongdoing. During the 1890s, investigative reporting was used to draw readers to newspapers, which began flourishing on a national scale. From 1900 to World War I (1914–18), magazines became increasingly popular, partly by featuring investigative reports.

Some journalists engaged in sensationalism, or "yellow journalism"—terms that refer to stories based on rumor, not fact; that aggressively highlight scandals; and that showcase the worst kinds of behavior, sometimes exaggerating the truth to make a greater impact on readers and to sell more papers. At the same time, responsible reporters were able to expose actual wrongdoing, backed with facts and thorough research.

"It is very necessary that we should not flinch from seeing what is vile and debasing. There is filth on the floor, and it must be scraped up with the muck rake. . . . But the man who never does anything else, who never thinks or speaks or writes, save of his feats with the muck rake, speedily becomes, not a help but one of the most potent forces for evil."

Theodore Roosevelt

917

President Roosevelt took the opportunity of a speech he delivered on April 15, 1906, at the Gridiron Club in Washington, D.C., to discuss journalists and reformers intent on exaggerating conditions in order to further their personal, financial, or political cause. He was using his authority to speak from the "bully pulpit": that term ("bully" refers to a show of power, "pulpit" is the place in a church where a sermon is delivered) is used to describe a situation when a president lectures on moral issues or general problems in the nation and tries to encourage improvement.

To underscore the theme of his address, Roosevelt quoted a passage from *Pilgrim's Progress,* a work by English writer John Bunyan, first published in 1678. That moral story became the second most widely read work in the English language after the Bible. Roosevelt likened sensational journalists and reformers to a character Bunyan called "the Man with the Muck Rake"—someone interested only in pleasures of the body and who sees only the seamy and vile parts of life.

Things to remember while reading an excerpt from President Roosevelt's "The Man with the Muck Rake" speech:

- Roosevelt acknowledged that the nation had problems. He began by noting that the population of the country had exceeded the nation's wealth—meaning that prosperity was not being enjoyed by all. The country faced very different problems than it had a century earlier, when most Americans were farmers. By 1906, when the speech was made, a majority of Americans lived in cities and worked in industrial-related jobs. Cities were growing overcrowded, creating health problems, and crime was on the rise.

- Stating that more reforms were needed, Roosevelt welcomed attempts to address the nation's problems. However, he was clear to define positive attempts for reform against those led by people interested in undermining public officials or the American system of government and economics. Singling out those who spread rumor, gossip, or lies as people who perpetuated evil, Roosevelt called them "the men with the muck rakes," a term he derived from the moral allegory *Pilgrim's Progress,* by John Bunyan.

- Roosevelt, himself a noted reformer, called for a balanced approach to the nation's ills. He was against "mudslinging"—a term that refers to character assassination through lies or exaggeration—and he was also against "whitewashing"—the attempt to cover up or ignore problems. He wanted people to expose the ills of society as a way toward improving the nation, rather than as a way to tear down the American system.

Excerpt from President Roosevelt's "The Man with the Muck Rake" speech

*Over a century ago Washington laid the **corner stone** of the Capitol in what was then little more than a tract of wooded wilderness here beside the **Potomac**. We now find it necessary to provide great additional buildings for the business of the government.*

This growth in the need for the housing of the government is but a proof and example of the way in which the nation has grown and the sphere of action of the national government has grown. We now administer the affairs of a nation in which the extraordinary growth of population has been outstripped by the growth of wealth in complex interests. The material problems that face us today are not such as they were in Washington's time, but the underlying facts of human nature are the same now as they were then. Under altered external form we war with the same tendencies toward evil that were evident in Washington's time, and are helped by the same tendencies for good. It is about some of these that I wish to say a word today.

In Bunyan's Pilgrim's Progress *you may recall the description of the Man with the Muck Rake, the man who could look no way but downward, with the muck rake in his hand; who was offered a **celestial crown** for his muck rake, but who would neither look up nor regard the crown he was offered, but continued to rake to himself the filth of the floor.*

In Pilgrim's Progress *the Man with the Muck Rake is set forth as the example of him whose vision is fixed on carnal instead of spiritual things. Yet he also typifies the man who in this life consistently re-*

Corner stone: A stone laid in a formal ceremony for a building under construction. President George Washington laid the corner stone for the nation's capitol in 1793, and the government officially moved into the District of Columbia in 1800.

Potomac: The river that runs through Washington, D.C.

Celestial crown: A colorful expression referring to the kingdom of heaven. In *Pilgrim's Progress,* the Man with the Muck Rake does not recognize the possibility of heaven because he is focused on the filth of the Earth. Likewise, according to Roosevelt, those who focus only on the ills of American society miss the opportunity the American system provides for improving society.

*fuses to see **aught** that is lofty, and fixes his eyes with solemn intentness only on that which is **vile and debasing.***

Now, it is very necessary that we should not flinch from seeing what is vile and debasing. There is filth on the floor, and it must be scraped up with the muck rake; and there are times and places where this service is the most needed of all the services that can be performed. But the man who never does anything else, who never thinks or speaks or writes, save of his feats with the muck rake, speedily becomes, not a help but one of the most potent forces for evil.

*There are in the **body politic**, economic and social, many and grave evils, and there is urgent necessity for the sternest war upon them. There should be relentless exposure of and attack upon every evil man, whether politician or business man, every evil practice, whether in politics, business, or social life. I hail as a benefactor every writer or speaker, every man who, on the platform or in a book, magazine, or newspaper, with merciless severity makes such attack, provided always that he in his turn remembers that the attack is of use only if it is absolutely truthful.*

*The liar is no whit better than the thief, and if his **mendacity** takes the form of slander he may be worse than most thieves. It puts a premium upon **knavery** untruthfully to attack an honest man, or even with hysterical exaggeration to **assail** a bad man with untruth.*

An epidemic of indiscriminate assault upon character does no good, but very great harm. The soul of every scoundrel is gladdened whenever an honest man is assailed, or even when a scoundrel is untruthfully assailed.

Now, it is easy to twist out of shape what I have just said, easy to affect to misunderstand it, and if it is slurred over in repetition not difficult really to misunderstand it. Some persons are sincerely incapable of understanding that to denounce mud slinging does not mean the endorsement of whitewashing; and both the interested individuals who need whitewashing and those others who practice mud slinging like to encourage such confusion of ideas.

*One of the chief counts against those who make indiscriminate assault upon men in business or men in public life is that they invite a reaction which is sure to tell powerfully in favor of the unscrupulous scoundrel who really ought to be attacked, who ought to be exposed, who ought, if possible, to be put in the penitentiary. If **Aristides** is praised overmuch as just, people get tired of hearing it; and **overcensure** of the unjust finally and from similar reasons results in their favor.*

Any excess is almost sure to invite a reaction; and, unfortunately, the reactions instead of taking the form of punishment of those guilty of the excess, is apt to take the form either of punishment of the unoffending or of giving immunity, and even strength, to offenders. The effort to make financial or political profit out of the destruction of character can only result in public calamity. Gross and reckless assaults on character, whether **on the stump** or in newspaper, magazine, or book, create a morbid and vicious public sentiment, and at the same time act as a profound deterrent to able men of normal sensitiveness and tend to prevent them from entering the public service at any price.

As an instance in point, I may mention that one serious difficulty encountered in getting the right type of men to dig the **Panama canal** is the certainty that they will be exposed, both without, and, I am sorry to say, sometimes within, Congress, to utterly reckless assaults on their character and capacity.

At the risk of repetition let me say again that my plea is not for immunity to, but for the most unsparing exposure of, the politician who betrays his trust, of the big business man who makes or spends his fortune in illegitimate or corrupt ways. There should be a resolute effort to hunt every such man out of the position he has disgraced. Expose the crime, and hunt down the criminal; but remember that even in the case of crime, if it is attacked in sensational, lurid, and untruthful fashion, the attack may do more damage to the public mind than the crime itself.

It is because I feel that there should be no rest in the endless war against the forces of evil that I ask the war be conducted with sanity as well as with resolution. The men with the muck rakes are often indispensable to the well being of society; but only if they know when to stop raking the muck, and to look upward to the celestial crown above them, to the crown of worthy endeavor. There are beautiful things above and round about them; and if they gradually grow to feel that the whole world is nothing but muck, their power of usefulness is gone. . . .

The fool who has not sense to discriminate between what is good and what is bad is well **nigh** as dangerous as the man who does discriminate and yet chooses the bad. There is nothing more distressing to every good patriot, to every good American, than the hard, scoffing spirit which treats the allegation of dishonesty in a public man as a cause for laughter. Such laughter is worse than the crackling of thorns under a pot, for it denotes not merely the vacant

On the stump: On occasions for speeches.

Panama canal: Roosevelt refers to the resistance he encountered in his efforts to build a canal in the nation of Panama that would link the Atlantic and Pacific oceans.

Nigh: Nearly.

*mind, but the heart in which high emotions have been choked before they could grow to fruition. There is any amount of good in the world, and there never was a time when loftier and more disinterested work for the betterment of mankind was being done than now. The forces that tend for evil are great and terrible, but the forces of truth and love and courage and honesty and generosity and sympathy are also stronger than ever before. It is a foolish and timid, no less than a wicked thing, to **blink the fact** that the forces of evil are strong, but it is even worse to fail to take into account the strength of the forces that tell for good.*

*Hysterical sensationalism is the poorest weapon wherewith to fight for lasting righteousness. The men who with stern sobriety and truth assail the many evils of our time, whether in the public press, or in magazines, or in books, are the leaders and allies of all engaged in the work for social and political betterment. But if they give good reason for distrust of what they say, if they **chill the ardor** of those who demand truth as a primary virtue, they thereby betray the good cause and play into the hands of the very men against whom they are nominally at war. . . .*

*We can no more and no less afford to condone evil in the man of capital than evil in the man of no capital. The wealthy man who exults because there is a failure of justice in the effort to bring some trust magnate to account for his misdeeds is as bad as, and no worse than, the so-called labor leader who **clamorously** strives to excite a foul class feeling on behalf of some other labor leader who is implicated in murder. One attitude is as bad as the other, and no worse; in each case the accused is entitled to exact justice; and in neither case is there need of action by others which can be construed into an expression of sympathy for crime.*

It is a prime necessity that if the present unrest is to result in permanent good the emotion shall be translated into action, and that the action shall be marked by honesty, sanity, and self-restraint. There is mighty little good in a mere spasm of reform. The reform that counts is that which comes through steady, continuous growth; violent emotionalism leads to exhaustion.

It is important to this people to grapple with the problems connected with the amassing of enormous fortunes, and the use of those fortunes, both corporate and individual, in business. We should discriminate in the sharpest way between fortunes well won and fortunes ill won; between those gained as an incident to performing great services to the community as a whole and those

Blink the fact: Not think.

Chill the ardor: Cool the intensity.

Clamorously: Noisily.

gained in evil fashion by keeping just within the limits of mere law honesty. Of course, no amount of charity in spending such fortunes in any way compensates for misconduct in making them. . . .

More important than aught else is the development of the broadest sympathy of man for man. The welfare of the wage worker, the welfare of the tiller of the soil, upon these depend the welfare of the entire country; their good is not to be sought in pulling down others; but their good must be the prime object of all our statesmanship.

Materially we must strive to secure a broader economic opportunity for all men, so that each shall have a better chance to show the stuff of which he is made. Spiritually and ethically we must strive to bring about clean living and right thinking. We appreciate that the things of the body are important; but we appreciate also that the things of the soul are immeasurably more important.

The foundation stone of national life is, and ever must be, the high individual character of the average citizen. (Speech Communication @ Texas A&M University *[Web site]*)

What happened next . . .

Roosevelt's speech helped start a backlash against sensational news stories. Such reporting continued but gradually began to lose popularity. Roosevelt, on the other hand, remained enormously popular and earned a reputation as a reformer. His successor, **William Howard Taft** (1857–1930; see entry in volume 3), is not remembered as a reformer, but Taft's administration actually had more success than Roosevelt's in breaking up companies that dominated a certain market. Those companies were illegal trusts (combinations of businesses): Roosevelt is remembered as the "trust-buster," though Taft had even greater success in breaking trusts. **Woodrow Wilson** (1856–1924; see entry in volume 4), another reformer, defeated Roosevelt and Taft in the election of 1912. By 1914, when World War I broke out, Americans became less interested in reform and more interested in staying out of the war, and then winning the war once America entered World War I in 1917.

Ironically, the term "Muckraking" became less negative than "yellow journalism" or sensationalism. A group of responsible writers began calling themselves "Muckrakers" after Roosevelt's speech. Those writers had begun thriving around 1900 and continued until about 1912. They are considered a historically significant group in American literature and journalism. Basing their stories on thorough research and documentation, Muckrakers presented conclusive evidence in stories about dishonest public officials, hazardous working conditions, social problems, worthless medicines, and dangerous foods.

Did you know . . .

- The writers often categorized historically as Muckrakers helped bring attention to several problems that were soon improved through legislation. The most famous Muckrakers were Upton Sinclair (1878–1968), whose novel *The Jungle* (1901) exposed unsanitary and dangerous work conditions in Chicago's meat-packing plants; Ida Tarbell (1857–1944), who exposed corrupt practices in big business and wrote *The History of the Standard Oil Company* (1904), about the trust that was later declared illegal and busted-up into smaller companies; Lincoln Steffens (1866–1936), whose series of articles on corruption in major American cities was published as *The Shame of Cities* (1904); and Samuel Hopkins Adams (1871–1958), whose exposure of ineffectual and dangerous medicines in *The Great American Fraud* (1906) helped spur passage of the Pure Food and Drug Act that continues to regulate medicine and health products in the United States a century after it was enacted.

Where to Learn More

Harbaugh, William H. *Power and Responsibility: The Life and Times of Theodore Roosevelt.* New York: Farrar, Straus and Cudahy, 1961. Reprint, Newtown, CT: American Political Biography Press, 1997.

Mowry, George. *Theodore Roosevelt and the Progressive Movement.* Madison: University of Wisconsin Press, 1946.

Schuman, Michael A. *Theodore Roosevelt.* Springfield, NJ: Enslow, 1997.

Texas A&M University, Department of Speech Communication. "The Man with the Muck Rake." *Speech Communication @ Texas A&M University.* [Online] http://www.tamu.edu/scom/pres/speeches/trmuck.html (accessed on August 7, 2000).

William Howard Taft

Twenty-seventh president (1909–1913)

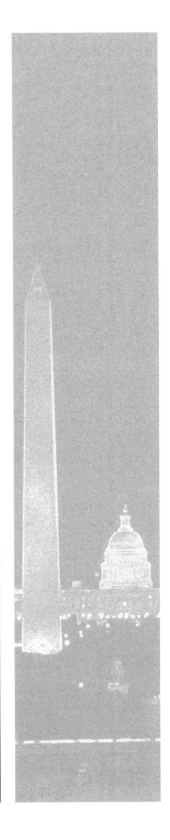

William Howard Taft

Born September 15, 1857
Cincinnati, Ohio
Died March 8, 1930
Washington, D.C.

Twenty-seventh president of the United States
(1909–1913)

Unsuccessful president fulfilled lifelong dream
when he became chief justice of the U.S.
Supreme Court

William Howard Taft had a long and distinguished career of public service. Four different presidents appointed him to judicial, diplomatic, or Cabinet (presidential advisory) positions. He achieved his main ambition when he was named chief justice of the U.S. Supreme Court in 1921.

Taft was less successful in his role as president. "I am entirely content to serve in the ranks," he wrote to a supporter who wanted Taft to run again for president in 1916. He had been soundly beaten in his bid for reelection in 1912.

The United States was undergoing tremendous economic growth during the first decade of the twentieth century when Taft was president. An increasingly profitable group of manufacturing, financial, and transportation corporations dominated American business. In response to such collection of wealth, a strong political trend called progressivism arose to promote legislation that would monitor business practices and improve social conditions for a growing urban population.

Taft considered himself progressive, but in reality he was a cautious leader. As president, he was quickly caught be-

"I am entirely content to serve in the ranks."

William Howard Taft

William Howard Taft.
Courtesy of the Library of Congress.

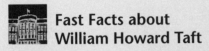

Fast Facts about William Howard Taft

Full name: William Howard Taft

Born: September 15, 1857

Died: March 8, 1930

Burial site: Arlington National Cemetery, Arlington, Virginia

Parents: Alphonso and Louisa Torrey Taft

Spouse: Helen Herron (1861–1943; m. 1886)

Children: Robert Alphonso (1889–1953); Helen Herron (1891–1987); Charles Phelps (1897–1983)

Religion: Unitarian

Education: Yale University (B.A., 1878); Cincinnati Law School (LL.B., 1880)

Occupations: Lawyer; law professor

Government positions: Judge; U.S. solicitor general; Philippines governor; secretary of war under Theodore Roosevelt; U.S. Supreme Court chief justice

Political party: Republican

Dates as president: March 4, 1909–March 4, 1913

Age upon taking office: 51

tween social activists wanting change and the powerful business sector that wanted to be left alone. Unable to please either, Taft suffered greatly during his term as one of the most criticized presidents of his era.

Taft was positioned—in his ideas, in his approach to governing, and in history—between two powerful and accomplished leaders. His predecessor, the popular **Theodore Roosevelt** (1858–1919; see entry in volume 3), vigorously promoted leadership in matters of business regulation and social improvement. Taft's successor, the forward-thinking Democrat **Woodrow Wilson** (1856–1924; see entry in volume 4), reformed financial practices and set the nation's agenda (list of things to do) through speeches, news conferences, and solid backing by a Democratic majority in Congress.

In comparison as a leader with Roosevelt and Wilson, who were able to rally support for their policies, Taft was unable to prevail against opponents. He allied himself with the more cautious and less popular side of his Republican Party. He did not possess the ability to inspire public support for his policies, nor did he show willingness to deal with the press. He was uncomfortable in the presidential office. Skilled as a lawyer, his highest ambition had always been an appointment to the U.S. Supreme Court.

Political roots

William Howard Taft was born September 15, 1857, in Cincinnati, Ohio. Both sides of his family had deep roots in

William Howard Taft Timeline

1857: Born in Ohio

1880: Admitted to Ohio bar and works as court reporter for the *Cincinnati Commercial* newspaper

1883: Works as attorney in private practice

1887–90: Serves in Ohio Superior Court

1890–92: Serves as U.S. solicitor general

1892–1900: Serves as judge in the U.S. Circuit Court

1901–4: Serves as civil governor of the Philippines

1904–8: Serves as secretary of war

1909–13: Serves as twenty-seventh U.S. president

1912: Loses presidential reelection bid to Woodrow Wilson

1921–30: Serves as chief justice of the U.S. Supreme Court

1930: Dies in Washington, D.C.

New England. His paternal grandfather (his father's father) had been a Vermont judge. Taft's father, Alphonso (1810–1891), set out on his own. First, he walked from Vermont to New Haven, Connecticut, when he was accepted at Yale University. Then, after graduation, he relocated west to Ohio as a young lawyer. He became a judge in Cincinnati and a leader in the Ohio Republican Party. Alphonso Taft later served briefly as secretary of war and as attorney general for President **Ulysses S. Grant** (1822–1855; see entry in volume 3). In the 1880s, he served as a diplomat in Russia and Austria under President **Chester A. Arthur** (1830–1886; see entry in volume 3).

Taft was raised in a household that included two older half brothers from his father's first marriage. Alphonso's first wife, Fanny, died in 1852. Taft's mother, Louise (1827–1907), bore four children. Always heavy as a child and throughout his life, Taft was sometimes called "Big Bill" or "Big Lub."

Taft excelled academically throughout his early life, first in Cincinnati's public schools, and then at Yale, which he entered in 1874. Returning to Ohio after graduating second in his class, Taft enrolled in Cincinnati Law School, from which he received his degree in 1880. He served for a time as assistant prosecuting attorney (the attorney who represents

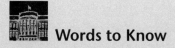

Words to Know

Brokerage firms: Businesses that invest money for clients.

Merger: The union of two or more businesses or corporations.

Philanthropic: Charitable.

Progressivism: A movement that began late in the nineteenth century whose followers pursued social, economic, and government reform. Generally located in urban areas, Progressivists ranged from individuals seeking to improve local living conditions to radicals who pursued sweeping changes in the American political and economic system.

Prosecuting attorney: The attorney who represents the government in a law case.

Solicitor general: An attorney appointed by the president to argue legal matters on behalf of the government.

Tariff: A tax placed on imported goods to raise their price and make them less attractive than goods produced by the nation importing them.

Trusts: A legal combination of firms and businesses formed to dominate a business sector and squash competition.

the government in a law case) in Hamilton County, Ohio, and as an attorney in private practice in Cincinnati. In March of 1887, Taft was appointed to an open superior court judgeship; the following year, he was elected to a five-year term for the same seat. It would be the only time he was elected to a position before he won the presidency.

Meanwhile, Taft met Helen Herron (1861–1943; see entry on **Helen Taft** in volume 3), a progressive-minded young woman. Taft and "Nellie," as he called Helen, were married in 1886. They would have three children.

When President **Benjamin Harrison** (1833–1901; see entry in volume 3) named Taft to the post of solicitor general of the United States in early 1890, the Taft family moved to Washington, D.C. (The solicitor general is an attorney appointed by the president to argue legal matters for the government.) Taft worried at first about his lack of experience with federal laws, but he soon mastered them. During his first year on the job, Taft argued eighteen cases before the Supreme Court and won fifteen of them. When the federal circuit court system was created by an 1891 act of Congress, Taft was named judge of the Sixth District, which encompassed Michigan, Ohio, Kentucky, and Tennessee. He spent eight productive years on the federal bench.

Governor of the Philippine Islands

President **William McKinley** (1843–1901; see entry in volume 3) invited Taft to head the newly created Philippines Commission in 1900. The United States had taken possession of the Philippine Islands, which had been ruled by Spain, following victory in the Spanish-American War in 1898. Taft aspired to become a Supreme Court justice and believed the appointment would not serve that ambition. Nellie Taft, however, urged her husband to take the post.

In the Philippines, Taft proved to be an able administrator and was made governor of the territory. One of Taft's main tasks involved bringing stability and economic growth to the Philippines. Great strides were made in education and other social programs during his governorship. Taft enjoyed his time in the Philippines despite ongoing fighting between U.S. Marines and rebels there who wanted independence for their island.

Vice President Theodore Roosevelt succeeded to the presidency in 1901 after the assassination of McKinley. He twice offered Taft a Supreme Court seat, but Taft declined. He wanted to complete his duty in the Philippines. By this time, he had come to enjoy being a political leader. Nellie Taft, who helped influence his career decisions, strongly supported his political pursuits. When Roosevelt was reelected to the White House in 1904, he offered Taft the Cabinet post of secretary of war. Taft accepted, and he and his family returned to Washington, D.C.

Taft served as one of Roosevelt's closest advisors during the next four years. He offered balance and caution to Roosevelt, who often sought quick solutions to the nation's problems. Taft also coordinated several foreign policy efforts: He traveled to Central America to supervise the start of construction of the Panama Canal (Roosevelt had told him to "make the dirt fly"), and in 1906, Taft sailed to Cuba when a rebellion there threatened stability in the Caribbean region. Taft negotiated a settlement that avoided U.S. military intervention.

William Howard Taft (right) served as one of President Theodore Roosevelt's most reliable advisors. In return, Roosevelt backed the reluctant Taft for the presidency.
Reproduced by permission of the Corbis Corporation.

Reluctant candidate

Taft quickly emerged as a favorite when President Roosevelt announced early in his second term that he would not seek reelection. With the encouragement of his wife, Taft overcame his personal reluctance and agreed to run for office. His highest ambition continued to be the Supreme Court, but all his friends and his family encouraged him to seek the presidency.

With New York senator James S. Sherman (1855–1912) as his running mate, Taft ran a mild campaign. He disliked stumping (traveling about making political speeches) to gain votes. Roosevelt's ringing endorsement (approval) helped him easily defeat Democratic nominee William Jennings Bryan (1860–1925; see box in **William McKinley** entry in volume 3). Taft had pledged to continue Roosevelt's aggressive policy of business regulation, but with his predecessor's approval, he surrounded himself with more moderate politicians.

Taft's first order of business was tariff reform (reform of laws on the taxing of imported goods). Many Americans wanted reductions in the taxes to slow the rising prices of consumer goods. Taft called a special Congressional session to address tariff reform during his first weeks in office. The Payne-Aldrich Act of 1909 originated in the House of Representatives as legislation to lower or eliminate many tariffs. However, a number of complex attachments (extra pieces of legislation) added in the Senate actually increased tariffs in many cases. Although there was widespread public disapproval of the bill, Taft felt compelled to support it. He undertook a cross-country trip in late summer of 1909 to promote the bill.

The enthusiasm that Taft showed in endorsing the bill came back to haunt him. The Payne-Aldrich Act was ridiculed in the press. So was Taft. Always overweight, he was usually depicted in cartoons as excessively portly. Taft was not

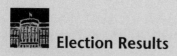

Election Results

1908

Presidential / Vice presidential candidates	Popular votes	Presidential electoral votes
William Howard Taft / James S. Sherman (Republican)	7,678,908	321
William Jennings Bryan / John W. Kern (Democratic)	6,409,104	162

Bryan lost for the third time as the Democratic nominee; he had lost in 1896 and 1900 to William McKinley, and did not run in 1904.

shrewd when it came to evaluating public opinion—a highly important talent for an elected politician. Teddy Roosevelt had used that talent to maintain his influence. Taft, on the other hand, was quickly overwhelmed and lost effectiveness as a leader.

A less-heralded trustbuster

An often overlooked feature of the Payne-Aldrich Act was its introduction of the first-ever-enacted corporate income tax. The tax, which was levied (imposed) on all corporations with revenue (income) above $5,000, became a significant source of new revenue for the government. Along with Taft's efforts to continue former President Roosevelt's trust-busting practices, Taft proved to be more of a business reformer than he gained credit for during his presidency.

In the late nineteenth century, many large companies had joined forces to overwhelm their competitors. Consumer activists blamed such industrial combinations—called trusts—for high prices of sugar, beef, and tobacco. Congress had enacted the Sherman Anti-Trust Law in 1890 specifically to abolish such entities, but the law was ineffective and was successfully challenged in the Supreme Court in 1895. Along with a growing popular press campaign against trusts, President Roosevelt had won great support by ordering the Justice Department to initiate a series of antitrust lawsuits against many dominant companies.

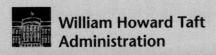

William Howard Taft Administration

Administration Dates
March 4, 1909–March 4, 1913

Vice President
James S. Sherman (1909–12)
None (1912–13)

Cabinet

Secretary of State
Philander C. Knox (1909–13)

Secretary of the Treasury
Franklin MacVeagh (1909–13)

Secretary of War
Jacob M. Dickinson (1909–11)
Henry L. Stimson (1911–13)

Attorney General
George W. Wickersham (1909–13)

Secretary of the Navy
George V. Meyer (1909–13)

Postmaster General
Frank H. Hitchcock (1909–13)

Secretary of the Interior
Richard A. Ballinger (1909–11)
Walter L. Fisher (1911–13)

Secretary of Agriculture
James Wilson (1909–13)

Secretary of Commerce and Labor
Charles Nagel (1909–13)

President Taft went after the largest trust of all—the Standard Oil Company of John D. Rockefeller (1839–1937). He supported the efforts of Attorney General George W. Wickersham (1858–1936) to break up the oil-refining conglomerate. Standard Oil dominated the industry through a series of corporate mergers that undermined competitors. (In a business sense, a merger is the union of two or more businesses or corporations.) In 1911, Wickersham went before the Supreme Court. In an historic decision, the court supported the government and ordered Standard Oil to disband. Rockefeller retired that same year. He began establishing philanthropic (charitable) bodies to dispense with $500 million of his personal fortune.

Taft and Wickersham lost the support of big business over the Standard Oil case. Nevertheless, they moved on to another big target—the U.S. Steel Corporation. The decision to prosecute the giant steel manufacturer and its prominent president, John Pierpont (J. P.) Morgan (1837–1913; see box in **Grover Cleveland** entry in volume 3), dated back to a Wall Street crisis of 1907.

Morgan, the most powerful banker in the country, had created U.S. Steel in 1901 after acquiring and merging several companies. It was the first billion-dollar corporation in history. During an economic crisis in 1907, Morgan was approached by the government to help prevent a financial collapse. The financier (a person who manages large-scale financial deals) and his U.S. Steel company were allowed to purchase several failing brokerage firms that owned stock in the Tennessee Coal and Iron Company. (A brokerage firm is a business that invests money for clients.) Morgan's purchase allowed the company and the brokerage firms to avoid bankruptcy (financial ruin).

In October 1911, Wickersham announced that his office would bring charges against U.S. Steel under the Sherman Anti-Trust Act for acquiring Tennessee Coal and Iron under false pretenses (false reasons). The threat of financial crisis, it was argued, had been a trick Morgan used to acquire another large energy company. The government's legal brief mentioned President Roosevelt: Although it did not hint of executive misconduct, the brief implied that the president had been fooled by Morgan. The government case failed. Incensed at what he felt was a betrayal by Taft, Roosevelt began campaigning for the 1912 presidential election and the long friendship between the two men was over.

 Taft and Sports

In 1910, William Howard Taft was the first president to throw out the ceremonial "first pitch" of a baseball season. He is also credited by some as having initiated baseball's "seventh-inning stretch." At one game he attended, Taft rose to his feet after the visiting team finished batting in the seventh inning. Thinking the president was leaving the game, fans around him rose in respect. But Taft simply stretched out and sat down again as the home team came to bat, and the fans around him did the same.

Taft also enjoyed golfing. He often played with Robert Todd Lincoln, Abraham Lincoln's son.

Dollar diplomacy

Taft's foreign policy efforts did not help his standing, despite good intentions. Upon taking office, Taft appointed former corporation lawyer Philander C. Knox (1853–1921) as secretary of state. Knox reorganized the Department of State geopolitically (geographically and politically)—Europe, the Far East, and Latin America each had its own division. This setup remained in place nearly a century later. Knox also established a Division of Information to improve communication between department sections, and he instituted a merit-based system for the promotion of Foreign Service officers. (A merit-based system looks at a person's skills and experience rather than a person's social standing or connections.)

Taft, as a policy aim, sought to stabilize troubled areas of Asia and Central America in order to protect and expand

William Howard Taft (center, seated) was appointed chief justice of the U.S. Supreme Court in 1921. The Court in 1930: (seated left to right) James C. McReynolds, Oliver Wendell Holmes, Taft, Joseph McKenna, and Willis Van Devanter; (standing left to right) Edward T. Sanford, George Sutherland, Louis Brandeis, and Pierce Butler. *Reproduced by permission of the Corbis Corporation.*

U.S. commercial interests. Taft was continuing policies begun by his predecessors, William McKinley and Theodore Roosevelt. Less politically clever, however, Taft saw his strategy referred to as "Dollar Diplomacy," which quickly became a negative term. The administration strategy combined financial aid or investment and increased trade to help stabilize the economy of a given country.

Nicaragua became the proving ground for this unsuccessful policy. That nation's leader, José Santos Zelaya (1853–1919), was viewed as an obstruction by the American business community with interests in Nicaragua. When an insurgency movement (rebellion, uprising) to unseat him arose in late 1909, the United States provided rebels with financial aid. Two Americans fighting with rebels were captured and executed by the Zelaya army. The United States severed diplomatic ties at that point and sent in troops. In the summer of 1910, American forces captured the nation's capital, Managua, and emerged victorious.

Complete American Presidents Sourcebook

The Taft administration strongly urged a new Nicaraguan government to accept a large loan from a coalition (partnership) of Wall Street banks. Meanwhile, U.S. military forces took control of Nicaragua's customs ports to back the loan. The situation still proved unstable: In 1912, another rebellion emerged and another force of Marines was dispatched to end it.

When similar unrest occurred in the Dominican Republic and then Mexico (the Mexican Revolution of 1910), Taft acted more cautiously. The administration adopted a neutral (showing allegiance to no sides) position on Mexico's problems, recognizing strong anti-American sentiment there. Still, Taft sent troops as a precaution to protect U.S. business interests. Internal strife increased considerably, and Mexico dissolved into relative anarchy (absence of any form of government). Oil firms with business in Mexico, politicians from the Southwest, and former president Roosevelt called for intervention, but Taft waited. His term came to an end as the situation worsened.

The last two territories within the continental United States, New Mexico and Arizona, entered the Union in early 1912.

A Republican disaster

More than a year before the election of 1912, Taft faced several challengers. His greatest political enemy in Congress was the nation's most prominent Progressive politician, Robert La Follette (1855–1925) of Wisconsin. The senator formed the National Progressive Republican League in early 1911 and began campaigning for the presidency. Meanwhile, the campaign of former president Roosevelt quickly gathered considerable momentum. Taft, however, still had much support among powerful figures within the Republican Party. They helped assure that Taft would win the presidential nomination at the Republican national convention of 1912.

Overwhelmed by more powerful party leaders, Roosevelt claimed that the nomination had been stolen from him. He took a number of reform-minded Republicans with him to form the Progressive "Bull Moose" Party.

The campaign of 1912 was hotly contested among split Republican factions and Democrat Woodrow Wilson, who had won national acclaim in his role as governor of New Jersey. Roosevelt's Bull Moose candidacy split the Republican

Robert A. Taft and the Taft Family

Several generations of Tafts have been influential in American politics since the Civil War years (1861–65). Alphonso Taft was a prominent Ohio attorney and Republican who served as secretary of war and attorney general under President Ulysses S. Grant and as minister to Austria-Hungary and then Russia under President Chester A. Arthur. His son, William Howard Taft, served as president and as chief justice of the U.S. Supreme Court. William Howard's son Robert Alphonso Taft was born in 1889, shortly before Alphonso Taft died. He served in the U.S. Senate from 1938 until his death in 1953. His son, Robert Alphonso Taft Jr., served three terms in the U.S. House of Representatives during the 1960s, and one term in the U.S. Senate during the 1970s. In 1998, Bob Taft, son of Robert Taft Jr., grandson of Robert Taft, and great-grandson of William Howard Taft, was elected governor of Ohio.

All the Tafts have been leading Republicans of Ohio, but it was the president's son, Robert Taft, who won the nickname, "Mr. Republican." He was a graduate of Yale University and the Harvard Law School (graduating at the head of his class). He returned to Ohio in 1913, was certified as a lawyer, and began practicing law in Cincinnati. On October 17, 1914, he married Martha Wheaton Bowers, whose father served as solicitor general in the Taft administration. They would have four sons.

During World War I (1914–18), Taft served his country as an assistant counsel for the U.S. Food Administration; after the war, he was a legal advisor for the American Relief Administration. Then, Taft returned to Cincinnati, where he established his own law firm with his brother, Charles Phelps Taft II.

In 1920, Robert Taft was elected to Ohio's House of Representatives. He was reelected three times and became Ohio Speaker of the House in 1926. He also served a term as a state senator. In 1938, he was elected to the U.S. Senate and quickly earned the nickname "Mr. Republican" for opposing much of Democratic president Franklin D. Roosevelt's New Deal program and foreign policy. Determined to keep the United States out of World War II (1939–45), Taft opposed such measures as trading fifty destroyers to Great Britain for leases of naval and air bases and the Selective Training and Service Act, which called for the first peacetime program of compulsory military service in American history. Taft believed that America should remain neutral, especially after the Soviet Union became involved in the war. "My whole idea of foreign policy is based largely on the position that America can successfully defend itself against the rest of the world," he explained. Once the United States became militarily involved in the conflict, however, Taft supported the war effort.

Robert A. Taft.
Courtesy of the Library of Congress.

In 1945, the year World War II ended, Taft began his second term in the Senate. Taft opposed the trial of several of the Nazi wartime leaders in Nuremberg, Germany. He had little sympathy for those tried, but he pointed to the U.S. Constitution, which prohibits the passage of *ex post facto* laws (laws made after a crime is committed). Taft perceived a "spirit of vengeance, and vengeance is seldom justice." **John F. Kennedy** (1917–1963; see entry in volume 5) would later include Taft in his Pulitzer Prize–winning book, *Profiles in Courage,* which included essays on U.S. senators who showed courage by sticking up for principles against popular opinion.

Taft showed similar principles during his second term as senator. When at the request of President **Harry S. Truman** (1884–1972; see entry in volume 4) the House of Representatives passed a measure allowing strikers in vital industries to be drafted for military service, Senator Taft vehemently protested. Convinced that such action was unfair and violated the civil liberties of a worker, he sided with progressive Democrats in opposing it. Taft led opposition to several initiatives by the Truman administration, including U.S. contributions to the international monetary fund and an international bank. Taft was concerned with balancing the national budget and limiting federal power and influence. In 1946, when Republicans gained control of both houses of Congress, Taft set about restoring what he thought was a better balance between management and labor. Out of this came legislation that bears his name, the Taft-Hartley Act. The act outlawed the closed shop (where all workers must join a union), provided that a union might be sued for breach of contract, and provided for delaying a strike eighty days if national health and safety seemed in jeopardy.

Even though he was a Republican Party leader, Taft never won his party's presidential nomination. Taft died of cancer on July 31, 1953.

A Selection of Taft Landmarks

Arlington National Cemetery. Arlington, VA 22211. Special burial site of President and Mrs. Taft. See http://www.arlingtoncemetery.org/historical_information/william_taft.html (accessed on August 8, 2000).

William Howard Taft National Historic Site. 2038 Auburn Ave., Cincinnati, OH 45219. (513) 684-3262. Birthplace and childhood home of President Taft. Museum of Taft memorabilia is in the house. See http://www.nps.gov/wiho/ (accessed on August 8, 2000).

Party's support and made Wilson an easy winner, with Roosevelt coming in second, and Taft third. Taft's Electoral College defeat was the worst in the twentieth century for an incumbent (in-office) president: He received only 8 electoral votes, compared with 88 for Roosevelt and 435 for Wilson. (For more information on the Electoral College, see boxes in **George W. Bush** entry in volume 5.)

Back to the bench

Taft was happy to leave Washington. He was appointed the Kent Professor of Constitutional Law at Yale University. During World War I (1914–18), he served as joint chair of the National War Labor Board. In 1921, another Ohio-born Republican president, **Warren G. Harding** (1865–1923; see entry in volume 4), appointed Taft as chief justice of the U.S. Supreme Court. Taft became the first former president to serve on the court in its history.

Taft instituted several reforms that reduced the backlog (the excess) of untried cases. He lobbied (sought to influence legislators) heavily for the construction of a new headquarters for the Court. His promotion of the new headquarters was commemorated by his successor when the cornerstone for the Court was laid in 1932. Taft retired from the court in February 1930 when his health declined; he died a few weeks later, on March 8, 1930.

Taft's son, Robert Alphonso Taft (1889–1953), became an influential Republican in Congress in the 1940s. Robert

Taft opposed the New Deal legislation of President **Franklin D. Roosevelt** (1882–1945; see entry in volume 4) as well as the creation of the North Atlantic Treaty Organization (NATO). The younger Taft coauthored the Taft-Hartley Labor Act of 1947, which restricted many labor union practices.

Legacy

William Howard Taft's presidential defeat in 1912 ended a virtual Republican lock on the White House. Between 1860 and 1912 eleven of thirteen elected presidents were Republican. After Woodrow Wilson's two terms from 1913 to 1921, three more Republicans were elected in succession as president.

Though not often linked with progressive politicians like Roosevelt, Wilson, or La Follette, Taft is credited with guiding through Congress several important pieces of progressive legislation. The Mann-Elkins Act of 1910 regulated railroad commerce and strengthened the powers of the Interstate Commerce Commission; it also included an attachment that established government regulation of the telegraph and telephone companies. Taft's Commission on Economy and Efficiency—the forerunner of the modern Office of Management and Budget—was the result of his impatience with a wasteful process through which the government departments obtained their annual funding through Congress.

In assessments of presidents, Taft often pales in comparison with Roosevelt and Wilson. Still, Taft maintained the momentum of Roosevelt's trustbusting. Wilson's foreign policy efforts in Central America and Asia were more modestly successful, but he failed when he took a more aggressive policy than Taft had toward Mexico. Wilson's foreign policy plans were completely disrupted by the outbreak of World War I in Europe in 1914.

Where to Learn More

Anderson, Donald F. *William Howard Taft: A Conservative's Conception of the Presidency*. Ithaca: Cornell University Press, 1973.

Anderson, Judith Icke. *William Howard Taft: An Intimate History*. New York: Norton, 1981.

Burton, David Henry. *William Howard Taft, in the Public Service.* Malabar, FL: R. E. Krieger Publishing Co., 1986.

Coletta, Paolo. *The Presidency of William Howard Taft.* Lawrence: University of Kansas Press, 1973.

Coletta, Paolo. *William Howard Taft: A Bibliography.* Westport, CT: Meckler, 1989.

Duffy, Herbert Smith. *William Howard Taft.* New York: Minton, Balch and Co., 1930.

Ross, Ishbel. *An American Family: The Tafts, 1678 to 1964.* Cleveland: World Publishing Company, 1964. Reprint, Westport, CT: Greenwood Press, 1977.

Helen Taft

Born June 2, 1861
Cincinnati, Ohio
Died May 22, 1943
Washington, D.C.

Ambitious politician's wife convinced her husband to turn down several offers of Supreme Court appointments and instead seek the presidency

W hen she was sixteen years old, Helen Herron visited the White House with her parents as private guests of President **Rutherford B. Hayes** (1822–1893; see entry in volume 3). She said later that the visit made such an impact on her that she vowed to return some day for a longer stay.

Years later, Helen became the wife of **William Howard Taft** (1857–1930; see entry in volume 3). She is credited by presidential scholars for possessing the ambition and providing the support that most assuredly landed her husband in the White House. Without her, Taft was unlikely to have ever pursued the office.

Few future prospects

Born on June 2, 1861, Helen Herron was one of eleven children of John and Harriet Herron of Cincinnati, Ohio. Her father, a former law partner of President Hayes, served in Congress and was influential in the Ohio Republican Party from which presidents Hayes and **James A. Garfield** (1831–1881; see entry in volume 3) emerged.

"My dearest and best critic [my wife]"

William Howard Taft

Helen Taft.
Courtesy of the Library of Congress.

"Nellie," as Helen was called throughout her life, attended a private Cincinnati school for young women. She studied music and languages and was known as an independent thinker with an adventurous streak. She wanted more than what was expected of her, but there were few opportunities open for females other than being a wife and mother.

She earned a living for two years as a teacher before realizing that she was not suited for that profession. In 1883, Nellie and two friends founded a "salon" designed to serve as a Cincinnati meeting place for intellectual, political, and cultural discussions. One of those attending the salon was William Howard Taft, a young lawyer and graduate of Yale University. "Will" Taft was impressed with Nellie's intelligence and forthright opinions. A courtship followed in which Nellie twice rejected Taft's marriage proposals. She eventually agreed, however, and the two were wed in June of 1886.

Nellie became a Cincinnati housewife and mother to three Taft children. She also began working for various causes as her husband became influential in state politics. Fond of classical music, Nellie used political connections to help found the city's Orchestra Association, the forerunner of the Cincinnati Symphony Orchestra.

Will and Nellie in Manila

In 1890, Taft was named to the post of solicitor general of the United States, and the Taft family moved to Washington, D.C. (The solicitor general is an attorney appointed by the president to argue legal cases on the government's behalf.) Ten years later, Taft was invited to lead a delegation to the Philippine Islands. The United States had taken possession of the islands following the Spanish-American War in 1898. Taft was uncertain whether to go to the faraway islands that were politically unstable. His wife convinced him it was a good opportunity.

The Tafts stayed for four years in the Philippines. Nellie Taft wrote extensively about that period in her autobiography. She enjoyed her husband's prominent role and eagerly participated in discussions with him about his duties as the territory's governor. She also battled prejudice among white

officials, who sometimes treated Filipinos with contempt. The Tafts urged tolerance and equality in official social occasions.

During her time in the Philippines, Nellie tried to improve the quality of life of the country's poor. She met with Filipino women to persuade them to accept food and medical supplies sent from the United States. She founded the Drop of Milk program, which instructed residents about methods of milk sterilization. Showing her adventurous spirit, Nellie became the first white female to tour the rugged and dangerous Luzon Mountain region.

The family returned to Washington, D.C., in 1904 when Taft was named secretary of war under President **Theodore Roosevelt** (1858–1919; see entry in volume 3). Nellie often traveled with her husband on his official duties, including a three-month world tour. Back in Washington, D.C., however, she disliked the social formalities of political life. She was not fond of the constant socializing expected of Cabinet wives. Taft was just as uncomfortable as a politician. He was more ideally suited for law. President Roosevelt twice offered him a seat on the Supreme Court, but Nellie convinced him to decline the offers. On the second occasion, she met with Roosevelt to explain why her husband should not accept the position. The Tafts had their eyes on a higher political office.

A bold beginning and a setback

In 1908, Taft won the nomination as the Republican presidential candidate. During his campaign tours, he wrote his wife daily, as was their custom when separated. At Taft's inaugural (official ceremony starting his presidency), Nellie became the first first lady to accompany her husband on the parade route back to the White House after the swearing-in ceremony. Traditionally, the outgoing president would ride with the newly inaugurated chief executive, but Roosevelt had already departed the capital. Nellie endured some criticism for her bold action, but she later said it was the proudest moment of her life.

But a setback struck the Tafts just two months after the inauguration. The first lady, at the age of forty-seven, suddenly became partially paralyzed and unable to speak. Severely restricting her public appearances, she was usually seen publicly only from a distance for several months. The White House never acknowledged the condition as a stroke (a broken or blocked blood vessel in the brain), preferring to call it a "nervous disorder." After a year, the determined first lady had regained much of her strength.

Returning to an active role as first lady, Nellie Taft quickly set about decorating the White House in a manner similar to the Tafts' arrangements at Malcanang Palace in the Philippines. Meanwhile, she continued to consult with the president, who asked her opinions on issues and invited her to his informal meetings with politicians. A 1909 *Ladies Home Journal* article mentioned the advisor role she played for her husband. She supported the women's suffrage (voting rights) movement, but she believed that women should not become office-seekers themselves.

The Tafts participated in a glittering round of social events. On their twenty-fifth wedding anniversary, the first couple hosted several thousand guests at a White House garden party that featured the novelty of a large, electrically lit sign that read "1886–1911." The occasion received negative press for its unnecessary extravagance, as well as for the many gifts given to the Tafts—some of which came from those courting the political favor of the Taft administration.

Springtime legacy

Nellie Taft enjoyed several successes as first lady. She personally interceded (became involved) on behalf of an immigrant woman whose young son was denied entry into the United States because of a speech disability. Mrs. Taft's efforts resulted in a reversal of the decision. On another occasion, she attended House committee hearings about dangerous workplace conditions facing young women in the nation's textile (cloth and clothing) factories. Her presence was noted in the press and she commented on the committee's findings. It was rare at that time for a first lady to be quoted in political matters in newspapers and magazines.

Nellie Taft was responsible for several civic improvement projects in the nation's capital. She pushed for the creation of West Potomac Park, preserving a natural setting along the Potomac River as it runs through Washington, D.C. She successfully campaigned for the construction of a bandstand by the river. Free weekly concerts by the Marine Band were instituted during her husband's administration.

Mrs. Taft's most enduring effort came about as a result of her past travels in Japan, when her husband had been secretary of war. As first lady, she gathered support to bring Tokyo's famous cherry blossom trees to the capital. The mayor of Tokyo presented three thousand trees as a gift to the first lady, which she then donated to the government. To this day, thousands of tourists plan trips to be in Washington, D.C., when the trees' pale pink petals blossom in the spring.

More joyous times

After Taft lost the 1912 presidential election, he happily retired from politics to teach law at Yale. Taft received his long-desired Supreme Court appointment in 1921. He served on the Court until 1930, the year he died.

Nellie Taft remained in Washington for the remainder of her life. She died on May 22, 1943, and was buried in Arlington National Cemetery, the first of two first ladies given that honor. (**Jacqueline Kennedy** [1929–1994; see entry in volume 5] is the other.) The Tafts' daughter, Helen Taft Manning (1891–1987), was able to fulfill some of the ambitions that had not been allowed her mother: She earned a doctorate degree from Yale University and became a history professor. The two Taft sons entered politics. Charles Phelps Taft (1897–1983) was a mayor of Cincinnati, and his brother, Robert Alphonso Taft (1889–1953; see box in **William Howard Taft** entry in volume 3), served in the U.S. Senate for several years.

Where to Learn More

Greenberg, Judith E. *Helen Herron Taft, 1861–1943*. New York: Children's Press, 2000.

Ross, Ishbel. *An American Family: The Tafts, 1678 to 1964*. Cleveland: World Publishing Company, 1964. Reprint, Westport, CT: Greenwood Press, 1977.

Taft's Final Annual Address to Congress

Delivered on December 3, 1912; excerpted from
The Annals of America

President Taft defends his foreign policy that opponents have called "Dollar Diplomacy"

During the early years of the twentieth century, many developing countries in Central and Latin America had unstable economies and governments. The United States, meanwhile, had enjoyed sustained prosperity since the mid-1890s. America had benefited from increased trade with other nations, which created new business opportunities and markets.

The administration of **William Howard Taft** (1857–1930; see entry in volume 3) pursued a policy of using trade and economic opportunity as a means for offering stability to troubled countries. Instead of helping nations maintain peace by using military force, the United States hoped to improve the economies and social welfare of developing countries through business investment and trade. A "developing country" refers to a nation that is only beginning to develop modern industries; a developed country, on the other hand, has reached an advanced stage of industrial progress.

Taft described his policy as "substituting dollars for bullets." He meant that the United States was creating business opportunities and offering financial assistance to troubled nations instead of using military force to maintain law and order. By

"With continuity of purpose we must deal with the problems of our external relations by a diplomacy modern, resourceful, magnanimous, and fittingly expressive of the high ideals of a great nation."

William Howard Taft

1912, however, Taft's policies had only enjoyed modest success. In reporting on Taft's policies, newspapers increasingly referred to the president's foreign policy as "dollar diplomacy" to suggest that the United States was attempting to buy friends.

Taft used the occasion of his final annual address to Congress to restate his foreign policy and to point out its successes. His address was delivered in December 1912, about one month after he finished a distant third in the presidential election. In the speech, Taft emphasized his belief that the United States can be a world leader by investing in smaller nations. He concluded by discussing a series of examples of nations that had achieved peace and improved economic conditions during his presidency.

Things to remember while reading an excerpt from President Taft's final annual address to Congress:

- Taft emphasized that trade and business investment were the best means for achieving and rewarding stability in developing countries. He pursued the theme that modern diplomacy was built on commercial interaction. Taft claimed that developing nations "need only a measure of stability and the means of financial regeneration to enter upon an era of peace and prosperity."

- Taft provided several examples of nations that either had internal conflicts or disputes with neighbors during the four years of his presidency. He did not always pinpoint the exact nature of the conflict or provide extensive information about the troubles of the nations he mentioned. The sheer number of examples, however, helps show how unstable the world was during that period. Taft discussed the nation of Nicaragua at length. In the case of Nicaragua, the Taft policy of substituting dollars for bullets failed. Taft blamed the failure on ruthless revolutionaries in that country and the inability of Congress to quickly approve loans the Taft administration wanted to provide to help counter revolutionary activities in that nation.

Excerpt from President Taft's final annual address to Congress

The diplomacy of the present administration has sought to respond to modern ideas of commercial **intercourse.** This policy has been characterized as substituting dollars for bullets. It is one that appeals alike to idealistic humanitarian sentiments, to the dictates of sound policy and strategy, and to legitimate commercial aims. It is an effort frankly directed to the increase of American trade upon the **axiomatic** principle that the government of the United States shall extend all proper support to every legitimate and beneficial American enterprise abroad.

How great have been the results of this diplomacy, coupled with the maximum and minimum provision of the Tariff Law, will be seen by some consideration of the wonderful increase in the export trade of the United States. Because modern diplomacy is commercial, there has been a disposition in some quarters to attribute to it none but materialistic aims. How strikingly erroneous is such an impression may be seen from a study of the results by which the diplomacy of the United States can be judged.

In the field of work toward the ideals of peace, this government negotiated, but to my regret was unable to **consummate,** two **arbitration** treaties which set the highest mark of the aspiration of nations toward the substitution of arbitration and reason for war in the settlement of international disputes. Through the efforts of American diplomacy, several wars have been prevented or ended. I refer to the successful **tripartite** mediation of the Argentine Republic, Brazil, and the United States between Peru and Ecuador; the bringing of the boundary dispute between Panama and Costa Rica to peaceful arbitration; the staying of warlike preparations when Haiti and the Dominican Republic were on the verge of hostilities; the stopping of a war in Nicaragua; the halting of **internecine** strife in Honduras.

The government of the United States was thanked for its influence toward the restoration of amicable relations between the Argentine Republic and Bolivia. The diplomacy of the United States is active in seeking to **assuage** the remaining ill feeling between this country and the Republic of Colombia. In the recent civil war in China, the United States successfully joined with the other interested

Intercourse: Exchange.

Axiomatic: Obvious; self-evident.

Consummate: Complete.

Arbitration: When two parties facing a disagreement allow a neutral party to settle their dispute.

Tripartite: Three-part.

Internecine: Marked by slaughter within a group.

Assuage: Ease.

powers in urging an early cessation of hostilities. An agreement has been reached between the governments of Chile and Peru. . . .

In China the policy of encouraging financial investment to enable that country to help itself has had the result of giving new life and practical application to the open door policy. The consistent purpose of the present administration has been to encourage the use of American capital in the development of China by the promotion of those essential reforms to which China is pledged by treaties with the United States and other powers. The **hypothecation** *to foreign bankers in connection with certain industrial enterprises, such as the Hukuang railways, of the national revenues upon which these reforms depended, led the Department of State, early in the administration, to demand for American citizens participation in such enterprises, in order that the United States might have equal rights and an equal voice in all questions pertaining to the disposition of the public revenues concerned.*

The same policy of promoting international accord among the powers having similar treaty rights as ourselves in the matters of reform, which could not be put into practical effect without the common consent of all, was likewise adopted in the case of the loan desired by China for the reform of its currency. The principle of international cooperation in matters of common interest upon which our policy had already been based in all of the above instances has admittedly been a great factor in that **concert** *of the powers which has been so happily conspicuous during the perilous period of transition through which the great Chinese nation has been passing.*

In Central America the aim has been to help such countries as Nicaragua and Honduras to help themselves. They are the immediate beneficiaries. The national benefit to the United States is twofold. First, it is obvious that the **Monroe Doctrine** *is more vital in the neighborhood of the Panama Canal and the zone of the Caribbean than anywhere else. There, too, the maintenance of that doctrine falls most heavily upon the United States. It is therefore essential that the countries within that sphere shall be removed from the jeopardy involved by heavy foreign debt and chaotic national finances and from the ever present danger of international complications due to disorder at home. Hence, the United States has been glad to encourage and support American bankers who were willing to lend a helping hand to the financial rehabilitation of such countries because this financial rehabilitation and the protection of their* **customhouses** *from being the prey of would-be dictators would re-*

Hypothecation: Assumption or interpretation of a situation that leads to action.

Concert: Union.

Monroe Doctrine: A policy statement issued during the presidency of James Monroe (1817–25) that explained the position of the United States on the activities of European powers in the western hemisphere; of major significance was the United States' stand against European intervention in the affairs of the Americas.

Customhouses: Buildings where customs and duties are collected.

Complete American Presidents Sourcebook

move at one stroke the menace of foreign creditors and the menace of revolutionary disorder.

*The second advantage to the United States is one affecting chiefly all the Southern and Gulf ports and the business and industry of the South. The republics of Central America and the Caribbean possess great natural wealth. They need only a measure of stability and the means of financial **regeneration** to enter upon an era of peace and prosperity, bringing profit and happiness to themselves and at the same time creating conditions sure to lead to a flourishing interchange of trade with this country.*

I wish to call your especial attention to the recent occurrences in Nicaragua, for I believe the terrible events recorded there during the revolution of the past summer—the useless loss of life, the devastation of property, the bombardment of defenseless cities, the killing and wounding of women and children, the torturing of noncombatants to exact contributions, and the suffering of thousands of human beings—might have been averted had the Department of State, through approval of the loan convention by the Senate, been permitted to carry out its now well-developed policy of encouraging the extending of financial aid to weak Central American states, with the primary objects of avoiding just such revolutions by assisting those republics to rehabilitate their finances, to establish their currency on a stable basis, to remove the customhouses from the danger of revolutions by arranging for their secure administration, and to establish reliable banks.

*During this last revolution in Nicaragua, the government of that republic having admitted its inability to protect American life and property against acts of sheer lawlessness on the part of the **malcontents,** and having requested this government to assume that office, it became necessary to land over 2,000 Marines and **Bluejackets** in Nicaragua. Owing to their presence the constituted government of Nicaragua was free to devote its attention wholly to its internal troubles, and was thus enabled to stamp out the rebellion in a short space of time. When the Red Cross supplies sent to Granada had been exhausted, 8,000 persons having been given food in one day upon the arrival of the American forces, our men supplied other unfortunate, needy Nicaraguans from their own **haversacks.***

I wish to congratulate the officers and men of the United States Navy and Marine Corps who took part in reestablishing order in Nicaragua upon their splendid conduct, and to record with sorrow the death of seven American Marines and Bluejackets. Since the

Regeneration: Renewal.

Malcontents: Those opposed to the current government.

Bluejackets: Enlisted men of the Navy.

Haversacks: Knapsacks worn over the shoulder.

reestablishment of peace and order, elections have been held amid conditions of quiet and tranquillity. Nearly all the American Marines have now been withdrawn. The country should soon be on the road to recovery. The only apparent danger now threatening Nicaragua arises from the shortage of funds. Although American bankers have already rendered assistance, they may naturally be **loath** *to advance a loan adequate to set the country upon its feet without the support of some such convention as that of June 1911, upon which the Senate has not yet acted. . . .*

It is not possible to make to the Congress a communication upon the present foreign relations of the United States so detailed as to convey an adequate impression of the enormous increase in the importance and activities of those relations. If this government is really to preserve to the American people that free opportunity in foreign markets which will soon be indispensable to our prosperity, even greater efforts must be made. Otherwise the American merchant, manufacturer, and exporter will find many a field in which American trade should logically predominate preempted through the more energetic efforts of other governments and other commercial nations.

There are many ways in which, through hearty cooperation, the legislative and executive branches of this government can do much. The absolute essential is the spirit of united effort and singleness of purpose. I will allude only to a very few specific examples of action which ought then to result.

America cannot take its proper place in the most important fields for its commercial activity and enterprise unless we have a Merchant Marine. American commerce and enterprise cannot be effectively fostered in those fields unless we have good American banks in the countries referred to. We need American newspapers in those countries and proper means for public information about them.

We need to assume the permanency of a trained foreign service. We need legislation enabling the members of the foreign service to be systematically brought in direct contact with the industrial, manufacturing, and exporting interests of this country in order that American businessmen may enter the foreign field with a clear perception of the exact conditions to be dealt with and the officers themselves may **prosecute** *their work with a clear idea of what American industrial and manufacturing interests require.*

Congress should fully realize the conditions which obtain in the world as we find ourselves at the threshold of our middle age as a

Loath: Reluctant.

Prosecute: Perform.

nation. We have emerged full grown as a peer in the great concourse of nations. We have passed through various formative periods. We have been **self-centered** in the struggle to develop our domestic resources and deal with our domestic questions. The nation is now too mature to continue in its foreign relations those temporary expedients natural to a people to whom domestic affairs are the sole concern.

In the past, our diplomacy has often consisted, in normal times, in a mere assertion of the right to international existence. We are now in a larger relation with broader rights of our own and obligations to others than ourselves. A number of great guiding principles were laid down early in the history of this government. The recent task of our diplomacy has been to adjust those principles to the conditions of today, to develop their **corollaries** to find practical applications of the old principles expanded to meet new situations. Thus are being evolved bases upon which can rest the superstructure of policies which must grow with the destined progress of this nation.

The successful conduct of our foreign relations demands a broad and a modern view. We cannot meet new questions nor build for the future if we confine ourselves to **outworn dogmas** of the past and to the perspective appropriate at our emergence from colonial times and conditions. The opening of the **Panama Canal** will mark a new era in our international life and create new and worldwide conditions which, with their vast correlations and consequences, will obtain for hundreds of years to come. We must not wait for events to overtake us **unawares**. With continuity of purpose we must deal with the problems of our external relations by a diplomacy modern, resourceful, **magnanimous**, and fittingly expressive of the high ideals of a great nation. (Adler, pp. 369–73)

Self-centered: In terms of a nation, self-centered is similar to isolationist—a national policy of avoiding pacts, treaties, and other official agreements with other nations in order to remain neutral and unbound.

Corollaries: Related polices or issues.

Outworn dogmas: Outdated points of view.

Panama Canal: A canal linking the Atlantic and Pacific Oceans built across the isthmus of Panama. After several failed efforts, work on the successful Canal began in 1905; the Canal opened in 1914.

Unawares: Unexpectedly.

Magnanimous: Courageous.

What happened next . . .

The instability of Central American and Asian nations that Taft tried to address during his presidency was a worldwide phenomenon. While the United States was concerned with nations in the Western Hemisphere, European nations were at odds over boundaries and over their colonies in Africa. The instability in the Western Hemisphere led to increasing tension between the United States and its nearest neighbors. The conflicts in Europe erupted into World War I (1914–18), which began the year after Taft left office.

Like the mixed success of Taft's foreign policy in Latin America, the United States continued to have successes and failures in dealings with Latin American countries. At times, some of the nations believed the U.S. businesses were trying to dominate their economy. On the other hand, political instability was ongoing in many of the countries. U.S. relations with Latin American countries gradually improved, in general, as the century progressed. Each president faced some crisis in a Latin American country, but Taft faced several in the increasingly unstable world that preceded the outbreak of World War I.

Did you know . . .
- **Woodrow Wilson** (1856–1924; see entry in volume 4), Taft's successor as president, did not fare much better in promoting better relations between the United States and its neighbors in the western hemisphere. Wilson and his secretary of state, William Jennings Bryan (1860–1925; see box in **William McKinley** entry in volume 3) attempted to forge better foreign relations, but their efforts were overwhelmed when World War I (1914–18) began in 1914.

Where to Learn More

Adler, Mortimer J., ed. *The Annals of America. Volume 1: Great Issues in American Life: A Conspectus.* Chicago: Encyclopedia Britannica, 1968.

Coletta, Paolo. *The Presidency of William Howard Taft.* Lawrence: University of Kansas Press, 1973.

Minger, Ralph Edwin. *William Howard Taft and United States Foreign Policy: The Apprenticeship Years, 1900–1908.* Urbana: Illinois University Press, 1975.

Pringle, Henry F. *The Life and Times of William Howard Taft.* New York: Farrar, Strauss, and Giroux, 1939. Reprint, Hamden, CT: Archon Books, 1964.

Where to Learn More

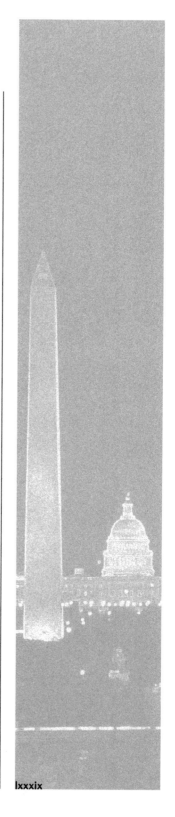

The following list of resources focuses on material appropriate for middle school or high school students. Please note that the web site addresses were verified prior to publication, but are subject to change.

Books

Bailey, Thomas A. *The Pugnacious Presidents: White House Warriors on Parade.* New York: Free Press, 1980.

Barber, James David. *The Presidential Character: Predicting Performance in the White House.* 4th ed. Englewood Cliffs, NJ: Prentice-Hall, 1992.

Barzman, Sol. *Madmen and Geniuses: The Vice-Presidents of the United States.* Chicago: Follett, 1974.

Berube, Maurice. *American Presidents and Education.* Westport, CT: Greenwood Press, 1991.

Boller, Paul F., Jr. *Presidential Anecdotes.* Rev. ed. New York: Oxford, 1996.

Boller, Paul F., Jr. *Presidential Campaigns.* Rev. ed. New York: Oxford, 1996.

Boller, Paul F. Jr. *Presidential Wives: An Anecdotal History.* Rev. ed. New York: Oxford, 1998.

Brace, Paul, Christine B. Harrington, and Gary King, eds. *The Presidency in American Politics.* New York: New York University Press, 1989.

Brallier, Jess, and Sally Chabert. *Presidential Wit and Wisdom.* New York: Penguin, 1996.

Brinkley, Alan, and Davis Dyer, eds. *The Reader's Companion to the American Presidency.* New York: Houghton Mifflin, 2000.

Brogan, Hugh, and Charles Mosley. *American Presidential Families.* New York: Macmillan Publishing Co., 1993.

Bumann, Joan. *Our American Presidents: From Washington through Clinton.* St. Petersburg, FL: Willowisp Press, 1993.

Campbell, Colin. *The U.S. Presidency in Crisis: A Comparative Perspective.* New York: Oxford University Press, 1998.

Clotworthy, William G. *Presidential Sites.* Blacksburg, VA: McDonald & Woodward, 1998.

Cook, Carolyn. *Imagine You Are the . . . President.* Edina, MN: Imaginarium, 1999.

Cooke, Donald Ewin. *Atlas of the Presidents.* Maplewood, NJ: Hammond, 1985.

Cronin, Thomas, ed. *Inventing the American Presidency.* Lawrence: University of Kansas Press, 1989.

Cunliffe, Marcus. *American Presidents and the Presidency.* New York: Houghton Mifflin, 1986.

Dallek, Robert. *Hail to the Chief: The Making and Unmaking of American Presidents.* New York: Hyperion, 1996.

Davis, James W. *The American Presidency.* 2nd ed. Westport, CT: Praeger, 1995.

DeGregorio, William. *The Complete Book of U.S. Presidents.* 4th ed. New York: Barricade Books, 1993.

Fields, Wayne. *Union of Words: A History of Presidential Eloquence.* New York: The Free Press, 1996.

Fisher, Louis. *Presidential War Power.* Lawrence: University of Kansas Press, 1995.

Frank, Sid, and Arden Davis Melick. *Presidents: Tidbits and Trivia.* Maplewood, NJ: Hammond, 1986.

Frost, Elizabeth, ed. *The Bully Pulpit: Quotations from America's Presidents.* New York: Facts On File, 1988.

Genovese, Michael. *The Power of the American Presidency, 1789–2000.* New York: Oxford, 2001.

Gerhardt, Michael J. *The Federal Impeachment Process: A Constitutional and Historical Analysis.* 2nd ed. Chicago: University of Chicago Press, 2000.

Goehlert, Robert U., and Fenton S. Martin. *The Presidency: A Research Guide.* Santa Barbara, CA: ABC-Clio Information Services, 1985.

Havel, James T. *U.S. Presidential Candidates and the Elections: A Biographical and Historical Guide.* New York: Macmillan Library Reference USA, 1996.

Henry, Christopher E. *The Electoral College.* New York: Franklin Watts, 1996.

Henry, Christopher E. *Presidential Elections.* New York: Franklin Watts, 1996.

Hess, Stephen. *Presidents and the Presidency: Essays.* Washington, DC: The Brookings Institution, 1996.

Israel, Fred L., ed. *The Presidents.* Danbury, CT: Grolier Educational, 1996.

Jackson, John S. III, and William Crotty. *The Politics of Presidential Selection.* 2nd ed. New York: Longman, 2001.

Jamieson, Kathleen Hall. *Packaging the Presidency: A History and Criticism of Presidential Campaign Advertising.* 3rd ed. New York: Oxford, 1996.

Kessler, Paula N., and Justin Segal. *The Presidents Almanac.* Rev. ed. Los Angeles: Lowell House Juvenile, 1998.

Kruh, David, and Louis Kruh. *Presidential Landmarks.* New York: Hippocrene Books, 1992.

Kunhardt, Philip B. Jr., Philip B. Kunhardt III, and Peter W. Kunhardt. *The American President*. New York: Penguin, 1999.

Laird, Archibald. *The Near Great—Chronicle of the Vice Presidents*. North Quincy, MA: Christopher Publishing House, 1980.

Mayer, William G., ed. *In Pursuit of the White House: How We Choose Our Presidential Nominees*. Chatham, NJ: Chatham House, 1996.

Murray, Robert K., and Tim H. Blessing. *Greatness in the White House: Rating the Presidents*. 2nd ed. University Park: Pennsylvania State University Press, 1994.

Neustadt, Richard E. *Presidential Power and the Modern Presidents: The Politics of Leadership from Roosevelt to Reagan*. New York: The Free Press, 1990.

Patrick, Diane. *The Executive Branch*. New York: Franklin Watts, 1994.

Presidents of the United States. A World Book Encyclopedia. Chicago: Field Enterprises Educational Corp., 1973.

Riccards, Michael, and James MacGregor Burns. *The Ferocious Engine of Democracy: A History of the American Presidency. Vol I: From the Origins through William McKinley. Vol. II: Theodore Roosevelt through George Bush*. Lanham, MD: Madison Books, 1996.

Robb, Don. *Hail to the Chief: The American Presidency*. Watertown, MA: Charlesbridge, 2000.

Rose, Gary L. *The American Presidency Under Siege*. Albany: State University of New York Press, 1997.

Sanders, Mark C. *The Presidency*. Austin, TX: Steadwell Books, 2000.

Shenkman, Richard. *Presidential Ambition: How the Presidents Gained Power, Kept Power, and Got Things Done*. New York: HarperCollins, 1999.

Shogan, Robert. *The Double-Edged Sword: How Character Makes and Ruins Presidents, from Washington to Clinton*. Boulder, CO: Westview Press, 2000.

Sisung, Kelle S., ed. *Presidential Administration Profiles for Students*. Detroit: Gale Group, 2000.

Smith, Nancy Kegan, and Mary C. Ryan, eds. *Modern First Ladies: Their Documentary Legacy*. Washington, DC: National Archives and Records Administration, 1989.

Stier, Catherine. *If I Were President*. Morton Grove, IL: Albert Whitman, 1999.

Suid, Murray I. *How to Be President of the U.S.A.* Palo Alto, CA: Monday Morning Books, 1992.

Truman, Margaret. *First Ladies: An Intimate Group Portrait of White House Wives*. New York: Ballantine, 1995.

Vidal, Gore. *The American Presidency*. Monroe, ME: Odonian Press, 1998.

Wheeless, Carl. *Landmarks of American Presidents*. Detroit: Gale, 1995.

Video

The American President. Written, produced, and directed by Philip B. Kunhardt Jr., Philip B. Kunhardt III, and Peter W. Kunhardt. Co-production of Kunhardt Productions and Thirteen/WNET in New York. 10 programs.

Web Sites

The American Presidency: Selected Resources, An Informal Reference Guide (Web site). [Online] http://www.interlink-cafe.com/uspresidents/ (accessed on December 11, 2000).

C-Span. *American Presidents: Life Portraits.* [Online] http://www.american presidents.org/ (accessed on December 11, 2000).

Grolier, Inc. *Grolier Presents: The American Presidency.* [Online] http://gi.grolier. com/presidents/ea/prescont.html (accessed on December 11, 2000).

Internet Public Library. *POTUS: Presidents of the United States.* [Online] http:// www.ipl.org/ref/POTUS/index.html (accessed on December 11, 2000).

Public Broadcasting System. "The American President." *The American Experience.* [Online] http://www.pbs.org/wgbh/amex/presidents/nf/intro/intro. html (accessed on December 11, 2000).

University of Oklahoma Law Center. *A Chronology of US Historical Documents.* [Online] http://www.law.ou.edu/hist/ (accessed on December 11, 2000).

White House. *Welcome to the White House.* [Online] http://www.whitehouse. gov/ (accessed on December 11, 2000).

The White House Historical Association. [Online] http://www.whitehousehistory. org/whha/default.asp (accessed on December 11, 2000).

Yale Law School. *The Avalon at the Yale Law School: Documents in Law, History and Diplomacy.* [Online] http://www.yale.edu/lawweb/avalon/avalon. htm (accessed on December 11, 2000).

Index

Note: *Italic* type indicates volume number; **boldface** indicates main entries and their page numbers; (ill.) indicates photos and illustrations.

Battle of Vicksburg, *2:* 568; *3:* 640, 644, 650, 667

Battle of Wisconsin Heights, *2:* 435

Seven Days' Battles, *2:* 566; *3:* 649

Baudelaire, Charles-Pierre, *5:* 1301

Bay of Pigs invasion (Cuba), *5:* 1283–84

"Bayonet Constitution," *3:* 831

Beanes, William, *1:* 158

"The Beauty of America" project, *5:* 1344

Bedtime for Bonzo (film), *5:* 1473

Beecher, Catherine, *2:* 470

The Beeches (Coolidge), *4:* 1076

Begin, Menachem, *4:* 1146–47, 1148 (ill.); *5:* 1445

Belgium, World War I, *4:* 973, 1091–92

Belknap, William W., *3:* 658

Bell, Alexander Graham, *3:* 724–25, 725 (ill.)

Bell, John, *2:* 468 (ill.), 562
election of 1860, *2:* 562

"Belle of Canton." *See* McKinley, Ida

Benton, Thomas Hart, *2:* 408, 468 (ill.)

Bentsen, Lloyd, *5:* 1515
election of 1988, *5:* 1519

Berlin airlifts, *4:* 1202

Berlin Wall, *4:* 1253; *5:* 1285, 1490 (ill.)

BEST Foundation for a Drug-Free Tomorrow, *5:* 1499

Bethune, Mary McLeod, *4:* 1163 (ill.), 1164

Betty Ford Center, *5:* 1425

Bewick Moreing, *4:* 1089

Bicentennial Celebration, *5:* 1417

Bierce, Ambrose, *3:* 854

"Big Bill" ("Big Lub"). *See* Taft, William Howard

"Big stick" foreign policy, *3:* 891–94, 895–96

Big Three (Paris, 1919), *4:* 975 (ill.)

Big Three (Potsdam, 1945), *4:* 1198 (ill.)

Bill of Rights, *1:* 20, 99, 106, 151, 152, 177

Bill of Rights proposal (Madison), *1:* 169–78

Bimetallism
Cleveland, Grover, *3:* 789, 860
McKinley, William, *3:* 795, 845–46, 848

Birmingham, Alabama, segregation protest, *5:* 1293

Birney, James G., *2:* 404

"Black Codes," *2:* 612, 635

Black Hawk, *2:* 434, 554

Black Hawk War, *1:* 275, 305; *2:* 431; *3:* 770

Black, Jeremiah, *2:* 526 (ill.)

"Black Monday" stock market crash, 1566–67

Blaine, James G., *2:* 442; *3:* 660, 689, 721, 722, 754, 756–57, 757 (ill.), 781 (ill.), 782–83
"Blaine from Maine," *3:* 756
election of 1884, *3:* 782, 783
Garfield's eulogy, *3:* 723

Blair, Francis P., Jr., election of 1868, *3:* 651

Blair House, *4:* 1207

"Bleeding Kansas," *2:* 500 (ill.), 501, 528

Bliss, Alexander, *2:* 590

Bliss, Mary Elizabeth (Betty), *2:* 448, 449

Bloody Angle, Battle of, *3:* 645

Bloomer, Amelia, *3:* 786

Bloomer, Elizabeth Ann. *See* Ford, Betty

Bolívar, Simon, *2:* 335

Bone, Scott C., *4:* 1029 (ill.)

Bones, Helen Woodrow, *4:* 992

Bonus Army March, *4:* 1103–4

Boom and bust cycles, *1:* 293, 309; *3:* 663

Booth, John Wilkes, *2:* 570 (ill.), 571, 578, 596, 610, 635; *3:* 677

Bootleg liquor, *4:* 1059

"Border states," *2:* 563

Borie, Adolph E., *3:* 652

Bork, Robert, *5:* 1379

Bosnia (Bosnia and Herzegovina), *5:* 1563, 1564

"The Boss." *See* Truman, Bess

"The Boss's Boss." *See* Truman, Margaret

Boston, Massachusetts
Adams, John, *1:* 57–58
during American Revolution, *1:* 10, 12, 33
police strike (1919), *4:* 1054

Boston Tea Party, *1:* 9, 76, 77 (ill.)

Boutwell, George S., *3:* 652

Boxer Rebellion (Righteous and Harmonious Fists), *3:* 858; *4:* 1089–91, 1110

Boys' Clubs of America, *4:* 1106

Braddock, Edward, *1:* 8

Brady, James, *5:* 1479 (ill.)

Brady, John R., *3:* 755 (ill.)

Braintree, Massachusetts, *1:* 223

Branch Davidians, *5:* 1570

Brandeis, Louis, *3:* 936 (ill.)

Brandt, Willy, *5:* 1295

Brandywine Creek, Battle of, *1:* 13, 14

Brazil, *3:* 900

Forsyth, John, *1:* 246
Fort Crawford, *2:* 431
Fort Detroit, *2:* 333
Fort Donelson, *3:* 644, 646
Fort Duquesne, *1:* 7–8
Fort La Boeuf, *1:* 7
Fort McHenry, *1:* 157, 158–59
Fort Necessity, *1:* 7
Fort Sumter, *2:* 563
Forty-ninth parallel, *2:* 405, 520
Foster Grandparents Program, *5:* 1496
Fourteen Points (Wilson), *4:* 976, 977, **997–1004**
Fourteenth Amendment, *2:* 609, 615; *3:* 787
Fourth World Conference on Women (United Nations, Beijing, China), *5:* 1585
Fox tribe, *2:* 431, 434
France
    Adams, John, *1:* 59
    American Revolution, *1:* 14, 16
    French Revolution, *1:* 22, 62, 105–6
    Great Depression, *4:* 1099
    Indochina, *5:* 1287, 1302, 1331, 1373
    Kennedys' tour, *5:* 1284, 1303
    Lafayette, Major General, *1:* 186–87, 187 (ill.)
    Lafayette, Marquise de, *1:* 206–7
    Mexico, *2:* 611
    Monroe, Elizabeth, *1:* 206–7
    Monroe, James, *1:* 188
    Napoleon I (Napoleon Bonaparte, emperor of France), *1:* 111–12, 189, 194–95
    Napoleonic war reparations, *1:* 274, 298–99
    Quasi-War, *1:* 66, 70
    Vietnam, *4:* 1245, *5:* 1287, 1331, 1373
    World War I, *4:* 973, 978
    XYZ affair, *1:* 66
Frankfurter, Felix, *4:* 1100
Franklin, Benjamin, *1:* 14, 15–16, 17, 17 (ill.), 133 (ill.), 190
    Committee of Five, *1:* 126
Franz Ferdinand, Archduke, *4:* 973
Frederick William III, *1:* 241
Fredericksburg, Battle of, *3:* 649
Free blacks, *1:* 199
"Free silver," *3:* 789, 845
Free Soil Party, *1:* 308; *2:* 439, 493
Free states
    California, *2:* 371, 439–40
    New Mexico, *2:* 439–40
Free trade policies, *3:* 858, 860
Freedmen's Bureau, *2:* 614

Freedom of speech, World War I, *3:* 893
Freedoms of individuals, applied to business, *4:* 1078
Freemasons, *2:* 462
Frelinghuysen, Theodore, election of 1844, *2:* 401
Frémont, John C., *2:* 408–9, 409 (ill.), 410, 469 (ill.), 522 (ill.), 524 (ill.); *3:* 792
    election of 1856, *2:* 409, 522, 523, 558
French and Indian War, *1:* 7–8, 8 (ill.)
French Empire, *1:* 194–95
French Revolution, *1:* 22–23, 62, 105–6
    Lafayette, Major General, *1:* 186–87, 187 (ill.)
    Lafayette, Marquise de, *1:* 206–7
    Napoleon I (Napoleon Bonaparte, emperor of France), *1:* 194
    Paine, Thomas, *1:* 190–91
Friedman, Milton, *5:* 1481
Fromme, Lynette "Squeaky," *5:* 1414
"Front porch" campaigns
    Bush, George W., *5:* 1631
    Garfield, James A., *3:* 742–43
    Harding, Warren G., *4:* 1024
    McKinley, William, *3:* 858; *5:* 1631
Frontier
    Homestead Act, *2:* 568, 573
    political development, *1:* 258, 275
Fuel conservation, *5:* 1445–48
Fugitive Slave Act, *2:* 371, 442, 455, 466–67, 479, 496–97, 509, 513, 541, 608
    Stowe, Harriet Beecher, *2:* 470
Fulbright, J. William, *5:* 1550
Fundamentalism, *3:* 856–57

G

Gable, Clark, *5:* 1495
Gadsden Purchase, *2:* 497–98, 503, 564
Gaines, Edmund, *1:* 304
Galt, Edith Bolling. *See* Wilson, Edith
Galt, Norman, *4:* 992
Gandhi, Mohandas, *5:* 1292
Gardiner, Julia. *See* Tyler, Julia
Gardiner, Lion, *2:* 379
Garfield, James A., *3:* **711–27,** 713 (ill.), 720 (ill.), 723 (ill.), 754 (ill.)

L

M

N

O

African safari, *3:* 899, 908
assassination attempt, *3:* 900
Brazilian expedition, *3:* 900, 908
conservation, *3:* 896–99
early years, *3:* 880–81
effectiveness as president, *3:* 901
election of 1900, *3:* 848, 858, 874
election of 1904, *3:* 894–95
election of 1912, *4:* 966; *5:* 1558
First Annual Address to Congress, *3:* 890–91, **909–16**
foreign policy, *3:* 891–94, 895–96, 903
governor and reformer, *3:* 888
"The Man with the Muck Rake" speech, *3:* **917–24**
marriage and family, *3:* 882, 883–84, 906–7
military service, *3:* 851, 887–88
Nobel Peace Prize, *3:* 879, 896, 903
political career, *3:* 882–86, 888–89
post-presidential life, *3:* 899–900, 907–8
presidency, *3:* 889–99, 907
Roosevelt Corollary to Monroe Doctrine, *3:* 891–94, 903
"trustbuster," *3:* 860, 874, 890–91, 910, 911; *4:* 1062
Root, Elihu, *4:* 1100
"Rose of Long Island." *See* Tyler, Julia
Ross, Edmund Gibson, *2:* 617, 617 (ill.), 619; *5:* 1279
Rough Riders, *3:* 887 (ill.), 888
Ruby, Jack, *5:* 1294, 1294 (ill.), 1325
Ruckelshaus, William, *5:* 1379
Rudolph, Lucretia. *See* Garfield, Lucretia
"Rugged Individualism" campaign speech (Hoover), *4:* **1115–22**
Rumsfeld, Donald H., *5:* 1414
Rural areas, 1920s, *4:* 1115
Rush, Richard, election of 1828, *1:* 267
Rusk, Dean, *5:* 1286
Russia, *1:* 195. *See* Union of Soviet Socialist Republics (USSR)
Adams, John Quincy, *1:* 223, 225–26, 241
Roosevelt, Franklin D., *4:* 1145
Russo-Japanese War, *3:* 895–96, 903; *4:* 970
World War I, *4:* 973
Russia (Republic, 1991), *5:* 1485, 1522, 1565
Ruth, Babe, *4:* 1049, 1063
Rutledge, Ann, *2:* 555
Rwanda, *5:* 1563
Ryan, Nolan, *5:* 1603
Ryan, Thelma. *See* Nixon, Pat

S

Sac. *See* Sauk tribe
Sacajawea, *1:* 115, 115 (ill.)
Sadat, Anwar, *4:* 1146–47, 1148 (ill.); *5:* 1445
"Safety fund system," *1:* 302
Sagamore Hill (Theodore Roosevelt), *3:* 884
Saigon evacuation, *5:* 1415
St. Albans (school), *2:* 538
Saint Helena, *1:* 195
St. Lawrence Seaway, *4:* 1061
St. Louis Post-Dispatch, *3:* 852
SALT. *See* Strategic Arms Limitation Treaty (SALT)
San Francisco Examiner, *3:* 854
San Francisco general strike (1934), *4:* 1143
San Jacinto, Battle of, *2:* 385
San Juan (Kettle) Hill charge, *3:* 888; *4:* 970
Sanborn Contracts scandal, *3:* 658
Sanderson, James, *2:* 381
Sandinistas (El Salvador), *5:* 1483
Sanford, Edward T., *3:* 936 (ill.)
Santa Anna, Antonio López de, *2:* 406, 436
Santo Domingo, *3:* 654
Saratoga, Battle of, *1:* 13
Sartoris, Algernon, *3:* 668
Satellite, first, *4:* 1248
Satellite nations (European), democratization, *5:* 1482
"Saturday Night Massacre," *5:* 1379
Saudi Arabia, *5:* 1523, 1537
Sauk tribe, *1:* 305; *2:* 332, 431, 434, 554
Sawyer, Charles, *4:* 1210
Saxton, Ida. *See* McKinley, Ida
Scalia, Antonin, *5:* 1483
Schenck, Charles, *3:* 893
Schlesinger, James, *5:* 1414
Schlossberg, Caroline Kennedy, *5:* 1302, 1305, 1305 (ill.), 1306 (ill.)
Schwarzkopf, Norman, *5:* 1544
Science and technology
Bell, Alexander Graham, *3:* 724–25
during Cold War, *4:* 1248, 1250, 1269
U.S. nuclear-powered submarine, *5:* 1439
Scopes, John T., *3:* 857
Scott, Caroline Lavinia. *See* Harrison, Caroline
Scott, Dred, *2:* 523–24
Scott, Winfield, *1:* 304–5, 305 (ill.), 306; *2:* 436, 468, 468 (ill.), 491, 494 (ill.)

U

U-2 aerial surveillance incident, *4:* 1250–51
United Nations, *4:* 977
Vietnam War, *5:* 1330–35, 1338, 1391–92, 1396–97
Watergate scandal, *5:* 1359, 1375–82
World War I, *4:* 973–76, 1005, 1092
World War II, *4:* 1147, 1150–52, 1221–23, 1226–27, 1240–42
United States Bank, *1:* 228
United States v. Susan B. Anthony, 3: 787
University of Virginia, *1:* 214
Upper Creek nation, *1:* 263
Urban areas, 1920s, *4:* 1115
Urban laborers, Populism, *3:* 823
U.S. citizenship, Native Americans, *4:* 1066
U.S. Civil Service Commission. *See* Civil Service Commission
U.S. Congress. *See* Congress
U.S. Constitution. *See* Bill of Rights; Constitution; specific amendments, e.g., Twenty-third Amendment
U.S. Forest Service. *See* Forest Service
U.S. House of Representatives. *See* House of Representatives
U.S. Housing Authority, *4:* 1140
U.S. Navy. *See* Navy
U.S. Senate. *See* Senate
U.S. Steel Corporation, *3:* 793, 934, 935
U.S. Supreme Court. *See* Supreme Court
U.S.S. *K–1, 5:* 1439
U.S.S. *Maddox, 5:* 1331
U.S.S. *Maine, 3:* 849, 850, 851 (ill.), 855, 887
U.S.S. *Mayaguez, 5:* 1417
U.S.S. *Missouri, 4:* 1199, 1199 (ill.), 1226
U.S.S. *Pomfret, 5:* 1439
U.S.S. *Seawolf, 5:* 1439
U.S.S. *Shaw, 4:* 1151 (ill.)
USSR. *See* Union of Soviet Socialist Republics (USSR)
Utilities
  federal regulation, *3:* 899
  New Deal legislation, *4:* 1140–41

V

Valley Forge, *1:* 11 (ill.), 15
  Washington, Martha, *1:* 33

Van Buren, Angelica Singleton, *1:* 167; *2:* 377
  hostess for her father-in-law, *1:* 311, 312
Van Buren, Hannah, *1:* **311–13,** 311 (ill.),
  marriage and family, *1:* 312
Van Buren, Martin, *1:* 266, 273 (ill.), 277, **291–310,** 293 (ill.), 303 (ill.), 308 (ill.); *3:* 690
  Adams, John Quincy, *1:* 246
  Calhoun, John C., *1:* 300
  early years, *1:* 294–95
  election of 1832, *1:* 267
  election of 1836, *1:* 301; *5:* 1612–13
  election of 1840, *2:* 336
  election of 1844, *2:* 401, 402
  election of 1848, *1:* 308–9; *2:* 439
  Inaugural Address, *1:* **315–21**
  Jackson, Andrew, *1:* 297–98, 300–301, 309, 315
  legal career, *1:* 295–96, 312
  marriage and family, *1:* 296–97, 312
  Mexican War, *2:* 425
  political career, *1:* 297–301
  presidency, *1:* 302–8
  retirement, *1:* 309
Van Devanter, Willis, *3:* 936 (ill.)
Van Ness, Marcia, *2:* 417
V-E Day (Victory-in-Europe Day), *4:* 1196
Venezuela, *3:* 791
Veracruz, Battle of, *4:* 969
Vermont
  Coolidge, Calvin, *4:* 1051–52, 1055–56
Veterans
  Vietnam War, *5:* 1338
  World War I, *4:* 1104, 1113
Veto Message Regarding the Bank of the United States (Jackson), *1:* **285–90**
Veto, presidential. *See* Presidential veto
Vice president
  becomes president after death of predecessor, *2:* 358, 364, 465, 607; *3:* 758, 890; *4:* 1056, 1196; *5:* 1323
  first, *1:* 60–62
  John Adams' view, *1:* 60
  resignation of predecessor, *5:* 1408–9
Vicksburg, Battle of, *2:* 568; *3:* 640, 644, 650, 667
Vicksburg, Mississippi, *2:* 565
Victoria, queen of England, *2:* 536; *3:* 660, 668

W